Legal Literacy and Communication Skills

Legal Literacy and Communication Skills
Working with Law and Lawyers

Jennifer Murphy Romig

PROFESSOR OF PRACTICE
EMORY UNIVERSITY SCHOOL OF LAW

Mark Edwin Burge

PROFESSOR OF LAW
DIRECTOR OF SAN ANTONIO PROGRAMS
TEXAS A&M UNIVERSITY SCHOOL OF LAW

CAROLINA ACADEMIC PRESS
Durham, North Carolina

Library of Congress Cataloging-in-Publication Data

Names: Romig, Jennifer Murphy, author. | Burge, Mark Edwin, author.
Title: Legal literacy and communication : working with law and lawyers /
   Jennifer Murphy Romig, Mark Edwin Burge.
Description: Durham : Carolina Academic Press, 2019.
Identifiers: LCCN 2019036974 | ISBN 9781531012618 (paperback) | ISBN
   9781531012625 (ebook)
Subjects: LCSH: Legal composition. | Communication in law--United States. |
   Law--United States--Language. | Courts--United States. | Justice,
   Administration of--United States.
Classification: LCC KF250 .R629 2019 | DDC 808.06/634--dc23
LC record available at https://lccn.loc.gov/2019036974

Carolina Academic Press
700 Kent Street
Durham, North Carolina 27701
Telephone (919) 489-7486
Fax (919) 493-5668
www.cap-press.com

Printed in the United States of America
2021 Printing

To my mom, Linda Kay Murphy, my inspiration
for embracing creativity plus valuing attention to detail
—JMR

To my wife, Rhonda West Burge, who has
an amazing talent for making life better
—MEB

Contents

Acknowledgments

Many colleagues and friends have given feedback and advice on this book and on the pedagogy that led to this book. We are extremely grateful for their time, wisdom, and specific advice. Thank you to the following:

Emory Law student research assistants Dakota Fraley, Christian Morbidelli, Josh Jackson, and Jenna Corcoran; and Emory Law student Mary Bryan. Special acknowledgments are in order for Christian Morbidelli and Josh Jackson, who played crucial roles in developing the story of Olivia Ralston for the case study in this book. Texas A&M Law faculty James McGrath, Susan Phillips, Lisa Rich, Frank Snyder, and Nancy Welsh played valuable roles—frequently unaware—in the curricular "proof of concept" reflected in so many aspects of this book. Thanks also to Emory Law Librarians Elizabeth Christian and Christina Glon. We are grateful to Rhonda Burge and Kay Murphy for their skillful proofreading. We are also grateful to Jeannette Livingston at Emory Law for her able and timely administrative support.

We are also grateful to many other colleagues and friends who shared their expertise, reviewed chapters, and answered questions that helped us shape the direction of this book:

Renee Allen
Lacy Bell
Alexa Chew
Nancy Daspit
Joe Fore
Iselin Gambert
Carl Gebo
Mindy Goldstein
Emmett Griner
Eve Powell Griner
Nicole Iannarone
Jennifer Judge
Scott Killingsworth
Katrina June Lee
Ellie Margolis
Jenn Mathews

Sue Payne
Robert Parrish
Kamina Pinder
Nancy Overholtzer
Sue Payne
Kamina Pinder
Rebecca Purdom
Jeremy Richter
Suzanne Rowe
Robert Schapiro
Julie Seaman
Allison Thornton
Sasha Volokh
Reynolds Wilson
Keely Youngblood

Google and the Google logo are registered trademarks of Google LLC, used with permission.

Legal Literacy and Communication Skills

Chapter 1

Foundations of Legal Literacy

> One can live in the shadow of an idea without grasping it.
>
> — Novelist Elizabeth Bowen

Many live in the shadow of the law without grasping it. Law reaches into every facet of life. At the highest level, the role of constitutional rights reaches from the right to speak in the public square to the legality of what happens in the bedroom. Statutory law affects every facet of life in specific and concrete ways: statutory law establishes federal Social Security and the framework for healthcare delivery, empowers the Securities and Exchange Commission to regulate sales of stock, defines copyright and trademark and other intellectual property rights, and requires workplace accommodations under the Americans with Disabilities Act—just to name a few examples. State and federal agencies also make regulations with significant input from the public and decide specific types of disputes. All these layers of law can be brought into the court system where, most commonly, licensed attorneys clash with other licensed attorneys on behalf of their respective clients, using legal arguments designed to persuade the experienced attorneys serving as judges to pick a winner. These clashes entail not only substantive legal questions about what a law covers or who can be responsible but also procedural questions about who can sue and where, and how the court should go about considering evidence and arguments about all of the above. With all these layers of possible arguments, it is no wonder that people with little to no legal training may have trouble understanding the legal forces affecting their lives.

But you will be different. You are already in the process of becoming legally literate. "Legal literacy" is both in the title of and at the core of this book. It means having the skills to grasp what the law is and how it works. Legal literacy empowers individuals to use their grasp of the law for personal and professional advancement. Licensed attorneys are legally literate, but legal literacy is broader than what licensed attorneys do for clients. Legal literacy empowers and benefits anyone whose life or work is affected by law. That "anyone" is you.

I. Literacy and Legal Literacy

The most basic concept of literacy is, of course, the ability to read and write. Literacy expands far beyond the basics, however, to include the idea of being "educated" and "cultured."[1] Thus, literacy in a community includes not only what an individual can actually do, but also how others in that community perceive and evaluate the individual's skills and performance. Thus, literacy covers a person's actual knowledge as well as the capacity to make others *perceive* the person as knowledgeable. In every field, literacy within that field is a matter of degree, ranging from minimally literate to extraordinarily erudite.

Legal literacy plays by the same rules as general literacy. It includes technical skills such as finding and reading the law. These skills require critical thinking, such as the ability to distinguish the law itself from biased representations of what others say the law is. Another skill is writing about the law clearly and accurately. Legal literacy is also deeply, thoroughly social. Attorneys are the original community defining legal literacy, and their community polices the boundaries today.

An example helps to show what we mean. On August 14, 2018, the *Washington Post* published an opinion piece[2] on the lawfulness of nondisclosure agreements between a campaign staffer and a presidential campaign, where the campaign proves successful and the staffer goes on to work in the White House. Here is the original passage from the op-ed that drew attention:

> Courts generally enforce private agreements, but under a well-established principle of contract law, one can also be voided if it goes against public policy — a term known in the legal community as "piercing the veil."

The problem with this statement is that it uses legal terms inaccurately. More bluntly, it's wrong. "Piercing the veil" refers to the legal concept that a corporation creates a protective "veil" around its officers, such that suing a corporation means suing the corporate entity itself, not its employees or officers or board members or shareholders. Piercing the veil means satisfying exceptional legal requirements allowing a party to sue

---

1. *Literate*, Merriam-Webster (June 3, 2018), https://www.merriam-webster.com/dictionary/literate#h1

2. *See* @JackByrom, Tweet, "that's…not what it's called," Aug. 14, 2018, 8:11 p.m. (attaching screen shot of original text from Deanna Paul, *Trump Accused Omarosa Manigault Neuman of Breaching Her NDA. Experts Say She Might Prevail in Court*, Washington Post, washingtonpost.com (Aug. 14, 2018, at 8:52 p.m.) available at The Wayback Machine, https://web.archive.org/web/20180815025540/https://www.washington post.com/news/politics/wp/2018/08/14/trump-accused-omarosa-of-breaching-her-nda-experts-say-she-might-prevail-in-court/).

not only the corporate entity but also one or more of its individual officers who would normally be protected by the corporate veil. That is a classic doctrine of corporate law that virtually every future lawyer studies in law school.

By contrast, a contract is "void against public policy" when some source of law (constitutional, statutory, or case law) prohibits enforcement of the contract because its subject matter stands against public policy. For example, a contract to sell human organs is void against public policy. These contracts are void and cannot be enforced because the law enforces public policy against selling organs. The mechanism for the law itself to enforce this policy is by making contracts to sell organs unenforceable. A person can sign a piece of paper that purports to be a "contract" to sell organs, but it will not actually be binding. No court will hold a party liable for not performing its duties stated in an unenforceable contract. The idea of a contract being "void against public policy" is a classic doctrine of contract law.

After the *Washington Post* editorial connected the term "piercing the veil" with the term "void against public policy," many lawyers went on social media to mock the author and the newspaper's editing process for making a clear legal error. The *Washington Post* then revised the article to quote a source and attempt to suggest an analogy:[3]

> Courts generally enforce private agreements, but under a well-established principle of contract law, one can also be avoided if it goes against public policy—analogous to a concept known in the legal community as "piercing the veil," Kitrosser offered as a point of comparison. Traditionally, the phrase is used when an individual is held personally liable for corporate action.

Lawyers continued with commentary, asserting that this clarification was not particularly clarifying, and criticizing the author and the *Washington Post*'s editorial process.

The point of discussing the brouhaha over "piercing the veil" is to show the social aspect of legal literacy. Lawyers recognized the incorrect use of the term and policed its usage through social media. But there are many more productive uses of legal literacy.

Law professor James Boyd White described literacy in the law as a spectrum, from just recognizing certain words as law-related and therefore outside one's own expertise (on the beginner side) to full competence (on the expert side).[4] At the very basic end of the spectrum, simply recognizing a word as unfamiliar and *potentially* legal in nature should be within the skill set of any college graduate. No special training should be needed to recognize that "piercing the veil" sounds specific and must have a meaning that can be verified. It is a rudimentary form of legal literacy to read these words, to

---

3. Deanna Paul, *Trump Accused Omarosa Manigault Neuman of Breaching Her NDA. Experts Say She Might Prevail in Court*, Washington Post, washingtonpost.com (Aug. 15, 2018).

4. James Boyd White, *The Invisible Discourse of the Law: Reflections on Legal Literacy and General Education*, 54 U. Colo. L. Rev. 143, 143 (1983).

understand that they have legal content, and to decide how to investigate further or consult an attorney if legal advice is needed.

At the other end of the spectrum, elite legal literacy requires not only formal schooling but also years of practice on top of it. For example, Lisa Blatt, a partner at the law firm of Williams & Connolly and head of that firm's Supreme Court and Appellate Litigation practice group, has argued 37 Supreme Court cases on a broad range of issues, the most of any woman in United States history. But the Supreme Court bar (meaning attorneys authorized to appear before the Supreme Court) is tiny, and these attorneys' skill set is highly specialized. Neither you nor most attorneys have need for that sort of elite specialization.

Realistic, practical, attainable levels of legal literacy are used every day by many others, including the 1.3 million licensed attorneys in the United States,[5] but legal literacy is certainly not limited to that group. The Model Rules of Professional Conduct, which are the American Bar Association's template for state regulations governing attorney conduct, allude to a number of "law-related" service areas where legal literacy is relevant: "A broad range of economic and other interests of clients may be served by lawyers' engaging in the delivery of law-related services. Examples of law-related services include providing title insurance, financial planning, accounting, trust services, real estate counseling, legislative lobbying, economic analysis, social work, psychological counseling, tax preparation, and patent, medical, or environmental consulting."[6] These service areas are quite broad, but they are still just selective examples of the many fields and professions where legal literacy is needed and beneficial.

II. Competent Legal Literacy

So where do you fit in for purposes of this book and this course? Mark Hannah, a professor of technical communication at Arizona State University, has helped to define what competent legal literacy looks like.[7] He argues that legal literacy is not just about recognizing the legal system as "an external, quantifiable entity" imposed on everyone; it is not "an after-the-fact phenomenon" that people "have no role in shaping."[8] Rather, legal literacy means recognizing that the people who read legal information, are affected by it, and use it are in fact "coproducers"[9] of law itself. For technical communicators, such as professionals writing product warnings, coproducing the law means at least two things: (1) understanding that their professional decisions may make case law, for

---

5. American Bar Association, *ABA National Population Lawyer Survey 1878-2018* (2018).

6. American Bar Association, Model Rule of Professional Conduct 5.7 comment [9] (as amended through August 2016).

7. Mark A. Hannah, *Legal Literacy: Coproducing the Law in Technical Communication*, 20 Technical Comm. Quarterly 5 (2010).

8. *Id.* at 9.

9. *Id.* at 10.

example if their product warnings are litigated; and (2) finding "opportunities for re-sisting or pushing against regulations, guidelines, or laws" that affect their field.[10] In both situations, Hannah argues, professionals "should not see themselves or their companies simply as subject to or victim to the limits and restrictions of the law."[11]

James Boyd White similarly emphasized action and participation in his definition of legal literacy:

> that degree of competence in legal discourse required for meaningful and active life in our increasingly legalistic and litigious culture.[12]

This view of legal literacy echoes the description of Canadian law professor Archie Zariski, who described legal literacy as "knowing the constraints and possibilities law offers for change, plus having the capability to use its tools and techniques to improve society for oneself and others."[13]

A core tenet of this book (and of legal masters programs such as Juris Master, Master of Jurisprudence, and Master of Legal Studies programs) is that other professionals can seek and attain "that degree of competence in legal discourse required for mean-ingful and active life in our increasingly legalistic and litigious culture." This degree of competence in legal discourse is a highly valuable asset for working effectively with li-censed attorneys. Non-attorney professionals who possess competent legal literacy can face legal language with an awareness of its history, flaws, and potential — and can also work with lawyers in a more effective, productive, collaborative manner. While legal literacy partly means developing good judgment about when to involve an attorney, it also means becoming empowered to understand legal information and communicate with confidence about matters that do not require attorney intervention.

White suggested that this middle ground of legal literacy has three basic functions:

- Advocating for oneself, such as in a zoning dispute
- Evaluating secondary sources, namely "news reports and periodical literature dealing with legal matters"
- Serving as a responsible leader, such as on a school board or neighborhood association[14]

White wrote these words in 1983. He had an incredibly strong imagination,[15] but even he may not have been able to imagine a regulatory world in which children receive

---

10. *Id.* at 13.

11. *Id.* at 14.

12. James Boyd White, *supra* note 4, at 144.

13. Archie Zariski, *Legal Literacy: An Introduction to Legal Studies* (2014).

14. James Boyd White, *supra* note 4, at 144.

15. In fact, he even wrote a book called *The Legal Imagination* (45th Anniv. ed., 2018).

aerial drones as holiday gifts and then ponder whether to register them with the FAA. He may not have been able to conceive of a transactional world where individuals routinely agree to pages and pages of licensing agreements for handheld devices that track their every move, and where businesses publish "smart contracts" on the "block-chain." He may not have even dreamed that non-lawyers could have easy, instant, free access to primary legal sources such as statutes, regulations, and cases. No social media and no Google existed in 1983, and even electronic bulletin boards were in a primitive state. And White may not have predicted the growing role of professionals not trained as lawyers in working on legal issues that arise within business, healthcare, government, and advocacy. But we can imagine you in that role today, and we hope you will increasingly imagine yourself there as you explore this book.

III. Legal Literacy Today

Today, legal literacy matters not just to people in their roles as citizens, but to professionals working in their roles in business, policy, government, and other functions outside the traditional practice of law. Legal literacy has never been more important and valuable in the workplace.

In some ways, legal literacy has never been easier to acquire, with the vastly improved availability of open-access digital legal resources in federal law, state law, corporate law, social justice, and other areas.[16]

Another hopeful sign for legal literacy is the continuing vitality of the Plain Language movement (also known as the Plain English movement). In the 1970s, UCLA professor David Mellinkoff, University of California-Davis professor Richard Wydick, and others began pushing for law to be written in plain language that the broader public could understand. The movement encouraged lawmakers, government workers, and lawyers to cut down on unnecessary jargon and write more concisely in general. The Plain Language movement remains vital today, with some of its best-known editing techniques highlighted in chapters 17 and 18 of this text. Writing in plain language is more than a set of techniques, of course, but by practicing editing in a few common scenarios, you can make your writing clearer, more concise, and more accessible to readers.

Despite lawyer jokes to the contrary, many lawyers do work hard to make their writing intelligible and useful for their audiences, including judges, other lawyers, opposing parties, sophisticated clients, unsophisticated clients, and the general public. Legally literate professionals working alongside lawyers also play a crucial role. Lawyers

---

16. *See, e.g.*, Franklin County Law Library, 50-State Surveys of Law and Regulations (Aug. 3, 2018), https://fclawlib.libguides.com/50statesurveys/surveysandhandouts (collecting 50-state surveys on issues including expungement of criminal records, ban-the-box laws in employment, indigent defendants' right to counsel in civil cases, state and local tenant protection, and other areas).

writing about law may, at times, be "cursed by their knowledge,"[17] which means losing touch with what non-experts need. Legally literate professionals working in and around lawyers can share some aspects of the lawyers' knowledge, while maintaining their connection to laypeople and the general public's needs.

For purposes of this book, the concept of "legal literacy" takes on a variety of meanings:

- Reading and understanding the law itself, such as statutes, regulations, and cases

- Reading and understanding material written about the law, such as newspapers, magazines, blogs, policy documents, and other resources

- Writing about the law in an accurate and useful way for a particular audience, such as another person who is also legally literate, or for a person who is not at all legally literate but is affected by the law

- Writing and creating law itself, such as by drafting a proposed regulation, policy, or contract

- Comprehending not just legal terminology but also the legal systems and processes in which legal terminology is used

- Learning in a community of students all working on their legal skills together, so as to gain a deeper understanding of how the law functions when explored in collective conversation

- Being "cultured" in the law, so as to use language and concepts that are consistent with how the law works

- Communicating about the law in a "polished" manner, with conventional and appropriate legal usage

Classes such as civics and U.S. government in high school and business law in college are all good steps toward legal literacy. Still, there is a large gap between the legal literacy one can attain from these basic classes and the literacy goals outlined above. It is a gap that — some would say — is unnecessarily large and beneficial to the attorneys who claim dominion over a larger-than-deserved area of expertise.[18] Being legally literate, and not dependent in all cases on licensed attorneys, benefits business executives dealing with complex issues of transactional and regulatory decision-making.[19] It benefits

---

17. See Lisa Cron, *Wired for Story: The Writer's Guide to Using Brain Science to Hook Readers from the Very First Sentence* 62 (2012) (describing the curse of knowledge by quoting communication scholars Chip and Dan Heath: "Once we know something, we find it hard to imagine what it was like not to know it").

18. Derek Denckla, *Nonlawyers and the Unauthorized Practice of Law: An Overview of the Legal and Ethical Parameters*, 67 Fordham L. Rev. 2581, 2599 (1998).

19. John Akula, *The Importance of Legal Literacy for Executives*, IEDP (August 14, 2012), http://www.iedp.com/articles/the-importance-of-legal-literacy-for-executives/.

people of modest financial means seeking access to justice.[20] Knowledge can be power, and legal literacy is a kind of knowledge that can serve as an empowering life skill. We want you to be empowered by the material we explore together in this book.

IV. Legal Literacy and the Structure of This Book

This textbook aims to give students the fundamentals of reading and understanding legal language, finding and evaluating legal information, and communicating about legal matters. The book begins with broad foundations:

- Chapter 2 gives an overview of the foundations of U.S. law, including some of the basics necessary to understand how law works in the United States, including the structure of the legal system and major sources of law.

- Chapter 3 summarizes the legal doctrine of the unauthorized practice of law and puts it into practical context for professionals working with law and lawyers.

- Chapter 4 introduces the skill of critically reading legal information. It addresses general skills for reading legal information and documents by skimming and then focusing on what matters most. The chapter then specifically covers how to read a case—in other words, a judicial opinion.

- Chapter 5 unpacks the skill of legal reasoning. It provides a behind-the-scenes look at how attorneys analyze the law they have researched, using it to make predictions and help their clients evaluate risks.

After this foundational section, the book delves into legal research and specific types of legal information. The focus in this book is on open-access legal information, meaning information that is not part of a fee-based commercial platform or behind a paywall, but the skills of finding and evaluating information covered in this book will also help with effective legal research in fee-based platforms.

- Chapter 6 explores general approaches to finding legal information on the Internet, evaluating the reliability of such information, and understanding what it means to be competent as a legal researcher.

- Chapter 7 specifically covers finding and evaluating secondary sources, which are *not* the law but can provide useful context and citations to primary sources of law.

- Chapter 8 covers legal research in statutes and legislative history.

---

20. Antony H. Barash et al., *Legal Literacy for Community Education, Policy Advocacy, Resource Development and More*, American Bar Association, https://www.americanbar.org/content/dam/aba/directories/pro_bono_clearinghouse/ejc_2014_063.authcheckdam.pdf (collected resources for presenters to use in promoting legal literacy).

- Chapter 9 covers legal research in regulations.
- Chapter 10 covers legal research in cases.
- Chapter 11 teaches the basics of reading, writing, and contextualizing legal citations to the sources covered in chapters 6 through 10, both formally and informally.

Much of the law that governs behavior is actually not public law found in statutes and regulations and cases, but private law such as that created by legally enforceable contracts. Thus, the next section of the book delves into crucial skills in reading and understanding contracts:

- Chapter 12 teaches the typical structure and parts of professionally drafted contracts.
- Chapter 13 covers the conceptual building blocks and types of substantive provisions commonly used in professionally drafted contracts.

The textbook then covers some specific contexts for communicating about the law:

- Chapter 14 provides basics about working with facts, such as recognizing legally relevant facts, distinguishing legal conclusions from facts, and summarizing fact investigations in a timeline or textual summary.
- Chapter 15 explores the broad topic of correspondence on legal matters, summarizing some key legal doctrines such as privilege and the importance of document retention. It then focuses on effective email practices.
- Chapter 16 introduces persuasive theory and types of legal arguments, then demonstrates persuasive legal writing through a study of persuasive comments filed in response to an administrative notice calling for comments on proposed regulatory action.

Finally, the book wraps up by covering editing skills:

- Chapter 17 focuses on accurate and consistent legal writing.
- Chapter 18 teaches principles of clear and concise legal writing.

Literacy in any specialized field is not easily acquired and must be built over time and through practice. The legal field is no different. Curious, persistent professionals may find deep satisfaction in discovering and reading the law governing a question. Those who work on a team may find that some legal writing techniques in fact benefit all of their professional writing with other team members, not just writing about law or legal issues. Gaining greater proficiency in understanding legal information can also mean asking better questions and thus working more efficiently with counsel. The benefits just discussed are somewhat individualistic or at least geared toward the effective internal mechanisms of private teams. More broadly, the journey toward legal literacy will, ideally, benefit not just individuals but society. Being legally literate means being able to advocate for better laws and regulations and even play a role in reforming the legal system itself.

As you work toward legal literacy, please remember the words of Professor White, reminding us that, like all literacy, legal literacy is a process:

> [T]he idea of perfect competence in legal language can never be attained; the practitioner is always learning about his language and about the world, he is in a sense always remaking both, and these processes never come to an end.[21]

Having studied this chapter, you should be able to:

- Apply the general concept of "literacy" to literacy in the law, or legal literacy
- Give examples of some situations in life where legal literacy plays a valuable role
- Formulate your own definition of legal literacy in your professional field
- Discuss how to move beyond basic to more advanced legal literacy

Introduction to the *Legal Literacy Case Study*

Olivia Ralston is a Colorado citizen at the center of the case study that runs throughout this book. Ms. Ralston will encounter a number of legal issues calling on legal literacy and communication skills. This is an outline of her situation and what she believes to be her legal issues.

Ms. Ralston and a cast of characters — including her family, friends, neighbors, coworkers, business partners, and others — will form many of the examples and the major case study you can work on to accompany the lessons in this book.

Olivia Ralston currently works as an account manager for Braggadocio, Inc., a global coffee manufacturer and retailer based in Denver, Colorado.

She is a dedicated family member who keeps tabs on her extended family in Texas such as her niece Tess Williams and nephew Sam Williams, both promising young people in the community. Her family knows Ms. Ralston has more legal knowledge than the average person on the street and looks to her for leadership and guidance. Ms. Ralston tries to be a supportive family member, but meanwhile

---

21. James Boyd White, *supra* note 4 at 143. The original uses the generic "he" to refer to all persons. This practice has come under scrutiny and criticism as sexist and unnecessary. *See* Joyce Rosenberg, *A Singular Understanding of They*, 85 J. Kan. B. Ass'n 20 (2016). Gender and pronouns will be addressed more fully in chapter 17.

may be facing a property dispute with her own neighbor at her backyard property line. Adding to her family responsibilities, Ms. Ralston's mother faces chronic pain and is looking into alternative homeopathic remedies. Ms. Ralston wants to make sure her mother does not ingest dangerous or illegal substances.

In her professional life, Ms. Ralston has an entrepreneurial streak: She wants to leave her job at Braggadocio, Inc., and start a new business in Denver, focused around the coffee industry. But she has a noncompetition agreement with Braggadocio and will be studying it closely to assess her situation.

She is excited by news such as a recent article in the *Inc.* business magazine, "Here's Why Venture Capitalists Are Pouring a Record $1 Billion Into Coffee Startups This Year."[22] She also hopes to infuse her own startup with a social-justice mission, acquiring coffee from micro-sellers who will be empowered by this new source of revenue. Ms. Ralston's own sense of social justice extends also to providing a safe environment for all her customers. Specifically, her family has dealt with severe food allergies, motivating her to source and sell non-dairy milks as an accompaniment to the coffee she hopes to serve.

Olivia Ralston also hopes to mentor and give opportunities to the next generation of young entrepreneurs through an internship program at her new business. Given the difficulty of funding a new business, this internship program will likely need to be unpaid, but Ms. Ralston is aware of legal concerns with unpaid internships and unsure whether she can proceed.

Ms. Ralston will be working with legal counsel to help her start these businesses, but she wants to do as much work as possible to establish her level of knowledge with counsel. By finding legal information and helping herself, Ms. Ralston expects to hold down her legal costs and remain fully connected to the management of her business.

---

22. Emily Canal, *Here's Why Venture Capitalists Are Pouring a Record $1 Billion Into Coffee Startups This Year*, Inc.com (Sept. 28, 2018) https://www.inc.com/emily-canal/national-coffee-day-startup-funding.html

Chapter 2

Foundations of the
United States Legal System

> If you have built castles in the air, your work need not be lost;
> that is where they should be. Now put the foundations under them.
>
> — Henry David Thoreau, *Walden*

Some foundational legal knowledge is crucial to develop and use legal literacy. This chapter reviews key points for understanding the United States legal system. If your program has a full introductory textbook or course, then some of this chapter may be review. That is okay. This foundational material is important because it quite literally affects everything else you will study in your legal education. The sections below discuss types of law, and they are followed by an overview of the structure of federal and state government and legal institutions in the United States.

I. Law: Relationships with Government and with Others

What does law address? What does it actually do? The idea of "the law" seems daunt-ingly monolithic. Is it possible to break down the law into categories? Thinking about categories of law means considering categories of relationships. Relationships in soci-ety affect the law, and the law affects relationships — relationships among people, busi-ness and other organizations, and governments.

Law provides background rules and creates duties and rights and remedies in an-cient situations such as property disputes among neighbors. But law also affects situa-tions never before seen in human history. How does law affect the relationships of people and "robots," such as driverless cars? Legislatures might seek to pass specific new laws on this type of question, but that does not mean there is currently *no* law affecting human-"robot" relationships. The general rules of product liability, a branch of tort law, are among the relevant laws structuring these questions even before specific new law can be enacted. Tort law sets forth liability rules for humans to collect money from other humans (including corporations treated as humans) for breaching a duty and causing damages. This is one example of a major category of law called civil law. Civil law governs relationships between people; for example, they can use the courts to pur-sue civil remedies, such as money damages. Civil law stands in contrast to criminal law, which is prosecuted by the government on behalf of the state or, as styled in many ju-risdictions, "the people."

Thinking about these categories of relationships is not just an academic exercise, but also a practical way of thinking about your own work: What categories are most inter-esting and important to you, as far as becoming more legally literate within your own industry, or developing a new expertise? When you think about working within the law or advocating to change it, what relationships would be relevant to that work? Where should you focus your attention and efforts?

A. The Distinction between Criminal Law and Civil Law

Criminal law is law that governs the minimal expectations of members of a society to one another. Violating a criminal law is not just violating an expectation of one party, but of the public. Prosecutors represent the public in enforcing criminal law. Because criminal law defines basic expectations such as "do not murder," the state funds the criminal justice system to enforce these basic expectations. The penalties for violating criminal law are often carried out through sentences of imprisonment in a local jail or a state or federal prison. Monetary fines and loss of rights, such as the right to vote or to drive or to practice a profession, may also serve as criminal penalties.

Civil law covers basically everything else about relationships and expectations be-tween people. Contract law and tort law are two classic examples. Contract law estab-lishes the rules for making binding agreements. Tort law establishes that people may sue one another to recover money for personal wrongs and injuries. These wrongs and injuries are described in legal terms as "intentional torts," such as battery; and "negligence," which broadly means failing to take reasonable care in certain situations. There are many other types of civil law beyond the classic areas of contract and tort, both of which originally derive from the English common law. Two examples include family law (dealing with marriages, divorces, adoptions, and other family-related situations) and probate law (dealing with distribution of property after death). Civil law can be created by statute, such as civil rights laws, health and safety laws, and privacy laws creating obligations between data collectors and consumers who provide data in the course of using services.

Because civil law provides the framework for relationships between people, it also provides the framework for litigation between people. That is, civil law is often the subject of private litigation, in which one party brings a lawsuit against another seeking a remedy from that person, often on the theory of making the plaintiff "whole." For example, a party to a contract who believes the contract has been breached can sue the other party for contract damages. But just as civil law includes a variety of statutory obligations between private parties, it also can be enforced by agencies in the pursuit of their legislative charge. Federal legislation defining individual rights and obligations typically includes an enforcement mechanism such as agency enforcement, a right of private action, or both. For example, individuals can sue their employers for employment discrimination after obtaining a "notice of right to sue" from the Equal Employment Opportunity Commission, but the EEOC can use its own agency resources to bring these suits as well. In contrast, anyone working in health care has probably heard of a "HIPAA breach," which refers to improperly releasing private health information in violation of the Health Insurance Portability and Accountability Act. HIPAA does not create a private right of action, so an individual whose health information has been released cannot sue for that harm. The only enforcement authorized by HIPAA is agency action by the Department of Health and Human Services.

With civil law as the framework for relationships between people, it's important to define what we mean by a "person." It includes natural persons, that is, human beings; but a corporation is treated as a person too, in many, many contexts—for example, a corporation has free speech rights under *Citizens United v. Federal Election Commission*, 558 U.S. 310 (2010). Corporate personhood exemplifies the concept of a "legal fiction," which basically means an artificial idea accepted in the legal system as a truth. Famous legal philosopher Lon Fuller described a legal fiction as "either (1) a statement propounded with a complete or partial consciousness of its falsity, or (2) a false statement recognized as having utility."[1] Another example is the "corporate veil," mentioned in chapter 1, which is the legal fiction that a corporation provides a "veil" around its shareholders protecting them from being individually liable (which essentially means financially responsible) for the actions of the corporation.

---

1. Lon L. Fuller, *Legal Fictions* 9 (1967).

Some areas of law are both civil and criminal. For example, an individual or business may hold a "trade secret," which is information that is economically valuable due to being a secret and that is subject to reasonable efforts to keep it secret.[2] If an employee leaves a business and starts a new business using the trade secret, the business can sue the employee civilly for misappropriation of a trade secret. But also under a relatively recent federal law, the Defend Trade Secrets Act, the theft of a trade secret used in interstate commerce may be a crime.[3] This is one example of how categories are useful ways to think about law, but they are not always formally separate. Sometimes different legal categories overlap in complementary ways, or in conflicting ways. That is part of what makes the law flexible but also complex.

B. The Distinction between Public Law and Private Law

The category of "public law" regulates relationships between people and government, and it imposes legal duties upon both. Criminal law is the most famous and well-known type of public law: It defines when government can prosecute and imprison members of society. Close behind it is constitutional law, which defines the structure of government and the rights of people that government cannot infringe.

Beyond criminal and constitutional law, there are other types of public law. The Internal Revenue Code is public law because it defines how the U.S. government collects taxes from individuals. The Freedom of Information Act is public law because it defines how individuals may seek and receive information from government. Administrative law is public law: It defines how administrative agencies use their statutory authority through the operation of the executive branch.

These forms of public law apply to everyone and cannot be modified — at least not unilaterally by the government. A police officer cannot change the scope of the Fourth Amendment in carrying out a search. A criminal suspect can, however, consent to the search, just as a criminal defendant can waive the right to a jury trial. A government employee can be disciplined or fired for disruptive words at work, but still has a zone of protected First Amendment rights to speak on matters of public concern.

---

2. Trade secrets law is a good example of the movement towards uniform laws. The National Conference of Commissioners on Uniform State Laws drafted and approved the Uniform Trade Secrets Act in 1985, and published it here: http://www.uniformlaws.org/shared/docs/trade%20secrets/utsa_final_85.pdf This is not an actual law; it is a model law available for state legislatures to consider and adopt, modifying if they wish. The Uniform Trade Secrets Act is the law in its exact or a slightly modified form in almost every state. See Uniform Law Commission, Trade Secrets Act, https://my.uniformlaws.org/committees/community-home? CommunityKey=3a2538fb-e030-4e2d-a9e2-90373dc05792 (interactive map of jurisdictions that have enacted the UTSA or whose legislatures have introduced it and are currently considering it).

3. 18 U.S.C. § 1832; see, e.g., John E. Drosick *Criminal Trade Secret Theft Charges Brought Against Silicon Valley Execs*, Lexology, (December 12, 2017), https://www.lexology.com/library/detail.aspx?g=1c8eed 5c-c535-42d9-ae3a-43e009cec77f (describing the possibility that executives who stole trade secrets from their company could suffer 10 years' jail time, as well as fines of up to $2.7 million).

In contrast, "private law" is a type of civil law for structuring individual relationships. Common examples include contracts, wills, and trusts, all of which are means by which parties create special law applicable to themselves, and not the public at large. The relationships forged by acts in a private law framework include relationships among actual human beings as well as among corporations and other business entities.

Private law is modifiable in many respects, although it is not completely malleable. Many bodies of private law (like the general law of contracts) set default rules, meaning the rules that apply in the absence of an agreement to the contrary. People can and do "contract around" those defaults all the time. The law of intestacy provides a default system for what happens when a person dies without a will, but a person can write a will that deviates greatly from the default rules of intestacy. The field of Law and Economics (capitalized because it is a famous school of thought like the Impressionists in art, but for law) focuses on the efficiency of default rules and arrangements to contract around them. A vast amount of law in this country is just that: private contractual arrangements between two or more parties. Private law is pervasive in U.S. society at both the business-to-business and business-to-consumer levels. Wall Street law firms create sophisticated custom lending and business transactions. Small businesses often use in-house lawyers and outside lawyers to craft their own deals. Everyone with a smartphone is a party to numerous licensing agreements for their smartphone apps.

Private law is highly modifiable because United States law generally prizes freedom of contract. That means parties are free to make contracts on a wide variety of matters, even if those contracts may look unwise or if one party is relatively powerless compared to the other. But freedom of contract is not unlimited. A contract to sell human organs is not enforceable, for example; and neither is a client's attempt to contract with a lawyer to assist a criminal enterprise. In a more subtle example, a ridesharing driver may sign a contract with the ridesharing provider that explicitly states she is an independent contractor. But a state's labor department, responsible for handling unemployment benefits when employees are terminated, may determine that the ridesharing driver in fact has the legal status of an employee for purposes of collecting unemployment taxes from the ridesharing provider and for purposes of her entitlement to unemployment benefits in the event she is terminated.

There are common themes in contracts that violate public policy, but you should be aware that state law can vary in certain respects. In many states, employees may sign and be bound to non-competition agreements prohibiting them from working for competitors after they leave the employer. Other states, such as California, prohibit these agreements as being against public policy. Many other states fall between these two extremes and will enforce noncompetition agreements only to the extent that they are "reasonable." The state-by-state variations of how public and private law interact can be a strength of the United States legal system, allowing experimentation and competition and efficient resolution of disputes. But they can also be a weakness, creating a race to the bottom where one way to compete is by deregulation that reduces cost and oversight to such a great extent that exploitation and other harmful consequences ensue.

These public policy exceptions to the freedom of contract show how public law can invade the domain of private law. Conversely, private law can invade the domain of public law. One major example is the role of dispute resolution clauses, often in the form of mandatory arbitration clauses. These clauses obligate the parties to the contract to use alternative dispute resolution, such as a specified arbitration service, while generally forfeiting the right to sue in court. In other words, the private law of the contract covers not only the substantive terms of the agreement but also the forum and procedure for resolving any disputes about that agreement. Arbitration can be faster and less expensive than litigation, but also has fewer procedural protections, such as very little latitude for appellate review of the arbitration result. Such clauses are commonplace not only in sophisticated business contracts but also in standard consumer contracts and even employment contracts. Throughout 2018, for example, a hotly disputed legal and political issue was the propriety of dispute resolution clauses for discrimination and sexual harassment claims.

Another current issue at the border of public and private law is the idea of "First Amendment rights" on social media platforms. In one sense, the arrangement between a social media user and the corporation offering the platform is pure private law—the terms of use accepted by the user when signing up. There are some restrictions on these arrangements, such as the Children's Online Privacy Protection Act,[4] and further regulating the data-related privacy practices of these businesses is an ongoing legal and policy issue. The corporation offering the platform does not, however, violate someone's First Amendment right of free speech by quarantining their posts or banning them from the platform. The corporation is not a government actor and is not responsible for protecting freedom of speech under the Constitution. Social media platforms are important and certainly can help to foster political speech, but their importance does not make a corporation into the equivalent of a governmental actor.

On the other hand, what about the scenario when a government official or agency uses a social media platform? Can an elected official block a constituent? That was the issue in *Davison v. Randall* 912 F. 3d 666 (4th Cir. 2019). The defendant was a county official who had banned a county resident from her Facebook page, which she categorized on Facebook as a "government official page" and titled "Chair Phyllis J. Randall" to indicate she was Chair of the Loudoun County Board of Supervisors. The plaintiff, a county resident, had posted something critical on her page in response to one of her posts, after which she deleted her post and the resident's comment, then blocked him on the page. The district court held, and the Fourth Circuit affirmed, that her use of the Facebook page for government business made it a limited-purpose public forum. Several passages in the opinion emphasized Randall's control over the page to reject her

---

4. Children's Online Privacy Protection Act of 1998, 15 U.S.C. §§ 6501-6506 (2018).

argument that Facebook was a private site. This judicial opinion is a worthwhile read and will surely be cited in future cases about how government officials utilize social media to interact with constituents especially if the United States Supreme Court continues to allow such issues to percolate at the circuit-court level.[5] *Davison*'s core holding was that the county official violated her constituent's First Amendment rights by—in her capacity as a government actor—engaging in viewpoint discrimination.

These two issues—mandatory arbitration clauses and public officials' use of social media—are just a few trending examples that illustrate the value of legal literacy. These examples also show that legal literacy is more than just knowing legal words and phrases like contracts that are "void against public policy." Understanding the functions of public and private law is a deeper type of legal literacy. Likewise, legal literacy entails understanding the structure of legal institutions. That is the topic of the next section.

II. The Legal Framework of United States Law

Developing legal literacy means building on a basic knowledge of civics. For instance, there are three branches of government, they check each other, and there are several levels of government including the state and federal levels. All of those basic statements that you have likely heard before are still true and are valuable in advanced legal training. By reviewing the structure of government and U.S. law, the legally literate professional can then move beyond basic knowledge into a deeper understanding. Knowing how to find and interpret the information they produce, seeing the primary evidence of how these branches interact, and being able to use legal knowledge and skills for professional work and self-advocacy—these are what we mean by legal literacy.

A. The Constitution and Branches of Government

In the United States, the founding document and master governing text is its national constitution. The U.S. Constitution is a relatively short document, consisting of 4,543 words in the main body and 7,591 words in the current list of amendments. The U.S. Constitution sets up three branches of government, as follows:

1. The Legislative Branch (Article I of the Constitution)

At the federal level, the legislative branch is the United States Congress, which consists of two chambers: the House of Representatives and the Senate. It is traditional to say that Congress makes the law; that is because, pursuant to Article I, Congress enacts legislation, also known as statutes. Congress makes laws under its enumerated powers in Article I, including laws that directly create, modify, or abolish legal rights and obli-

---

5. The United States Supreme Court has begun to address these issues. *See Packingham v. North Carolina*, 137 S. Ct. 1730 (2017) (holding that the state of North Carolina violated sex offenders' First Amendment rights by banning them completely from using or accessing social media); *Manhattan Community Access Corp. v. Halleck*, 139 S. Ct. 1921 (2019) (holding that Manhattan's public access channel was not a state actor subject to the First Amendment).

gations, as well as laws that influence the administrative state, such as by charging an agency with a legislative mandate. In the process of making legislation, Congress generates reports and other documents known as "legislative history." Research into statutes and legislative history is discussed in chapter 8.

2. The Executive Branch (Article II of the Constitution)

The federal executive branch consists of the President, Cabinet, and administrative agencies (main agencies represented in the Cabinet, plus other independent agencies). Article II sets out the general rules defining the U.S. presidency and describes the president's powers in leading the executive branch. The administrative agencies of the executive branch make rules (commonly known as *regulations*) as well as less formal guidance. Some agencies also adjudicate cases before administrative law judges. Research into administrative law is discussed in chapter 9.

3. The Judicial Branch (Article III of the Constitution)

Pursuant to Article III, the federal judiciary — that is, the federal courts — decide cases when they have jurisdiction (legal authority) to do so. Article III actually only requires the existence of a Supreme Court, but it delegates authority to Congress to create lower-level courts. Congress has exercised this authority many times in American history, resulting in the robust and extensive federal judicial branch that exists today. The judicial branch is unique in that the only way it creates law is by the courts writing opinions as they resolve the cases brought before them.[6] The important skill of reading judicial opinions is discussed in chapter 4, and the structure of the court system is further discussed in chapter 10.

4. Other Key Constitutional Features

Beyond its first three Articles, the Constitution also sets out the relationships of states to each other (Article VI), creates a process for its own amendment (Article V), and establishes that the Constitution and federal law hold supremacy over state laws when they conflict in areas of shared authority (Article VII).

The three branches of U.S. government are, famously, subject to "checks and balances" by one another. A well-known example is presidential veto power as a check on Congress, which in turn is checked by Congress's ability to override that veto. Another famous example of checks and balances is judicial review, most famously established in the Supreme Court case of *Marbury v. Madison*.[7] In *Marbury*, the U.S. Supreme

---

6. Proving that every rule has an exception, even the judicial branch implements the law like a regulatory agency in a few instances. For example, the United States Sentencing Commission is a bipartisan agency created by Congress but structured within the judicial branch of government, with seven voting members appointed by the President. Three of these members must be federal judges, and *all* federal judges must use the Sentencing Guidelines issued by this Commission in determining criminal sentences in federal court.

7. Chapter 11 discusses legal citations. Here is the formal legal citation: *Marbury v. Madison*, 5 U.S. 137 (1803).

Court first claimed and asserted its own power to strike down a law passed by Congress as unconstitutional. (*Marbury* also stands for the proposition the Supreme Court can order the President to obey the law.) But the Court is checked by the Executive as well because the President nominates federal judges for a lifetime appointment, and the Court is checked by Congress because Supreme Court nominees must be confirmed by the Senate. Congress can also "pack the court" by enacting legislation enlarging the number of judges that sit on a court, or have the opposite effect by holding up judicial nominations. Federal judges (as well as the President) can also be impeached by Congress. In addition, Congress funds the courts, and the Department of Justice — an executive agency — shapes federal law, especially federal criminal law, by how it represents the U.S. government as a litigant.

Beyond the formal checks and balances, the structure of U.S. government is not as clear-cut as one might expect from the three-part framework of legislative, executive, and judicial. Article II executive agencies are subject to the president's authority to nominate and to remove the agency's head officer, but Congress has established some independent agencies whose head officer is not appointed or removable by the President. Executive Orders and nonenforcement of laws and regulations have been discussed in recent years as ways the executive branch may effectively make law or control law's effect without congressional action. And even the courts are not neatly contained in Article III. Most courts are known as "Article III courts" and subject to the structural framework in Article III of the Constitution, but there are courts created by Congress and known as Article I courts: the United States Bankruptcy Courts, the Patent Trial and Appeal Board, and the Trademark Trial and Appeal Board. Many disputes and hearings are handled through administrative adjudications before administrative law judges carrying out the adjudicative function of administrative agencies. These examples illustrate that while the three-part structure of the U.S. government is a useful way to think about government, the model is not a strict set of inviolate and impermeable categories.

B. Federal and State Legal Systems

A key feature of the United States legal system is federalism itself: the idea that the federal government is not the only layer of government. State government is extremely important in U.S. law. Overall, federal and state law exist in different but overlapping circles, which you might envision like this:

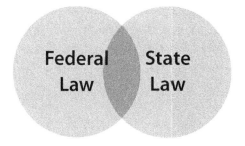

Two provisions of the U.S. Constitution are most important in setting up the interplay between federal and state law. First, under the Supremacy Clause, federal law supersedes any conflicting state law on the same subject:[8]

> This Constitution, and the Laws of the United States which shall be made in Pursuance thereof; and all Treaties made, or which shall be made, under the Authority of the United States, shall be the supreme Law of the Land; and the Judges in every State shall be bound thereby, any Thing in the Constitution or Laws of any State to the Contrary notwithstanding.

Under the Supremacy Clause, the U.S. Constitution sets a minimum, often called a "floor," for constitutional rights. What this means is that state government cannot establish lower or less protective constitutional rights than those guaranteed by the Constitution. Remember that the Constitution does not protect anyone against other private citizens' decisions and actions, but it does protect against government action such as interfering with free speech and the free exercise of religion, conducting unreasonable searches and seizures, and invading other Constitutional rights, especially those secured by the Bill of Rights (the first 10 amendments to the Constitution). Thus, for example, the state of Maryland could not, in its state constitution, require appointed government officials to declare their belief in God as a requirement to take office; this requirement violated the First Amendment of the U.S. Constitution, specifically the First Amendment's Free Exercise Clause.[9] State constitutions can, however, establish higher protections. For example, Montana is among several states whose constitution mentions environmental rights alongside other types of individual rights:

> All persons are born free and have certain inalienable rights. They include the right to a clean and healthful environment and the rights of pursuing life's basic necessities, enjoying and defending their lives and liberties, acquiring, possessing and protecting property, and seeking their safety, health and happiness in all lawful ways. In enjoying these rights, all persons recognize corresponding responsibilities.[10]

In sum, states *must* provide the minimum constitutional protections from government action that are guaranteed in the U.S. Constitution, and they *may* provide higher protections from their own state government action via their own state constitution.

In addition to this overlap in the constitutional rights that federal and state constitutions protect, there is also some overlap in statutory law. The federal Constitution

---

8. U.S. Const. art. VI, cl. 2.
9. *Torasco v. Watkins*, 367 U.S. 488 (1961).
10. Mont. Const. art. II § 3.

does not hoard every power of government; under the Tenth Amendment, every area of lawmaking power not enumerated to Congress is reserved to the states or to the people.

But when Congress does have the enumerated power to legislate, the Supremacy Clause gives Congress the power not only to overlap with state law, but also to blot it out through *preemption*. Preemption occurs when federal law covers an area and sets the bar in a way state law cannot change, even to make it more protective. Federal law that preempts state law sets one uniform standard for the country in that area. Federal patent law is an example; there is no state patent law, nor can there be. Copyright is another example; state copyright law has been preempted since 1972. (There are actually still some current cases addressing pre-1972 rights under state copyright law, such as old sound recordings from the 1960s.[11]) Patent and copyright law are now completely preempted by federal law. Sometimes Congress legislates in an area but does not preempt state law in that same area. Thus, some areas of law are covered by Congress *and* by state legislatures. For example, some states have antidiscrimination laws that provide broader protections against discrimination in employment and public transportation than their federal counterparts.[12] And some areas of law are traditionally reserved to state legislatures, particularly family law, property law, and the law of trusts and estates. But these areas are still subject to the constitutional protections of Equal Protection and Due Process. For example, the Supreme Court held in *Obergefell v. Hodges* that the Fourteenth Amendment requires states to recognize same-sex couples' right to marriage.

What does this dual, partially overlapping system mean for people, organizations, and companies trying to find and understand the law? Recognizing a potential legal issue means also recognizing it may be subject to federal law only, state law only, or both federal and state law. The intertwined state and national roles in a federal system like that of the United States mean that many legal issues can be very complex. Legal literacy means being able to take an educated guess at whether an issue is federal, state, or both, and to find and use information from whatever layer (or layers) of government may apply.

C. Local Government

Many legal issues that affect people, organizations, and companies are governed at the local level, rather than at the national or state level. Local governments in the United States are created and authorized by the applicable state government. Typically, a state legislature charters a city, giving it the authority to enact its own municipal ordinances. Ordinances cannot exceed the scope of the charter. Most states are also divided into geographic regions known as counties — another level of local government.

---

11. *E.g.*, *iHeart Media v. Sheridan*, 300 Ga. 771, 798 S.E.2d 223 (2017).

12. *See, e.g.*, New Jersey Civil Rights Law 10:5-1.

Local governments, being part of the state in which they are located, are subject to state open records and sunshine laws requiring them to make requested documents available and hold open meetings. They may publish their laws online and in printed, bound form at government offices. A detailed treatment of legal research into municipal ordinances is outside the scope of this book, but the general research skills covered here will help with work in local government.[13]

III. How Law Changes Over Time

As we noted in chapter 1, competent legal literacy means not just knowing about the legal system, but participating in it. Reaching this level of literacy means understanding two things:

The law is much more than what is written down in statute books and judicial opinions and regulatory codes. Importantly, in a democratic system of government, the law changes in response to people's efforts to make it change.

The law is comprised of text (i.e., words), and textual arguments are highly valued in legal reasoning. But valid legal arguments can arise from the effects of law in the real world. Working with the law means seeking to understand its practical effect in the real world, and using tools of legal reasoning to influence that effect. The law changes through the efforts of people who set out to reach results. This section gives an overview of how the law changes, and how advocacy and other efforts play a role in that change. Chapter 16 discusses persuasive advocacy using legal reasoning in more detail.

A. Changing Statutes and Regulations

Legislation changes, most obviously, through more legislation—new laws and amendments to old laws. The election cycle influences the policy goals of each legislature, bringing in new legislators and re-electing incumbents. Lobbyists and constituent interests seek to influence legislation through action and support, as well as inaction and opposition. Legislators may also draw ideas from legal institutions such as the Uniform Law Commission, whose stated goal is providing states with "non-partisan, well conceived, and well drafted legislation that brings clarity and stability to critical areas of state statutory law."[14]

Regulation and administrative law also change from both the top down and bottom up. The election cycle brings in a new or re-elected chief executive (president or gov-

---

13. A source to consult for further information is Barbara Bevis and Robert Brammer, *Municipal Codes: A Beginner's Guide*, In Custodia Legis Blog hosted by the Law Librarians of Congress (Nov. 21, 2013), https://blogs.loc.gov/law/2013/11/municipal-codes-a-beginners-guide/; see also the University of Buffalo, Municipal and Local Government Law: Books, Treatises, and Practices Guides (last updated October 24, 2018), https://research.lib.buffalo.edu/municipal-and-local-govt .

14. The Uniform Law Commission (also known as the National Conference of Commissioners on Uniform State Laws), http://www.uniformlaws.org/

ernor), which in turn influences administrative appointments and policy priorities in administrative agencies. Agencies also must adhere to their statutory mandate, which of course can be modified by the legislature. And agencies considering new regulations must follow the applicable administrative procedure, which generally will provide a forum for the public to comment on and advocate for their interests.

B. Cases and the Changing Common Law

The *case law* in a jurisdiction is the collection of that jurisdiction's judicial opinions. In one sense, case law is constantly changing. Every time a new judicial opinion is published, it adds something to the law. But in a more meaningful sense, the case law in a jurisdiction usually changes very, very slowly. U.S. courts are deeply influenced by the English common law system. One of the key features of the common law is the principle of *stare decisis*—Latin for "to stand by things decided."[15] Under the principle of stare decisis, courts must follow precedent from courts that are above it, and courts must also follow their own precedent absent a compelling reason to do otherwise. Following precedent can be very direct: Suppose a state's supreme court has decided a legal issue, including how that issue applies to a certain set of facts. The trial courts and intermediate appellate courts in that state must follow that decision. If the same or very similar facts arise in a new case, those courts should follow that case and reach the same result. In this way, the principle of stare decisis gives the court system stability and predictability. Those affected by the law—both in the litigation and in the general public—can manage their conduct accordingly.

Stare decisis does not mean that case law never changes. The common law's influence over United States courts still leaves substantial flexibility. The most traditional way that case law changes is when new factual scenarios arise and the court must consider whether and to what extent stare decisis compels the result. If the facts are exactly the same as in a precedent case, the court should follow stare decisis. But what if the facts are different in some way? What if the new facts present a new type of argument for a different result? Different facts present opportunities for courts to follow precedent by *distinguishing* it: that is, to decide cases by explaining that the old precedent is still "good law" but that the different facts lead to a different result.

Attorneys representing their clients in litigation play an important role because they are professionally obligated to advocate for their client. Their arguments may say that the new facts are just like existing precedent; the new facts are different from but consistent with precedent; or the new facts are so different from precedent that there really is no precedent on point. Here it is important to note that making precedent is not just about arguments lawyers come up with after the facts have happened; as Professor

---

15. *Stare decisis*, Wex, Cornell Legal Information Institute, https://www.law.cornell.edu/wex/stare_decisis

Mark Hannah argued in his article on legal literacy, the parties themselves begin to make precedent with their decisions before any lawyer or judge gets involved.[16]

C. The Interplay of Cases and Statutes

Case law also changes because of its relationship to legislation. Courts must follow their legislature's enacted law — statutes — unless they are holding a statute *unconstitutional*, in other words, violating a higher legal authority (which is quite rare). Courts interpret statutes and decide cases involving statutory disputes, and then they try to follow their own precedent — how they previously interpreted the statute. But case law changes very quickly when legislation changes. When the legislature changes statutory law, the cases decided under the prior version of the statute are questionable at best. Case law from before the statutory change may no longer be valid law, or it may still have some validity, depending on the nature of the change. The legislation itself may specify that the new statute supplants and replaces old law, or that the new statute continues old law with clarifications — or it may be silent, leaving courts to interpret this question too.

Apart from new facts and new legislation, sometimes case law changes because courts themselves drive the change, or at least recognize it and modify or overrule their precedent in light of new circumstances. In the famous 1954 case of *Brown v. Board of Education*, the Supreme Court considered historical circumstances at the time the Fourteenth Amendment was ratified and when the 1896 case of *Plessy v. Ferguson* permitted racial segregation into so-called "separate but equal" public facilities. On its way to overruling *Plessy* and holding that racial segregation was unconstitutional, the Court cited current circumstances: "We must consider public education in the light of its full development and its present place in American life throughout the Nation."[17]

Changed circumstances also played a role in the Supreme Court's recent consideration of sales tax on internet sales. In 2018, the court reversed earlier precedent that states could not collect sales tax from businesses with no physical presence in the state.[18] New circumstances render the old law unworkable, as the Court recognized: "[T]he real world implementation of Commerce Clause doctrines now makes it manifest that the physical presence rule as defined by [the prior precedent] must give way to the 'far-reaching systemic and structural changes in the economy' and 'many other societal dimensions' caused by the Cyber Age."[19] When circumstances change substantially, courts then must consider arguments that following precedent is worse and less legitimate than changing course.

---

16. Mark A. Hannah, *Legal Literacy: Coproducing the Law in Technical Communication*, 20 Technical Comm. Quarterly 5, 13 (2010).

17. *Brown v. Board of Educ.*, 347 U.S. 483, 492–493 (1954).

18. *Wayfair v. South Dakota*, 138 S. Ct. 2080 (2018).

19. *Id.* at 2097.

IV. The Rule of Law

The government structures and processes discussed above are intended to serve the purpose of implementing an <u>overarching democratic value: the rule of law</u>.

In countries based on the rule of law, politicians and bureaucrats and citizens shape their actions based on something other than force. <u>Rule of law requires integrity, fairness, and consistent application of the law</u>. People are accountable for their actions and inactions. And government, including the individuals acting on government's behalf, can be subject to lawsuits for their own violations of the rule of law. In other words, the governors are accountable to the governed not just through democratic processes, but through lawsuits as well.

The rule of law plays a role in every branch of government. Judges must recuse themselves if they have a conflict of interest. Congress has enacted the Freedom of Information Act, giving people the right to request information from the government. Administrative agencies must follow a strict process for making rules, allowing the public ample opportunity to comment on proposed regulations before they are implemented.

Increasing legal literacy among the populace thus ideally enhances the populace's ability to participate in and preserve the rule of law. Legally literate individuals can use their literacy skills in many ways that maintain and strengthen the rule of law:

- write clearer laws, contracts, and policies
- understand and interpret laws even when the laws fall short of being ideally clear
- find law where it is published and accessible
- help others access and understand legal information
- recognize when the law is stable and evenly applied—or not
- participate in or criticize government
- serve as a representative or neutral arbiter to resolve disputes
- advocate to a representative or neutral, thus providing better information for the dispute resolution process

Having a <u>strong rule of law</u> should benefit everyone in a country, increasing conditions for economic opportunity and creating an (accurate) sense of stability and fairness in people's dealings with one another and the government.

V. Conclusion

Law is everywhere. It inspires aspirational beliefs and cynical disappointment; it causes concrete effects. Law defines punishment, rights, remedies, and procedures for dealing with disputes. Law is a process, an ongoing evolution of people's relationships with each other and the government. It is text on paper, but it also affects the world beyond the paper.

Law is simultaneously stable and dynamic. It is political, but with limits on political influence. Disputes should be decided fairly based on each new set of facts, but the law should also apply consistently in similar situations. These constant tensions are not a side effect to be tolerated; they help maintain the legal system's vitality and legitimacy. These tensions sometimes also cause dissatisfaction with the legal system—arguments that the law is too stable or too dynamic, too political or too apolitical, too individualized or too categorical. The law is neither completely certain, nor completely uncertain. Whatever effectiveness it may or may not have is derived from the work of people collectively playing their roles in the legal system.

Having studied this chapter, you should be able to:

- Describe the functions of public and private law
- Explain to a friend or colleague the basic structure of state and federal legal systems in the United States
- Identify areas where contracts create a massive body of private law deviating from the default legal rules set by legislatures
- Discuss how law is not a static framework but is subject to change in individual results and, to an extent, its very structure
- Explain the concept of the rule of law and why it is an important foundation in a legal system

··

Case Study: U.S. Legal Structure and Uses

Olivia Ralston, a resident of Denver, Colorado, faces a variety of personal and professional issues that legal information and skills can help her manage. For this segment of her case study, choose one of the following situations. Think about, discuss, and/or write about the law's role in the situation:

- What parts of the legal system are relevant to this situation?
- How does the legal system contribute to the problem, or provide means to solve it, or both?
- How could legal institutions and legally knowledgeable professionals help address and resolve each specific person's problem?
- Are there any legal reforms that could alleviate or prevent the problem in the first place? If so, what might those be?

Situation 1

Ms. Ralston hears from her sister Angela that her 19-year-old niece, Tess Williams, has been traumatized by an event at work. She was accused of shoplifting—falsely—and held in an interview room and not allowed to leave for two hours. Her manager, a former football star in the community, along with two security guards, were present during this ordeal. Ms. Ralston, her brother, her brother's wife, and the rest of the family are outraged. They want to use the legal system against the store, and prevent this kind of thing from happening to others.

Situation 2

Tess's older brother, Sam Williams, has earned excellent grades at Texas A&M University and has political aspirations. He now has the opportunity to do an internship in Washington D.C. This internship, however, is unpaid. The family will be able to financially support Sam in this unpaid internship, but they know other promising students who would not be able to muster such support. Ms. Ralston is interested in this issue because she herself may want to invite interns (unpaid) at her new business venture in Denver, Colorado. She wants to learn the rules of unpaid internships so she can understand more about her family's own situation and make decisions for her small business.

Situation 3

In starting her small business, Ms. Ralston wants the business to make money, of course. But she also wants to imbue it with a specific social purpose: providing a safe place for people with severe environmental and food allergies to work, and providing products that people with environmental and food allergies can buy and eat. She is curious about potential business structures that would help express these goals. She wants to inform potential investors this is a business with a positive mission, and inform them that some of her decisions will help further the business's social purpose. She believes the social mission will make the business more attractive and profitable, and wants to investigate business structures that would best fit her goals.

Chapter 3

Foundations of the Practice and Unauthorized Practice of Law

"Are you planning to follow a career in Magical Law, Miss Granger?" asked Scrimgeour.

"No, I'm not," retorted Hermione. "I'm hoping to do some good in the world!"

— J.K. Rowling, *Harry Potter and the Deathly Hallows*

We confess to being far more optimistic than Hermione about the capacity for law to do some good in the world. Law sets up a framework for problem solving that cuts across and is relevant to all industries and professions, including but not limited to law. Problem-solving is ultimately part of the job of all working professionals. It is how individual and group efforts are successful: identifying needs and conflicts and other situations to work on, generating strategies, choosing a strategy, involving others when appropriate, executing the strategy, and assessing whether all of it worked. Problem-solving helps institutions adjust to challenges and carry out their work, and it helps individuals gain recognition and advancement at work.

Categorizing the expertise needed to solve a problem is part of actually solving it. This chapter addresses some of the legal ramifications when working professionals face a *legal* problem. The goal is to encourage engaged legal literacy and effective legal problem-solving but to discourage the unauthorized practice of law, which is illegal and can lead to a variety of consequences discussed below. Please note that throughout this chapter we use the term "lawyer" as shorthand for a licensed attorney in the relevant jurisdiction.

I. The Legally Literate Professional

What sorts of things can a person who does not have a law license do without venturing into the minefield of the unauthorized practice of law? Although the complete answer to this question varies from state to state, a few guiding principles apply most everywhere in the United States.

First, you can use any and all legal skills in helping yourself. You can freely use legal information and legal skills to try to solve your own problems. You can use your own expertise to analyze the law; you can think and decide what to do; you can even represent yourself in court. The technical term for a self-represented layperson is one of the few Latin terms still routinely used in legal language: *pro se*, as in "*pro se* litigant." It means proceeding on your own behalf. Representing yourself is allowed (even when doing so is unwise) because if you make a mistake, the only person hurt is you. Giving advice to others raises the possibility of harming them, which is the basic justification for prohibiting the unauthorized practice of law.

Second, you can use legal skills under the supervision of a lawyer. Most employees of law firms and in-house corporate legal departments who are not lawyers fit in this category. The lawyer in these situations has an independent ethical duty to supervise professionals doing delegated work and to make sure they do not engage in unethical conduct (actions the lawyer could not accomplish directly under the applicable rules of legal ethics). From an enforcement standpoint, the lawyer's law license is the one being put on the line because he or she is responsible for the actions of the supervised employees.

Third — and probably most importantly for students reading this book — within an organization or agency or corporation, you can satisfy the duties in your job description. Some jobs provide, indeed require, significant leeway to perform law-related services and handle legal issues not under the direction of a lawyer. For example, the typical duties of a contract administrator or contracting officer involve a variety of legal tasks and roles, possibly including drafting contract provisions and assessing whether a contract has been violated in a manner that justifies terminating it. Other jobs involve occasional contact with lawyers. A company risk manager may, for example, be asked to review lawsuits being handled by outside counsel in the course of making a decision on whether to continue in a certain line of business.

As with many legal issues, there are gray areas. Suppose a startup faces its first unemployment claim by a former worker. Can its Human Resources director attend the unemployment compensation hearing on behalf of the company?[1] The discussion be-

---

1. *See* Allen Smith, *When Does HR Cross Over Into the Practice of Law?*, Society for Human Resource Management (July 6, 2017).

low of the unauthorized practice of law should help professionals recognize when their work might overlap into applying the law to the facts using legal judgment or representing another person or entity before a tribunal. We hope this chapter also facilitates effective problem solving by professionals called upon to assess situations that may require or benefit from legal advice.

II. Bridging the Gap with Lawyers

The very mention of the illegality of the unauthorized practice of law may lead some readers to want to drop this book and run far away. Don't. You need to be aware that the legal profession has an enforceable monopoly over the practice of law, and it is a monopoly with teeth because acts constituting the unauthorized practice of law are a crime in some jurisdictions. Such acts can also trigger consequences such as not being able to enforce a contract for services later determined to be the unauthorized practice of law. A contract that entails paying for legal representation by someone who is not a licensed attorney is void against public policy. While parties are free to *sign* such a contract or enter one verbally and perform such a contract, neither side will be able to *enforce* it—even if one side fails to deliver agreed-upon services or the other side refuses to pay for services rendered.

Whether the consequences are civil or even possibly criminal, the most important lesson to draw here is that the core of the prohibition on unauthorized practice of law is that a person who is not a licensed attorney cannot take on and represent clients. Period. A licensed attorney's job is to practice law for clients, and the state-sanctioned monopoly over that job exists to protects the public for reasons (arguably) analogous to the state-sanctioned monopoly on licensing doctors to practice medicine for patients.

Even outside of any legal consequences for overlapping into lawyers' domain of practicing law, we want you to understand that lawyers bring to the table a great deal of expertise. A licensed attorney has completed three years of law school, passed the state's bar exam, and kept up to date on the law by completing the state's annual continuing legal education requirements.[2] When dealing with questions that do not technically require the practice of law, it still may be wise to seek legal advice. When people who lack legal knowledge attempt to dig into legal issues, they can sometimes do more harm than good. In-house counsel and other practicing lawyers sometimes become frustrated with speculative inquiries such as "Hey, I Googled this and I think…" Part of the lawyer's ethical responsibility is to inform and communicate legal issue with the client, giving the client the information and advice necessary for the client to make decisions. Having

---

2. In four other states, it is still possible to "read the law," instead of attending law school—an option recently brought back into the public eye by celebrity Kim Kardashian's statement to *Vogue* magazine that she is reading the law in California. Jonathan Van Meter, *The Awakening of Kim Kardashian West*, Vogue (April 10, 2019).

a lawyer's advice and representation will in some cases be the ideal approach to solving a problem with a legal dimension, even if not required by law.

A. Roles in the Legal Landscape

This book is premised on the firm belief that there is a middle ground between proceeding at your own risk with little to no legal savvy on the one hand, and relying completely on a lawyer's legal advice for any "law-sounding" question, on the other hand. The law applies to everyone, and everyone is operating within its complexity. Professionals from all fields need the ability to collaborate effectively and efficiently on legal issues. Expertise in such a collaborative field is not a zero-sum game. Effective collaborations do not require one party to have all the information and her counterpart to have none. Legal literacy, rather than usurping the lawyer's role, actually encompasses working with lawyers more effectively and with a better understanding of why they do what they do and how to collaborate with them. An informed client has a better and more effective lawyer when those interactions arise. Yet lawyers do maintain a special role in giving legal advice, drafting legal language in contracts, and representing clients in court.

The goal of this chapter and this book is to empower professionals from various fields of expertise in their collaboration and problem-solving. With those goals and understandings in mind, let us next try to better define some boundaries.

B. The Practice of Law and the Unauthorized Practice of Law

State courts and legislatures define the practice of law, which in turn defines the *unauthorized* practice of law ("UPL"). The American Bar Association, a national association for lawyers that studies and advocates on issues affecting lawyers nationwide, influences states' approach to UPL, even though the ABA is a trade association and does not make law. A few historical notes on the ABA's work in this area show the challenges in clearly and simply defining what the practice of law actually is. The 1981 version of the ABA's suggested ethical rules for lawyers provided a "functional" definition of the practice of law:

> [T]he practice of law relates to the rendition of services for others that call for the professional judgment of a lawyer. The essence of a lawyer's professional judgment is the educated ability to relate the general body and philosophy of law to a specific legal problem of a client.[3]

In 2002–2003, an ABA Task Force tried to develop a model definition of the practice of law. That task force ultimately decided not to set out one definition, instead

---

3. ABA Model Code Ethical Consideration 3-5 (1981), quoted in Derek Denckla, *Nonlawyers and the Unauthorized Practice of Law: An Overview of the Ethical and Legal Parameters*, 67 Fordham L. Rev. 2581, 2586-2587 (1999).

recommending that each state set its own definition based around the idea of applying law to fact for another:

> [E]ach state's and territory's definition should include the basic premise that the practice of law is the application of legal principles and judgment to the circumstances or objectives of another person or entity.[4]

The report supporting this recommendation noted that legal advice is inherent not only to representing others in court but also selecting and drafting legal documents.[5] In reaching the very general statement above, the task force emphasized the balance of harm and benefit in how jurisdictions go about defining and policing the practice of law:

> The process of balancing harm and benefit is not an easy one. There is no simple formula. It requires an exercise of discretion and judgment based on the best available evidence. Each jurisdiction should weigh concerns for public protection and consumer safety, access to justice, preservation of individual choice, judicial economy, maintenance of professional standards, efficient operation of the marketplace, costs of regulation and implementation of public policy.[6]

The current version of the ABA's Model Rules of Professional Conduct suggests a policy rationale behind these different definitions: "Whatever the definition, limiting the practice of law to members of the bar protects the public against rendition of legal services by unqualified persons."[7] Others have suggested that a more significant rationale for guarding the practice of law is to prevent competition.[8]

The ethics rules acknowledge that some professionals are also experts in law-related matters: As early as that 1981 set of ethics rules, the ABA recognized and accepted that some occupations "require a special knowledge of law in certain areas," such as police officers, court clerks, and many governmental employees.[9] And the ethics rules acknowledge a wide range of "law-related services" that can be performed in conjunction

---

4. ABA Task Force on the Model Definition of the Unauthorized Practice of Law, *Recommendation as adopted August 11, 2003*, cited in Michele DeStefano, *Compliance and Claim Funding: Testing the Borders of Lawyers' Monopoly and the Unauthorized Practice of Law*, 82 Fordham L. Rev. 2961, 2968 (2014).

5. Lish Whitson, Chair, *Report Supporting ABA Task Force Recommendation on the Model Definition of the Unauthorized Practice of Law* (August 2003).

6. *Id.* For more analysis, we recommend Catherine Lanctot, *Does Legal Zoom have First Amendment Rights: Some Thoughts About Free Speech and the Unauthorized Practice of Law*, 20 Temple Pol. & Civ. Rights L. Rev. 255 (2011).

7. Comment [2] to ABA Model Rule 5.5.

8. Kimberly Ann Clemsen, *The Unauthorized Practice of Law: Overstepping the Boundary*, 1 Fla. Coastal L. J. 535, 538 (2000).

9. Derek Denckla, *Nonlawyers and the Unauthorized Practice of Law*: An Overview of the Legal and Ethical Parameters, 67 Fordham L. Rev. 2581, 2587 (1999).

with the practice of law but are "not prohibited as unauthorized practice of law when provided by a nonlawyer."[10]

A broad range of economic and other interests of clients may be served by lawyers' engaging in the delivery of law-related services alongside the practice of law. Examples of law-related services include providing title insurance, financial planning, accounting, trust services, real estate counseling, legislative lobbying, economic analysis, social work, psychological counseling, tax preparation, and patent, medical, or environmental consulting.[11]

While performing law-related services, lawyers must take reasonable measures to inform people using these services that they are not legal services and do not have the protections of the client-lawyer relationship such as the attorney-client privilege.[12] The rules contain a useful reminder for all professionals providing law-related services: "When the full protections of all of the Rules of Professional Conduct do not apply to the provision of law-related services, principles of law external to the Rules, for example, the law of principal and agent, govern the legal duties owed to those receiving the services."[13] For example, a social worker may have separate legal and ethical boundaries on the duty of confidentiality, and the trustee administering a trust has a fiduciary duty to the trust.

C. State Variations

In spite of (or perhaps because of) this very general guidance from the ABA, American states vary quite a bit in how they define the practice of law (which in turn defines the unauthorized practice of law). For example, Arizona's Rule of the Supreme Court 31(a)(2) defines the practice of law as follows:

The "practice of law" means providing legal advice or services to or for another by:

A. Preparing any document in any medium intended to affect or secure legal rights for a specific person or entity;

B. Preparing or expressing legal opinions;

C. Representing another in a judicial, quasi-judicial, or administrative proceeding, or other formal dispute resolution process such as arbitrations and mediations;

D. Preparing any document through any medium for filing in any court, administrative agency or tribunal for a specific person or entity; or

E. Negotiating legal rights or responsibilities for a specific person or entity.

---

10. Model Rule of Professional Conduct 5.7(b).
11. Model Rule of Professional Conduct 5.7, comment [9].
12. Model Rule of Professional Conduct 5.7(a).
13. Model Rule of Professional Conduct 5.7, comment [11]

More broadly, the Maryland Supreme Court has defined the practice of law as "the using of 'legal education, training, and experience' to apply legal analysis to a client's problems."[14]

Consequences for the unauthorized practice of law (or UPL) also vary, ranging from being unable to enforce the contract and obtain payment[15] to facing criminal charges, usually a misdemeanor.[16] In New York, however, the unauthorized practice of law can constitute a felony when it causes damages of more than $1000 or other material damage from the impairment of a legal right.[17] The New York law addressing unauthorized practice of law has numerous exceptions and does not apply to pre-paid legal plans, non-profits that provide incidental legal services, and legal aid services for the indigent.[18] Legislation was introduced in 2017 to reduce the penalty back to a misdemeanor, but the legislation appears to have stalled in a legislative committee and had not been enacted into law as of this writing.

Beware that a caveat such as "I'm not a lawyer and this is not legal advice, but..." does *not* prevent the advice itself from meeting a state's definition of the practice of law. You may wonder why this is the case. Consider what would happen if a simple disclaimer like this could defeat a state's effort to enforce its UPL statutes. Strong free-market advocates would argue that the resulting market for legal services would be *better* than the status quo. But state courts and state bar associations, citing the policy of protecting the public from unreliable, unqualified advice, do not agree.

III. Problem Solving in the Shadow of the Unauthorized Practice of Law

Understanding the rough boundaries of legal advice should help working professionals brainstorm ways that legal advice may fit in with — or conflict with — problem-solving in their industries and their organizations. In some situations, teams made up of various professional disciplines like law, business, engineering, policy work, medicine, and so on may work together very productively. In other situations, the various professionals' differing goals, vocabularies, and risk tolerance may cause clashes and collaborative difficulties. Below, we discuss two diametrically opposed options — basically delegating everything to the lawyer and, alternatively, keeping the lawyers out of it as much as possible. You should immediately see where this is going: We want to explore the middle ground.

---

14. DeStefano, *supra* note 4, at 2968 (quoting *Kennedy v. Bar Ass'n*, 561 A.2d 200, 208 (Md. 1989)).

15. E.g., *Linder v. Insurance Claims Consultants, Inc.*, 560 S.E.2d 612 (2002) (voiding contract for public insurance adjuster since some of his services were the unauthorized practice of law, but allowing adjuster to recover the value of services he provided to client that did not constitute UPL).

16. *E.g.,* Tex. Penal Code § 38.122 (prohibiting non-lawyers from holding themselves out as lawyers to gain an economic benefit).

17. N.Y Consol. Judiciary Law 485-a.

18. N.Y. Consol. Judiciary Law 495(7).

A. The "Hot Potato" Approach

A legal problem should be handed off to a lawyer or in-house department, right? That, after all, is their entire purpose—to handle legal issues. Some clients may enter their working relationship with a lawyer hoping they can hand off a problem and not think about it again until it is resolved.

The "hot potato" approach is not effective or realistic for a variety of reasons. First, when a lawyer begins to represent a client—solving a problem, working on a transaction, or otherwise practicing law—the lawyer does not take over the whole process. The ethical rules governing lawyers preserve the client's power and authority to set the objectives of the representation and make key decisions. The lawyer has authority over some of the day-to-day details of a representation, but the client sets the objectives of the representation, such as negotiating a contract or pursuing litigation to obtain a monetary reward. And the client must make key decisions such as settling a case at a certain amount or giving up the right to a jury trial.

In sum, a lawyer works on behalf of a client and must communicate with that client and implement the client's decisions in key areas. For corporate and organizational clients, the organization itself is the client, but the lawyer still communicates with its officers about the objectives and decisions of the organization. Thus, problem-solving with legal issues may involve bringing in "legal," but when that happens, the client still makes the crucial decisions. Legal literacy helps the client to fulfill that role.

B. The "Lone Wolf" Approach

The opposite route is to keep the lawyers out of the loop, either intentionally or unintentionally. It is probably rare for a business team to intentionally exclude in-house lawyers from information and conversations about known legal problems, but people can sometimes make shockingly bad decisions. What seems more common is not recognizing a problem as "legal" at all, and trying to implement business solutions that exacerbate related legal problems.

Legal advice can provide crucial support to an individual or organization negotiating contract terms that have legal consequences, making decisions that bring risk on the organization, or proceeding with a difficult situation. (One example that comes to mind is handling the last months or year of a long-term outsourcing contract that the company intends to terminate and transfer to another vendor. Contact with the outsourcing provider about to be dropped may be fraught with business and legal issues that would benefit from legal advice.) Legally literate professionals should be able to recognize when a lawyer's advice is needed, communicate with the lawyer to explore options, set the objectives of the representation, and make key decisions. Professionals in a corporation or other organization should be able to effectively communicate with lawyers performing their advisory role within the organization.

C. The Middle Ground: Working on Legal Issues with Law and Lawyers

While practicing law for others is a role reserved for lawyers, "thinking like a lawyer" is open to anyone who wants to do it, lawyer or not. So what is "thinking like a lawyer"? Among other things, it means recognizing legal issues. We can informally define a *legal issue* as **a situation where the facts may fit into a legal category with consequences.** Let us break down this informal definition into smaller concepts and discuss the roles of various professionals at each step:

1. "The Facts"

Facts include written words, statements, objects, recollections, and all forms of evidence. The facts are what has happened, as well as what has not happened. For example, when a neighbor erects a fence near the property line, the fence is a fact. And if the other neighbor did not object to the fence, that is also a fact.

The facts may be a dynamic situation that can be planned and influenced. For example, an employer may be planning an internship. Will the internship be paid or unpaid, and how long will it last? Here the facts are yet to be determined. The employer will be generating facts by establishing the internship program.

Legal problem solving includes gathering relevant facts in an appropriate manner. There are legal issues embedded in both of these concepts: what is relevant, and what is the appropriate approach gathering facts? Chapter 15 explores working with facts in more detail.

2. "Fit into a Legal Category"

The next question is: What do the facts mean? According to all the laws that might apply, do they fit into a category, such as the definition of a crime, a tort, a breach of contract, a trade secret? A more practical way to ask this question focuses not on definite conclusions but on risk: Is there a realistic risk that these facts *might* fit into a legal category? Asking whether the facts do — or could — fit into a legal category is essentially asking how the law applies to the facts.

Applying a rule to facts can be simple. For example, burglary typically means breaking and entering the dwelling of another with the intent to commit a felony. Does the term "dwelling" include the median of a busy highway? No. It does not require legal judgment or skill to know this. Does the term "dwelling" include a single-family home where four people live? Yes. That is not a difficult question either, and it does not require legal judgment or skill to answer. But what about a vehicle? You might instinctively answer, "No, of course a vehicle is not a dwelling." But that conclusion is sometimes incorrect. Understanding whether a vehicle is a dwelling, or has a risk of being determined to be a dwelling, requires legal skill, and in fact was recently argued at the

United States Supreme Court. The term "dwelling" may actually include a vehicle, if that vehicle is "adapted or customarily used for lodging."[19]

Part of legal literacy means recognizing that facts *could* fit into a legal category. A recruiting department that is discussing targeting job ads to age groups should immediately recognize that doing so *could* qualify as age discrimination. This realization is useful because it enables the next step of redirecting to a different strategy or pursuing a modified approach to the idea, after consulting with the legal department.

As noted above, *using legal judgment to apply the law to the facts for another person* is the practice of law. A licensed attorney can be helpful, and may be the only professional who can lawfully advise another on how a rule applies to facts. Thus, an important part of legal literacy in practical problem-solving situations is the ability to recognize that a situation calls for the application of legal judgment to a factual situation.

3. "With Consequences"

Closely connected to whether facts fit into a legal category is the further inquiry: What happens as a result? Obligations of public law are often enforced by government actors such as prosecutors or regulators. Consequences may range from imprisonment to fines to civil forfeiture to nothing. Enforcement of law is also a function of government resources and priorities. Issues of private law are generally enforced by individual lawsuits seeking a range of remedies. Remedies include monetary damages, which compensate or punish; injunctions, which force or forbid actions; declaratory judgments, which state and thereby legally establish a certain right or obligation; and specific performance, for example, forcing a transfer of property. In public and private situations, attorney's fees may be a consideration as well, because the party that sues and loses may be liable for the other party's attorney's fees for defending the suit.

Thus, legal problem-solving involves not just thinking about investigations of facts and legal possibilities, but also strategic and practical consequences. Within each step of this process, there are related questions that lawyers think of as procedural:[20] Which parties can and must be included in resolving the situation? Is it necessary, wise, or unwise to write a letter attempting to informally resolve a dispute? Where would the dispute be handled? How closely do the facts have to fit the rule? Who decides—judge or jury? Are alternative dispute resolution mechanisms a possibility or a requirement? How much proof is required (also known as the burden of proof)? As far as the remedies, are they required or discretionary? And once it appears that the law applies to the facts in a certain way, is there any corresponding defensive rule that could apply and thereby avoid the consequences? What is the best way to record and document what has happened, in case there is an appeal? Can negotiations take place without keeping

---

19. *United States v. Stitt*, 403–404, 139 S. Ct. 399 (2018).

20. James Boyd White, *The Invisible Discourse of the Law: Reflections on Legal Literacy and General Education*, 21 Michigan Quarterly Review 420, 432 (1982).

records so that everyone is incentivized to come forward and resolve the dispute? These procedural questions may not have precise answers, but involving a lawyer can help with decision-making.

With this background in mind, the rest of this chapter discusses some specific scenarios and then delves deeper into the process of legal analysis that lawyers perform.

IV. Working with Law as an Employee

Rules governing the practice of law inside an organization such as a corporation have some twists and turns affecting both licensed attorneys and other professionals. To understand just how aggressive state bar associations can be about policing the bounds of law practice in their states, you need to know even a licensed attorney in one state can face professional discipline by moving to another state to join a corporation as in-house counsel without becoming licensed to practice law in the new state.[21] The argument for this type of enforcement is that the attorney is now advising a client in that jurisdiction on an essentially permanent basis and, to best serve the client's interest, needs to know the law of the licensing jurisdiction (i.e., the new state). The best way to ensure the client is protected is to require the lawyer to either take the bar exam and become licensed there or, if possible, use the custom of "reciprocity" by which some states allow reciprocal licensing for attorneys with a certain amount of experience.

So if a *licensed attorney* can face discipline for giving legal advice outside his or her own jurisdiction, what about a *non-licensed* professional dealing with legal issues? As we noted above, many jobs call for law-related services, and lawyers' ethical rules themselves acknowledge that government workers, lobbyists, and many other professionals provide law-related services. A major benefit to having non-bar-licensed professionals study the unauthorized practice of law is so they themselves can know when an employer might unintentionally be asking its employees to do something close to giving legal advice. A professional who spots such an issue can then decide how and whether to escalate the issue in the organization. Here, judgment and intuition, informed by legal literacy, can be helpful.

Common UPL situations involve services offered to consumers for a price. Thus the interest served by enforcement is consumer protection. But for employees who are doing legal tasks in their official duties, there is no consumer and arguably no "other" party at all because the tasks are done for the corporate employer, which explicitly directs the employee to act on its behalf. Also, at a more practical level, who would be the complaining party? Unlike with LegalZoom and other innovations that arguably threaten law firms' livelihoods and have prompted vigorous complaints by lawyers and bar associations, it seems doubtful that lawyers would complain about the decisions of corporations (i.e., potential clients) to allocate responsibility inside the business. For-

---

21. Model Rule of Professional Conduct 5.5.

mer employees aren't injured and seem an unlikely complainant. And if the organization itself doesn't have in-house lawyers, it will be hiring outside counsel if and when legal issues can no longer be handled internally.

No matter how legally literate a professional may become within his or her organization, it remains extremely important to know and follow explicit chains of command. This is especially true when an organization has devoted the resources to having a legal or compliance department, or both. In these organizations, legal literacy can help a professional collaborate effectively across those lines. It's also crucial to understand the organizational culture; common practice and implicit norms of the workplace supplement explicit policies in every organization. In addition to understanding both official policy and unofficial cultural norms in the organization, working professionals need to exercise good judgment.

V. Sharing Information and Solving Problems for Others

Disseminating legal information is not the same as providing legal advice to another person about how the law applies to the facts. In a famous case within the world of legal ethics and the law of law practice, a non-lawyer fought for his right to publish a book about the probate process (the legal mechanism for handling a dead person's assets). In *New York County Lawyers' Association v. Dacey*, 234 N.E.2d 459 (1967), the New York County Lawyers' Association sought to prevent non-lawyer Norman Dacey from publishing his book *How to Avoid Probate!* The Association won at the trial and intermediate appellate levels, but the highest court in New York State (the New York Court of Appeals) reversed and adopted the dissenting opinion in the intermediate appellate court below. The dissent had argued that Dacey had a First Amendment right to publish the book unless it was false and misleading, which it was not. Nor was it the unauthorized practice of law: "At most the book assumes to offer general advice on common problems, and does not purport to give personal advice on a specific problem peculiar to a designated or readily identified person."[22]

As the *Dacey* case shows, bar regulators aggressively police what they consider false or misleading information. And lawyers themselves regularly tangle with bar regulators about their own First Amendment rights. Ohio attorney Andrea Burton was held in contempt and jailed for refusing to remove a Black Lives Matter lapel pin after a judge ordered her to do so.[23] Attorney Andrew Dwyer used his website to post accurate quotes from judges saying he was a good lawyer, leading the judges to complain and the New Jersey Supreme Court to forbid such practices.[24] Dwyer sued for a First Amendment

---

22. *New York Cnty. Lawyers' Ass'n v. Dacey*, 283 N.Y.S.2d 984, 998 (Stevens, J., dissenting).

23. Cleve R. Wootson, Jr., *This Attorney Wore a Black Lives Matter Pin to Court—and Went to Jail for It*, Washington Post (July 26, 2016).

24. Debra Cassens Weiss, *Restriction on Quotes in Lawyer Ads Violates First Amendment, 3rd Circuit Rules*, ABA Journal (August 12, 2014).

violation and ultimately won in the United States Court of Appeals for the Third Circuit.[25] Those who are not subject to bar regulation of course maintain their own First Amendment rights. But they may still face legal consequences involving state bar discipline committees and others if their legal information suggests the application of legal judgment to specific facts, or if their information is arguably false or misleading.

VI. Legal Analysis and the Practice of Law

For legal masters students, studying the core concepts of legal analysis should enhance your judgment about legal judgment. If you have studied legal analysis that uses legal judgment to apply law to facts, then you will know when a situation calls for it. Likewise, you will be able to avoid doing it when inappropriate.

Legal research and writing by a lawyer must meet the ethical standard of competence, subjecting them to professional discipline and malpractice liability if they fail to meet this standard. The baseline standard of competence is found in the American Bar Association's Model Rule of Professional Conduct 1.1:

> A lawyer shall provide competent representation to a client. Competent representation requires the legal knowledge, skill, thoroughness and preparation reasonably necessary for the representation.

These standards address the attorney's depth and breadth of legal research: the attorney must find not just *a* statute or "a relevant case" but *the* statute or statutes on point (all of them) and *the* key cases on point. The comprehensive nature of competent legal research is an important focus of the mandatory legal research class all Juris Doctor law students take in accredited United States law schools. Legal analysis by lawyers also means setting aside personal opinion, belief, speculation, or wishes; competent research must uncover the reasonable range of possibilities for what the law *is*, not a biased picture of what the researcher wishes it would or could be.

Applying the law to the facts also means using the skills of legal reasoning to try to reason as a court would reason when presented with the facts, and then to predict what that court would decide. As explored in Chapter 5, predicting how a court would decide a new case may require detailed legal reasoning, such as comparing and contrasting the facts of the current case to the facts of relevant precedent. Therefore, a lawyer's memorandum of law may go into more detail than professional writing in other settings.

At the same time, clients want efficient and concise legal advice, not a sequel to *War and Peace*. Clients value clear advice that gets to the point, doesn't "hedge," and omits extraneous detail. Thus, formal legal writing should be as concise and as certain as

---

25. *Dwyer v. Cappell*, No. 13-3235 (3d Cir. Aug. 11, 2014), http://www2.ca3.uscourts.gov/opinarch/133235p.pdf

possible. Clients really want to know the bottom line, ideally expressed at the top in some type of executive summary.

Yet legal advice should not irresponsibly promise certainty where it does not exist. A lawyer who presents an unrealistically simple, certain, or optimistic view of the client's risk is likely trading short-term client satisfaction for long-term dissatisfaction. However, a lawyer who relentlessly emphasizes an unlikely worst-case scenario is probably turning a short-term risk aversion into a long-term loss for the client. Focusing on the worst case can sometimes hinder practical problem-solving and frustrate a positive client outcome. Chapter 5 further explains how legal analysis works to predict risk, and chapters 17 and 18 summarize editing techniques for accuracy, consistency, clarity, and conciseness.

The preview of legal analysis in this chapter seeks to connect the legally protected role of giving legal advice to the legal analysis that undergirds it. For situations where you have no client and are advising yourself, studying legal analysis is a model for trying to address your own legal issues. The line between appropriate self-help and unnecessarily risky independence can be extremely difficult to recognize. We hope the legal literacy skills in this book help bring it into better focus.

Having studied this chapter, you should be able to:

- Discuss problem solving in a legal setting
- Provide an overview of how lawyers solve problems
- Avoid the unauthorized practice of law
- Describe the basic analytical steps of applying law to facts
- Provide informed warnings to others about the consequences of giving legal advice where doing so is not specifically allowed by law
- Contribute as a team member while working with lawyers to solve legal, business, and other problems

Case Study

Olivia Ralston accompanied a family member to court in Adams County, Colorado. There she found resources on Colorado's "Self-Represented Litigant Coordinators." These coordinators, or "Self-Help Personnel," are known informally as "Sherlocks." They help unrepresented parties navigate the legal system by assisting with specific roles authorized by the Colorado Supreme Court's Chief Justice Directive 13-01. That Directive provides boldface text of a "Notice to Self-Represented Litigant," shown below. Ms. Ralston checked the websites of various county courts in Colorado and has seen a variety of brochures and websites offering this information. She is intrigued by the idea of volunteering as a Sherlock to gain more insight into the legal system and help people who don't have a lawyer. She has an appointment with a local court administrator for an interview to become a Sherlock. In preparing for that interview, she is going to do two things:

- Research the full guidelines on Self-Help Personnel in Colorado and evaluate how they compare with similar programs in other states. The National Center for State Courts' Self-Representation Resource Guide is one source to help gather information, available at: https://www.ncsc.org/Topics/Access-and-Fairness/Self-Representation/Resource-Guide.aspx
- Evaluate the full text of the Notice below and redesign it to provide the information in a more consumer-friendly format.

Notice to Self-Represented Litigant

Self-help services are available to all persons who seek information to file, pursue, or respond to a case without the assistance of a lawyer authorized to practice before the court, within the resources available to Self-Help Personnel.

Self-Help Personnel are neutral information providers and will provide the same services and information to all parties in a case, if requested.

Self-Help Personnel are employees of the court or volunteers for the court and are available to provide information about court procedures, practices, rules, terminology, and forms, as well as community resources and services. They will assist you by providing information in a neutral way, but cannot act as your lawyer or provide legal advice.

Self-Help Personnel will explain the court process, will help you to understand what information is needed to fill in the blanks on a form, and will review your forms for completeness, but cannot tell you what your legal rights or remedies are, represent you in court, or tell you how to testify in court.

Self-Help Personnel will listen to you to help you locate forms and understand the information you need for your case, but because the Self-Help Personnel are court employees or court volunteers, any information you share with them is not confidential or privileged.

No attorney-client relationship exists between Self-Help Personnel and you as a Self-Represented Litigant. If you need a lawyer or legal advice, Self-Help Personnel will help you find community resources and services without recommending a specific lawyer or law firm.

Self-Help Personnel are not responsible for the outcome of your case.

Self-Help Personnel are not investigators and cannot provide investigative services.

Self-Help Personnel are court employees or court volunteers not acting on behalf of any particular judge. The presiding judge in your case may require that you change a form or use a different form. The judge is not required to grant the relief you request in a form.

In all cases, it is best to obtain the assistance of your own lawyer, especially if your case presents significant or complicated issues. If requested, Self-Help Personnel will help you find community resources and services without recommending a specific lawyer or law firm.

For more information about the court's self-help assistance, see Chief Justice Directive 13-01, which is available at http://www.courts.state.co.us/Courts/Supreme_Court/Directives/Index.cfm.

Traditions and Trends

The nineteenth century provides a distinct historical prelude to today's environment with state-by-state enforcement of unauthorized practice of law statutes and debates on every front about what UPL actually is and what it should be. Not to sound clichéd, but that was a simpler time, when there were few to no boundaries dividing the permissible roles for lawyers and non-lawyers. In fact, Massachusetts had a state statute *protecting* the rights of anyone of "decent and good moral character" to bring or defend a suit for another.[26]

Unauthorized practice of law became a legal concept in the early twentieth century: Legal historians and bar association studies have identified catalysts which coalesced to enhance professionalism of the bar. Specialization became increasingly common as lawyers embraced new "law as business" pressures, while business corporations and administrative agencies were on the rise. Elsewhere active bar associations began lobbying for restrictions on unauthorized practice. Frequently cited as the first organized effort to restrict lay activity, the New York County Lawyers Association began its campaign in 1914 to limit competition; the American Bar Association followed suit in 1930, forming a standing committee on unauthorized practice.[27] This standing committee stated as its objective "the elimination of the unauthorized practice of law."[28] The legal concept of UPL was *somewhat* defined (but not all that clearly) and had *some* degree of enforcement (but not consistently) from the beginning.

---

26. Alexis Anderson, *"Custom and Practice" Unmasked: The Legal History of Massachusetts's Experience with the Unauthorized Practice of Law*, 94 Mass. L. Rev. 124, 128 (2013).

27. *Id.* at 128–129.

28. *Id.* at 131.

As soon as the legal community began to define and enforce UPL, other interests emerged to challenge tight regulation of law-related work. A tax preparation company challenged Massachusetts UPL laws in 1936, prompting a judicial opinion that foreshadows many themes still crisscrossing the legal landscape today. The court described an area that is "[p]lainly ... reserved exclusively for members of the bar," and that is "the commencement and prosecution for another of legal proceedings in court and the advocacy for another of a cause before a court."[29] Yet the court also noted that many professions know and use the law in their everyday work: "For example, an architect cannot advise a landowner properly, or plan for him intelligently, without an adequate knowledge of the building laws and regulations. In practice, an architect prepares the building contract, and drafts the specifications that accompany it and determine to a great extent the rights and liabilities of the landowner. An insurance agent or broker, in order to be of service, must know the legal effect of different forms of policies and of various provisions in them."[30] But then, just as today, "[w]hen we pass beyond these propositions we enter debatable ground."[31]

Today's debatable ground includes similar business-related issues about what UPL does and does not include. Disputes over online contracts and forms are exemplified by events in North Carolina, where the North Carolina State Bar opposed the activities of LegalZoom. LegalZoom brought a counterclaim for antitrust violations—essentially the allegation that the State Bar was engaging in anticompetitive activities in violation of federal law. As of 2018, the bar association lawsuits appear to have all been settled, with North Carolina's claim for UPL and LegalZoom's counterclaim for antitrust violations being services in conjunction with North Carolina lawyers.[32] North Carolina updated its statutory definition of the unauthorized practice of law with a detailed focus on document preparation.[33]

Today's debatable ground also extends to UPL's possible detriment to access to justice. If UPL is broadly defined, then the availability and cost of legal representation will necessarily be higher, and individuals' access to justice, especially for individuals with limited means, will be lower. To enhance access to justice yet still protect consumers, the state of Washington authorized the creation of "Limited License Legal Technicians," professionals who are expressly authorized to handle certain law practice tasks despite not having a J.D. degree and not having taken

---

29. *Lowell Bar Ass'n v. Loeb*, 52 N.E.2d 27, 32–33 (Mass. 1943).

30. *Id.* at 33.

31. *Id.*

32. Joan C. Rogers, *Settlement Allows LegalZoom to Offer Services in N.C.*, BNA News (Nov. 16, 2015) https://www.bna.com/settlement-allows-legalzoom-n57982063694/

33. North Carolina Bar Association, Unauthorized Practice of Law Statutes (2017) https://www.ncbar. gov/media/299201/unauthorized-practice-of-law-statutes.pdf

the bar exam. In contrast, consider actions taken by Financial Industry Regulatory Authority ("FINRA"), a non-profit, quasi-governmental organization that plays a key role in regulating broker-dealers in the private investment industry. FINRA has proposed ending its prior practice of allowing compensated non-attorneys to represent parties in FINRA arbitrations, effectively mandating that only licensed attorneys can perform that work for compensation.[34] The proper role of professionals working in the legal industry without carrying a law license will continue to be a complex and contested issue.

---

34. News Release, Report from FINRA Board of Governors Meeting – December 2018 (Dec. 21, 2018).

Chapter 4

Foundations of
Reading Legal Information

Never trust anyone who has not brought a book with them.
— Lemony Snicket, *Horseradish: Bitter Truths You Can't Avoid*

Working with legal issues means lots of reading. The better you are at reading legal information, the more legally literate you will be. But reading legal information requires flexibility and discretion. Knowing how to read thoroughly, accurately, *and* efficiently distinguishes poor to average readers from excellent ones. Reading skills are extremely important to practicing lawyers, as an ethnographic study of lawyers at work recently showed:

[L]awyering for these junior associates was fundamentally about reading. They read constantly, in digital and hardcopy form. What they read and why was determined by the client, though client contact was limited for the junior associates, and the clients' needs were typically conveyed through the supervising attorney, usually a senior partner. They read primary authority, but they also read more broadly, frequently accessing secondary authority and non-legal texts. They frequently read closely, but more often than not, we observed these attorneys skimming and scanning documents, trying to hone in on the most relevant information as quickly as possible. They were focused and read with a purpose.[1]

Close reading skills benefit anyone who works with legal information, and close reading skills are essential to anyone who works with legal information in a high-stakes environment. This chapter focuses first on the general process of reading legal information, including primary authority, secondary authority, factual documents, and contracts and other legal instruments. Then it gives an overview of how to read a case, which has some unique terminology and is a specialized skill of legal literacy. The chapter ends by emphasizing that legal reading is a skill to develop over time.

I. Close Reading of Legal Texts: A Process

In a widely publicized case that ran from 2014–2017, a group of truck drivers in Maine and their legal team carefully read a new overtime statute in Maine and eventually won a $5 million settlement as a result. The drivers delivered milk and cheese; thus, they were involved in the distribution of perishable goods. The statute made workers exempt from receiving overtime pay on the following jobs:

> The canning, processing, preserving, freezing, drying, marketing, storing, packing for shipment or distribution of: (1) Agricultural produce; (2) Meat and fish products; and (3) Perishable foods.

The argument hinged on first part of the list laying out the duties that were exempt. The list was clear about duties such as "canning" and "processing" of produce, meat and fish, and perishable foods. But the words "packing for shipment or distribution" were not as clear. The state argued that this phrase referred to two items: (1) "packing for shipment" or (2) "distribution." Because the drivers were involved in distribution, they were exempt from overtime. The drivers argued that because "packing for shipment or distribution" had no comma, it was really one item—basically "PACKING (for shipment or distribution)." If they could persuade a court that the statute covered only packing for shipment or distribution, not distribution by itself, then they would not be exempt from overtime and they would be owed a substantial amount of money. The U.S. Court of Appeals for the First Circuit agreed with the drivers, beginning its opinion with a rhetorical flourish that also foreshadowed the holding:

> For want of a comma, we have this case.[2]

---

1. Ann Sinsheimer and David J. Herring, *Lawyers at Work: A Study of the Reading, Writing, and Communication Practices of Legal Professionals*, 21 J. Legal Writing 63, 72 (2016).

2. *O'Connor v. Oakhurst Dairy*, 851 F.3d 69 (1st Cir. 2017), available at https://cases.justia.com/federal/appellate-courts/ca1/16-1901/16-1901-2017-03-13.pdf?ts=1489437006

The *Oakhurst Dairy* case illustrates the economic value of microscopically close reading. But if people read that closely all the time, scrutinizing every word and punctuation mark in every legal document they came across, there would be no time to grow food and eat and sleep and generally maintain human society. A study by Aleecia M. McDonald and Lorrie Faith Cranor found that if everyone using websites took the time to read their privacy policies, each person would need 25 days out of the year to do so. The lost value of this time—in other words, "the national opportunity cost for just the time to read policies"—would be "on the order of $781 billion."[3] Deciding when and how to read legal information is therefore crucial for personal and professional efficiency.

Reading and understanding legal information can be challenging in a number of different ways. Legal information often comes packaged in a document with one or more of the following characteristics:

- Long documents
- Lots of extraneous information
- Unclear authorship
- Complex, interconnected provisions
- Openly persuasive agenda and biased arguments about the law
- Marketing rhetoric to sell a product or idea
- Subtle, hidden persuasive agenda
- Outdated or simply wrong information about the law
- Tangentially relevant
- "Click-bait" content with revenue generated by clicks rather than the quality of the content

To deal with all these challenges and get the information you need, you need strong reading skills. This section outlines some basic steps for reading legal information effectively.

A. Step 1: Determine the Document Context

Legal information and legal documents are created in a vast range of situations. Gaining a sense of the basic context of what you're about to read will help you read it more effectively and efficiently. One of the most basic and helpful contextual questions to ask is whether it is *general* or *specific*. Are you reading general legal information—for example, a statute or set of federal agency guidelines? Or are you reading specific factual documents created and sent by someone to someone else to achieve the sender's

---

3. Aleecia McDonald & Lorrie Cranor, *The Cost of Reading Privacy Policies*, 4 ISJLP 543 (2008), http://lorrie.cranor.org/pubs/readingPolicyCost-authorDraft.pdf

particular goal? Are you reading specific factual documents—for example, a contract or demand letter?

This section gives an overview of the major types of general legal information—primary and secondary authorities. The general section is followed by an overview of more specific legal documents, such as contracts and demand letters.

1. Primary and Secondary Sources

In reading legal information, a basic skill everyone should master is distinguishing between primary and secondary sources. Primary sources are the law itself: Constitutions, statutory codes, cases, regulations, other administrative guidance, municipal codes, and the like. A contract could be a sort of primary source since it is the law of a particular contractual relationship. These sources are very different from secondary sources, which are information from unofficial sources *about* the law, but are not the law itself.

Both types of sources need careful reading. Primary sources need careful reading because they often provide the most important information. At the same time, they may be out of date or otherwise off point. For example, the legislative history leading up to a statute's passage carries different and lesser weight than the final textual language of the statute itself.

Secondary sources need careful reading for different reasons. They may look like primary sources. For example, the Restatements of Law are an influential secondary source divided into short sections, each of which contains a short statement of law. Each of these short statements is expressed as a legal rule that looks a lot like a statute or regulation, but these Restatement rules are not actually law. They express the Restatement authors' view of what the common law actually is—or, if there are a variety of approaches among U.S. jurisdictions, the best approach among the options. Here is an example from the Restatement (Second) of Contracts § 261 (1981):

> Where, after a contract is made, a party's performance is made impracticable without his fault by the occurrence of an event the non-occurrence of which was a basic assumption on which the contract was made, his duty to render that performance is discharged, unless the language or the circumstances indicate the contrary.

In many situations, courts have adopted rules from the Restatement. But a Restatement section by itself is still a secondary source. And just because a secondary source like a Restatement is quoted in a primary source, that does not mean the secondary source automatically becomes the law. For example, the Restatement (Second) of Contracts is quoted in a federal district court opinion by a Russian boxing promoter against Don King, *World of Boxing LLC v. King*, 56 F. Supp. 3d 507, 512 n. 33 (S.D.N.Y. 2014):

[T]he Second Restatement suggests that "[t]he fact that the event was foreseeable, or even foreseen, does not *necessarily* compel a conclusion that its non-occurrence was not a basic assumption." Second Restatement § 261 [comment b] (emphasis added). But New York law is crystal clear: the supervening event must have been "unanticipated" for an impossibility defense to prevail.

This example shows that a source may be quoting another source to disagree with it! Thus, be cautious and do not simply quote a source found within another source as a true statement of law. A source quoted within another source may be quoted in order to set up agreement or disagreement. To effectively read any type of source — a primary source quoting a secondary source, a secondary source quoting a primary source, or any other permutation like this — you should carefully assess the source you are reading, how it relates to the sources it quotes, and whether to find and read the original sources quoted within it.

More will be said about using secondary sources effectively in chapter 7. Legal literacy means using secondary sources to maximize their benefit to the reader while minimizing wasted time and other risks.

2. Contracts and Other Legal Instruments

Contracts create private law. When you read a contract, you are not reading the law for *everyone* (like a statute) but the law for *certain people* (those who are parties to the contract). Both contracts and wills are types of legal instruments. A *legal instrument* is a written document that itself constitutes a legal act by creating a legal obligation or right. When you read a legal instrument, you will want to pay close attention to the terms of that instrument. The meaning of the text itself is very important.

In reading the terms of a legal instrument, you should also be aware that the instrument itself may vary — sharply — from what the law would be in the absence of the instrument. That is a major benefit to contract law itself: setting the terms of your own deal even if that's not the "default rule" for this situation. Generally, in the United States there is freedom of contract and wide latitude to draw up terms that depart from the default rules. But it is not unlimited. For example, a signed contract between a borrower and a lender may say the borrower will pay 200 percent interest if she defaults on the loan, but that interest rate is likely to be unenforceable under any state's usury laws. ("Usury" means exploitative lending.) Similarly, a married individual may write a will disinheriting his or her spouse from receiving any part of the estate, but state probate law protects the spouse's right to some portion of the estate through the concept of an "elective share." By signing a separate prenuptial or postnuptial agreement, a spouse can contractually forfeit the right to the elective share. But one spouse's will alone cannot unilaterally deprive the other of that share. Thus, reading a contract or other legal instrument means not only reading the explicit terms, but also having enough contextual knowledge to perceive that certain matters could be important and need further investigation, including consultation with an attorney. Chapters 12 and 13 say more about reading and working with contracts.

3. Factual Documents

Working with law effectively often means working with facts too. Working with facts includes a variety of activities such as collecting relevant facts, communicating about them without characterizing them or drawing conclusions, and recognizing when to involve legal counsel. Interwoven within all of these activities is the skill of reading documentary evidence.

Factual documents could include almost anything that is potentially legally relevant. Here are a few examples:

- An employee's emails could be relevant to an employment-related claim by or against the employee.
- A term sheet laying out the basic terms of a contract to be drafted and signed later could be relevant to a commercial dispute.
- A police report could be relevant to a civil rights claim or to a broader policy-based advocacy effort.
- A set of accounting documents could be relevant to assessing potential damages in a business dispute.
- A summary of a translated interview with a child migrant detained at a national border could be relevant to an advocacy letter to members of Congress.

This book delves into analyzing and communicating about facts in more detail in Chapter 15.

4. Negotiation Documents

Some documents suggest or explicitly state a position in a negotiation or dispute. An email may demand that a certain action be taken. A cease-and-desist letter is a type of formal demand. In some legal contexts, a cease-and-desist letter has legal ramifications. For example, sending a cease-and-desist letter before suing may allow the sender to seek extra damages or attorney's fees under the relevant law. Negotiation documents have the purpose of asserting a legal position and perhaps establishing a legal right in the process. A lawyer may be silently involved in drafting negotiation documents behind the scenes, or a lawyer may be the named author of a negotiation document.

5. Blurred Lines

The *general* and *specific* categories are useful for evaluating context but do not fit neatly into every situation. An employment policy that applies to situations within a corporation is both general (because it is a policy intended to apply across many situations) and specific (because it is customized to that corporation's human resources structure and titles). *Primary* and *secondary* sources often cross over in networks of references. A demand letter is a type of legal document from one party to another, but it might quote a statute, which is a type of legal information. A secondary source is general legal information, but it might quote and analyze a contract term from an actual legal document. As noted above, a judicial opinion might quote a secondary source such as a Restatement either as authority for a rule being adopted or as an example of what the court is rejecting—or something in between.

By analyzing the type of information or document you are reading, you will begin to analyze its intended purpose and audience. And you can then make decisions on whether and how to use the information or document for your own purpose in communicating with your own audience.

B. Step 2: Skim the Text

Once you've determined context, you need to figure out a reading strategy. To do that, assess the basic structure and purpose of what you are reading.

1. Skimming for Structure

One excellent method for finding structure is to look for the beginning, middle, and end. The beginning and end often tell you particularly useful information: what the source is about and what it concludes. Then you can decide whether and how to read the middle—which typically would be the part that develops the topic in detail and supports the conclusion.

Another method is to skim over the visual markers in the source, such as headings and subheadings. These should indicate the author's intended purpose and organization for achieving that purpose.

If the source is dense and text-heavy with few or no visual markers, you can try a different version of this strategy: Read the first sentence in each paragraph.

Some legal sources use a law-specific structure. A statutory code, for example, will generally be organized by sections. You will see this sign: § or the word "section." Sections separate one statute from the next. For example, Figure 4.1 shows some sections from Colorado's workers' compensation statutes:[4]

---

4. The Colorado Revised Statutes are available in free, digital format online. Colorado law can be found in a number of ways, such as through the Cornell Legal Information Institute's website, which leads to the Lexis-sponsored page providing the statutory text free of charge. You will learn more about researching statutes in Chapter 8.

Figure 4.1

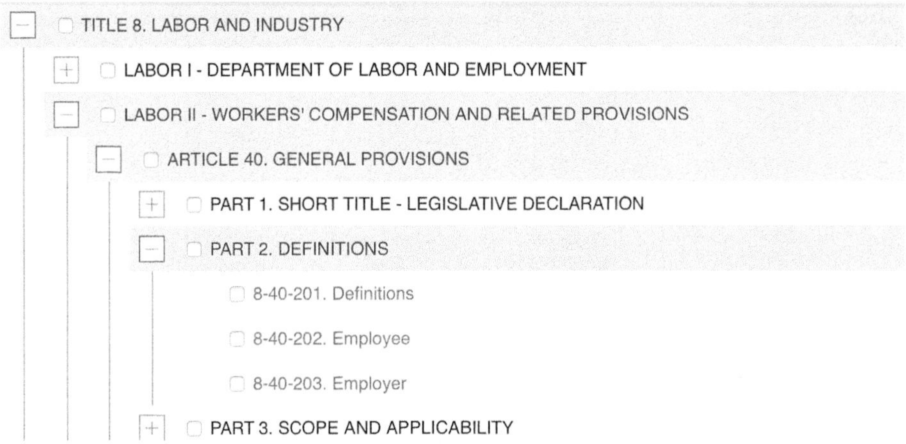

Section 8-40-201 contains "Definitions" for this area of the law. It contains a specific provision for the definition of "employee," which as you can see refers readers to another section:

> (6) "Employee" has the meaning set forth in section 8-40-202 and the scope of such term is set forth in section 8-40-301.

This is one of many examples in which legal information references other legal information. Read with curiosity and persistence to track down these types of references. Here, Section 8-40-202 defines "employee." This section, with the full definition of "employee," is much longer than the short definition of "employee" in the definitions section. Here is an excerpt from section 8-40-202:

> (1) "Employee" means:
>
> (a) (I) (A) Every person in the service of the state, or of any county, city, town, or irrigation, drainage, or school district or any other taxing district therein, or of any public institution or administrative board thereof under any appointment or contract of hire, express or implied; and every elective official of the state, or of any county, city, town, or irrigation, drainage, or school district or any other taxing district therein, or of any public institution or administrative board thereof; and every member of the military forces of the state of Colorado while engaged in active service on behalf of the state under orders from competent authority....
>
> (b) Every person in the service of any person, association of persons, firm, or private corporation, including any public service corpora-

tion, personal representative, assignee, trustee, or receiver, under any contract of hire, express or implied, including aliens and also including minors, whether lawfully or unlawfully employed, who for the purpose of articles 40 to 47 of this title are considered the same and have the same power of contracting with respect to their employment as adult employees, but not including any persons who are expressly excluded from articles 40 to 47 of this title or whose employment is but casual and not in the usual course of the trade, business, profession, or occupation of the employer....

(2) (a) Notwithstanding any other provision of this section, any individual who performs services for pay for another shall be deemed to be an employee, irrespective of whether the common-law relationship of master and servant exists, unless such individual is free from control and direction in the performance of the service, both under the contract for performance of service and in fact and such individual is customarily engaged in an independent trade, occupation, profession, or business related to the service performed. For purposes of this section, the degree of control exercised by the person for whom the service is performed over the performance of the service or over the individual performing the service shall not be considered if such control is exercised pursuant to the requirements of any state or federal statute or regulation....

Reading for structure means paying attention to organization, such as the titles, articles, and sections shown in the example above. It also means going beyond the outward organization. For example, section 8-40-202 provides catch-all language including "any individual who performs services for pay for another." But then it gives an important exception, describing a class of workers *not* included in the definition of an employee: "unless such individual is free from control and direction in the performance of the service, both under the contract for performance of service and in fact and such individual is customarily engaged in an independent trade, occupation, profession, or business related to the service performed." This exception is not separately numbered. The careful reader should see this exception even though it is contained within a larger section about who *is* an employee.

2. Skimming for Purpose

Legal information is generated for many reasons — some neutral, some disguised as neutral, and some openly argumentative. How can a reader critically assess the purpose of author and publisher? To evaluate an author's or publisher's purpose, consider a series of questions:

- Why did the author write this?
- Why would a reader need or want to read this?
- Why did the writer choose to publish on this platform (such as a magazine or website or email newsletter), and why is the reader reading on this particular platform?
- What words did the author use that indicate a position (or attempt to take no position) on the topic?
- Why did the publisher make this available, and what were its incentives to do so?

For example, using a search engine to look for "Colorado workers' compensation employee independent contractor" can lead one to find a legal blog post *Are You an Employee or an Independent Contractor?* by the Denver law firm Burg Simpson.[5] Here are the first two paragraphs:

In today's economy, the popularity of independent contractors has ascended for several years. Whether it's driving around strangers for money or building Web pages from home, it seems like more people than ever are forgoing employee status and embracing life as an independent contractor. In fact, a recent Intuit study claims that slightly more than 40 percent of the nation's workforce will be composed of freelancers in just three years.

Of course there is a dark side to this as well. During the economic downturn many employers were looking to cut costs and avoid paying for benefits like health insurance or unemployment. This led to a decision by some to start calling some former, current or future employees independent contractors so that they could give them a 1099 and avoid paying benefits that were federally mandated. We have found that this practice was particularly prevalent in the construction trades.

The post goes on to provide more information about the definition of employee and independent contractor, and the pros and cons of each, under Colorado law. Burg Simpson's website contains a tag line "Colorado Workers' Compensation Attorneys." It also links to other states where the firm does business, and has a form one can fill out to get a "Free Case Evaluation." From these details about the website, can you form an opinion about the purpose of this post?

C. Step 3: Pick Your Strategy

Now that you've analyzed the source's basic type, its structure, and its purpose, you are ready to decide whether: (1) you're done with this source and need to move on, (2) you should skim it again for more information, or (3) you should read it carefully.

---

5. Burg Simpson, *Are You an Employee or an Independent Contractor?* https://www.burgsimpson.com/colorado/2017/08/employee-independent-contractor/ (Aug. 23, 2017).

The most common reasons to stop and move on are that the source is irrelevant, duplicative, or relevant but unlikely to make a difference.

Common reasons to continue with the skimming strategy are to be efficient with time, to find more important sources cited within this one, and to decide whether to involve others in interacting with this source. The downsides of skimming are possibly missing important information, misinterpreting it, and not remembering and retaining the information.

Some common reasons to read a source thoroughly are because it is obviously highly relevant, it has high stakes, or it strongly influences other related sources. Reading thoroughly has many benefits: gaining relevant information, not missing information, accurately interpreting it, and remembering and retaining it. But reading thoroughly is not always the right answer; sometimes there's just too much information to deal with. Reading thoroughly risks time and may waste effort if the wrong person is trying to understand something that needs to be delegated or shared elsewhere. Reading a source in detail can, paradoxically, distort context by focusing the reader too much on the one source, and miss connections with other sources.

D. Step 4: Identify Key Legal Language

A critical skill in reading the law is recognizing legally significant language — in other words, recognizing key terms. Key terms may be substantive or operative.

1. Finding Substantive Key Terms

A single word or a short phrase may function as a key term. Key terms are well-known terms with a fairly stable, predictable meaning. The sections of Colorado workers' compensation law above give detailed definitions for "employee" and "employer." Here are some more examples of legal terms with specific meanings:

Directors and officers of the corporation are protected by the *business judgment rule.*

The state must prove the defendant *guilty beyond a reasonable doubt.*

To qualify as a *trade secret*, information must have *actual or potential value from not being known or readily ascertainable and must be the subject of reasonable secrecy efforts.*

Some of the words above are further defined by statute or contract. For example, the directors and officers of a corporation incorporated in a state would be defined by that state's body of corporate law (statutes and cases).

Some of the words and phrases above are further defined by case law. In trade secret law, what it means for information to be the subject of "reasonable secrecy efforts" has been explored in many different cases where parties litigated whether a business idea was in fact a protectable trade secret. Likewise, the "business judgment rule" in corporate law is the subject of many cases. The case law developing these terms shows that their meaning is not mathematically precise. Legally literate readers encountering legally significant terms will know that these terms should not be taken simply at face value.

Although these terms mean more than just what their literal textual language says, that textual language is still extremely important. Being legally literate means knowing that key terms should not be changed. In writing about reasonable secrecy efforts and trade secret law, a legally literate person would never change the words "reasonable secrecy efforts" to "justifiable methods of covert maintenance." Developing writers are taught to use the thesaurus and write with variety, to avoid boring repetition. But in legal language, writing with unnecessary variety is not only *not* beneficial but in fact could be harmful when it changes the terms and confuses the meaning. For example, a legal writer should feel comfortable about a document that repeats the phrase "reasonable secrecy" 10 or more times! Changing that term to something similar such as "justifiable methods of covert maintenance" creates far more problems than leaving the term as is. That phrase is wordy and awkward, and it also changes the meaning of the law. By not using the words "reasonable secrecy," this phrase signals the intent *not* to use the body of law and common understanding about what reasonable secrecy means.

This type of brainstorming — imagining what it would be like to change a word and whether that would change the meaning of the text — is another good way to recognize whether a word or phrase is a legally significant key term.

2. Finding Operative and Relational Key Terms

Some words do not seem substantive, yet they are still extremely important. Some words have important operational meaning. In other words, they express and define the legal relationship of concepts.

Examples of operative key terms

Verbs	Connecting words
May	And
Must	Or
Shall	All
Will	Any
Can	Unless
Allow	Except
Prohibit	
Violate	
Exempt	

Look for any other grammatical and punctuation choices that convey meaning. For example, a provision referring to "a default" may refer to any default, but a provision referring to a "Default" may refer to default as defined with an initial capital letter somewhere else.[6]

E. Step 5: Read Actively by Interacting with the Text

A study of first-year law students in a J.D. program showed that the most successful students actively read their course material, annotating it with notes in the margins and imagining questions and challenges to the reading's content.[7] The same is true for professionals who read legal information. Simply running your eyes over the text from the first word to the last is not likely to help you or others you may be collaborating with.

To read actively, you should interact with the text. Here are some possible methods of interaction:

- Highlight or underline important passages.
- Make notes in the margins summarizing paragraphs, allowing you to see the overall framework and content of the text.
- Make notes in the margins that ask questions:
    - Ask questions of yourself, e.g., "Need to find out more on covered entity."
    - Ask questions of the text, e.g., "What is formal definition of covered entity in definitions §?"
    - Ask questions of others: e.g., "Ask Faroud whether we should seek covered entity status."
- Analyze sources in the text, distinguishing its use of quotes and paraphrases from other sources from its own contribution.
- Evaluate the argument in the text, separating what it claims from how it supports those claims.
- Think about what the text does *not* say. What did the writer leave out? What is missing but potentially relevant? What unanswered questions do you have?

F. Step 6: Read Mindfully

Professionals read legal documents for practical reasons — that is, to accomplish a goal (including nested goals such as research the law then use it to investigate the facts, or discover another party's position and analyze whether to support that position or

---

6. This example is one reason legal writing does not capitalize words just because they are important. Capitalizing a word indicates it is a proper noun or defined term.

7. Anne Enquist, *Unlocking the Secrets of Highly Successful Legal Writing Students*, 82 St. John's L. Rev. 609 (2008).

submit a competing argument). Thus, part of legal reading is deciding what to do as a result of what you read. There are both analytical and emotional aspects to this question. Analytically, you may decide to take an action like one of the following:

- Respond to an email
- Write a formal letter
- Forward the information to another team member
- Scan the document and distribute it broadly such as by social media
- Print out the source and place a copy in the file
- Write a memo to yourself (or "the file") about what you just read
- Write a memo to another person about what you just read

But the emotional response to reading should not be ignored. When you read a legal source—especially a specific document targeted to your organization or even you personally—you may also experience an emotional reaction, such as:

- Confidence (or lack thereof) in how to proceed
- Frustration at a lack of clarity
- Defensiveness at an accusation
- Resignation at an ongoing issue that shows no sign of resolution
- Anger at a falsehood
- Motivation to argue against each and every point being raised
- Worry about a strong argument that is difficult to counter, or a bad fact that is difficult to refute
- Celebration at good news
- Confusion at overly complex information
- Self-doubt interpreting information that seems too simple or too good to be true
- Desire to avoid the situation
- Eagerness to handle a matter by yourself without involving others

Reading legal information and deciding what to do means acknowledging the emotions that may come along with this process. It's common advice that, in these situations, you should write something, put it in a drawer, then come back to it a day or two later with fresh eyes. Likewise, if you are reading legal information that is prompting an emotional response, consider making a tentative plan for responding, then set that tentative plan aside for a period of time to gain more perspective before responding.

II. Reading Cases: A Special Skill

Reading a judicial opinion — or "case" — has a somewhat specialized vocabulary and approach. Judicial opinions can be clear and concise or lengthy with many sub-sections addressing various sub-issues. Therefore, reading cases deserves special attention as part of legal literacy.

A. The Parts of a Case

To read a case effectively, you first need to know some basic vocabulary for the parts of a typical case. Here is a condensed version of *Teller County v. Industrial Claim Appeals Office*, 410 P.3d 567 (Colo. App. 2015), showing you the parts of a case. The context for this case is that it is a judicial opinion from the intermediate court of appeals in Colorado — that is, the first line of appeals after the trial court. The immediate court of appeals sits in an intermediate position between the trial courts and the Colorado Supreme Court.

Claimant Michael Smith is the president of Teller County Search and Rescue (TCSAR), which is composed entirely of volunteers who receive no compensation for their service. As president of TCSAR, claimant attends numerous meetings to prepare for disasters such as floods and fires.

> Context, factual history, and brief procedural history.

On May 10, 2013, Smith left his home to attend a fire chiefs meeting in Divide. Before departing, he notified Teller County that he was en route. As he was traveling to the meeting, he was struck head-on by an approaching vehicle and sustained severe injuries. He filed a claim for workers' compensation benefits, asserting that as a volunteer, he fell within the scope of the definition of an "employee." Teller County contested the claim.

> The beginning of the opinion's analysis, identifying the issues to be discussed. This listing of the issues is often called a "roadmap" and is seen throughout legal writing.

Teller County contends that (1) Claimant Smith's actions did not fall within the statutory definition of "employee"; [and] (2) the Worker's Compensation Panel's inclusion of "planning and preparation" activities broadened the scope of the provision beyond the General Assembly's intent. We are not persuaded by these arguments to set aside the Panel's order.

> A preliminary statement of this court's holding. (Keep reading to see the court expand upon and clarify its holding.)

First, we interpret statutory provisions de novo, giving considerable weight to the Panel's interpretation of the statute it administers. If the language is clear and unambiguous, we look no further and enforce it as written. The Act defines "employee" to include: volunteer rescue teams while they are "actually performing duties" as members of such teams and while

> The reasoning for the first issue begins here. This sentence focuses on procedural legal reasoning.

This reasoning states the statutory rule and then applies it to the facts of this case. See Chapter 5 for more on rules.

engaged in organized drills, practice, or training necessary or proper for the performance of such duties. § 8-40-202(1)(a)(I)(A). Here, attending fire chief meetings was part of Smith's position and duties as president of TCSAR. As a commander with the Teller County Sheriff's Office acknowledged, coordinating with the fire chiefs is "important," as is coordination between TCSAR and the Sheriff's Office.

The opinion now moves to precedent to show that it also supports the application of the statute above.

Other cases involving volunteers have reached similar conclusions. In one case, a division of this court upheld the Industrial Commission's finding of compensability for injuries sustained by a search and rescue volunteer while traveling by private plane to a meeting. See *Colo. Civil Air Patrol v. Hagans*, 662 P.2d 194, 196 (Colo. App. 1983). In that case, the commander testified that the volunteers were on duty "from the time they leave home to attend a meeting until they return." Id. Thus, traveling to attend a meeting satisfied the requirement of "actually performing duties."

The reasoning for the second issue begins here.

Second, Teller County argues that looking to custom and practice expands the statutory language of "performing duties" beyond its plain meaning. However, a division of this court observed that "as a result of custom and practice, other activities have become part of the normal activities of volunteer fire departments, and when injuries have occurred in the course of these activities, compensation has been allowed." *Nw. Conejos Fire Prot. Dist.*, 39 Colo. App. at 369–70, 566 P.2d at 719–20

Here the opinion uses analogical reasoning to compare the facts of this case to the facts of a relevant precedent.

An agency can also acquiesce in the compensability of certain acts by knowingly permitting them to occur. For example, in *Capano v. Bound Brook Relief Fire Co.* #4, 811 A.2d 510 (N.J. Super. Ct. App. Div. 2002), a ninety-three-year-old volunteer firefighter [fell] while putting a log in a wood-burning stove. Although the claimant had never been ordered or instructed to stoke the firehouse's wood-burning stove, his injuries were held compensable because the fire department acquiesced in his activity and benefited from the claimant's habit of keeping the fire burning. Id. at 513. Similarly here, Smith attended numerous meetings as president of TCSAR and regularly attended the fire chiefs meeting. Nothing in the record suggests Smith was ever instructed not to attend the various meetings, and Teller County admittedly benefited from Smith's attendance.

> We therefore conclude that Smith was performing duties pursuant to a custom and practice in which Teller County acquiesced when he was involved in the accident. The Panel thus did not err in finding Smith an "employee" at the time of his accident.

Here, the court fully states its holding.

B. "Briefing" a Case

Some of your legal training may involve assignments or projects to "brief a case." Case briefs are summaries. In three-year Juris Doctor programs, briefing a case is an essential skill because law students create case briefs to prepare for class, to contribute to small group discussions, and to study for final exams. A case brief is an internal document for you, generally not a product you show to others. But some law classes may require or encourage students to turn in their case briefs to reveal their learning process. Eventually many law students become skillful enough at reading and briefing cases that they stop writing out separate briefs and begin to annotate the margins and accomplish the same goals. Briefing a case is thus a worthwhile exercise for beginners to build legal reading and reasoning skills.

Here's a general overview of what goes into a case brief, with notes from the *Teller County* case as a demonstration:

THE PARTIES

Who sued whom, as listed at the top of the case?

(You can use shorthand such as last names and a short version of a long name.)

The original claimant in the case is Michael Smith, the individual who was injured. He won his case in the worker's compensation panel below, so the parties on appeal are Teller County (the defendant) and the Industrial Claim Appeals Office.

THE COURT

What court decided the case, such as the United States Supreme Court, the supreme court of a particular state, or another federal or state court?

This case was decided by the Colorado Court of Appeals, specifically Division I. The fact it is "Division I" indicates the three judges assigned by the chief judge, as shown in the Colorado court system's website. It does not appear to control any particular jurisdiction; all Colorado Court of Appeals cases are binding over the whole state. States such as Florida, New York, and Texas have jurisdictional districts in their intermediate appellate courts.

THE YEAR

When was the case decided?

The case was decided in 2015. It would have been appealed by now if the county was going to take the case to the Colorado Supreme Court, so it is effectively final.

THE ISSUE

What legal issue was at the core of the case?

The core legal issue was whether Smith, a volunteer, was acting as an "employee" and performing duties when he was injured on the way to a meeting of volunteer fire chiefs.

THE FACTS

What were the facts that prompted the case?

Smith volunteered for the county search and rescue operation. He was on his way to a meeting in another town in Colorado when he was hit by a car and severely injured. He sued for workers' compensation.

THE REASONING

What did the court emphasize in reaching its result?

The court emphasized the plain language of its definition of "employee." It also relied on deference to the panel's decision below interpreting the statute. The court compared Smith's case to prior cases about employees on their way to a meeting by private plane, who were also held to be employees. The court also noted that the county acquiesced to and benefited from Smith's attendance even if it never explicitly told him to attend.

THE HOLDING

You already identified the legal issue earlier in your case brief. As a result of what the court has stated in this opinion, what is the legal test for deciding this issue in the future? That's the holding.

Sometimes the court is kind enough to say "We hold …." In such cases, most of the time what follows is the actual holding of the case. But the most effective readers do not depend on an explicit signal in the opinion. The most effective readers can read the case and analyze what it stands for — its holding — without the benefit of an explicit signal.

Note that the holding must be a statement that is essential to the actual result of the case. If it's a tangential note or background information that could be deleted from the opinion without changing the result, it's not the holding. Here is one way to state the holding in *Teller County*:

The claimant volunteer was actually performing his duties, and thus an employee, for purposes of gaining workers' compensation, where he was driving to a meeting when injured, even if the county did not directly instruct him to attend that meeting.

RELEVANT DICTA

Did the court say anything interesting or potentially important that was not actually necessary to its holding and the result it reached? These statements are *dicta*. Most Latin words are falling out of favor in legal vocabulary, but the word "dicta" is a Latin word that has sticking power. It means statements in the opinion that are not essential to the result. Dicta is a side note for the parties in the case; the result in their case is what it is no matter what extraneous statements the court may have made. But dicta can influence the law over time by expressing the court's view about side issues not raised. In this way, dicta can speak to future parties who may bring a case making an argument that builds on dicta from a prior case. Dicta may help future readers understand the law more thoroughly because the dicta provides context, or dicta may just confuse people and seem to plant seeds that ultimately do not bear fruit. This is one example of how legal reading is not formulaic but is subject to argument and interpretation.

This case had two major arguments and the court limited its reasoning to both. It did not offer dicta on tangential, alternative issues.

THE RESULT (SOMETIMES KNOWN AS THE DISPOSITION)

What result did the court reach for the particular parties before it? For example, was the case below affirmed or reversed? Was it remanded for more factual findings? Was it remanded for the trial court to do exactly what the appellate court instructed?

The court affirmed the panel's decision that the claimant was an employee.

III. Becoming a Better Reader Over Time

The more legal sources, documents, and information you encounter, the stronger you should become as a legal reader. This learning process will happen naturally as you take more classes and complete more law-related projects. But you can help it along by seeking feedback and reflecting on your own practices, habits, and overall effectiveness.

A. Obtaining Guidance from Others

Seeking feedback on how well you do as a reader may sound strange. Reading skills are difficult to see and measure. The other receptive communication skill, listening, is also difficult to measure. Contrast that with the productive communication skills of talking and writing, which are much easier to notice and assess.

Another challenge is that you certainly already know how to read. Reading for decades as a child, teenager, and then working adult professional can create ingrained habits that are hard to even recognize and assess, much less change and improve. We suggest reflecting on your legal work up to this point, examining it with a trusted professor or through your own independent study. The goal is first to reveal the strengths and weaknesses of your own reading practices.

One possibility is to meet with a trusted professor, mentor, or academic advisor to focus specifically on your reading techniques. Make an appointment to go over a class assignment or other legal project that required reading. Bring your notes for that assignment or project. If you worked on an assignment that involved a key text such as a statute, bring the printout of that key text with your highlights and annotations. (If you didn't make any highlights or annotations, say no more; this is step one for you to work on!) Talk with your professor about how you read the key text and what you got out of it: which section did you identify as most important, and which words did you zoom in on? If you remember being confused by some part of the text, or if you are confused when revisiting the text, share your thought process and discuss the possibilities. In addition to analyzing different possibilities, try to summarize the overall key point of what you read in a sentence or two. Does your summary accord with what the professor says? Take detailed notes on what you learn and review them in detail later.

B. Self-Improvement

Without involving any professor or mentor, you can also coach yourself on becoming a stronger reader. Again, because your approach to reading is probably an ingrained set of practices you don't think about much, the key is to reflect on your work thus far. The goal is to get a more objective look at your own reading practices—what you do, specifically, when you read.

One way to do this is to choose a single project to focus on, ideally a project that required you to read and process what you read to make the final project. Gather all the materials you used for the project—what you printed, what you skimmed, what you read, your outline or other preparatory writing, your final product, and any feedback or assessment on the project. As with gathering your material to meet with a professor, this step alone can generate good insight. The outward signs of your reading—such as note-taking and highlighting—are not a complete picture of your mental steps, but they offer important clues.

As you look at your own materials, examine them critically to see what they show about your reading. Here are some things to think about in this examination:

- **Were you multitasking when you read the text?** Have you ever compared your notes on reading while multitasking to your notes on reading while not multitasking?

- **When and how did you skim the materials for context?** Skimming allows prioritizing and focus; by contrast, diving in without context may lead to too much focus on the first part of a text and loss of focus on what really matters.

- **How actively did you read the text?** Active reading means engaging with what is there, such as by noting key terms, relating parts of the text to other parts of the text, and connecting the text with your prior knowledge. Active reading also means asking questions, a step so important that we address it in the next bullet point.

- **What questions did you notice yourself asking while you read?** Active reading means generating a lot of questions—questions about the words, questions about how the text is organized, questions about the overall meaning, and questions about what seems would be relevant but is not actually mentioned in the text. You may not be able to answer all your questions while reading, although some, such as the meaning of a particular word, could be answered with a quick Internet search. *Having* questions is important because it shows active reading. A reader with questions about a text can accomplish more simply by having these questions, as compared with a reader who passively takes in text without question. A reader with questions can gain a deeper understanding by researching answers to the questions or asking an expert. A reader with questions can better collaborate with a team to try to resolve important areas of uncertainty. A reader with questions can avoid overconfidence and false certainty. A reader with questions can earn the right to be confident by grappling with uncertainty and arriving at a more certain understanding of some aspects of a text, even if all aspects still cannot be definitively pinned down.

- **How did you know you were done reading?** Effective reading means more than starting at the first word and ending at the last. Effective reading means achieving your goals from the time spent reading a text. If your goal was to understand the text for a project, how did you actually know you had understood it?

- **How did you use the reading?** In legal education and in professional work, reading is always done for a purpose. Even if that purpose is to eliminate a text as relevant, that is still an accomplishment. Why did you read this text in the first place, and what did you expect to use it for? How in fact did you use it? Did you quote key parts, paraphrase segments of text, or incorporate it into your background knowledge without explicitly using it? Did you compare and contrast it with other reading? Did you read it for class and then use the knowledge gleaned from that text to help with notetaking and listening to classmates discuss the same material? Reading without an intentional focus is unlikely to be effective. Reading with intent to use the text is much more likely to work. By studying how you actually used a text and the knowledge you generated from reading it, you will be more prepared to read the next text and do the next project.

C. Outside Resources

Whether meeting with a mentor or studying your own work independently, time spent reflecting on your legal reading will benefit all of your legal communication skills. For more information on legal reading, we suggest the following resources:

Orin S. Kerr, *How to Read a Legal Opinion: A Guide for New Law Students*, 11 The Green Bag 51 (2007), https://papers.ssrn.com/sol3/papers.cfm?abstract_id=1160925

Jane Grise, *Critical Reading for Success in Law School and Beyond* (2017)

Ruth Anne McKinney, *Reading Like a Lawyer: Time-Saving Strategies for Reading Law Like an Expert* (2d ed. 2012)

Having studied this chapter, you should be able to:

- Approach an unfamiliar legal document with a plan for how to read it
- Locate key terms and concepts from a legal text
- Become a more effective legal reader over time by seeking feedback and engaging in self-reflection
- Read and brief a judicial opinion (a case)

....

Case Study

Olivia Ralston is continuing to think about her niece, Tess Williams, and the experience she had with her former employer detaining her for two hours on an allegation of shoplifting. Ms. Ralston heard from her brother that her 19-year-old niece, Tess Williams, had been traumatized by an event at work. She was escorted to an interview room, falsely accused of shoplifting, and not allowed to leave for two hours. Her manager and two security guards were present during this ordeal.

Ms. Ralston has found a case in the jurisdiction and is reading it for her own education on this area of law. That case is *Cuellar v. Walgreens Co.*[8] Ms. Ralston is reading this case to better understand the legal background with her niece's possible legal claim. The case is reproduced below. In the role of Ms. Ralston,

---

8. The opinion here in *Cuellar v. Walgreens Co.* is based on a real case decided by an intermediate Texas Court of Appeals that was not selected for publication in the *South Western Reporter*, Third Series. For educational purposes, we have edited and modified the case, including by converting it into a fully "published" case that was decided by the Texas Supreme Court. In the interest of full disclosure, we want you to know this is not a case actually decided by the Texas Supreme Court. The cases cited in the opinion, however, are all real.

read this case actively, adding notes and highlights. Then write a concise case brief summarizing its key parts such as the facts, holding, and reasoning, as taught throughout this chapter.

···

93 S.W.3d 458 (Tex. 2002)

Case No. CV-02-094
SUPREME COURT OF TEXAS

DULCINEA N. CUELLAR, Appellant,
v.
WALGREENS CO. AND JIM LINDSEY, Appellees.

On review from the Fifteenth Court of Appeals of Texas, Bluebonnet

PER CURIAM

Dulcinea Cuellar petitions this Court based on the Bluebonnet Court of Appeals' affirmation of a summary judgment granted by the trial court in favor of the appellees, Walgreens Company and its loss prevention specialist, Jim Lindsey. Cuellar contends generally that the trial court erred in granting summary judgment on her claim for false imprisonment and that the court of appeals erred in its affirmation. We affirm the judgment of the court of appeals.

Background

The summary judgment evidence, viewed in the light most favorable to Cuellar, shows that Cuellar began her employment with Walgreens on February 13, 1999. According to Cuellar, cashiers routinely rang up items priced as "two for" a particular amount by entering the first item at the listed price and the second item at one cent. In late April, Cuellar purchased some items at the store. In accordance with the recommended practice, the purchases were entered by another Walgreens cashier. The price entered for a purchase of photographs was one cent. On June 2, 1999, in response to a request from the store manager, Lindsey arrived at the store to investigate the incident. Lindsey escorted Cuellar to the "tape room," a room at the rear of the store used by employees to review training tapes, and interviewed her for approximately an hour and fifteen minutes. Cuellar contends Lindsey threatened that she would be charged with theft and taken away in handcuffs by the police unless she confessed to stealing store merchandise. According to Cuellar, she was not specifically informed of the nature of the allegations against her, nor was she given an opportunity to explain. Lindsey accused her of "grazing," a term used to describe a store employee's taking of a product from the store and consuming it without paying for it. Cuellar admitted she had eaten two candy bars without paying for them. Although Cuellar denies that she ever stole any items from the store, at the end of the two-hour interview, she was so distraught that she signed a statement confessing to "passing" $350 in store merchandise, plus four dollars for the two candy bars.

Cuellar filed suit against Walgreens and Lindsey on June 23, 1999, alleging causes of action for negligence, defamation, and intentional infliction of emotional distress. (1) On July 11, 2000, the trial court granted a "take nothing" summary judgment in favor of appellees. Appellate proceedings followed.

Standard of Review

In a traditional summary judgment proceeding, the standard of review on appeal is whether the successful movant at the trial level carried the burden of showing that there is no genuine issue of material fact and that judgment should be granted as a matter of law. *M. D. Anderson v. Willrich*, 28 S.W.3d 22, 23 (Tex. 2000); *Am. Tobacco Co., Inc. v. Grinnell*, 951 S.W.2d 420, 425 (Tex. 1997); *Nixon v. Mr. Prop. Mgmt. Co., Inc.*, 690 S.W.2d 546, 548 (Tex. 1985). In resolving the issue of whether the movant has carried this burden, all evidence favorable to the non-movant must be taken as true and all reasonable inferences, including any doubts, must be resolved in the non-movant's favor. *Willrich*, 28 S.W.3d at 23-24; *Nixon*, 690 S.W.2d at 548-49; *Noriega v. Mireles*, 925 S.W.2d 261, 266 (Tex. App.—Corpus Christi 1996, writ denied). When the defendant is the movant and submits summary judgment evidence disproving at least one essential element of each of the plaintiff's causes of action, then summary judgment should be granted. *Grinnell*, 951 S.W.2d at 425; *Science Spectrum, Inc. v. Martinez*, 941 S.W.2d 910, 911 (Tex. 1997). If the movant has established his or her right to summary judgment, the burden shifts to the non-movant to present evidence that would raise a genuine issue of material fact. *Fojtik v. Charter Med. Corp.*, 985 S.W.2d 625, 629 (Tex. App.—Corpus Christi 1999, pet. denied). If a summary judgment is granted generally, without specifying the reason, it will be upheld if any ground in the motion for summary judgment can be sustained. *Bradley v. State ex rel. White*, 990 S.W.2d 245, 247 (Tex. 1999) (citing *Star-Telegram, Inc. v. Doe*, 915 S.W.2d 471, 473 (Tex. 1995)).

Issues which the non-movant contends preclude the granting of a summary judgment must be expressly presented to the trial court by written answer or other written response to the motion and not by mere reference to summary judgment evidence. *McConnell v. Southside School Dist.*, 858 S.W.2d 337, 341 (Tex. 1993). Issues not expressly presented to the trial court in writing shall not be considered on appeal as grounds for reversal. Tex. R. Civ. P. 166a(c).

Errors Alleged

Cuellar contends the trial court erred in granting summary judgment because there are material fact issues regarding: (1) whether holding her against her will for two hours constitutes false imprisonment; (2) whether appellees' conduct in accusing her of theft and firing her after a forced confession was sufficiently "outrageous" as to constitute intentional infliction of emotional distress; (3) whether the accusations of theft constitute defamation per se; and (4) whether appellees acted negligently in conducting the investigation.

False Imprisonment

The elements of false imprisonment are: (1) a willful detention; (2) performed without consent; and (3) without the authority of law. *Randall's Food Markets, Inc. v. Johnson*, 891 S.W.2d 640, 644 (Tex. 1995); *Wal-Mart Stores, Inc. v. Cockrell*, 61 S.W.3d 774, 777 (Tex. App.—Corpus Christi 2001, no pet.). A willful detention may be accomplished by violence, by threats, or by any other means restraining a person from moving from one place to another. *Randall's*, 891 S.W.2d at 644-45. In a false-imprisonment case, if the alleged detention was performed with the authority of law, then no false imprisonment occurred. *Cockrell*, 61 S.W.3d at 777 (citing *Wal-Mart Stores, Inc. v. Resendez*, 962 S.W.2d 539, 540 (Tex. 1998)). The plaintiff must prove the absence of authority in order to establish the third element of a false-imprisonment cause of action. *Id.* An employer has a common-law privilege to investigate reasonably credible allegations of the dishonesty of its employees. *Randall's*, 891 S.W.2d at 644.

Where, as here, it is alleged that a detention is effected by a threat, the plaintiff must demonstrate that the threat was such as would inspire in the threatened person a just fear of injury to his person, reputation, or property. *Fojtik*, 985 S.W.2d at 629 (citing *Randall's*, 891 S.W.2d at 645). Threats to call the police are not ordinarily sufficient in themselves to effect an unlawful imprisonment. *Id.* In determining whether such threats are sufficient to overcome the plaintiff's free will, factors such as the relative size, age, experience, sex, and physical demeanor of the participants may be considered. Id. (citing *Black v. Kroger Co.*, 527 S.W.2d 794, 800 (Tex. App.—Houston [1st Dist.] 1975, writ dism'd)).

Even when we consider the evidence in the light most favorable to Cuellar, we find she has not raised a fact issue as to whether she was willfully detained without her consent and without authority of law. Appellees contend Cuellar's false imprisonment claim fails because: (1) she consented to the interview by never attempting to leave the room; and (2) they were privileged to investigate the suspected theft. As summary judgment proof, Cuellar "incorporate[d] by reference all of the depositions, documents, and exhibits attached to [appellees'] Motion for Summary Judgment." In particular, Cuellar pointed to her deposition testimony, in which she testified that she signed the statement saying she had "passed" $350 in merchandise because she was "scared to death." Cuellar testified that what "scared [her] the most" was Lindsey's statement that she had a choice between riding home in her own car or in a "cop car." She noted that as a twenty-two-year-old, she had "never had to do this before."

Cuellar points to *Skillern & Sons v. Stewart*, 379 S.W.2d 687, 689-90 (Tex. App.—Fort Worth 1975, writ ref'd n.r.e.), as "factually similar" to the instant case. The facts in *Skillern* are distinguishable. The plaintiff, who was accused of theft, was taken by the arm and led to a room for questioning. *See Skillern,*379 S.W.2d at 689. At one point, she left the room to call her son, but was physically escorted back to the room. *See id.* She denied the accusations and asked to see a lawyer, but was not allowed to do so. *See id.* When she tried to get up, one of the men put his hands on her shoulders and prevented her from leaving. *See id.* at 689-90.

We have reviewed Cuellar's deposition testimony in its entirety and conclude she has failed to raise a fact issue regarding whether she was willfully detained without her consent. According to Cuellar, when Robert Pena, the assistant store manager, told her Lindsey needed to speak with her, she went into the tape room. She testified Lindsey never physically touched her, physically threatened her, or restrained her from leaving the room. Cuellar did not ask if she could call her parents. Although Cuellar described Lindsey's manner as "rude," "abrupt," and "short," he remained "calm," and did not touch her, yell at her, call her a thief, call her bad names, or curse at her. Although he did not tell her she could leave, he never told her she could not leave. Lindsey was not in the room when Cuellar wrote her statement confessing to the "passing" of merchandise and "grazing."

Cuellar testified she is a journalism major, with two-and-a-half years of college. Prior to her employment at Walgreens, she worked as a reporter at a television station and at two newspapers. At the time of her deposition, she was employed as a newspaper reporter. As a journalism major, Cuellar testified that she enjoys writing and believes she has strong grammar and vocabulary skills. When Lindsey asked her about "grazing," she asked him to define it. She stated she "asked him to define a lot of things that evening." We conclude that viewing the evidence in the light most favorable to Cuellar, she has failed to raise a fact issue as to whether she was unreasonably detained without her consent. We hold the trial court properly granted summary judgment as to Cuellar's claim of false imprisonment.

We AFFIRM the judgment of the court of appeals.

Traditions and Trends

Reading is, traditionally, a skill learned in grammar school and strengthened in high school, but assumed to be set and stable — neither diminishing nor improvable — by college and graduate school. Advanced degree programs were premised on the idea their admitted students had strong reading skills and would then proceed to use them in their course of study.

Reading material itself was, traditionally, a commodity to be sought after and purchased. Books, magazines, newsletters, and newspapers cost money and generated revenue for publishers from these sales. Reading material — what we now call "content" — was costly to produce and purchase. The fact that content was published at all provided some indication that the source was credible. Reading was an old-school "analog" experience, both isolated and potentially isolating. In a book or magazine or newsletter, the reader had the printed text and nothing more—no computer code behind the scenes in the printed item, and no connections to other information via hyperlinks.

The major trend, of course, is online reading. Now everyone is reading all the time. Reading material is easily available and free, offered through online sources that use cookies and other tech-enabled mechanisms to build a picture of its audience. Content's economic value is more in the reader's attention than in any direct sale and purchase of the content itself. Reading material is easy to share and can reach a wider audience than ever before; but the source and credibility of information are much more difficult to pinpoint.

The experience of online reading is somewhat different from the experience of reading print. Studies have revealed an "F" pattern to readers' eye movements as they read online; thus, many web pages are designed to accommodate this pattern.[9] Studies suggest that readers retain more from reading real books than text online, although claims that any one medium is superior to another are hotly contested. Online text is interactive and multimedia, connected to other information, and often provides the immediate opportunity to interact with the text or author or both.

In graduate and professional education, there is some sense that reading skills—at least as applied to extended, complex material—have diminished. Some graduate educational programs now offer additional resources and training related to reading. But the claim that anyone is "worse" at reading because of pervasive online exposure is a hotly debated claim.

---

9. *See* Kara Pernice, *F-Shaped Pattern of Reading on the Web: Misunderstood, But Still Relevant (Even on Mobile)*, Nielsen Norman Group (Nov. 12, 2017), https://www.nngroup.com/articles/f-shaped-pattern-reading-web-content/

Chapter 5

Foundations of Legal Analysis

Thinking like a lawyer ... means exercising judgment, distinguishing among those arguments, sifting good from bad. Just as you will come to understand that there are arguments made in good faith on opposing sides, you must also learn to reject some arguments, or at least to choose among them.

— Anne-Marie Slaughter, *On Thinking Like a Lawyer*, Harvard Law Today (May 2002)

Brevity may be the soul of wit, but it isn't the soul of rigorous analysis.

— U.S. Circuit Judge Gregory Phillips[1]

---

1. *Harper v. C.R. England, Inc.*, No. 17-4008, 2018 WL 3860471 (10th Cir. Aug. 14, 2018). The reason the case citation here is to Westlaw rather than a free public source is that this opinion was "unpublished," meaning the deciding court designated not for publication, which means it is binding on the parties in the actual case, but not binding precedent for future cases. Unpublished cases lack citations in the case reporters that collect published binding cases.

Solving legal problems requires legal analysis — in other words, "thinking like a lawyer." But what does that actually entail? One answer focuses on prediction. It means taking a certain situation or question, thinking about the legal rules and relevant precedent, and then applying that law to the facts of the client's case to predict an outcome: how would a court make the same decision? This is often a hypothetical exercise because the situation will never end up in court, and that's a big part of the point: by predicting how a court would apply the law to the facts, the lawyer helps the client choose a course of action.

The lawyer's prediction must be multilayered, not just accurately evaluating the substance of the law but also accurately evaluating the lawyer's own prediction about that substance. The latter evaluation requires the lawyer to assess and communicate what parts of the prediction are relatively certain because they are grounded in well-accepted legal authorities, and what parts are less certain and riskier because they arise in new or uncharted legal territory. Law students in J.D. programs spend three years learning and practicing these skills so they can use legal analysis to advise clients. Professionals who work with and around lawyers and legal systems can benefit from understanding why lawyers do what they do. This chapter will introduce you to common approaches to legal analysis and empower you to recognize these approaches and to understand their value in legal problem solving.

I. Introduction to Predictive Legal Advice

The idea of "legal analysis as prediction" is fundamental to legal reasoning and deserves more elaboration before we unpack the steps of legal reasoning. A client begins seeking a lawyer's advice by providing information and relevant documents. This communication is generally protected by the attorney-client privilege, so the client can fully share all of the facts — good, bad, and ugly. The documents that the client shares are not themselves privileged just because the client gives them to the lawyer, but the communications between the lawyer and client about the client's situation are privileged.

Sometimes an experienced lawyer can learn the facts and immediately advise the client that the answer is a clear "yes" or "no." There actually are some easy questions in law. But more often, the lawyer recognizes that legal research and analysis are needed. Resisting the temptation to share a guess or rely upon gut reaction is part of what good lawyering should be.

The next step is legal research and analysis, which an attorney may do individually or by delegating the task to another lawyer (typically a more junior one). This research and analysis may be internal, from the junior lawyer to the senior lawyer, or it may be produced and shared directly with the client. It may be highly formal or not even committed to writing. Either way, it informs the advice given to that client. Legal writing professor Kirsten Davis has argued that even with diminishing attention spans and proliferating digital communication tools like email and texting, this core analytical approach is fundamental to the lawyer's task:

The rest of lawyers' practice—giving advice, making arguments in trial, negotiating contracts, or mediating claims, for example—is based upon this carefully considered analysis of how the law governs the client's facts. Without this foundation, a lawyer's work may prove incompetent.[2]

This analysis and the advice it supports are fundamentally about predicting what a court would do if presented with the client's situation. Sometimes the situation is an idea about what to do—a proposed course of action. Should the client go forward with what it is thinking about doing? If the court would likely agree with the client's proposed course of action, then the client may feel more comfortable proceeding with it. If the court would likely disagree with the client, then the client may feel less comfortable doing so. This task is a form of *risk assessment*; the lawyer's prediction is not an actual determination or decision. Ultimately, a court or arbitrator or other authority authorized to decide the dispute will determine the result. Because the lawyer's analysis is predictive and not determinative, the lawyer cannot guarantee results, as we will explore in more detail below.

Sometimes the advice centers on facts that have already occurred. The situation could be a car accident, an issue at work, a family dispute, a business conflict, or anything else where the key events have already taken place. The client may be the person who believes he or she has suffered a legal wrong, or the person who has been served with a lawsuit alleging that he or she committed a legal wrong. The lawyer's question now is what these facts mean. The lawyer uses the tools of legal analysis to predict what a court would do. Is this claim likely to be meritorious? The prediction helps the client on the plaintiff side evaluate whether the difficulty of a lawsuit may be worth it. The prediction helps the client on the defendant side evaluate how meritorious the lawsuit is and whether to pursue settlement before trial.

The idea of trial brings up an important point about litigation. Legal analysis predicts "what a court would do" if presented with the facts. But sometimes it's the jury, not the court, that decides. Lawyers' detailed legal analysis characteristically focuses on "what a court would do" because in litigation, a court makes many decisions before the case could possibly reach a jury trial, and the courts' preliminary decisions are bound by precedent. Crucial decisions by the court include whether to grant a motion to dismiss and whether to grant a motion for summary judgment. If the plaintiff's claim survives both of these stages, the case will reach a jury. As a result, lawyers' predictions on the strength of a claim really focus on whether that claim is likely to survive a motion for summary judgment motion and get to trial. Lawyers who litigate become very animated when substance and procedure come together like this. Others may find the procedural

---

2. Kirsten K. Davis, "*The Reports of My Death Are Greatly Exaggerated*": *Reading and Writing Objective Legal Memoranda in a Mobile Computing Age*, 92 Or. L. Rev. 472, 478 (2014) ("Just because lawyers might want 'shorter' memos, on-screen or otherwise, this does not mean that shorter memos are suitable for either legal readers or legal writers.").

dimension more confusing than helpful, and tune out completely. That is why fully formed legal analysis is sometimes not shared with the client directly but is rather "translated" through meetings or shorter summaries. This chapter goes in more depth regarding legal analysis and, at the end, returns to the value of these translation skills.

II. IRAC: The Typical Legal Analysis Method

Whether the issue is simple or complex, at its core there is a basic logic to legal analysis. This basic logic forms the model for analysis that every law student learns: "IRAC." The letters in IRAC stand for the following steps of logical analysis:

The "IRAC" Model	
I	Issue (the legal question and its ultimate answer)
R	Rule Statement (the unapplied statement of the law)
	Rule Explanation (examples of the rule in action)
A	Application (supporting analysis)
	Application (counter-analysis)
C	Conclusion (concluding thesis)

What this IRAC model really represents is deductive reasoning. Deductive reasoning means starting with a logical premise, then drawing a conclusion. It is also sometimes described as reasoning from the general to the specific. The IRAC idea generates a vast range of reactions from gratitude for having a simple framework to frustration at having a simple framework. Both reactions are common, yet incomplete.

The best reaction to IRAC may be encapsulated in a quote by statistician George Box: "All models are wrong, but some models are useful." IRAC is a model that is imperfect but useful. Indeed, the IRAC acronym itself is not that important. Many different variations on the IRAC acronym for legal analysis are being taught in U.S. law schools today,[3] but every law student studying for a J.D. learns *some version* of what IRAC represents. Thus IRAC remains the sort of uber-acronym for this concept. Whatever the acronym or phrase used for this logical framework, it is a means to an end, guiding the analysis through the deductive process.

Consider the following scenario: Olivia Ralston drove her Corvette through the intersection while the traffic light was red. The legal issue is: Did Olivia violate a traffic law? Most people know from their personal experience and governing traffic law that vehicles must stop at intersections when the traffic light is red. That's the rule. And we know that here, Olivia was driving a Corvette, which as a car qualifies as a "vehicle" under the law, and he entered the intersection while the light was red but did not stop

---

3. A few of the many variations on IRAC are CREAC, CRuPACC, TREAT, TO REACT, and PREACH. You can be sure that even more such acronyms are running around out there in U.S. law schools.

as required by law. That's the application. Thus, Olivia violated the law. That's the conclusion.

As the scenario above demonstrates, the IRAC model of legal reasoning is simple yet powerful. It clarifies and organizes the thought process, raising questions that need to be answered. This model could be used by a judge deciding a case (Olivia's guilty), or by a lawyer advising a client whether to pay a traffic ticket or try to argue it (no, just pay it). Some judges advocate the idea that a judge applying the law is like being a baseball umpire who calls balls and strikes; indeed, the Chief Justice of the United States, John Roberts, used this analogy in his Supreme Court confirmation hearing.[4] When the rule is more complicated or the facts rest at the edge of what the rule seems to cover, the umpire analogy may not work as well. For example, what if Olivia was riding an e-scooter, like a Bird or a Lime available through app-based rentals in many cities? Does a person controlling an e-scooter have to follow traffic rules that definitely apply to cars and trucks, such as stopping at a red light? A legal analysis of this fact situation would be more complicated than the steps outlined above. And legal analysis can expand or contract to fit a simple situation or a very complex one.

The rest of this chapter explores some different types of rules, and you will see that IRAC can be applied to any of them. When one rule is actually a series of separate smaller rules, an IRAC-style analysis can be done for each of the smaller rules. In that regard, it's a huge benefit for helping legal writers do something so simple but so important — talking about just one point at a time, and finishing that point before moving on to the next. The IRAC model also expands or contracts to fit the needs of the moment. IRAC can be concise and streamlined for a simple, clear issue; or it may spread out over several pages to fit more complex and detailed issues with lots of relevant cases and the need for an in-depth application of law to fact. Whether an IRAC analysis is short or long, it centers on a "rule" — the "R" in IRAC. We turn to rules next.

III. Rule-Based Reasoning

Legal analysis is, at its core, *rule-based reasoning*. What exactly is a rule? One well-known formulation states that "[a] rule is a formula for making a decision."[5] A legal rule thus provides formulaic structure to legal analysis and helps to answer crucial questions:

- What is the test for the issue?
- Is that test broken up into smaller parts?
- If so, how do those parts relate?

---

4. At hearings on his nomination to be Chief Justice of the United States, John G. Roberts Jr. famously — and to some criticism — said that "judges are like umpires" and "it's my job to call balls and strikes and not to pitch or bat." Dana Milbank, *Hey, Batter, Hold the Chatter*, Washington Post Online (Sept. 15, 2005).

5. Richard K. Neumann, Jr., Ellie Margolis, and Kathryn M. Stanchi, *Legal Reasoning and Legal Writing* 9 (8th ed. 2017).

Thinking of law as rules has many practical benefits. Perhaps the greatest benefit of all is the ability to break big questions into individual, logical pieces. Once a rule is broken into individual pieces, those pieces can be analyzed individually and in relation to one another.

The parts of a rule can operate in different ways. The most common two roles are the *element* and the *factor*:

- An **element** is a mandatory requirement.
- A **factor** is a consideration that is not necessarily required by itself but is balanced against all the other factors in a test.

In legal vocabulary, some words have very distinct meanings. The difference between an element and a factor is one of these distinctions, because the use of one or the other in a rule may completely change the analysis and result, as shown in the examples below.

A. Elemental Tests

In a rule with elements, each element must be satisfied in order for the entire rule to be satisfied. The statement below is from a judicial opinion from Texas stating the basic rule for *false imprisonment*, an intentional tort creating a civil legal claim by the injured party against the party that committed the tort. Here is the rule:

> False imprisonment is the direct restraint by one person of the physical liberty of another without adequate legal justification. Its elements are: (1) a willful detention of the person; (2) a detention without authority of law; and (3) a detention without the consent of the party detained.

These sentences communicate a great deal of information to a legally literate reader. The reader now knows that a civil cause of action exists for a person in Texas who is unlawfully deprived of his or her liberty. The reader also knows that three elements are necessary for a plaintiff to prove the claim against a defendant:

1. willful detention of the plaintiff by the defendant,
2. without the defendant having legal authority, and
3. without the plaintiff consenting to be detained.

In many statutes, regulations, and judicial opinions, the elements of a test are explicitly numbered (as they are above), but that is not always the case. The basic concept is a list of requirements joined by "and." The "and" is a crucial connector that expresses the mandatory relationship of these parts.

Because the rule sets out parts joined by "and," *all* of the elements must be proven for a claim to succeed. Think of an elemental test as one in which only two scores are possible: 100% or 0%. Legally speaking, proving two out of three gets the same recovery as zero out of three because anything less than full credit gets no credit. That characterization may sound harsh for a plaintiff, but it actually makes sense. Any set of facts that does not fulfill all three elements does not actually qualify as false imprisonment, and it is not actually the kind of situation this particular rule was intended to deal with.

Thus, for example, a police officer who detains a suspected shoplifter cannot face civil liability for false imprisonment even if the police officer is ultimately wrong. Why? Government officials (like police officers) usually detain people on the basis of their special legal authority to do so. The second element, which requires the absence of "authority of law," is the specific reason this claim would fail. Instead, the tort of false imprisonment commonly arises in situations where shopkeepers detain a person suspected of stealing from a store.

Understanding that proving false imprisonment involves an elemental test provides some deductive tools for a legally literate reader as well. Since prevailing on the claim for false imprisonment requires proof of every element, a claim is only as strong as its weakest element.

A lawyer advising a client should be thorough and consider each element, but the legal advice will rest most heavily on the "weak link"—the element that is the least likely to be satisfied. And if one element cannot be successfully proven, then the whole claim cannot succeed.

B. Factor Tests

In contrast to the check-every-box logic of an elemental test, some legal rules are looser and built around *factors*, considered in relation to the other factors in the test.

For example, courts have used the "primary beneficiary test" to determine whether an intern or student is, in fact, an employee under the federal Fair Labor Standards Act (FLSA). In short, this test allows for examination of the "economic reality" of the intern-employer relationship to determine which party is the "primary beneficiary" of the relationship. The following seven factors are part of the test:

1. The extent to which the intern and the employer clearly understand that there is no expectation of compensation. Any promise of compensation, express or implied, suggests that the intern is an employee—and vice versa.

2. The extent to which the internship provides training that would be similar to that which would be given in an educational environment, including the clinical and other hands-on training provided by educational institutions.

3. The extent to which the internship is tied to the intern's formal education program by integrated coursework or the receipt of academic credit.

4. The extent to which the internship accommodates the intern's academic commitments by corresponding to the academic calendar.

5. The extent to which the internship's duration is limited to the period in which the internship provides the intern with beneficial learning.

6. The extent to which the intern's work complements, rather than displaces, the work of paid employees while providing significant educational benefits to the intern.

7. The extent to which the intern and the employer understand that the internship is conducted without entitlement to a paid job at the conclusion of the internship.

Courts have described the "primary beneficiary test" as a flexible test, and no single factor is determinative. Accordingly, whether an intern or student is an employee under the FLSA necessarily depends on the unique circumstances of each case.[6]

This test has seven parts, but each is not required. Indeed, the U.S. Department of Labor (DOL) explicitly states in its own interpretative guidance that "no single factor is determinative." This language explains the test for the general public. As a professional with enhanced legal literacy, you will know from the word "factor" that no single factor is determinative.

This factor test is longer and more detailed than the elemental example above. It provides flexibility and discretion for both employers and the Department of Labor to use when assessing an unpaid internship program, and for courts to use when they follow this test. Notice that the factors do not function as checkboxes to satisfy or not satisfy. Instead, they provide a list of considerations, each of which contributes in some way to the ultimate determination. The first factor explicitly states how it contributes: an express or implied promise of compensation suggests the intern is an employee, and no express or implied promise of compensation suggests the intern is not an employee. The other factors articulate considerations and leave it to the reader to infer which way they cut. For example, the fourth factor requires consideration of "the extent to which the internship accommodates the intern's academic commitments by corresponding to the academic calendar." A legally literate reader can deduce that an internship that corresponds to the academic calendar is more likely to be acceptable as an unpaid internship. In contrast, an internship with no relationship to the academic calendar, such as a consistent workload throughout finals and academic breaks, suggests the intern is actually an employee.

Elements and factors are logically different, but both require thorough analysis. A thorough analysis of whether an internship program qualifies to be unpaid will address every factor, just as complete analysis of an elemental test will address each element. A test based on the totality of circumstances from seven factors is more flexible than an elemental test, which is helpful in some ways but also more difficult to predict.

---

6. United States Department of Labor, Fact Sheet #71: Internship Programs Under the Fair Labor Standards Act (updated January 2018), https://www.dol.gov/whd/regs/compliance/whdfs71.htm.

C. Other Rule Variations

Elemental tests and factor tests are the two major categories of rules, but rules come in other variations as well. Some tests rely on a disjunctive "either/or" relationship rather than a list of elements joined by "and." For example, under lawyers' ethical rules, attorneys must protect confidential information gained in the course of representing a client, but there are several exceptions giving the lawyer the discretion—although not the duty—to reveal the information:

> A lawyer may reveal information relating to the representation of a client to the extent the lawyer reasonably believes necessary:
>
> (1) to prevent reasonably certain death or substantial bodily harm;
>
> (2) to prevent the client from committing a crime or fraud that is reasonably certain to result in substantial injury to the financial interests or property of another and in furtherance of which the client has used or is using the lawyer's services;
>
> (3) to prevent, mitigate or rectify substantial injury to the financial interests or property of another that is reasonably certain to result or has resulted from the client's commission of a crime or fraud in furtherance of which the client has used the lawyer's services;
>
> (4) to secure legal advice about the lawyer's compliance with these Rules;
>
> (5) to establish a claim or defense on behalf of the lawyer in a controversy between the lawyer and the client, to establish a defense to a criminal charge or civil claim against the lawyer based upon conduct in which the client was involved, or to respond to allegations in any proceeding concerning the lawyer's representation of the client;
>
> (6) to comply with other law or a court order; or
>
> (7) to detect and resolve conflicts of interest arising from the lawyer's change of employment or from changes in the composition or ownership of a firm, but only if the revealed information would not compromise the attorney-client privilege or otherwise prejudice the client.[7]

As this rule shows, *any one* of the reasons listed would justify the lawyer in using discretion to reveal the information.

Balancing tests compare competing values—typically two contrasting elements. For example, a public employee who is terminated from employment because of his or her speech may be able to pursue a civil rights claim based on retaliation. That test has several logical steps: It balances the employee's right to speak "as a citizen on a matter of public concern" against the employer's interest in regulating speech to "promote the efficiency of the public services it performs through its employees."[8] And if that balanc-

---

7. American Bar Association, Model Rule of Professional Conduct, Rule 1.6 (b).
8. *Moss v. City of Pembroke Pines*, 782 F.3d 613 (11th Cir. 2015).

ing test suggests the employee does have a First Amendment right that outweighs the employer's interest in managing the workplace, then "the third stage of the analysis requires Plaintiff to show that [the speech] was a substantial motivating factor in his termination." (Note here that the word "factor" means essentially "reason" for the termination.) And if *that* part of the rule is satisfied, *then* there is *another* step that can override the employee's First Amendment rights: "[T]he burden shifts to the City to prove that it would have terminated Plaintiff even in the absence of his speech."[9] Thus, this rule has a (sort of) exception: Even if an employee speaks as a citizen on a matter of public concern so as to outweigh the employer's interest in regulating and managing the workplace, and even if that speech is a substantial motivating factor in the termination, the employer can still prevail by showing that it would have fired the employee anyway.

Rules come in many forms. Knowing some basic terminology such as "element" and "factor" helps a reader interpret legal rules accurately. Practice with some basic types of rules like those shown here can help as well. Because rules come in variations and are not always enumerated in obvious ways, the best approach is to develop and use strong critical reading skills, as discussed in chapter 4.

IV. Reasoning by Analogy

Deductive analysis is not always enough to support a legal prediction. What if a lawyer faces a new factual situation that does not clearly fit within the wording of the legal test and does not have a case precedent exactly on point? Is an e-scooter like a Lime or Bird rented by smartphone app a "vehicle" in the same sense as a Corvette?

Here, deductive reasoning is not enough, because neither the language of the rule nor the facts and holding of clear precedent help the lawyer predict what a court would do with the new situation. In situations like these, where deductive analysis is not enough, the lawyer adds analogical reasoning. Analogical reasoning means comparing and contrasting precedent to current facts:

- Are the facts similar to the facts of cases where the rule was held to be satisfied?
- Are the client's facts similar to the facts of cases where the rule was held *not* to be satisfied?
- Are there relevant similarities or differences that seem likely to affect how a court would decide the client's case?

Analogical reasoning is not just about what the case *says* in textual rules, but also about what it *does* in deciding that these facts do or do not satisfy this rule. Analogical reasoning helps to fill gaps in the language of a rule and adds flexibility in legal analysis

---

9. *Id.*

to deal with situations to which the legal answer is not obvious. But again, as with the factor tests discussed above, with that flexibility comes some uncertainty. The lawyer as counselor endeavors to predict what would happen with the client's current facts. The lawyer as advocate takes those same analytical skills to navigate the range of arguments and uncertainties, seeking a particular result. Many consider analogical reasoning to be the quintessential skill of lawyers trained in the Anglo-American legal system. Let's pull back the curtain and see how the process works.

V. Predictive and Persuasive Analysis Amidst Uncertainty

Lawyers provide a flexible set of services to clients, but two roles stand at the core of what they do: counseling and advocating on clients' behalf in court. Legal analysis informs *both* of these roles. In counseling, the lawyer gives legal advice. This advice may take the form of a prediction: "Client, if you pursue this lawsuit, you will probably not prevail. Here is why." In advocating, the lawyer acts as an advocate. The lawyer speaks and writes to persuade a decision-maker — the jury or trial judge, and if necessary the appellate judges — to decide in favor of the client. These roles of advice and advocacy share a common basis in legal analysis. To make a solid prediction, the lawyer must understand the arguments on both sides. To make a solid argument, the lawyer must imagine a court's legal research and thinking behind the scenes in trying to decide the case objectively.

Everyone in this scenario is trying to do the same thing, which is assess how close the fit is between the law and the facts. The closer the fit, the more certain the prediction: A very close fit between law and facts will support a more confident and certain prediction. The lawyer's advice will be more like an "If ___, then ___" statement, and the court's decision may come at a very early stage in a case because the law and facts so clearly point to what the judge sees as the appropriate conclusion. In contrast, a loose or questionable fit will support a less confident and more uncertain prediction. The lawyer's advice will be more like a discussion of options with caveats about risk and uncertainty. And the court may deal with uncertainty by permitting the case to proceed to trial (if the uncertainty is mostly about the facts) or writing an order deciding the legal issue, with the awareness the case may be appealed and is at risk of being reversed (if the uncertainty is mostly about the law).

In your professional career, you may deal with lawyers acting as counselors, advocates, or both. Lawyers seek to provide practical advice that is valuable to clients. To provide practical, valuable advice, the lawyer must balance the uncertainty inherent in prediction with the strong desire for certainty that is natural and understandable in clients wanting to make decisions and structure their conduct based on sound legal advice. However, overconfident advice that creates unrealistic expectations is not valuable. When receiving legal advice, formulating questions, giving input on strategy, or otherwise collaborating with lawyers, be aware: **Applied legal analysis can assess, describe, and (to an extent)**

even minimize legal uncertainty, but not eliminate it. A lawyer counseling a client should recognize and communicate about which parts of the advice are well-supported and what parts are more risky or untested. A lawyer making an argument should understand which arguments are more solidly grounded in legal principles and precedent, and which arguments are more of a stretch. Arguments may be a stretch for many reasons—for example, the rule language does not precisely cover the situation, or precedent cases create analogies both for and against the client's side of the argument.

Lawyers are not only unwise to promise a specific outcome, but they are ethically prohibited from making such a promise. Lawyers are prohibited from making "false or misleading" statements about their services.[10] False or misleading statements include material misrepresentations, material omissions, and statements about results in past cases unless those statements make very specific qualifications. These restrictions on speech about past results are intended to protect consumers from believing that a lawyer's results in past cases imply success in future cases. For the same reason, a statement is false and misleading and therefore prohibited if it "is likely to create an unjustified expectation about results the lawyer can achieve."[11] That would include promising an outcome when the fit between law and fact leaves room for uncertainty, as is so often the case.

This truth about the uncertainty inherent in legal analysis can lead to frustration for those who are dealing with lawyers. "Why can't you promise that we will win?" "Why can't you guarantee that we will recover all our damages?" And, for the quantitatively minded such as engineers and accountants, "We need a percentage for exactly how likely each outcome will be." Legal analysis is a valuable tool for empowering informed decision-making, but no lawyer can assure a result under all possible circumstances, much as no doctor should guarantee a cure. Whether medical or legal or any other field, professionals use the tools of their trade to assess the circumstances and guide those they serve.

VI. Legal Analysis in Action: An Example

You may recall from the end of Chapter 2 that Olivia Ralston's sister, Angela Williams, along with her husband, Garrett, has a 19-year-old daughter named Tess. Tess has had a problem with her employer, the retailer MegaMart. The family, including Tess's parents, ultimately decided to consult with an attorney, Amanda Way, regarding Tess's situation. Some documents resulting from that consultation can be found in Appendix A, and we will excerpt parts of them here. Way is a named partner in the firm of Way & Wynne, L.L.P. Ms. Way is working with a new associate attorney at her firm, Joshua Mansfield, and has asked him to prepare a legal memorandum.

---

10. American Bar Association, Model Rule of Professional Conduct 7.1.

11. For the full text of Texas's version of ABA Model Rule 7.1, locate and read Tex. Disc. R. Prof. Conduct 7.02(a). The Texas rule is typical of the limitation on attorneys in other American jurisdictions.

The goal of this section is to show legal analysis both behind the scenes and in the lawyer's role advising the client directly. Behind the scenes, Way, Mansfield, and other lawyers in the firm conduct in-depth legal research and analysis. They feel comfortable using legal terminology and concepts in their work because they are writing to one another and to themselves (as in the idea of a "note to the file" documenting events and information). This behind-the-scenes work is a lawyer-to-lawyer collaboration for the client's benefit, but is not directly addressed to the client. The client may never see the lawyer's full file created while working on the client's behalf, but the client has a property interest in that file and has the legal right to demand and receive a copy of the entire file. Formally demanding a file typically happens when a client is dissatisfied with the lawyer's work and wants to transfer the representation to another lawyer or consider a malpractice suit. What is more common, and what lawyers should be doing, is using the analysis in the file to summarize and explain all of that work to the client in appropriate language and the right amount of detail for the client. Ultimately the lawyer has an ethical duty to "explain a matter to the extent reasonably necessary to permit the client to make informed decisions regarding the representation."[12] And informed consent, in turn, "denotes the agreement by a person to a proposed course of conduct after the lawyer has communicated adequate information and explanation about the material risks of and reasonably available alternatives to the proposed course of conduct."[13] The legal analysis in the file is how the lawyer investigates the law and fact necessary to give that explanation.

A. Prelude to IRAC: Collecting the Facts

Applying the law to the facts requires knowing the facts, at least to the extent possible under the circumstances. In this example, after senior attorney Way interviewed the client, Tess Williams, Way wrote the following factual summary that she passed along to junior attorney Mansfield:

> Tess Williams is nineteen years old. She is unmarried and lives at the home of her parents Garrett and Angela Williams. In high school she was a member of the drill team. Since she was only five feet tall, she was always on the front line for the team. During her school years, she also worked part time at the concession stand at the movie theater. After graduation from high school, she began working as a cashier at MegaMart. Her MegaMart job was her first full-time job. After one year of service, she was promoted to the cosmetics counter.
>
> MegaMart is part of a national chain of "super-sized" drug stores with separate photo-developing and cosmetics counters. Several of the MegaMart stores are open twenty-four hours. Rocky Malone is the store supervisor at the MegaMart where Tess worked. He is a local hero as he was a lineman on the high school's state championship

---

12. American Bar Association, Model Rule of Professional Conduct 1.4(b).
13. American Bar Association, Model Rule of Professional Conduct 1.0(e).

team twenty years ago and was voted most valuable player on the team. Rocky is now thirty-eight years old, married with two children, and he has been an employee of MegaMart for the last ten years. He has regularly received promotions to positions of increasing responsibility at MegaMart, and hopes one day to work his way into a corporate leadership role.

At approximately 3:00 p.m. on July 15, 20XX, Tess was at the cosmetics counter helping her best friend, Caroline, decide on appropriate cosmetics for Caroline's upcoming wedding. Rocky approached the cosmetics counter. He interrupted Tess and Caroline and in a stern voice said, "Tess–I need you to come with me, right now." Tess followed Rocky and claims that she was too surprised and confused to ask any questions about where they were going or why. Rocky had never been so abrupt with her or, to her knowledge, with anyone else in the past.

Rocky, without any explanation, led Tess to a back room. The room was about fifteen feet wide by fifteen feet deep. It had no windows and only one door. The room had a small table and one chair. After they entered the room, Rocky shut, but did not lock, the door. In the room, there were two men dressed in dark suits. Without introduction, one of the men ordered Tess to sit down. The other man, shaking his finger at Tess, demanded: "What did you do with the goods? How long have you been stealing cosmetics?"

Tess was shocked by the demand. She did not know how to respond or defend herself. The man repeated the questions. Tess stammered, "I don't know what you're talking about." The men continued to grill her with similar questions. After about ten minutes, Tess asked to call her dad. The men ignored her request and told her, "If you confess now, the company will go easy on you and it will not be necessary to call the police." Although neither Rocky nor the two other men ever physically restrained Tess, she did not try to leave the room.

After two hours of unremitting questioning, one of the men slapped a typed confession statement on the table in front of Tess and demanded that she sign it. Reluctantly, Tess signed the confession, and one of the men told Tess to go home. Tess claims she signed the confession so that she could leave the room.

This statement of facts demonstrates a crucial observation for anyone who works with law and lawyers: Legal analysis is only as thorough as the facts that feed into that analysis. Sound legal analysis relies not only on accurate, complete, and correct *law* but also on accurate, complete, and correct *facts*. Professionals who work with and around lawyers play a crucial role at this point in a case, such as by assisting with or taking primary responsibility for investigating the facts. Chapter 15 discusses working with facts in further detail.

Attorney Way recorded her initial assessment of the Tess Williams facts and gave instructions to her junior associate Mansfield on how to proceed with them.

These facts have me wondering about the viability of a false imprisonment claim against MegaMart. I recall from a prior matter that the "willful detainment" element is often where false imprisonment claims fail. Please get me a memorandum on that first element, and let us discuss the results so we can help the Williams family decide whether they wish to proceed further. I also need to determine if this claim is one our firm would be willing to take on a contingent fee basis as the family requested. Your analysis should be helpful on that point.

For purposes of the present illustration, we have limited the law to two cases, *Cuellar v. Walgreens* and *Black v. Kroger*. You may have read *Cuellar* for Chapter 4's exercise in reading a judicial opinion. If not, you can find it at the end of Chapter 4 and read it now. (That case is a somewhat fictionalized case adapted for your learning purposes.) You can also read a judicial opinion in its original format, *Black v. Kroger Co.*, 527 S.W.2d 794 (Tex. App. — Houston [1st Dist.] 1975) from one of the many sources where it is available.[14]

Based on what you know so far, what do you think the outcomes of *Cuellar* and *Black* mean for Tess Williams? An attorney in Mansfield's position will read the applicable cases using the techniques described in Chapter 4 to determine both the legal rule and how the rule was applied to the facts in these prior cases. With that knowledge, Mansfield has the tools he needs to reduce his legal analysis to writing an objective memorandum following the IRAC organizational paradigm.

The first part of Appendix A contains both Attorney Way's assignment and Attorney Mansfield's written analysis that ultimately resulted from his review. Before proceeding in the chapter, take a few minutes to review Mansfield's complete memo. With that big picture in mind, we will next review the substance of the memo paragraph by paragraph, to see exactly what this attorney did.

B. Issue — Stating the Thesis

The I in IRAC refers to the "issue" being analyzed; other variations of the legal analysis paradigm call it the "conclusion" or "thesis." Taken together these terms refer to the fact that the opening paragraph of an IRAC analysis is a tell-all roadmap for what is yet to come. Put another way, a memorandum is not like a murder mystery, where the author's big reveal is saved until the end after much buildup. In fact, "suspense is the enemy of good legal writing" as quipped by Professor Mary Beth Beazley.[15] Legal writing is a species of technical writing where clarity, context, and direct signposting of the author's intent are valuable traits; indeed, such traits are expected by a law-trained reader. Think about how much information is packed into the issue paragraph of Mansfield's memo:

Tess Williams can likely prove she was willfully detained by MegaMart and its employees. In a false imprisonment claim, the element of willful detention "may be ac-

---

14. You can find and read *Black* in the free online sources Google Scholar and Court Listener, as further demonstrated in Chapter 10 on researching cases.

15. Mary Beth Beazley, *A Practical Guide to Appellate Advocacy* 362 (5th ed. 2018).

complished by violence, by threats, or by any other means of restraining a person from moving from one place to another." *Cuellar v. Walgreens Co.*, 93 S.W.3d 458, 459 (Tex. 2002). Williams was detained in a small room by three men who prevented her from using a phone and who interrogated her, using harsh tones and threatening gestures, until she signed a prepared confession and was permitted to leave. These facts are sufficient to establish willful detention by threat.

Notice that this issue paragraph accomplishes three tasks: First, it identifies and predicts the probable outcome of the legal problem (the willful detention element of a false imprisonment claim) that will be the subject of the analysis to follow. Second, the issue paragraph summarizes the core rule controlling the analysis. Finally, the paragraph highlights the facts that support the prediction. When an issue paragraph summarizes the (1) prediction, (2) rule, and (3) factual reasoning, the result is an informative roadmap leaving the rest of the IRAC analysis as proof of what was stated up front. If this memo were a murder mystery, we would already know who the villain was and (basically) how he accomplished his nefarious plot! In a very real sense, the remainder of the IRAC analysis is devoted to elaboration and proof of matters stated in the first paragraph.

C. *Rule*

The R in IRAC refers to the applicable legal rule, which is the cornerstone of legal analysis. A rule ultimately has two parts: the *rule statement* and the *rule explanation.* Joshua Mansfield's analytical memo illustrates both parts of the rule below.

1. Rule Statement: Isolating the Basic Legal Test

As noted in our discussion of legal rules above, the rule is the "formula" for deciding the issue. The rule statement in a legal memorandum is the place to state that formula in as clear and succinct a fashion as the law allows. The rule statement should be as clear as possible without sacrificing accuracy or completeness. That is one of the central difficulties of all legal communication. A complete quotation of the legal authorities would be unclear, over-inclusive, and not very useful. But a one-sentence paraphrase would be too simplistic and general, compromising the usefulness of the legal advice. The Mansfield memo addresses this challenge in part by relying on a mix of quoted language and paraphrasing for the rule statement in its second paragraph:

> False imprisonment in Texas is the willful detention of a person without his or her consent and without the authority of law. *Id.*; *Black v. Kroger*, 527 S.W.2d 794, 796 (Tex. App.—Houston [1st Dist.] 1975). "A willful detention may be accomplished by violence, by threats, or by any other means restraining a person from moving from one place to another." *Cuellar*, 93 S.W.3d at 459. When claiming willful detention by threat, the plaintiff must prove that the threat put her "in just fear of injury to... her person, reputation, or property." *Black*, 527 S.W.2d at 796. Threats to call the police "are not

ordinarily sufficient in themselves to effect an unlawful imprisonment." *Cuellar*, 93 S.W.3d at 459 (emphasis added). The threat also must be strong enough to overcome a person's will to leave. *Black*, 527 S.W.2d at 800. Factors that may be considered in assessing whether a person was detained by a force that overcame her free will include the relative age, size, education, experience, sex, and demeanor of the participants, as well as any relationship between interrogator and accused. Courts also consider the physical environment in which the person was confined and any attempts the person made either to leave or to call for help. *Id.* at 800–01; *Cuellar*, 93 S.W.3d at 460.

This rule statement starts at the top level of the three-element test. The statement then drills down for detail on the willful detention element that is the focus of this memo. The rule stated in both *Black* and *Cuellar* shows, for instance, that there are three possible ways to prove willful detention: violence, threats, or other means of restraint. The rule statement then narrows its scope further to "willful detention by threat," which requires not just any old threat, but a threat sufficiently strong to overcome the plaintiff's free will to leave.

The final two sentences of this rule statement may come as something of a surprise. In a false imprisonment claim, proving that the element of willful detention is satisfied because of sufficient threat requires a factor test. What? Yes! An elemental test can, as one or more of its elements, have a factor test embedded inside of it. Here, the factors relevant to analyzing willful detention by threat expressly include "the relative age, size, education, experience, sex, and demeanor of the participants, as well as any relationship between interrogator and accused," along with "the physical environment" of confinement and "any attempts the person made either to leave or call for help."

Despite all we have learned at this point from the attorney's memo, the rule is still fairly general. The next section of the legal analysis goes into more detail.

2. Explaining the Rule in Action

Everyone—lawyers and other professionals alike—learns from examples. Here, if you imagine the rule as a wild animal, we need to know what it does when released into the wild. What do courts actually do when they apply that rule to facts to decide cases? After the rule statement above, the legal analysis provides a set of examples of how the rule has actually worked in the past. These examples are often called the *rule explanation*. The explanation typically consists of precise, real-world stories drawn from prior cases that have applied the rule. A lawyer has typically followed four steps to create this explanation:

- researched the relevant cases,
- selected the cases most relevant to the client's situation,
- put the key cases in the most logical and efficient order for the analysis, and

- encapsulated them in a concise way that still covers their key facts and holding, plus detailed citations.

The third and fourth paragraphs of the Mansfield memo show what a rule explanation looks like:

> Factors of age, experience, and education of the claimant relative to her interviewer contributed to a successful false imprisonment claim by the *Black* plaintiff where her counterpart in *Cuellar* failed. Cuellar, a twenty-two-year-old college student and journalist, had worked as a reporter for a television station and two newspapers before beginning her job at Walgreens. She had worked for Walgreens for four months when the store accused her of theft, and she participated in the interview with the Walgreens loss-prevention specialist on terms of intellectual equality. *Cuellar*, 93 S.W.3d at 460–61. Black, in contrast, was eighteen at the time of the accusation made against her, with a tenth-grade education. Her job at Kroger was the only job she ever held, and she had worked for Kroger for approximately two years when she was accused of theft. *Black*, 527 S.W.2d at 796. Black's mother and husband also worked for Kroger. *Id*. The court in *Black* noted that her limited business experience and the relationship of her family to the store could have made Black particularly unable to resist the authority of her employer. 527 S.W.2d at 800.
>
> The number, gender, demeanor, and relative size of the participants, as well as the physical surroundings in which each interview took place can also aid in establishing willful detention by threat. Black, for example, was taken by her male boss to a small room with one door and no windows, crowded with furniture, in which another man (plus a woman) both claiming to represent Kroger Security were already present. In sharp tones, they accused her of theft, and they threatened that unless she confessed and repaid the money, she would be handcuffed and taken to jail and would not see her family "for a long time." *Id*. at 797. Cuellar, on the other hand, was taken to a room normally used for training employees. Her lone interviewer answered her questions calmly, and the only time Cuellar felt intimidated was when her interviewer threatened to call the police. *Cuellar*, 93 S.W.3d at 460. In fact, her interviewer was not in the room when Cuellar wrote her confession. *Id*. at 461.

These paragraphs are the lawyer's effort to distill the most relevant facts from precedent cases and organize them to illustrate important aspects of the rule. Note that the result of this explanation is considerably shorter than the actual judicial opinions being cited here. The lawyer's job in explaining the rule is not to parrot large swaths of the prior cases or even to tell a complete story of what happened. Rather, the goals are *distillation* and *synthesis*:

- Written analysis of cases should distill from the story primarily the facts that are legally relevant, supported by enough contextual facts that the reduced story makes sense and is efficiently communicated even to a reader who has not seen the source cases.

- Synthesis is important because that is how the lawyer takes numerous cases dealing with the same rule and harmonizes them into a single, complete picture of how the rule operates based on the outcomes from diverse sets of facts.

The Mansfield memo deals with only two precedent cases, but another legal problem might require meaningful consideration of a dozen or more cases, plus multiple statutes. Legal analysis and the IRAC model can expand or contract to fit both relatively clear or relatively unclear situations, and situations with few relevant legal authorities as well as situations with numerous relevant legal authorities.

In this sample rule explanation, notice that the paragraphs do not just *list* the cases. Law students in J.D. programs are taught—sometimes a bit painfully—not to write a "book report" of cases in a list.[16] Rather, the paragraphs are organized by the common thread of analysis between the two cases:

- The first paragraph addresses the comparative "age, experience, and education" of each plaintiff as compared to their alleged captors. This collection of factors makes sense to consider together, as they all relate to the plaintiff's internal personal situation at the time of her claimed captivity. In *Black*, the disparity in these areas between Cathy Black and her employer's representatives was significant and ultimately supported a successful false imprisonment claim. Dulcinea Cuellar, in contrast, was comparatively older and had more education and work experience than did Black. Cuellar's claim failed where she had greater personal ability to protect herself and resist her employer's threat. These facts will be useful in predicting whether Tess Williams's age, experience, and education tend to prove willful detainment by threat.

- The second paragraph addresses the factors of "number, gender, demeanor, and relative size of the participants, as well as the physical surroundings in which each interview took place." Notice these considerations have a commonality: the setting where the interrogation event occurred. These facts will also be useful in predicting whether the setting of what happened to Tess Williams tends to prove willful detainment by threat.

Through these two paragraphs, the lawyer has isolated facts that are relevant and therefore provide the basis for useful comparisons to the Tess Williams episode. The analysis is not able to cover everything in equivalent detail. For example, neither the *Black* nor *Cuellar* opinion provides height and weight statistics for the people involved

---

16. *E.g.*, Kristen Konrad Tiscione, *Paradigm Lost: Recapturing Classical Rhetoric to Validate Legal Reasoning*, 27 Vt. L. Rev. 483, 498 (2003) (describing how "the Book Report" is a common error with several related effects such as missing information and incomplete analysis).

in those cases. The lawyer may wish to know those statistics and believe they would be relevant. The lawyer can mention height and weight statistics as a supplement to the legal analysis. But if the height and weight statistics were not used as a key fact in the prior cases, they are unlikely to play a key role in Tess Williams's case either. Lawyers drafting legal analysis are basically at the mercy of the case law here: they must do the best they can with what they have. They must think creatively about facts that seem relevant, such as height and weight. But they must also think realistically about what type of facts matter in the precedent. An argument that seems "creative" because no one has ever thought of it before is probably going to be weakly predictive at best, and risky as an argument. A client might *need* the lawyer to make a new or risky argument, and lawyers are explicitly permitted by the ethical rules to advocate for changes in the law. But lawyers dealing with uncertainty will recognize and advise clients that an argument based on stretching the law or changing the law is far more uncertain than an argument grounded in what the law already *is*, right now. Thus, the rule and rule explanation hew closely to the details of what the case law has actually said and done, while distilling and synthesizing it for relevance to the client.

Having stated the rule and explained it, Mansfield is ready for the main event of IRAC: the Application of law to his client's facts.

D. Application — Analogical Reasoning in Action

The real purpose of setting forth a detailed statement of a rule is to use it. In IRAC organization, the application paragraphs are where that occurs. Application can be quite simple if the language of the rule unequivocally covers or does not cover the facts. But for factual situations with nuance or complexity, rule application means *analogical reasoning*—the use of specific fact-to-fact comparisons and rationale from prior cases as the means to establish the truth of a prediction. Analogical reasoning means, essentially, relying on relevant similarities and differences between the key facts of prior cases and the new set of facts.

Because the traditional legal memorandum is a tool for objective analysis, it must do something that careful lawyers have been trained to do—consider both sides of the argument. As a consequence, the application paragraphs in many IRAC analyses, including the Mansfield memo, come in two types: supporting analysis and counter-analysis.

1. Supporting Analysis

The beginning of rule application in the Mansfield memo can be found at paragraphs five and six:

> Tess Williams's claim of willful detention, like Black's, will likely succeed in part because of her relative youth, inexperience, and education as compared to her supervisor. Williams is twenty years old with a high-school education. Her job at MegaMart, for whom she worked for two years, was her first full-time job, so she had limited experience in business or in the world. Williams, like Black and in contrast to Cuellar, has very little

business experience and is much more submissive to company authority. Williams was so intimidated by the interrogator's threats and actions that, like Black, she was "unable to exercise her free will to leave the interview and that she was unreasonably detained." *Black*, 527 S.W.2d at 801. In *Cuellar*, the plaintiff's employment and professional experience in journalism enabled her to ask questions and request clarifications, showing she voluntarily remained in the room, a situation unlike that of Williams who asked only to call her father. *See Cuellar*, 93 S.W.3d at 461.

The number, gender, demeanor, and size of MegaMart's employees in the cramped interview space also created an environment in which Williams would reasonably have felt threatened. Williams, the only female in the room, was ordered to sit in the only chair in the room while three men stood around her. In addition, one of the men shook his finger at Williams, accusing her of being a thief by asking her about what she had done with the store's property. These direct accusations continued for two hours without pause before the men "slapped" a pre-written confession on the table and demanded Williams sign it, strongly implying that she could not leave unless she did so. In *Cuellar*, the court determined that because the interrogators did not yell at the plaintiff, call her a thief, or remain in the room when the plaintiff wrote her confession — a notable contrast to Williams's experience — Cuellar was not willfully detained. *See Cuellar*, 93 S.W.3d at 461. Williams's experience more closely parallels the plaintiff's circumstances in *Black*, where the interrogators spoke in a loud tone of voice, called her a thief, and told her to sign "a statement admitting" she took money from the store. *Black*, 527 S.W.2d at 797–98. In fact, Black faced less of a threat of physical harm because another female was in the room and all parties were seated during questioning. *Id.* at 796. The comparative size of the parties — Williams being five feet tall while her supervisor is a former high school linebacker — increased the perceived threat to Williams.

These paragraphs summarize important fact-to-fact comparisons between her case and the court decisions that came before her. By "important," we really mean "legally relevant." The facts that Williams was outnumbered three-to-one and that her interrogators were all men are legally relevant because they relate to prongs of the rule dealing with number and gender. Suppose in contrast that we knew Williams's interrogator was wearing a blue shirt, but the interrogator in Cathy Black's successful false imprisonment case was wearing a white shirt. Would that matter? Nothing in the rule on willful detainment suggests that the color of a person's clothing has any impact one way or the other. Thus, the differing shirt colors, even if they are true facts, are not legally relevant facts. We would not expect legal analysis to be focused there.[17]

The rule application tracks the same concepts and the same structure as the rule statement and rule explanation earlier in this memorandum. The first of the supporting analysis paragraphs is based upon the factors of relative age, experience, and edu-

---

17. See Chapter 15 for an extended discussion of facts and legal relevance.

cation. Similarly, the next supporting paragraph deals with another previously explained group of factors: number, gender, demeanor, relative size, and the nature of the detention area.

This consistency shows how important the legal rule is for organizing analysis. Imagine if the lawyer's memo introduced a new idea and new case about the law right in the middle of the rule application. That new information would distract from this segment's key purpose, which is focusing on what the facts mean in light of the law as already explained. These two paragraphs of supporting analysis may look simple, clear, and comprehensible — but much mental labor went into producing this highlight of the memo. Easy reading is frequently the result of hard writing!

2. Counter-Analysis

A skilled lawyer must be able to perceive and account for arguments that would undermine the main prediction. The purpose of counter-analysis, such as that in the seventh paragraph of Mansfield's memo, is to poke holes in and highlight weaknesses in the writer's prediction. Why would a lawyer do that? As noted earlier, legal analysis predicts what a court would do if presented with the facts the lawyer is now analyzing. The memorandum uses thorough analysis to estimate a probability. Lawyers and their clients need to anticipate and be prepared for the uncertainty inherent in this predictive role. Robust counter-analysis is part of that preparation. It also vividly illustrates why a lawyer predicting a result cannot properly also promise that result.

A second reason to document counter-analysis in a memo is to reveal the lawyer's reasoning so that other readers can read and question it, possibly criticizing the lawyer's own work, but improving advice to the client in the process. Writing counter-analysis may prompt the lawyer to realize that the counter-analysis actually describes the more likely result in the case. Thus, a lawyer drafting an internal office memorandum might actually switch sides from a first draft to a final draft! Overall, the process of writing a memorandum does not merely document a lawyer's thinking; writing will itself serve to move the thinking forward.

In his Tess Williams memo, attorney Mansfield highlights a particular point on which the Williams case is weaker than the plaintiff's position in *Black*. He also notes statements in the cases that are ripe for use against Williams.

Nonetheless, MegaMart will likely argue that the threat against Williams to call the police was inadequate to prove willful detention by threat because it was not made alongside a threat to Williams's family. Indeed, in *Black*, willful detention was based not only on a threat to call the police, but on such a threat made in the context of a long conversation about Black's family. *Black*, 527 S.W.2d at 801. In Williams's situation, there was no implied threat to her family and, by itself, the threat to call the police would not have been sufficient to establish willful detention. *Cuellar*, 93 S.W.3d at 459. The threat to Williams, however, unlike the threat to Cuellar, did not stand completely alone. The threat to Williams occurred in a context of superior numbers and authority on the employer's side, superior education and experience, cramped surroundings, and the intimidating manner of her interviewers. Furthermore, Williams asked for permission to call for help; not only was the request denied, but followed up by MegaMart's threat to call the police. Such a response would have had a chilling effect on any further attempts by Williams to defend herself. Thus Williams can argue that in context, MegaMart's threat to call police is more like the threat in *Black* than in *Cuellar* and supports her claim for false imprisonment.

While counter-analysis paragraphs in the Application part of IRAC can take various forms, this example accomplishes the writer's important goals. The first sentence articulates a legal argument that is in opposition to the memo's prediction. The paragraph then documents legal support — specific case references — for the opposing prediction. The latter half of the paragraph completes the circle by explaining why the counter-analysis is not likely to prevail. Objective legal analysis requires proof that the attorney has considered the strongest arguments counter to the prediction, and this paragraph accomplishes that mission.

E. Conclusion — Meaningful Summation

The Conclusion in IRAC is the bookend to the opening Issue. In Mansfield's memorandum, the opening and closing paragraphs actually have a great deal in common. While the Issue is a forward-looking roadmap, the Conclusion is a backward-looking summation. Both are ultimately a thumbnail sketch of the lengthier analysis contained in the IRAC's R and A sections.

> The circumstances of Tess Williams's detention are supported by most of the factors Texas courts consider to establish willful detention by threat: the age, experience, and education of the participants; the size and number of participants; the room in which she was detained; and her accusers' demeanor, coupled with their refusal to allow her to call for help. *Id.* at 460; *Black*, 527 S.W.2d at 800–01. Williams accordingly can likely prove the willful detention element of her claim of false imprisonment against MegaMart.

IRAC-style analysis in a legal memorandum often has much in common with the timeworn advice on how to make a speech: "Tell them what you're going to tell them, then tell them, and then tell them what you told them." The beginning and ending of an IRAC unit are repetitive, but for a reason: The opening and closing summaries create context that supports and reinforces the intensive analytical information that the attorney seeks to communicate in a memorandum. Legal writing prizes usefulness and reader convenience, so it begins and ends in the same place.

VII. Client Follow-Up: Now What?

We have now walked through the lawyer's process of analyzing a legal problem, in this case a personal injury[18] case for Olivia Ralston's Texas relatives, the Williams family. In this example, the detailed legal analysis above was done *from* one lawyer *to* another lawyer. That memorandum is the internal work product of the law firm, and although it belongs to Tess Williams because she is the client, she may never see it. Whether the lawyer offers detailed legal analysis to a client depends on the situation. Sophisticated corporate and government clients are much more likely to see unfiltered lawyer-to-lawyer analysis than individual consumer clients and personal-injury clients.

Imagine that Tess Williams and her parents have briefly spoken by telephone with Joshua Mansfield about his initial findings. Here in the style of a "choose your own adventure," let us imagine three possible scenarios for the attorney's interaction with the family.

- **Scenario 1:** The attorney reviews the detailed legal analysis and schedules a meeting with the family. In the in-person meeting, he explains the gist of the analysis, gives them time to ask questions, and presents them with options for proceeding with their possible lawsuit against MegaMart.

- **Scenario 2:** The attorney reviews the detailed legal analysis and writes a more concise version of it, omitting the formal legal detail and "translating" it for a non-lawyer audience. He emails this version to the family and schedules a meeting to ask questions and discuss options.

- **Scenario 3:** The family requests the file to review it, and the attorney Mansfield provided Tess with a copy of key documents including the legal memorandum assessing her false-imprisonment claim. He then schedules a meeting so they can ask questions and discuss options.

Through any of these scenarios, the purpose of the legal analysis above is to enable the client to make decisions. The expert analysis comes from the lawyer, but it serves the client's interest in managing life, business, and other important choices.

Whether the family receives the legal advice in a spoken summary, a concise version by email, or a full review of the file, the analysis will probably prompt questions. What questions might they now have before deciding how to proceed? Based on the analysis discussed throughout this chapter, here are a few questions that the family might ask:

---

18. Be careful not to make the common mistake of equating "personal injury" to "physical injury." A physical injury is one type of personal injury, but it some personal injuries are not physical. Here, Tess Williams is complaining of a legal harm — being unjustifiably deprived of liberty — that is a personal injury, even though the harm does not involve physical harm.

- The memo is focused on the one element of the false imprisonment claim about which you were most concerned. Are you confident in the other two?

- What else would you need to know to make your analysis more definite?

- On what fee basis would you be willing to handle the case? Would you be willing to handle this on a contingent fee, and how would that work?

- Our discussion has focused on the possibility of filing a lawsuit. Do we have other options short of actually suing? Is there any way to fight what happened without actually going to court?

- How long would you estimate this lawsuit would last?

- I have heard that many lawsuits settle before trial. Do you think that is likely here? Why or why not?

- How much involvement would you need from Tess or others in any litigation?

- Would Tess have to testify in her case? Could MegaMart dig into our private business if we sue them?

What other questions might you suggest the Williams family ask? A few of the questions above deal with the substance of Tess's claim, but many more relate to understanding the process. When the family asks about pursuing their goals without actually going to court, one way to possibly do that is by first writing a "demand letter"—a formal letter, often written under a lawyer's signature and letterhead, asking the recipient to do or not do something. When the family asks about giving testimony and possibly having their private business intruded upon, they are really asking about "civil discovery," meaning the process of requesting documents and taking testimony from potential witnesses and preparing the case for trial. Here, Tess would likely have to give a deposition under oath and then give testimony at trial as well if the case did not settle before then. MegaMart's lawyer would try to find ways to "impeach" her or make her testimony look inconsistent, flawed, or misleading. These considerations are important in the complete picture of legal analysis and legal advice. None of those "outside" matters are addressed in the analytical memo. The memo's legal analysis is most interested in the legal outcome. The life questions, however, are just as important to the family's decision, and will certainly be worth discussion time with the attorney.

VIII. Tying It All Together

Applying the law to the facts is the core of legal analysis performed by lawyers for clients. It is a broad skill set requiring legal research, critical reading skills, logical reasoning skills based on rules and analogies, and detailed application of law to the facts—including both strengths and weaknesses. One of our quotes to begin the chapter was that "brevity may be the soul of wit, but it is not the soul of rigorous analysis." We hope you see now why some legal analysis goes into length and detail.

Another goal of this chapter was to show the *steps* of legal analysis and the detailed thought process behind researching and analyzing the law. Even if the lawyers do not actually document their analysis in a formal legal memo as shown here, competent legal analysis and advice still demands thorough research and the application of legal judgment to make a prediction. Thus, the steps shown here may not be captured in writing in a memo, but they still need to happen. For example, legal analysis is often condensed into the format of an email, but the steps of reasoning should not be incomplete just because the final written product is a shorter piece of writing. The steps of legal reasoning should not be incomplete even if there is no writing at all, because the lawyer's legal research and analysis funnel directly into an in-person discussion between lawyer and client. Legal analysis is a set of flexible analytical approaches that should expand or contract to meet the needs of the situation and the needs of the client.

Having studied this chapter, you should be able to:

- Describe the core concept of legal analysis: the use of rule-based reasoning to explain the law and then apply it to facts
- Recognize and identify the modular components of legal rules, including the differing functions of elements and factors in those modules
- Articulate the parts of the common IRAC framework for shaping legal analysis: issue, rule, application, and conclusion
- Recognize how legal analysis shapes the way lawyers advise clients
- Anticipate how to interact with lawyers performing their role of giving legal advice by explaining and applying the law to facts
- Use the core concepts of legal analysis to ask questions and work productively with lawyers

....

Case Study: Working with Legal Analysis

INTERNAL MEMORANDUM

To:	Risk Manager
From:	Olivia Ralston
Date:	October 3, 20XX
Re:	Earth Foods Contract Issue

I know you haven't been with Olivia's Beans for very long, but I have been impressed with the extent to which you have learned the ins and outs of our business. Let me bring you up to speed on a legal predicament that is going to require us to make some far-reaching business decisions over the next several weeks. I want your input, and I have been distracted from this matter more than I should have been.

As you probably recall, I incorporated Olivia's Beans in Colorado two years ago, hoping to combine my love of coffee with my interest in sustainable agriculture. My business model is to buy fresh, sustainably sourced coffee beans from small growers, roast and package them at our facility using proprietary methods, and sell them to retailers or directly to consumers via our online store. At first I was the sole shareholder, but I've since accepted funding from several investors in exchange for significant ownership interests. I manage the company's day-to-day affairs and report to the outside investors periodically.

On July 29 of last year, I started corresponding with Raul Proteus, the Chief Logistics Officer at Earth Foods, concerning a long-term supply contract for our Pure Colombian blend. He'd tried it at a local coffee shop and said he was "hooked." I was excited to finally land a contract with a major retailer; before this, we were mainly roasting small batches for boutiques and cafés.

I knew that Earth Foods would expect Olivia's Beans to offer a volume discount for buying at the scale we were discussing, so I decided to cut out the middleman and contact Colombian farmers' co-ops directly. I ultimately received an excellent bid from Federación de Cafeteros Pequeños de Colombia (FCPC), a small Colombian co-op, at $6.50 per pound. On August 12, after Olivia's Beans had received the bid, I executed a contract with Earth Foods for 100,000 pounds of the Pure Colombian blend at $7.05 per pound. Then, on August 14, I executed the contract with FCPC.

The Earth Foods contract called for bimonthly shipments of 10,000 pounds, starting on September 1. Because this far exceeded Olivia's Beans' current capacity, I've been contracting the roasting out to a third-party facility.

The contract seemed like a great deal for everyone at the time — maybe more so for Earth Foods than for Olivia's Beans. I visited my local store and saw that Pure Colombian was the most reasonably priced blend in its category, so I think they would have been willing to pay even more than the price we agreed to.

Unfortunately, FCPC dissolved in late-September, not long after our first shipment to Earth Foods. I think the farmers couldn't agree on profit-splitting or something and decided they'd be better off on their own. Right now I can't find anyone claiming to be acting on behalf of the co-op, and I don't know whether Olivia's Beans could eventually have an actual, enforceable remedy for FCPC's breach. Maybe that's why there are professional coffee brokers.

In the meantime, no individual farmer is willing to give Olivia's Beans the same discount, or provide shipping. For the foreseeable future, I'm facing costs of about $8.25 per pound from substitute sources for Colombian beans. Olivia's Beans' only major contract will be money-losing! I was willing to live with a narrow profit margin (I expected we'd come out ahead about $55,000 on the whole 100,000 pounds when all was said and done) because of the benefit of having Olivia's Beans associated with such a well-regarded upscale market as Earth Foods. Taking a large hit is another matter entirely. At this moment, on the remaining 90,000 pounds of beans to be delivered on the Earth Foods contract, Olivia's Beans will suffer a loss of $108,000 instead of getting its expected profit of $49,500. As you can see, I need a way out of this deal if at all possible.

The contract says that any disputes are governed by New York law, and our outside counsel told me a while back about a law—section 2-615 of New York's Uniform Commercial Code—that excuses non-delivery of goods if performance becomes "impracticable"—whatever that means. The outside counsel analyzed the legal issue and prepared a memorandum on the topic, though I'm not confident that he understands our company as well as you do.

I've requested a copy of the company file from Olivia's Beans' attorneys. You can find it in Appendix B. Please review those materials and prepare a 3- to 5-page report for me that does the following:

1. Summarize and explain the attorney's memorandum on whether Olivia's Beans can be excused from performing the Earth Foods contract. Be concise but accurate, and make sure you (briefly) describe the attorney's reasoning.

2. Describe the business risk Olivia's Beans would face from breaching the Earth Foods contract.

3. Describe the business risk Olivia's Beans would face from *not* breaching the Earth Foods contract.

4. Make recommendations on how our company should handle the situation. What is the best way for us to proceed from here?

Your report should have headings and corresponding sections reflecting each of the four areas I have asked you to address. Use anything you know about the company and our current position as you consider the business risk surrounding our situation.

I appreciate your assistance regarding this matter.

Traditions and Trends

Traditional legal analysis rests on traditional legal reasoning techniques and ideas. Such techniques include approaches such as close reading of statutes, regulations, and other text, and the use of case precedent for analogies and distinctions. Traditional ideas include a rich and well-established body of concepts such as stare decisis, canons of statutory interpretation, and procedural frameworks such as claims and affirmative defenses.

These strong traditions are now influenced and supplemented by broad cross-disciplinary analysis such as sociological studies of law, law and economics, and cognitive psychology. Beginning in the late 1960s, law professors and think tanks began conducting empirical studies of the legal system's patterns and results. Recently, studies in cognitive psychology have both enriched and challenged this cross-disciplinary work in legal studies. For example, Nobel Prize recipient Daniel Kahneman and his longtime co-author Amos Tversky studied the decisions of Israeli parole-board judges, revealing different outcomes on essentially the same decision, depending on what time of day it was. (This and other studies are recounted for a popular audience in Kahneman's book *Thinking Fast and Slow* (2013).) The J.D. course of legal education continues to inculcate traditional approaches to legal analysis in its students, especially during foundational classes, with some upper-level elective options covering cross-disciplinary and empirical ideas.

In the world of law practice, empirical methods are making their way toward the standard suite of client services. Quantitative thinking is already well established in specific contexts such as financial calculations of damages, statistical sampling in employment cases, and large-scale text analysis of massive document productions in litigation. But empirical methods have not, to date, spread into general use by lawyers analyzing law and fact to advise clients. As of 2019, legal research providers are developing and promoting "artificial-intelligence-based" toolkits to supplement traditional legal research and analysis. Lawyers, sophisticated clients, and others involved in delivering and consuming legal analysis will need to be aware of these new tools, study them closely, and use them when they are cost-effective and worthwhile for enhancing client advice.

On the writing side, the delivery of legal analysis was traditionally accomplished via lengthy, detailed, comprehensive intra-office memoranda written by junior lawyers to senior lawyers. The standard legal memorandum has a highly stylized and set formula: a Question Presented giving the legal issue and key facts being analyzed in the memo; a Brief Answer summarizing the analysis and conclusion; a Statement of Facts comprehensively including every relevant fact plus necessary background; a Discussion providing the "meat" of the memorandum, meaning all of the law and fact analysis; and a Conclusion restating the memo's prediction and perhaps sharing recommendations for future action. These memos would require significant expenditure of billable hours for attorneys to produce and would be stored in a searchable law firm database to be retrieved later if the same or a related issue arose with any other client of the firm.

Economic pressure on clients and lawyers now means clients are less willing to pay tens of thousands of dollars for junior associates' comprehensive and stylized legal memoranda. Law firms need to produce analysis and recommendations efficiently, reducing the amount of billable time they charge clients or write off before finalizing client bills. The rise of email has helped to address this pressure, with legal analysis now often delivered by email in shorter, less formal messages. Client expectations for reliable analysis and competent legal advice, however, have not changed.

Chapter 6

Using the Internet for
Legal Research

If all you have is a hammer, everything looks like a nail.

— Abraham Maslow

It's rectangular. It glows. When you start typing, it wants to help by guessing what you're thinking. What is it? The search box in an internet search engine, of course. It's the answer to every researcher's dream, right? The internet search engine—for example, Google, Bing, Yahoo Search, and DuckDuckGo—is an extremely valuable tool for finding online information, including legal information—but the search engine is not the only answer or the best answer in every case. Legal literacy overlaps with information literacy; specifically, gaining knowledge of well-respected sources for legal information and developing skills in searching through unfamiliar legal information.

This chapter explores the process of preparing to research using online legal resources, including but not limited to effective use of search engines. This approach is consistent with the book's overall focus on open-access online research into legal information. Open-access legal information makes the law more accessible than when it could be found only in hard-copy books in law libraries. Open access to legal information may provide far-reaching benefits not only for individuals seeking answers, but also for community and society, as hypothesized by law librarian Virginia Wise and legal philosopher Frederick Schauer:

> Legal information, especially legal information to the public in "raw" form, may thus, we hypothesize, be a significant driver of the creation of the norms, habits, networks, and institutions of coordination, cooperation, and reciprocity that collectively go by the name of social capital.[1]

But state websites providing free legal information are not always easy to use, and researchers may experience barriers from "minor annoyances to users" to "real impediments to retrieving materials" such as poor or nonexistent search functionality.[2] Thus, free legal information is both idealistic and flawed. We resolve these tensions with a practical mindset: Researchers should prepare themselves to cope with these limitations and maximize the benefits of free legal information. In contrast to free legal information, fee-based platforms provide robust access to a large variety of legal information including primary law and deeply researched secondary sources—but at a price. The focus here is on free resources, but the information and skills discussed in this chapter and this book are valuable for research on a fee-based platform too.

I. Getting Started with Legal Research

When starting a legal research project, first identify your goal, and then design a strategy to achieve that goal. Goals for legal research vary widely, for example:

- **Gain context:** Find general context for an area of law to understand it better
- **Follow trends:** Learn about recent developments in an area of law

---

1. Virginia J. Wise & Frederick Schauer, *Legal Information As Social Capital*, 99 Law Library Journal 267, 272 (2007).

2. Kimberly Mattioli, *Access to Print, Access to Justice*, 110 Law Library Journal 31, 37 (2018) (quoting Sarah Glassmeyer, *Access to Law in the Twenty-First Century: Current Barriers to Access and the Future of Legal Information*, AALL Spectrum, Nov./Dec. 2016, at 34, and Sarah Glassmeyer, *State Legal Information Census: An Analysis of Primary State Legal Information: Search*, http://www.sarahglassmeyer.com/State LegalInformation/barriers-to-access/search/ [https://perma.cc/5MMT-4D3F].)

- **Find a specific piece of information:** Find a statute or regulation or a small group of sources relevant to an issue
- **Conduct a comprehensive search:** Gain comprehensive knowledge of a topic and ensure all research is up-to-date and reliable in a high-stakes situation

Open-access legal information can help with each of these research goals, as discussed with brief examples below.

A. Finding a Contextual Framework

Many research projects, not just in the legal field, begin with a conundrum: The researcher has a question to investigate. But doing an effective investigation requires some baseline knowledge about the question. How can you know enough to effectively research something you don't already know? People understand information when they have a "schema" for mentally organizing that information. That is cognitive jargon that means having a framework to organize new details that you learn, or having pre-existing knowledge you can use as a comparison for new details. Gaining context for an area of law means finding helpful sources that provide a reliable framework for understanding the law's details.

Imagine Olivia Ralston is part of a small group about to attend a meeting with the Braggadocio General Counsel's office. The purpose of the meeting is to discuss the idea of using age targets on social media for job advertisements. Ms. Ralston does not want to simply be a passive observer or source of facts in this meeting. She wants to learn more about age discrimination law generally.

Online legal research often turns up very helpful sources for gaining context. To gain context, a researcher does not need to find a single specific source, but does need to find a handful of useful, reliable general sources. Thus, Ms. Ralston could use an internet search engine to find news articles taking a legal angle and recent legal blog posts on this question. She can conduct separate searches for overviews of age discrimination law generally using a term like "primer" or "overview" in her search. From these sources, Ms. Ralston could gain context for understanding this question and asking questions.

B. Spotting Trends

Online legal information can be excellent for covering new developments in the law. Many law professors post articles before their hard copy publication on the Social Science Research Network (www.ssrn.com), and legal bloggers and legal journalists explore new issues as they arise.

Imagine that Ms. Ralston has a teenage son, and he has expressed an interest in using a scooter rental app to get around the city of Denver. Scooter rental outfits such as Bird and Lime have been embraced in some cities and rejected in others. Ms. Ralston wants to find out the legal situation and trends concerning these scooters, especially as they concern teenage users.

Internet search engines are an effective way to find legal information and some legal analysis on trends. Search algorithms tend to bring newer articles to the top of search results. A search for legal issues with Bird and Lime scooters would lead Ms. Ralston to articles covering various legal issues from municipal ordinances to tort liability and class actions and special considerations for unlicensed teens using the scooters.

C. Finding Specifics

Online resources can be excellent for quickly pulling up a single source — especially when you already know some detail about its key words or citations. Entering key words in a search engine will help identify a single targeted source when the source itself uses those words and the webpage for that source is advantaged by the search engine's algorithm.

For this example, imagine that Ms. Ralston is evaluating her startup idea's business structure. She wants to build in a social justice mission from the very start, and make it not just a value or mission but a part of the corporate structure. In searching online for social justice in corporate law, she came across the idea of "public benefit corporations." She has read a magazine article on public benefit corporations that dropped a footnote to "Section 7-101-503(2), C.R.S."

To use online resources to find a specific statutory or regulatory source, Ms. Ralston could use official government sources in Colorado, such as the Colorado legislature's website. She finds the official source for the Colorado Revised Statutes and pastes in the citation from the article to pull up the statute itself.

D. Getting Comprehensive

Online legal information's weakest contribution is in comprehensive legal research, particularly when the issue involves a lot of case law. Comprehensive legal research into cases is a classic example of what a lawyer would do when giving legal advice to a client. To find all the binding sources on a question using free online resources, the researcher may need to search multiple sites. Also, online information may not always be up-to-date, and case research platforms do not tag cases as "overruled" or "vacated" or otherwise questionable. Thus, while cases can be found online in many useful ways, it is difficult for researchers to know that their case law research is complete and up-to-date.

As an example here, imagine Ms. Ralston has a property dispute with her neighbor, who has sued her for encroaching on the back lot line with a fence Ms. Ralston built many years ago. She will be representing herself in court. She knows the key concept here is "adverse possession" and wants to find any statute plus every case decided in Colorado applying the doctrine of adverse possession.

For a comprehensive search into case law on adverse possession in Colorado, Ms. Ralston can try to use free online legal research. For example, Findlaw allows her to search Colorado Supreme Court cases since 1997. She has concerns that adverse possession is an old idea in property law, and 1997 might not be far enough back to give her all of the cases. Using Findlaw's search function, she finds 14 cases with the exact phrase "adverse possession." She is not sure whether these cases are overruled or reversed; all she has is the text. She also notes that she would need to do a separate search to find Colorado Court of Appeals cases, which could also be binding or at least influential on a trial court. To find Colorado Supreme Court and Colorado Court of Appeals cases in a single search, Ms. Ralston turns to Google Scholar for cases. Using Google Scholar, Ms. Ralston finds 250 cases in Colorado with the term "adverse possession." She is overwhelmed by the idea of reading 250 cases.

In each of the examples above and for each research goal, online legal research is useful, with many benefits and some limitations. Understanding whether you want context, trends, one specific resource, or a comprehensive answer will help you decide how to proceed.

II. Identifying the Standard for Successful Legal Research

Designing a legal research strategy means setting a standard for competence: what is "good enough" for your purposes? Of course, truly superb legal research—the best this world has ever seen—might be wonderful, but it also might be out of the question because of limited time and resources. Defining competence means setting the standard for what is acceptable and what is not acceptable.

For licensed attorneys working with clients, the relevant state bar sets that standard: a lawyer has a duty of competence. That duty, when breached, can result in bar discipline—a reprimand or other sanctions. The lawyer also may be liable to the client for the tort of legal malpractice.[3] For a non-bar-licensed professional—who by definition cannot give legal advice to others—the standard for legal research competence is more flexible and individualized. Professionals working in "law-adjacent"[4] fields or law-

---

3. Licensed attorneys have a professional duty to perform competent legal research. "Competent handling of a particular matter includes inquiry into and analysis of the factual and legal elements of the problem, and use of methods and procedures meeting the standards of competent practitioners." Stated in negative terms, being less than competent at legal research can lead to public sanctions by the relevant bar association or the state Supreme Court that enforces attorney discipline: "An attorney's failure to perform adequate research and write well can violate the attorney's professional responsibility." Debra K. Hackerson, *Access to Justice Starts in the Library: The Importance of Competent Research Skills and Free/Low-Cost Research Resources*, 62 Maine L. Rev. 473, 477 n. 20 (2010) (listing cases where attorneys were sanctioned for poor legal research).

4. Harvard Law School Center on the Legal Profession, *Introduction to Volume 2, Issue 3: Drawing Your Own Path: Forging New Identities in the Profession*, The Practice (March 2016), https://thepractice.law.harvard.edu/article/drawing-your-own-path/ (noting that many law graduates "are entering positions that

yer-adjacent positions may not have a clear industry standard defining what legal research competence looks like, or how it might be enforced.

To define a standard of competent legal research, this textbook relies on a general definition of "information literacy" from the American Association of Law Libraries (AALL):

> The ability to "recognize when information is needed and have the ability to locate, evaluate and use effectively the needed information."[5]

1. Do you recognize when legal information is needed?
2. Do you know what information is needed?
3. Do you know how to locate the needed information?
4. Do you know how to evaluate the needed information?
5. Do you know how to use the needed information?
6. Do you know how to use the needed information effectively?

For professionals working with legal information, this definition can be broken down into separate questions:

Below are more thoughts on each step. This approach may seem abstract, and it is; but thinking abstractly about your approach to legal research and legal information will help you when it comes time to use your skills concretely. Anyone can just start typing words into a search bar. One thing that differentiates the expert from the amateur is having a larger conceptual framework for understanding what to do.

A. Recognizing When Legal Information Is Needed

There is a psychological phenomenon called the Dunning-Kruger Effect. It describes the situation when a person is so ignorant that the person does not even realize how ignorant he or she really is. The Dunning-Kruger Effect can describe not just a state of ignorance, but also incompetence. A person who is bad at a task and unable to recognize that fact may be quite confident — unjustifiably yet remarkably confident.

Avoiding the Dunning-Kruger Effect with law and legal issues means being able to recognize a legal issue in the first place. Becoming information literate and, specifical-

---

might be considered 'law adjacent,' resting at the intersection of law and other fields, such as technology, business, and education.")

5. Ellie Margolis & Kristen Murray, *Using Information Literacy to Prepare Practice-Ready Graduates*, U. Haw. L. Rev. 1, 24 n. 147 (2017) (quoting Presidential Committee on Information Literacy: Final Report, Am. Libr. Ass'n (Jan. 10, 1989), http://www.ala.org/acrl/publications/whitepapers/presidential).

ly, legally literate, means being able to recognize that an issue is legal and that more information is needed. The legally literate professional recognizes that a question calls for legal information. The legally literate professional also recognizes that a question may call for law-related judgment or the involvement of a lawyer. This recognition may be immediate: someone in a meeting pipes up with a shocking statement, and it is immediately clear that general counsel needs to be involved as soon as possible. Or this recognition may dawn slowly as a team of professionals works on a problem over time and the solution becomes more and more intertwined with legal advice.

Litigators benefit from Dunning-Kruger because when unjustifiably confident people forge ahead without spotting legal issues, they make decisions that create legal risks they don't even realize they are causing. Yes, this is a cynical view, but when legal risks are unexpected or disproportionate, disputes happen and (sometimes) litigation follows. Thus, understanding when legal information is needed is really about a form of judgment — spotting issues and beginning to solve them using the appropriate information and professionals, including licensed attorneys. Issue spotting for situations that require legal judgment (applying law to fact) is discussed more specifically in chapter 3. But the material throughout this book and in your other law-related classes should help you to develop that judgment.

B. Knowing What Information Is Needed

Being in a situation and recognizing the need for legal information is just a first step. Knowing *what* information is needed starts the road to being effective at dealing with the situation. Here again, having legal training and context is enormously valuable. For example, when someone in a meeting starts discussing social media ads targeted by age, another professional with a baseline knowledge of law will recognize that age targeting could raise issues of age discrimination under federal and possibly state law. Just knowing that the issue is potentially federal is a form of wisdom because beginning in federal case law would quickly lead any researcher to the statutory source.

Knowing *what* information is needed also entails knowing *how much* is needed. In certain situations, having *some* reliable, up-to-date information is valuable; in other situations, having *all* the relevant binding information is necessary. Knowing what information is needed relates back to understanding the initial goals and stakes of the research project.

Knowing what is needed also means knowing what is *not needed*. Using a search engine is particularly likely to provide some distracting, unnecessary, unreliable, biased, tempting, or irrelevant results. Recognizing what is needed means discerning what seems potentially relevant but is unnecessary, distracting, or even harmful and wrong. Recognizing what is needed also means being able to wade through sources that are *somewhat* helpful, and to extract only the parts that are helpful.

C. Knowing How to Locate the Needed Information

Knowing how to locate the needed information has at least two subparts:

- knowing about the most popular and reliable and respected research sources for general legal research
- knowing how to craft searches and recognize the attributes of respected sources (without preexisting knowledge of what they are)

As to the general goal of knowing popular research sources, this chapter and the rest of this book provide basic knowledge about where to find legal information. By reading this book and practicing legal research, you should gain a good sense for the most popular and reliable and respected research sources for general legal research. Keep in mind that legal research sources can and will change after this book is printed. Stay on top of trends in your field of interest, and be aware when you use any type of research tool that it will likely change over time. This chapter started with a legal cliché, "it depends," and now is a good time for a more general cliché: in legal research, as in life, "the only constant is change."

The other general goal is knowing how to conduct good research in an unfamiliar area. At the highest level, the way to achieve this goal is actually quite simple:

At each step, you are balancing the goal of finding everything relevant with the goal of finding only the relevant things. These are known in expert research terminology as "precision" and "recall." Being effective at locating the needed information means gathering all the sources you need and not missing anything important, while also filtering out irrelevant sources and gathering only the sources that matter:

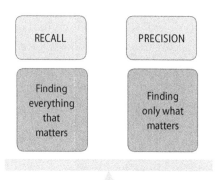

Balancing the need for comprehensive recall against the need for precise results is a constant tension, akin to balancing the importance for accurately describing law against the importance of communicating concisely and in a manner the audience will understand. As has been noted at other points throughout this book, learning to balance these goals will come with time and practice.

D. Knowing How to Evaluate the Needed Information

The evaluation step moves out of pure research and into reading the results. Here, the researcher assesses what the research efforts have produced.

A first step here is skimming the results and planning next steps. Skimming allows a researcher to immediately identify what a source is: Is it a primary source from the government (in other words, is it actual law?), or is it a secondary source from a lawyer or advocacy group or someone else describing the law? Skimming allows a researcher to quickly recognize where a source comes from. Thus the researcher can discard sources from irrelevant jurisdictions and print or save sources from the binding jurisdiction. Skimming allows a researcher to notice that a source mentions the key term only in passing and thus the source should be de-prioritized and perhaps not read in full.

Skillful researchers adjust their strategy as they go. A logical and reasonable initial search strategy might end up generating nothing. Initially failing to find relevant sources does not mean they don't exist. Before drawing such a conclusion—which is an increasingly uncommon conclusion in a world filled with information at least tangentially relevant to almost any inquiry—a skillful researcher would try again with another reasonable search strategy.

E. Knowing How to Use the Needed Information

Using the information has at least two separate meanings.

First, do you know how to use the information you find in the form it is presented? For example, when you find an unannotated statute, do you know how to use that statute for further legal research? Second, do you know how to use the information for your own professional purposes? Legal literacy means not just reading information, but also communicating about it appropriately.

As to using the information by understanding its form, you are skimming and reading to ascertain what you've found and how to use it. Reading skills are addressed in chapter 4 and throughout this book. Keep in mind that when you read a source as a researcher, you should be particularly curious about research-related questions:

- How recent is this source?
- How authoritative is this source?
- What is this source's bias or point of view?
- Does this source contain links or citations to other valuable legal information?
- Is this source worth actually reading with detailed attention?

As to how you use the information for your own professional purposes, it should not be surprising that legal information has a large variety of potential uses. Some sources may be filed away in an online folder to be dug up months later when the topic arises. (Side note: as you work on your legal research skills, consider adopting a long-term strategy for saving interesting websites you find. OneNote, Evernote, Pocket, Google Keep, or simply bookmarking in your browser are all tools to consider.)

Some sources may be so relevant that their discovery almost creates an emergency, prompting the researcher to catapult directly into the CEO's office much as Joan Cusack's character sprinted through the news desk, skidding under open file cabinets and hurdling over mothers and toddlers, to deliver a tape to the news desk in less than 84 seconds in the movie *Broadcast News*.[6]

This book focuses on less dramatic forms of communication. For example, a researcher might write an email that summarizes something she found, or pick up the phone to share preliminary questions and schedule a meeting with the legal department.

F. Knowing How to Use the Needed Information Effectively

Effectiveness requires a combination of knowledge, skills, and ways of thinking. It means *knowledge* about how the law works and what legal information may be available. It means *skills* in recognizing what is complete and up to date and what is not; creativity in generating questions from what you already know; reading to skim, focus, and interpret; and communicating to share information in writing or other appropriate method of communication. And it means *ways of thinking* such as curiosity, critical assessment, persistence, record-keeping, flexibility at stretching a concept more broadly or funneling it down more narrowly, imagination at picturing what might be out there and where it might be, and discipline to stay focused on the project at hand. Another way of thinking is the practice of humility and recognizing one's own capabilities and boundaries, and the role played by each member of a working team or larger organizational hierarchy. Along these lines, using legal information effectively means knowing when to consult an attorney because doing so is necessary or would be perceived as necessary.

Overall, the good news about this definition of information literacy is that it's useful and wise. The bad news is, you won't be able to finish this chapter and declare yourself satisfactory on every part of this definition. Competence at legal information literacy is a function of everything you know how to do with legal information. By studying legal literacy and communication in this book, you will learn much more about legal information and legal analysis. Information literacy is not something you can acquire in a one-day training and declare your knowledge "complete." Like all of legal literacy and any effort to gain expertise in a challenging field, it is a process.

---

6. *Broadcast News* (Twentieth Century Fox, 1987) — *Tape Scene*, YouTube (Jan 14, 2014), https://www.youtube.com/watch?v=AYCEkqH0NQQ.

III. Choosing a Starting Point

Now that we have connected the overview of information literacy to legal literacy, we are ready to discuss the practical steps of conducting online legal research. This section is a general introduction setting up more specific coverage in chapters 8–10 on statutes, regulations, and cases.

You have two basic choices for how to start an online search—the URL bar or the search box.

At the very top of any web browser page, you have a URL bar that looks something like this:

> http://

The URL bar is easy to overlook. It's narrow—and it takes things literally. For example, in a search for the New York Department of Motor Vehicles, if you type www. dmv.gov you get nothing, but www.dmv.ny.gov takes you to the New York State Department of Motor Vehicles.

The drawbacks of the URL bar attract internet users to the big beautiful search box that is a part of any search engine such as Google, Bing, Yahoo Search, or DuckDuck-Go:

As noted at the outset of this chapter, the search box is tempting and easy. With autofill, the box is active and wants to help you fill in the blank to start your research! For example, when you start a search by typing the word "legal," Google fills in some ideas: *legal zoom*, *legalshield*, *legal seafood*, and *legally blonde*, among other suggested searches. (How helpful is that?)

You've done it a million times, and mostly good things have happened—like finding a restaurant or a movie review or the distance between your hometown and where you want to go. But before you start typing a word or phrase into that tantalizing empty space, stop and think about what you are looking for. As part of this reflection, consider writing out your research strategy with some or all of the following prompts:

Once you have clarified some of your strategic goals and methods, you are ready to start researching. And the question is: "Where do I start?" Here are some options:

> The issue I'm researching is ___.
>
> The type of information that will best answer my question is ___.
>
> I have (little/a lot) of previous knowledge about this issue.
>
> What I know about this issue can be summarized as follows: ___
>
> I already know about several authoritative sites for this type of issue, and they are __.
>
> I am going to start my research in the following source(s): ____.
>
> My reason for starting there is ____.
>
> My plan for keeping track of my research is ___.
>
> I will be able to judge my research to be complete when ___.
>
> I will be able to judge my research to be a success if ____.

Option 1: *Consider using an official website (or a quasi-official website) if you know exactly what you want and know it's there.*

Option 2: *Consider using a reliable research portal site or other well-known research website.*

Option 3: *Search using a search engine such as Google.*

Option 4: *Pay a fee or purchase an ongoing membership to use a proprietary legal research platform.*

We now turn to considering the merits of these four options.

A. Official Websites

If you know exactly what you want, consider using an official website (or a quasi-official website). Remember that legal research balances two big goals — getting everything you want (recall) and nothing you don't want (precision). Using a search engine is certainly good for recall, as you can go through screen after screen of possible results; what you are looking for is probably in there somewhere. But using a search engine may not be precise enough — that is, finding only what you want. A search engine will often — though not always — err on the side of being over-inclusive and may bury the information you want among other unhelpful results.

If you have a firm idea of what you are looking for and where to find it, you may want to go straight to a specific source offering that type of legal information. For example, someone researching the regulations for emotional support animals on airplanes could do an internet search and would find many news articles about emotional support squirrels and alligators as well as, maybe, the actual regulations. Or that researcher could avoid the general search and go directly to the relevant government website, which, in this case, is the U.S. Department of Transportation, https://www.

transportation.gov/. Many have .gov as their top-level domain identifier, but sites with .edu and .com and .org may function as quasi-official sites in some contexts.

Here are three more examples of research situations where the researcher might opt for the URL bar to go directly to an official or quasi-official source.

- A patent agent wishes to find examples of patented inventions in the field of solar energy. She types in the URL for the Public Patent Application Information Retrieval website (what patent agents and patent lawyers refer to as "Public Pair"): https://portal.uspto.gov/pair/PublicPair/

- A policy analyst for a nonprofit called Safe Food for America wants to check any recent nationwide recalls on food products. His goal is to write press releases on the Safe Food for America website amplifying the message and providing additional context and resources for food producers and consumers. He types in the URL for the Food and Drug Administration, www.fda.gov and checks the front page for recall news, as well as checking news releases and searching the site for the word "recall."

- A government contracts specialist is researching developments surrounding the Federal Acquisition Regulation. This specialist navigates directly to the well-known and well-maintained (private) website for government contractors, www.wifcon.com. The specialist then clicks on its "contents" page http://www.wifcon.com/mapindex.htm. From there, the specialist finds lists of Federal Acquisition Circulars and FAR cases going back to 1989.

Official and quasi-official websites may be especially appropriate as a starting point under the following conditions:

- Do you already know a lot about your legal issue?
- Do you know what type of information you are looking for?
- Do you know of an official website or quasi-official website where that information is very likely to be found, and that is commonly used for this type of question? (If you told a legal expert you were looking on this website for this specific information, would the expert feel comfortable trusting your research and the information?)

Part of legal information literacy therefore means knowing about useful official websites. Of course there is no single all-encompassing official source of official sources. At the federal level, the closest thing to a complete list may be the Library of Congress's page with an alphabetical list of each and every federal agency from the most obvious (perhaps the Department of Justice) to the most obscure (perhaps the Pantex Plant within the Department of Energy), available here: https://www.loc.gov/rr/news/fedgov.html. This list also provides links to each agency's website.

At the state level, some quasi-official associations collect state law resources by category:

- The National Conference of State Legislatures publishes a list of state legislative websites at http://www.ncsl.org/aboutus/ncslservice/state-legislative-websites -directory.aspx.

- The National Center for State Courts publishes a list of state court websites at http://www.ncsc.org/Information-and-Resources/Browse-by-State/State-Court-Websites.aspx. As noted above, state court websites may not be the best way to conduct legal research into state cases on a particular topic; state court websites' search capacity, historical records, and overall purpose for interacting with the public vary widely.

- The National Association of Secretaries of State publishes a list of state administrative rules at http://www.administrativerules.org/administrative-rules/.

You can expand this strategy to include quasi-official and well-known, reliable research websites as well. The best quasi-websites are those that are well-known and used in a particular field all the time. Thus, one way to test whether you should go directly to a quasi-official website to search for legal information is to consider its reputation among experts in this particular area of law.

For example, if you want to find out more about a current United States Supreme Court case, you might think, "Obviously, I should go to the Supreme Court's website!" But actually, you should probably not use the Court's official website, https://www. supremecourt.gov/. This site is meant for news and up-to-date information on cases and judges and court procedures. It is a reasonable site for researching the docket of *pending* cases. (A docket is essentially a list of pending cases, and it also functions as a sort of tracking or filing system. When someone files a lawsuit in a certain court, the court clerk assigns the case a docket number, which everyone on all sides of the case then uses to identify documents in that case.) In 2017, the Supreme Court's official website was redesigned to make it more usable.[7]

But for researching pending cases as well as decided cases back to 2007, another website has attained quasi-official status: SCOTUSblog.com, a website started by attorney Tom Goldstein. SCOTUSblog contains the docket information for each case, including copies of all briefs filed in the case in an easily accessible format. It also provides scholarly commentary on cases and links to oral argument transcripts in the cases. Within the legal community, SCOTUSblog is well-known as a reliable, useful, and up-to-date resource. SCOTUSblog is so well-known that when the Supreme Court releases a controversial decision, SCOTUSblog receives many angry messages excoriating it for what

---

7. Andrew Hamm, *Supreme Court Unveils New Website*, SCOTUSblog (July 30, 2017) http://www.scotusblog.com/2017/07/supreme-court-unveils-new-website/

the Supreme Court did.[8] Any experienced lawyer or legal journalist would be comfortable using SCOTUSblog for up-to-date information on a pending Supreme Court case.

The obvious thought in your mind at this point may be, "Great! Now I'd like a list of official and quasi-official sources." One problem with doing that is the nature of print resources themselves — i.e., the decision whether to print a list of resources in this particular book you are holding.

If this book includes a list of official and quasi-official resources, it risks being out of date as soon as the book is published. Moreover, the more sources the book includes to try to cater to everyone's needs, the less useful it is to any one person's needs. A professional working in school administration and education compliance needs very different sources from a professional working in health law and policy. This book does not try to list every official or quasi-official source that students in legal masters programs may want to know about. A few other research-focused texts may be good resources on this question:

- Carole A. Levitt & Judy Davis, *Internet Legal Research on a Budget: Free and Low-Cost Resources for Lawyers* (American Bar Ass'n 2014).
- Carole A Levitt & Mark Rosch, *The Cybersleuth's Guide to the Internet: Conducting Effective Free Investigative and Legal Research on the Web* (14th ed. 2017).

In addition to sources like these, you could consult a law librarian at a law school or courthouse or other law library and ask about official sources for your research needs. As noted at the beginning of this chapter, law libraries may be somewhat few and far between in some areas of the country, but phone calls and email inquiries may work if walking in is not an option.

B. Reliable Legal Research Portals

Consider using a reliable research portal site or other well-known research website. Sometimes you have a solid, specific idea of what you're looking for, but an official website doesn't provide the information. Let's take the Supreme Court example above and change it a little bit. Suppose you need all the Supreme Court cases on a topic — like all the cases decided in the Supreme Court's history on the fair use defense to copyright infringement. SCOTUSblog is excellent for recent cases, but it only goes back to 2007. A key theme throughout the legal-research coverage in this book is this: When you use a website for legal information, check how up-to-date it is. Look for clues on when the site was last updated, as well as how far back its resources reach. If you need all the cases on point in a particular court's history, make sure the research site you are using provides cases since the beginning of that court's history.

---

8. Staci Zaretsky, *Angry Mob Takes to Twitter to Scream at SCOTUSblog for Hobby Lobby Decision*, Above the Law (July 1, 2014) https://abovethelaw.com/2014/07/angry-mob-takes-to-twitter-to-scream-at-scotus blog-for-hobby-lobby-decision/

To look for all Supreme Court cases on a topic, you would need a reliable website that provides *all* of the cases in Supreme Court history, in a searchable format. Here are some examples of websites that provide free, searchable databases of Supreme Court cases going back further than 2007:

- Cornell Legal Information Institute
- Google Scholar for cases
- Court Listener
- FindLaw
- Justia

You could navigate to any of these pages and enter the term "fair use" to search for cases on that topic. You would get cases back to the beginning of U.S. Supreme Court history with this technique.

The same strategy can work with research into legislation and administrative law. For example, imagine Ms. Ralston is dealing with a medical and legal issue affecting her mother. Her mother is 85 years old and suffering from chronic pain. Her mother is extremely concerned about taking opioids and wishes to avoid them if possible. A friend has told Ms. Ralston's mother about a substance called "kratom." Kratom is a substance that some argue is healthful and others argue is addictive and unsafe.[9]

Ms. Ralston wants to find out if kratom is legal in Colorado. (She has already done a quick search using an internet search engine, and found a number of potentially unreliable sources. Thus she is starting over with law-focused research on well-known platforms.) She will start by researching statutes that mention "kratom" somewhere in the text. Does the Colorado legislature outlaw, permit, or otherwise govern kratom, or delegate its regulation to an agency? For this project, using the official website strategy outlined above, she could go to the Colorado legislative website providing the full text of the Colorado Revised Statutes. (Incidentally, the Colorado Revised Statutes are published on a Lexis Advance website, but this portion of Lexis Advance's platform is free and open to the public.) With the ability to full-text search the Colorado Revised Statutes, Ms. Ralston could search the word "kratom" in the statutes.

What if Ms. Ralston wanted to get involved in promoting — or trying to prohibit — kratom at the national level. To do this, she would need more information about kratom in all 50 states. Could she research all state statutes at once in free open-access research? It appears that the answer is no; no single free online source appears to do this.[10] Instead, she could individually search all 50 states and track the work in a spreadsheet or other document. Beyond the National Association of Secretaries of State and

---

9. *Drug Facts: Kratom*, National Institute of Drug Abuse (July 2018), https://www.drugabuse.gov/publications/drugfacts/kratom

10. A premium legal-research platform such as Bloomberg, Fastcase, Lexis, or Westlaw would allow you to search all state codes all at once for the word "kratom."

other resources listed above, other portals that list state websites for statutory and administrative research like this include the following:

- Cornell Legal Information Institute
- FindLaw
- Justia

C. General Purpose Search Engines

Search on a popular general-purpose search engine, such as Google. Search engines have many benefits and often will be the best place to start. Even if you skip through options 1 and 2 above, being aware of them before you open a search engine will help with filtering results from a search.

1. Basic Searching

Using the search engine is a realistic and appropriate place to start if you don't already know which websites or sources are likely to provide the sought-after information. When you have a question and don't know what type of information would answer it or where that information would be, you have to search everything. In the example above about gaining context, the whole point of the research is to escape a state of ignorance by developing a framework to understand the law. A search engine is also particularly advantageous when a question will be answered by different categories of information. If the best information on a topic would derive from a wide variety of sources, a search engine will excel. Here are more specifics on the advantages and disadvantages of search engines:

Advantages	Disadvantages
Searches everything not beyond a paywall	Yields practically infinite search results
Uses the search engine's algorithm to bring quality results to the top of the search	Algorithm's definition of quality of information does not give special weight to legal information or legal sources; top results may not be legal at all
Includes date as a factor in the search algorithm, so more recent information should rise to the top of searches	Includes many factors in how results are sorted, so results can be difficult to sort (by date or otherwise)
Prioritizes in-depth pages with reliable links and other pages linking to them	May be vulnerable to some manipulative linking practices
Provides a short snippet of the relevant text in the initial search results	Provides a snippet of the relevant text around the key word in the search box; heavily text-driven rather than driven by content and meaning

2. Advanced Search Techniques

You can always type a phrase into the search box on Google or Bing or Yahoo! Search or some other search engine. But information literacy includes the ability to conduct more precise research.

One hallmark of a truly strong researcher is the ability to use Boolean search terms. Boolean search terms are "operators" that shape your word search into a kind of computer code. Here are some typical Boolean operators:

- " "(to enclose an exact phrase)
- And
- Or
- /10 (within 10 words)
- Not or % (to exclude any sources containing a particular term)

Beyond Boolean search terms, you can also search more precisely by controlling which domains you are searching. You will recognize the most common top-level domains: .com, .gov, .edu, and .org.

For example, in the Bing search engine, you can use advanced terms to limit your search just to government sites with the .gov extension. To search for government sites with the exact phrase "skilled nursing facility," you could type the following phrase in the box:

"skilled nursing facility" (site:.gov)

At the time of this book's publication, Google contains an advanced search page at www.google.com/advanced_search with a menu of options for more precise searching. Here too, you could enter a search of just websites ending in the .gov domain.

The URLs and techniques for advanced searching change too quickly to be listed in detail in a printed book. For whatever search engine you are using, use the search box to discover advanced search techniques.

D. Proprietary Fee-Based Platforms

The most powerful legal research platforms are fee-based. Lexis and Westlaw are the most historically "famous" (in the legal industry). Bloomberg is well-known for its powerful Bloomberg terminals in the business world. Bloomberg Law is an extension of the Bloomberg research enterprise into legal information. Fastcase is another legal research platform with robust capabilities, available for use by lawyers and law firms and offered to bar-licensed attorneys as part of their bar membership in many states. The Fastcase app for ios, Android, and Windows is free for use by anyone (with no bar membership or fee required other than to create an account, as of late 2018). Casemaker is another legal research platform offered through many bar associations, billing itself as "the value leader in legal research."[11] Even beyond these platforms, new players continue to enter the proprietary legal research space. Casetext.com is a relatively new platform that offers some free case research and fee-based enhancements.

Fee-based sites excel at providing efficient searches, up-to-date information, and the ability to validate your research. When you pull up a statute on a fee-based research platform, the screen will tell you whether that statute has been superseded by another statute, and it will provide annotations to cases and other sources citing that statute. The same is true for other primary sources; they are surrounded with additional information such as related secondary sources and citations back to the main primary source. These sites are also fee-based; that is, they are not a service of the government or a nonprofit, but commercial sites designed to make money for their publishers. Lawyers and law firms typically pay significant sums for access to one or more fee-based legal research platforms. These platforms are powerful and thorough, and provide comprehensive, up-to-date legal information with multiple sophisticated searching mechanisms. Thus, a good legal researcher should do a cost-benefit analysis of when and how to pay for legal information. If you have access to a fee-based platform, use its tutorials and other "help" options as needed to supplement the introduction to legal research in this book.

All of the above information has been about choosing where to start your research, based on your prior experience and baseline knowledge about what you are researching. Whether you do your research in a courthouse law library or online and whether you pay for information or get it from free open-access sources, the goal should be the same — *to do competent legal research*. Getting started is indeed half the battle — but legal research has not only a beginning, but also a middle and an end.

IV. Conducting Legal Research as a Process

Legal research demands not only the knowledge and creativity to get off to a good start, but also persistence and organization to execute the research process.

During the research process, a few key methods should help:

A. Taking Good Notes

There is no strict formula; effective research notes are notes that accomplish their purpose — or, in this case, purposes. Law librarians have described several purposes for note-taking during legal research:[12]

---

11. Casemaker, https://public.casemakerlegal.net/

12. Penny A. Hazelton, Peggy Roebuck Jarrett, Nancy McMurrer, and Mary Wisner, *Develop the Habit: Note-Taking in Legal Research*, Perspectives: Teaching Legal Research and Writing (Winter 1996), https://info.legalsolutions.thomsonreuters.com/pdf/perspec/1996-winter/1996-winter-3.pdf

- Notes record the researcher's sources in order to use them, find them again, and cite them.

- Notes record the research path so the researcher knows what has been checked.

- Notes help the researcher to think about what is being done and keeps the focus on the correct issue.

- Notes aid the researcher in communicating with colleagues, supervisors, and others the researcher may want to ask for help.

- Notes allow the researcher to demonstrate her thoroughness, especially when there are incomplete answers to the questions posed.

- Notes help the researcher or a reader to understand, replicate, and update results.

- Notes serve as reinforcement to everything the researcher learns during a particular project and provides a "tips and tricks" resource for future projects.

A good note-taking system will combine all of these purposes in an efficient and fluid way. The researcher will keep track of the process, collect information on the sources (including enough citation detail to find them again later), and begin to read and synthesize the sources' meaning.

B. Applying Strong Legal Reading Skills

Legal research and reading legal information go hand in hand. Research helps you find information. Then you evaluate that information according to your purposes—including the decision about whether it is relevant and whether you need to adjust your strategy or keep going. Experts in working with law seamlessly weave together legal research and legal reading.

As you begin the process of researching legal information, avoid these two extremes:

Reading Everything   Reading Nothing

The sweet spot in the middle is skimming the sources and making a solid judgment on what to do with each one of them as well as with your overall legal strategy. Review chapter 4 on legal reading as a general reminder. When skimming and reading as a legal researcher, your functional questions can be pretty specific:

- Is this source a "keeper" that fits what you are looking for? If so, save or print it to read later.

- Should you continue in this category of research to get more sources like this one?

- Are there other search terms or strategies suggested in this source to consider later in your process?
- If you are keeping this source, where should you file it in your records?

Once you've amassed a solid group of sources, you can stop to carefully read them. At this point, you are stepping out of the research process and focusing carefully on each source for its content, how it connects to the content in other responsive sources, and what you want to use it for. These are major analytical steps and they demand focus. Thus, during this analysis stage, you are not also actively researching as well. You may take notes on the side about additional research ideas, but those are tangential to the focused reading and analysis.

As you make your way through the solid group of sources using close reading and note-taking skills, you will need to assess whether to do more legal research, gather more sources, and repeat the process. Deciding whether your research is complete is addressed more fully below.

C. Balancing Persistence with Flexibility

Legal research that is too persistent will end up being inefficient. You don't need to read everything ever written in any jurisdiction that has your key word in it. And even within a single jurisdiction, if your search is producing source after source that just has nothing to do with what you're looking for, it is likely time to adjust and try something else. At the same time, legal research that is too flexible will end up missing key information. Adjusting your strategy too soon and too often will cut off productive approaches.

One key to maintaining this balance between persistence and flexibility is to force yourself to explain your strategic decisions every step of the way. For example, in researching whether a corporation can claim a mission other than maximizing profit for shareholders, you might research "social justice corporations." After examining a few sources found with this search, you might reflect on the process thus far and jot down "Using the term 'social justice' is not productive. I keep finding factual material about social justice advocacy groups, which is not the point at all. I need to adjust the search to something else like 'social mission' or 'public mission' or 'public interest.'" Or you may discover a rich vein of sources that themselves offer many more ideas for researching the topic.

D. Staying Organized, Both with Hard Copies and Online Material

To stay organized, a legal researcher should create a filing system for both online information and any hard copies generated from the research process. For example, you might create folders — on a computer hard drive, in hard copy, or both — for the following categories of information:

- blog posts, news articles, and other secondary sources
- statutory language
- regulations
- cases

To stay organized, you might think it's better to be completely consistent with a paperless approach, or going the opposite route and printing everything. But legal research is an example where the best approach is probably a hybrid. Just as you want to stay in the middle between being too persistent and too flexible, you also may want to try staying in the middle of all-digital and all-hard-copy approaches. Print out the key sources, then use pens and markers to highlight their key language and make notes and questions. Active reading is more likely to be effective and help the reader comprehend the material and make connections with other material. While it is possible to do active reading on a computer screen, legal researchers should experiment with online and hard-copy reading of key sources to see what works best for them.

V. Completing the Legal Research Process

When will you know that your legal research is complete? The common answer in J.D. legal research classes for future lawyers is this: "Your research is complete when you have closed the loop—that is, when you have gone in a circle of research and are now finding the same things over and over. When your research becomes repetitive and redundant, then you're ready to stop." Another way to describe this phase of research is exhaustion—the researcher has exhausted all reasonable sources and has gone as deeply into each type of source as needed to ensure everything (and the right things) has been found. The researcher may feel mentally exhausted as well, but the concept is more about exhausting the available information. So long as the research keeps revealing more relevant sources that could make a difference, the research is not done.

This approach is the best answer for high-stakes legal research. High stakes could mean a lot of things, but essentially if the legal research will support analysis that has major consequences, then the research should continue until exhaustion. Facing a legal issue that is high stakes in this way may mean it is necessary or wise to seek advice from a lawyer.

Some legal research issues do not require exhausting all available types of sources. There are narrow inquiries that create a different approach to completing the work. When you already know essentially what you are looking for, efficient legal research means going directly to the place where the information should be and using tailored research techniques to retrieve that information. But even there, when you think you've retrieved exactly what you came for, it still may benefit your legal research to expand the search.

Having studied this chapter, you should be able to:

- Plan a legal research project that will rely on free online tools
- Evaluate the strengths and weaknesses of free online legal research tools
- Locate some well-established free online sources for legal research
- Use general search engines more effectively
- Recognize the value of fee-based legal-research websites and their capabilities in certain situations

Case Study: Planning Internet Research

Ms. Ralston is proceeding with her business idea to start a new small coffee company that will also serve the needs of customers and possibly employees who struggle with severe allergy and anaphylaxis health issues. She has heard that it is possible to start a corporation with an express purpose to benefit the public—like a social justice corporation. She wants to research this possibility for her business idea, under Colorado law.

The issue I'm researching is ____.

The type of information that will best answer my question is ____.

I have (little/a lot) of previous knowledge on this issue.

What I know about this issue can be summarized as follows: ____

I already know about several authoritative sites for this type of issue, and they are ____.

I am going to start my research in the following source(s): _____.

My reason for starting there is _____.

My plan for keeping track of my research is ____.

I will be able to judge my research to be complete when ____.

I will be able to judge my research to be a success if _____.

Traditions and Trends

Throughout the nineteenth century, legal education was grounded in the theory that law operates rationally and predictably, and legal information can be categorized in a logical top-down framework. Influenced by the prevailing sense of legal formalism in the late nineteenth century and the fundamentals of library science, legal information itself was organized in categorical fashion and available in print in law libraries. The West Publishing Company began publishing cases in 1876, and debuted the National Reporter System for collecting and publishing state courts' appellate opinions. Because of West's market domination, cases began to be cited according to West's publishing conventions: 12 A.3d 456 refers to volume 12 of the Atlantic Reporter, Third Series at page 456 of that volume. West's domination over case reporters and citation forms continued until well into the early 2000s.

Legal information is less expensive to find, harvest, and organize online than it used to be, with the full text of statutory language and the full text of many cases now freely available online in multiple locations. Whether a researcher is working in a traditional fee-based legal research platform, an upstart platform, or with free online sources, strong search skills are crucial. Effective legal researchers do not just enter a few key words, see what the search engine produces, and stop there. Strong skills include proficiency in using Boolean connectors such as "and" and "or" and retrieving exact text in quotations. Strong Boolean skills provide a researcher with more control over the search results than relying on the search boxes with their changing proprietary algorithms.

In the fee-based legal research space, premium services compete to offer new information such as artificial-intelligence-inspired search capabilities, advanced visualization tools for showing patterns in legal information, and predictive data analytics. Other commercial research businesses have positioned themselves to offer legal research with premium features such as comprehensive citations to cases and statutes (revealing if they are overruled or superseded). Fastcase and Casemaker are two examples; they have partnered with many bar associations as a low-cost option for lawyers doing legal research and are also available for others to subscribe and use. Casetext is another example of an upstart legal research business, offering a fee-based service called "CARA," in which users can upload a document with legal citations to receive more relevant legal research suggestions based on the sources cited in the uploaded document. Many more product features driven by algorithms are sure to follow.

Chapter 7

Finding and Reading
Secondary Sources

> If I have seen further than others, it is by standing upon the shoulders of giants.
>
> — Sir Isaac Newton, Mathematician and Physicist
>
> Don't reinvent the wheel, just realign it.
>
> — Anthony J. D'Angelo, Writer and Motivational Speaker

Legal research begins with a conundrum. But doing an effective investigation requires some baseline knowledge about the question. How can you know enough to effectively research something you don't already know? Secondary research breaks through this conundrum.

Secondary sources come from a variety of authors and publishers, ranging from the "the single most important essay ever written by an American on the law,"[1] an article in the Harvard Law Review called *The Path of the Law* by then-future Supreme Court Justice Oliver Wendell Holmes Jr.,[2] to scores of legal blogs produced by lawyers or even by professional legal content writers that sell articles to lawyers and firms for

---

1. Albert Alschuler, *The Descending Trail: Holmes' Path of the Law 100 Years Later*, 49 Fla. L. Rev. 353, 354 (1997).

2. Oliver Wendell Holmes, Jr., *The Path of the Law*, 10 Harv. L. Rev. 457 (1897).

publication on their websites. Regardless of the author and influence of a secondary source, remember that *secondary sources* are sources *about* the law; they are not the law themselves.

Secondary sources can make your life much easier because sometimes you will find a source that is up-to-date with a credible author that thoroughly and clearly answers your question. On the other hand, consider this well-known cliché to be cautionary advice: *You get what you pay for.* Some free secondary sources may not be as up-to-date or thorough or reliable as one would hope. Some web pages and blog posts are there to generate business, make a political case, or express a lawyer's personal reflections. These types of sources may—or may not—be a good use of your time in executing a legal research project. But neither is looking through 100-plus possibly relevant cases when a solid, recent, credible, free secondary source summarizes them in 800 well-written words.

This chapter gives an overview of secondary research: why and how to do it, and what to look for.

I. Basics of Secondary Research

The purpose of conducting research in secondary sources is to help the researcher find out enough basic information to get started effectively. An excellent secondary source will help the researcher do two things: (1) gain context for researching the issue; and (2) begin gathering useful citations to primary sources.

Step 1: Find credible secondary sources to gain context.	Step 2: Work your way toward primary sources for authoritative information.

Let's discuss each of these functions in turn.

A. Gaining Context

Context could include a variety of ideas. Secondary research can provide many or even all of these benefits:

- Basic definitions

What does an unfamiliar legal term mean? A secondary source aimed at non-expert readers may explicitly define basic important terms. A secondary source aimed at experts may not explicitly define basic terms, but often will make them clear in context.

- Important key terms and closely related terms

Online legal research can be is often controlled by the exact search terms used. Full-text searching depends on the terms entered into the full-text search, so knowing the right key terms is crucial for effective research. Secondary sources can help you do that by identifying key terms as well as closely related terms. For example, employers are liable for the actions of their employees working within the scope of employment under the doctrine of "respondeat superior," a tort doctrine that is closely related to and sometimes (but not always) synonymous with the doctrine of "vicarious liability." A researcher would need familiarity with *both* terms to do complete legal research in this area. For research tools that rely entirely on the exact text of search terms, it's even more important to know synonyms and other relevant terms.

- What type of legal source governs the issue

Is the issue governed by constitutional law or statutes or regulations or cases, or a mixture? Is it controlled by an administrative agency, or is it an issue that transcends different legal authorities and sources?

- What level of government controls the issue

Is the issue governed at the state or federal level, or both? You can extend this idea to international law with many issues, such as data privacy and use of Internet cookies to track website viewers.

- The most important legal sources

What are the key legal sources or authorities, for example a statute or regulation or case?

- The basic structure of the law

How is the law organized in this area? For example, does it define terms and then set forth legal obligations followed by consequences for violating those obligations?

- Historical trends and recent developments with the issue

How has this area of law developed over time, and what has happened very recently? What are the key issues on the horizon?

B. Finding Primary Sources

Many secondary sources will provide not only context, but also citations to primary sources. Indeed, a secondary source's use of legal citations — or at least clear source attributions and/or working hyperlinks — is one indicator of a quality secondary source. While reading through a secondary source, make a note of citations to statutes, regulations, cases, and other sources the author relied upon.

While such citations can provide a major jump-start to legal research, a careful researcher should also evaluate them critically. Specifically, take care to update, verify, and expand on them. Updating them means acknowledging, for example, that a secondary source dated 2015 is going to have primary sources as of 2015. An amazing blog post written by an expert in the field in 2017 could be completely wrong if the relevant government agency changed the rule in 2018. Verifying the primary sources cited in a secondary source means going to the originals and seeing them for yourself. Like everyone else, secondary source authors can make mistakes. Working with legal information means verifying it carefully before relying on it. Expanding on the primary sources cited in a secondary source means independently researching primary sources for yourself.

All of these actions are mutually reinforcing: updating is consistent with verifying, and expanding helps to verify and update.

II. Types of Secondary Sources

Secondary sources for law come in several broadly recognizable categories: dictionaries, encyclopedias, periodicals such as magazines and academic journals, and books. The broad category of "books" includes both single-volume monographs on a topic and multivolume treatises comprehensively describing a body of law. Many of these sources are available online, but the categories remain modeled upon traditional print formats for secondary materials.

This section focuses on the secondary sources most likely to be available in online, open-access legal research. Commercial legal research platforms have a wealth of highly credible and updated secondary sources; such sources are valuable intellectual property, unlike the actual text of the primary law, which cannot be copyrighted, held exclusively, or licensed. Although secondary research with free and open-access sources can require more sifting and critical assessment, freely available sources can in many cases meet the goals of providing context and starting the researcher on a path to primary sources.

A. Legal Dictionaries

Legal dictionaries provide basic definitions of legal words and phrases. The most well-known is *Black's Law Dictionary*. A search for the exact phrase "Black's Law Dictionary" in all federal cases revealed 9,883 federal cases citing it, including 63 United States Supreme Court cases, 2,122 federal circuit court cases, and more than 6,000 district court cases.[3]

The good news is that a version of *Black's Law Dictionary* is available for free online at The Law Dictionary, www.thelawdictionary.org. The bad news is that the free online version is based on the Second Edition from 1910, which is now in the public domain and thus not subject to copyright law. Additionally, searching the terms on this website

---

3. These results were generated by searching "Black's Law Dictionary" on Westlaw Next, July 10, 2018.

generates a mix of dictionary entries and what appear to be paid advertisements to potentially relevant commercial links. As with all legal research in free sources, here it is particularly important to proceed with caution, obtaining information that helps you while filtering out irrelevant content.

A selection of other free legal dictionaries include:

- Merriam-Webster's Law Dictionary at https://www.merriam-webster.com/legal
- Wex, crowd-sourced and maintained by the Cornell Legal Information Institute at https://www.law.cornell.edu/wex
- Law.com's legal dictionary at https://dictionary.law.com/
- The Free Dictionary's legal dictionary at https://legal-dictionary.thefree dictionary.com/

The usefulness of these free dictionaries versus purchasing or paying to access the current edition of *Black's Law Dictionary* will be a matter of personal taste and resources for each legal researcher. Some researchers may think they can get all they need from these basic online dictionaries. Others may feel more confident using an updated, copyrighted dictionary, such as *Black's*, edited by Bryan A. Garner, a highly respected figure in legal vocabulary, legal writing, and legal interpretation.

B. Wikipedia

Wikipedia is a famous collaborative encyclopedia that is often referred to as a "crowdsourced" encyclopedia. Some of the content is quite helpful; other content is incomplete or questionable. Both Wikipedia's strength and its weakness are its reliance on collaboration, as shown in its About page:

Wikipedia is written collaboratively by largely anonymous volunteers who write without pay. Anyone with Internet access can write and make changes to Wikipedia articles, except in limited cases where editing is restricted to prevent disruption or vandalism. Users can contribute anonymously, under a pseudonym, or, if they choose to, with their real identity.

Courts have varied widely on how they approach Wikipedia as a source to rely on — or not — within judicial opinions. In a 2016 case, the Texas Supreme Court extensively reviewed Wikipedia's characteristics, coming to a pragmatic conclusion:

At the least, we find it unlikely Wikipedia could suffice as the sole source of authority on an issue of any significance to a case. That said, Wikipedia can often be useful as a starting point for research purposes.[4]

---

4. *D Magazine Partners, L.P. v. Rosenthal*, 529 S.W.3d 429, 436 (Tex. 2016). The court went on to criticize the Texas Court of Appeals, whose decision it was reviewing on a final appeal, for relying on Wikipedia as a

While a court preparing a judicial opinion interpreting the law and applying it to facts for the parties before it (and all future parties relying on the decision) has a higher standard for secondary sources than a researcher sitting at a computer screen about to embark on an individual project, the Texas Supreme Court's cautious approach is appropriate in both cases. Wikipedia can be useful as a *starting point* for research purposes. You should not use it as an ending point, however.

C. Scholarly Secondary Sources

Both law professors and practicing lawyers have been in the business of writing scholarly commentary on the law for centuries. These resources can often be useful, containing analysis and synthesis that could cost a great deal of time and money if done for just a single case. Here are some examples of common types of secondary sources generated by legal scholars describing and analyzing the law:

Treatises	A treatise is a book by an author or authors (usually with some prestige behind their names) that attempts to comprehensively cover a legal topic. Examples include McCarthy on Trademarks, Chisum on Patents, Freer on Civil Procedure, and Prosser on Torts.
Restatements and Uniform Laws	Restatements are influential statements of law that scholars of the American Law Institute develop to describe the law in a variety of jurisdictions. Uniform Laws are drafted by the Uniform Law Commission to provide statutes and overall legal frameworks that state legislatures may choose to adopt. Restatements and Uniform Laws are not officially the law in any jurisdiction, but state courts may adopt Restatement sections, and state legislatures may adopt Uniform Laws.
Law Review Articles	Law review articles are in-depth articles that are written most frequently by law professors but sometimes by judges and practitioners. The articles are published in scholarly law journals maintained by law schools. Some law review articles analyze what the law actually is, and others focus more on what it should be, or what is problematic about the law as it is. Law review articles typically range from 14,000–25,000 words.

These secondary sources were traditionally available in law libraries and on fee-based legal research platforms such as Westlaw and Lexis and Bloomberg and Fastcase. Now some of them are available online without a password or fee, at least to some extent. Here are some examples of ways you can access these secondary sources:

- Uniform Laws are available at http://www.uniformlaws.org/. The Uniform Law Commission also tracks which states have adopted various Uniform Laws at http://www.uniformlaws.org/Legislation.aspx.

"lynchpin of its analysis on a critical issue." *Id.* at 442.

- Law review articles are available in various open-access sources. Some journals publish their own full articles on their websites, and many have an additional online spinoff of their journal that publishes shorter articles exclusively online. Many journal articles are available on the Social Science Research Network, www.ssrn.com. SSRN was acquired by Elsevier Publishing in 2016, and some articles are now available for a fee, but many drafts and final versions remain freely available on SSRN. Bepress.com is another source for some law review articles. Google Scholar's article-searching feature may be somewhat helpful, but many of its citations are behind paywalls on academic sites such as Hein Online and JSTOR.

- Treatises are often commercial publications paid for by law libraries that order them in hard copy or negotiated to be included in fee-based platforms. Likewise, Restatements are available at law libraries and on fee-based platforms.

D. Legal Blogs and Bar Journal Articles

Legal blogs and similar content produced by law firms can provide up-to-date information. They can provide in-depth analysis of a topic, as well as insight into possible trends and ongoing legal developments. Here are some of the types of law firm content you may find:

- Chronological blog posts on a legal blog by an individual lawyer
- Chronological blog posts on a legal blog by various lawyers within a firm
- Semi-permanent analytical content providing an overview of an area (sometimes referred to as "explainers" and "evergreen" content)
- Client alerts published online that purport to speak to law firm clients but in fact can be accessed by anyone, sharing a new development in the law and possible next steps for those affected

This type of content has a mix of upsides and downsides. Legal blogs and similar content produced by law firms may become outdated when individual posts languish and remain unchanged even after the law changes. Legal blogs may not offer in-depth analysis at all, but rather tempt readers with a small segment of analysis; the hidden (or not-so-hidden) message is to contact the law firm and pay for more in-depth personalized information.

E. Government Guides

Government agencies may publish legal guides to certain areas of law. An excellent example is the Department of Justice's Guide to the Freedom of Information Act.[5] This guide, in its entirety, is equivalent to a scholarly treatise in length and detail.

---

5. Department of Justice FOIA Guide, https://www.justice.gov/oip/doj-guide-freedom-information-act-0 (updated July 11, 2016)

You will know you have a genuine government guide because of the website where it is published and its top-level domain, .gov.

F. Advocacy and Policy Guides

Some advocacy and policy groups may take the time and effort to research and publish a detailed guide on an area of law. These guides may contain useful analysis and ideas. They are also likely to represent one side of an issue. It is not possible to comprehensively catalog all advocacy and policy groups, but good lists can be found on the National Association for Law Placement's website and Wikipedia's entry for Legal Advocacy Organizations in the United States.

The name *advocacy* guide should alert you that such a source is, by its very nature, advocating for a position. An advocacy guide is explicitly, openly biased toward some particular angle on the law and how it works or should work. This does not mean you should avoid advocacy guides as a possibly useful secondary source. Frankly, an advocacy guide that is open and transparent about its point of view is more reliable and trustworthy than an article strategically published to *look* neutral and objective but with the underlying purpose of pushing for a particular point of view. Skillful, critical reading and legal literacy will help you evaluate this type of information and decide whether and how to use it.

III. Practical Considerations for Evaluating Online Secondary Sources

Understanding the categories of secondary sources is a good start. Then there are some broader steps and skills that will help any researcher get the most out of online secondary sources.

A. Dates and Updates

Legal research is only as up-to-date as the date it is published. Thus, one challenge of using any information published online is trying to find the most updated version. Sometimes it is difficult even to locate any date at all on an online source. Authors and publishers of law reviews and blog posts are under no obligation to update their work. The burden falls on legal researchers to assess information's *recency* (how up-to-date it is) and reliability.

For example, the Department of Justice's FOIA Guide (mentioned above) is an excellent resource and is regularly updated. But several editions of this Guide have been released, and earlier editions are still available online. Thus, a researcher would want to make sure to look at the 2016 edition of the FOIA Guide rather than 2004 edition, both of which are available online and turn up in search results for "FOIA Guide."

To check for updates or determine an online resource's date, you can take some or all of the following steps:

- Look for a date on the individual source—such as the date of a blog post at the top or bottom.

- Look for a date on the website as a whole—such as the copyright date at the bottom (if there is one) or the About page.

- Look for the most updated content posted anywhere on the website. Dormant or abandoned blogs and sites are generally not something you should rely on.

- Look for a date in the information itself. For example, a blog post touting a case update from 2012 may seem like exactly what you need but, if accessed in 2018, would be missing at least six years' worth of legal developments.

B. Descriptive or Normative?

In working with secondary sources in print or online, you should constantly evaluate the perspective of what you are reading. Secondary sources have an author, and every author writes with some purpose. In reading a secondary source, evaluate what the author's purpose appears to be:

- Does it aim to describe what the law *is*?
- Does it aim to argue what the law *should* be or how it *should* work?

This distinction—what *is*, versus what *should be*—is the difference between a descriptive source and a normative source. Descriptive sources attempt to be objective at covering the law as it is. Normative sources suggest or argue what the law should be. Any time you find a website that appears to be useful, read it critically to understand its perspective and its possible biases. Those are matters you will want to take into account when weighing the value of its information.

IV. Using Good Secondary Sources to Your Advantage

When you find a good secondary source, your next question is often what to do with it. Here are some recommended steps:

- Make a record of what you are looking at so you can return to it later. Save the link or the page in a set of notes or in a web-clipping service such as Evernote.

- If possible, make a copy you can annotate or mark up. Print out a hard copy, or save a PDF and use PDF annotation software to make highlights and notes.

- Skim the Table of Contents and overall structure when possible.

- Skim around any areas that include the search term that led you to the source.

- Decide what sections (if any) to read closely.

- Read actively. Highlight key terms. Make notes of your reactions and questions.
- Take advantage of the head start on primary research that a good secondary source can provide. Circle or make a list of the primary sources mentioned in the secondary source you are reading.
- Distinguish between direct quotes from primary law and paraphrases or summaries of law. Some legal paraphrases are oversimplified or inaccurate.
- *Never* quote a primary source solely from a secondary source—not even if you provide a citation to indicate where you got the law from. You must find the law in a primary source and verify it. Secondary sources can help you understand the law better and find it faster, but they do not substitute for actually verifying and reading the law.

Sometimes in researching a topic, you may find the relevant primary sources very quickly. Secondary sources could be a waste of time when it is easy to go directly to the law itself. If, for example, your company has been accused of violating a specific statute, you would not dawdle in blog posts about the statute; you would track down the statute post-haste.

But even in that scenario, you may go directly to the primary source, read it, and discover it is impossible to understand. When this happens, remember that secondary sources are still there for you. Secondary sources can be useful at any time during the research process. Thus, you might go back to secondary sources after finding one or more primary sources, seeking help and perspective to cut through complex details. Or you might formulate your own viewpoint from reading the primary sources, then go to secondary sources at the end to glean whether others share your interpretation. Legal research is not a formulaic one-way street; it is a fluid process. Expert legal researchers move back and forth among types of sources to work efficiently and enhance their own independent critical thinking.

V. Writing about and Sharing Secondary Sources?

Some situations call for not just reading secondary sources, but also writing about them. Writing about secondary sources in a legal context could come about for any number of reasons—for example, sharing the context to decide what to do next or combining the background secondary research with your own primary research to offer a more complete analysis.

A basic concept to remember—always—is that secondary sources are not the law. Thus, it is important to be very accurate in what you say about a secondary source, as well as any assertions you have gleaned from that source. A few additional considerations can help with effective communication at this point.

- Be selective when sharing links. Share only what seems reliable. Share what the reader needs, not every single thing unearthed in research so far.

- Be careful about putting a period, comma, parenthesis, or anything else after a link because punctuation may break the link or confuse readers who cut and paste it with the punctuation and then get a non-functional "404" error message.

- Give context for the sources being shared. Don't just provide a list of URLs and expect someone to click and understand them. Context can include things like the source and date — essentially some of the same functions as a legal citation.

VI. Conclusion

Secondary sources are a crucial part of any legal researcher's skill set. They help the researcher work efficiently to avoid "reinventing the wheel" and effectively to understand complex issues. Strong legal research in secondary sources will be grounded in knowledge of the traditional categories of secondary sources, as well as strong skills in finding and evaluating online legal information.

Online legal information certainly reduced the barriers to publication, so now secondary sources may analyze important new legal authorities within 24 hours of their issuance. The ease of publishing an article online is almost matched by the ease of removing it. "Link rot," where a source is no longer found at its previous URL, is a significant problem with online legal information. We advise finding a reliable method of saving important web pages as well as becoming familiar with archiving tools such as the Wayback Machine.

Having studied this chapter, you should be able to:

- Distinguish between secondary and primary legal sources
- Locate and evaluate some secondary sources online
- Use secondary sources to gain context and find relevant primary sources
- Think critically about the purpose and scope of secondary sources found online
- Recognize the characteristics and value of traditional secondary sources available in law libraries and on fee-based platforms

Case Study

In her business endeavors, Ms. Ralston continues to pursue the idea of incorporating her coffee business as a public benefit corporation. She is still learning about the ins and outs of these types of business entities. She has found two websites and is studying them carefully. She will evaluate these sites and make notes about their usefulness and point of view.

- Colorado Secretary of State, Business FAQs, Public Benefit Corporations, https://www.sos.state.co.us/pubs/business/FAQs/pbc.html
- Fairfield & Woods, P.C., https://www.fwlaw.com/news/428-colorado-public-benefit-corporations-qa

The text of these websites as of January 2018 is reprinted below for convenience, but you can still check the current version of each website.

Site 1: Colorado Secretary of State[6]

CONTENTS

Attachments	Missing, illegible, or incorrectly indexed records
Beginning a business	Noncompliance and delinquency
Business survey information	Periodic reports
Certificate of Good Standing	Personal identifying information
Certifications	Professional service companies
Delayed effective date	Public benefit corporations
Dissolution and reinstatement	Registered agent
Electronic filing	Secure business filing
Email notification	Tax information
Entity names	Trademarks
Filing documents and finding information	Trade names
Foreign (outside of Colorado) business entities	
Glossary	

Public benefit corporations

Q1. What is a Public Benefit Corporation?

A1. A public benefit corporation (PBC) is a for profit corporation or domestic cooperative that is intended to produce one or more public benefits and to operate in a responsible and sustainable manner. A PBC must be managed in a manner that balances the shareholders' pecuniary interests, the best interest of those

---

6. Reprinted with permission of the Colorado Secretary of State.

materially affected by the corporation's conduct, and the public benefit identi-fied in its articles of incorporation.

Q2. What is a public benefit?

A2. Section 7-101-503(2), C.R.S., defines public benefit as "one or more positive ef-fects or reduction of negative effects on one or more categories of persons, en-tities, communities, or interests other than shareholders in their capacities as shareholders, including effects of an artistic, charitable, cultural, economic, edu-cational, environmental, literary, medical, religious, scientific, or technological nature."

Q3. What requirements must an entity satisfy in order to be a public benefit cor-poration (PBC)?

A3. An entity must satisfy several requirements to be a PBC, including the following:

- The articles of incorporation must identify one or more specific public benefits that the entity will promote,
- The articles of incorporation must state at the beginning that the entity is a PBC,
- The entity's name can include the words "public benefit corporation" or the abbreviations "Pub. Ben. Corp.", "P.B.C." or "PBC", and
- Share certificates issued for a PBC must clearly indicate that the entity is a PBC.

For other requirements, see the Public Benefit Corporation Act of Colorado (HB 13-1138 & HB 17-1200).

Q4. How do I form a public benefit corporation (PBC) entity?

A4. You should complete the appropriate form depending on whether you are cre-ating a new entity or changing an existing entity through amendment, conver-sion, or merger.

Q5. Does a public benefit corporation (PBC) or other entity that designates a charitable purpose in its organizational documents need to register under the Colorado Charitable Solicitations Act?

A5. In some cases, the specific public benefits a PBC identifies in its articles of incor-poration may also fit the definition of a "charitable purpose" under the Colorado Charitable Solicitations Act. This may be the case with any other entity formed under Colorado law or the law of other states where the organizational docu-ments reflect that a purpose of the entity fits within the "charitable purpose" definition. If the PBC or other entity intends to solicit funds in Colorado for that purpose, it may need to register as a charitable organization. See the charities FAQs.

Site 2: Website of Fairfield and Woods P.C.

Colorado Public Benefit Corporations: Q&A[7]

February 2, 2015
Author: Ryan M. Tharp/https://www.fwlaw.com/attorneys/ryan-m-tharp

Colorado's benefit corporation statute became effective on April 1, 2014, allowing socially conscious entrepreneurs another entity option when starting a business. If you are interested in a Colorado public benefit corporation, contact an attorney at Fairfield and Woods, P.C., and we can help you decide which entity type is right for you.

What is a Colorado public benefit corporation?

A Colorado public benefit corporation is a for profit corporation that requires the company be operated in a manner that is sustainable and beneficial to society and the environment. As compared to a regular Colorado corporation, a Colorado public benefit corporation has these key differences:

The articles of incorporation must list one or more public benefits which the company must strive to achieve.

The company must be managed to balance (1) the pecuniary interest of the shareholders, (2) the best interests of those affected by the company's conduct, and (3) the public benefits listed in the articles of incorporation.

The company must prepare an annual benefit report with (1) a description of how the company promoted the public benefits listed in the company's articles of incorporation and any obstacles the company faced in promoting those public benefits and (2) an assessment of the overall social and environmental performance of the company against a third-party standard.

What types of things can be "public benefits"?

The definition is of "public benefit" is very broad. The Public Benefit Corporation Act of Colorado defines "public benefit" as "one or more positive effects or reduction of negative effects on one or more categories of persons, entities, communities, or interests other than shareholders in their capacities as shareholders, including effects of an artistic, charitable, cultural, economic, educational, literary, medical, religious, scientific, or technological nature."

How is the management of a Colorado public benefit corporation different than the management of a regular Colorado corporation?

Colorado law requires that the business and affairs of all for profit corporations be managed by the corporation's board of directors.

A regular Colorado corporation must be managed in the company's best interests. While there is some debate about what constitutes the company's best interests,

---

7. Copyright © 2015 Fairfield and Woods, P.C., ALL RIGHTS RESERVED. Reprinted with permission.

many believe this means that directors must manage a regular Colorado corporation in a manner that maximizes corporate profits and stock price, without giving consideration to other interests. [1] Others believe that the "best interests of the company" is broader than solely the maximization of profits and share price, instead arguing that directors can (but are not required to) consider certain other interests, provided those interests align with the best interests of the company.

In contrast, the directors of a Colorado public benefit corporation must consider and balance three different interests: (1) the pecuniary interest of the shareholder, (2) the best interests of those affected by the company's conduct, and (3) the public benefits listed in the articles of incorporation. This is a major change from a regular corporation, where directors are required to only consider the best interests of the company — which many believe is limited to the maximization of profits and stock price.

What is a benefit report?

The idea behind an annual benefit report is that the company can be more effective in promoting its public benefits and sustainability.

Every Colorado public benefit corporation must annually prepare a written report with (1) a description of how the company promoted the public benefits listed in the company's articles of incorporation and any obstacles the company faced in promoting those public benefits and (2) an assessment of the overall social and environmental performance of the company against a third-party standard. The company is required to submit the report to every shareholder and to post the report on the company's website. If the company does not have a website, the report must be made available to the public upon request.

Benefit reports have been criticized as being redundant, expensive and time consuming, and of little value to the public.

- **Benefit Reports Can Be Redundant.** Most public benefit corporations are likely to be small companies with a few shareholders and where the shareholders are active in the management of the company (this is known as a "close corporation"). The shareholders in a close corporation likely know what is going on with the company — they wouldn't need a report to keep them informed. If there are shareholders who are less active in the company's management, such shareholders could simply contact the other shareholders who do manage the company to get any desired information.

- **Benefit Reports Can Be Expensive and Time Consuming.** Small companies often do not have the time or resources to annually create a benefit report — rather, such companies are busy running a business and creating public benefits. Every minute spent drafting a benefit report is a minute that cannot be spent on the company's business (or spent enjoying Colorado).

- **Benefit Reports Can Be of Little Value to the Public.** The selection of a third party standard is a choice left to the company. The only requirement is that the company not participate in the creation of the standard and the standard must define the criteria and the weightings of those criteria in measuring the company's performance. Beyond those requirements, the company can select any standard it desires, or switch the standard every year. Interested members of the public will have difficulty comparing different company's benefit reports because it is likely the reports will use different standards, which could make the reports to be of little value to the public. It is also possible that directors of public benefit corporations will select the standard by which their company performs the best — again making the reports of little value to the public.

Are there any risks involved in a Colorado public benefit corporation? If I don't consider one of the required interests, can someone sue me?

Colorado law specifically protects directors of public benefit corporations from law suits by people who are interested in the public benefits listed in the articles of incorporation, and by people affected by the corporation's conduct.

However, this does not mean that public benefit corporations are risk free. In regular corporations, creditors of a company may "pierce the corporate veil" and hold shareholders of the company liable for corporate debts in certain limited situations. One such situation is the failure to follow corporate formalities, *i.e.*, the failure to do the things required for corporations under Colorado law. Since benefit reports are required for Colorado public benefit corporations, the failure to annually prepare and distribute the benefit reports may constitute a failure to follow corporate formalities and could result in liability for the shareholders. Since Colorado public benefit corporations are so new, and are not particularly common at this point, there have been few cases in Colorado courts dealing with these and other issues.

What's the difference between a Colorado public benefit corporation and a Certified B Corporation?

A Colorado public benefit corporation and a Certified B Corporation are not the same thing. A Colorado public benefit corporation is a legal entity organized under Colorado law. A Certified B Corporation (often referred to as a "B Corp") is a special designation that was created by a non-profit organization called B Lab. Any company that meets B Lab's requirements can apply for and become a Certified B Corporation. A Colorado public benefit corporation is eligible to become a Certified B Corporation by meeting B Lab's requirements.

Are there other entity options besides Colorado public benefit corporations for socially conscious entrepreneurs?

Colorado public benefit corporations are not the only entity options for socially conscious entrepreneurs. Colorado public benefit corporations may be a good choice for some types of endeavors, but there are also other viable options, some of which may be a better choice.

- **Limited Liability Companies ("LLCs").** Limited liability companies do not have many statutory obligations. They were created with the principal of "freedom of contract" in mind. The owners of a limited liability company can agree to operate the company in any way they desire, including by requiring the managers of the company to manage the company as if it were a Colorado public benefit corporation. The owners could accomplish this by signing a written operating agreement setting forth the obligations of the managers. One major advantage to a limited liability company is that the owners could agree that the company is not required to annually produce a benefit report — that way, the company could have the benefits of a public benefit corporation without the time consuming obligation to produce a benefit report.

- **Regular Corporations.** Regular corporations are the traditional choices for businesses, but the directors of a regular corporation may not be able to consider the full range of interests that directors of public benefit corporations are required to consider. Nonetheless, there are many ways to promote public benefits in a regular corporation.

- **Non-Profit Corporations.** For certain undertakings, a non-profit corporation may be the appropriate choice, but if your goal is to make money and promote public benefits, a non-profit corporation is probably not the appropriate choice.

[1] For example, in a decision between two options — one option promises great profits but would harm the environment or society, and the other option would result in lower profits but benefit the environment or society — the maximization of shareholder value theory suggests a director is required to pick the option with greater profits.

This Article is published for general information, not to provide specific legal advice. The application of any matter discussed in this article to anyone's particular situation requires knowledge and analysis of the specific facts involved.

Traditions and Trends

Traditionally, secondary sources were available in law libraries that had purchased the secondary sources and continued to pay for regular updates. These secondary sources were divided into five traditional categories: (1) book-length or multivolume treatises; (2) *Restatements of Law* published by the American Law Institute; (3) law review articles; (4) legal encyclopedias; and (5) American Law Reports, also known as A.L.R. Annotations. The American Law Reports is a unique combination of notable case opinions with secondary research on the important issue in that case. Legal researchers used hard copies in law libraries and would design an explicit strategy on where to start, based on what they already knew about the topic. Because traditional legal research was highly formalized through legal publishers, there could be a lag time in how quickly cutting-edge legal issues were discussed in the literature. Traditionally, in commercial legal research software such as Lexis and Westlaw, researchers would navigate many folders to choose the relevant database and then conduct a search from there. Thus, a researcher heavily invested in secondary research might conduct five searches in the corresponding database for the five categories listed above. Secondary research for researchers without access to a commercial database would include finding a local law library open to the public, and using the print sources.

Today, the main research method for secondary sources and all other information retrieval is a search. Typing a search query in a search box is a way of life for anyone, anywhere, looking for any type of information. In the legal field, the commercial legal research platforms have gravitated toward the search box, giving it prime real estate on the main research page. It is now commonplace for researchers to enter a search query in the search box and then filter the multitude of sources in the results. Indeed, the search box on commercial research platforms suggests search terms just as Google and other search engines have "autocomplete" suggestions once you begin to type in a term.

These search boxes are not controlled only by the actual search terms; they also use proprietary algorithms to draw from the research platforms' databases. In a study based on 2015 data, the research results of doing the same search across several different commercial platforms varied more widely than expected, with "hardly any overlap" in the top 10 results returned for identical searches done across six platforms.[8] The possible differences in search results using the search box reinforces the importance — for all legal researchers — of developing strong skills in using Boolean connectors. Strong Boolean skills can supplement use of a search box because Boolean searches give the researcher more control and transparency with search mechanics.

Beyond the traditional secondary sources, which remain available on fee-based platforms, free sources on the internet contain legal information serving some of the same purposes. For example, many law review articles are published on the law-review's webpage and on platforms such as the Social Science Research Network (SSRN). In 2016, SSRN — an open-access collaborative platform — was acquired by Elsevier, a large publisher of fee-based academic journals, causing controversy. Concern about publishers acquiring and charging high rates for scholarly and practical information is a continuing trend and hot-button issue among law librarians, as well as other librarians and information experts.

---

8. Susan Nevelow Mart, *Results May Vary in Legal Research Databases*, ABA Journal (March 2018).

Chapter 8

Finding and
Reading Statutes

> When you are writing laws you are testing words to find their utmost power.
> Like spells, they have to make things happen in the real world, and like spells,
> they only work if people believe in them.
>
> —Hilary Mantel, *Wolf Hall*

The legislature makes the law; the other branches administer it and use it to decide disputes. Competent legal research frequently must begin with finding the statute or statutes on point.

Most of the time, you will be looking for statutes in force right now. Thus, you will be searching "the code" of the relevant jurisdiction. A code is a jurisdiction's collected current statutes, usually organized by topic.

After finding the relevant statute or statutes, the next step is reading and understanding them. Statutory interpretation is a fascinating discipline all of its own, and this chapter gives a short introduction, with recommended resources.

Beyond the text of the statute, another kind of legal information is generated through the legislative process. "Legislative history" is comprised of the documents produced in the legislative process. Most statutes go through a multi-step process on their way from bill to law. They are introduced, often considered by a legislative committee, perhaps debated on the floor of the legislature, voted on, transferred to the other chamber of the legislature in a bicameral system, considered and voted on again, then signed by the chief of the executive branch (governor or president, in the state and federal systems respectively). The reports and other documents created as a bill progresses collectively constitute its legislative history, and these documents can be helpful in understanding statutory law. They can also be helpful in tracking pending legislation: legislative documents are available, practically in real time, for bills that have not yet become law but still could, and failed bills from past Congresses that will never become law. (The reference to "past Congresses" brings up a fact necessary to understanding federal legislation: Every two years, we have an election and a new Congress. The 2017–2018 Congress was the 115th Congress, and the Congress that sits in 2019–2020 is the 116th Congress.[1]) This chapter introduces techniques to research legislative history, while also acknowledging the well-known debates on what role, if any legislative history should play in courts' work interpreting statutes and deciding cases.

I. The Basic Path of Legislation

A bill can eventually become a law, but there are many different ways for a bill to get from point A to point B. Let's take a generic, idealized version of how a bill becomes a law. Here is what the process of enactment might look like:

- Draft bill text is filed in one chamber of a bicameral legislature. For this example, let's assume the bill was introduced in the U.S. House of Representatives (though for another bill, the originating house could also be the U.S. Senate).
- The bill is referred to a House committee.
- The House committee holds hearings on the bill, perhaps including witnesses testifying for and against the bill.
- The House committee makes changes to the original bill in the form of "markups" and amendments.
- The House committee issues a report based on its hearings and the bill markup.
- The bill is then referred out of committee to the floor of the House.
- The House holds floor debate on the bill.
- The bill is passed by the House, and sent to the Senate for consideration.
- The bill referred to a Senate committee.
- The Senate committee holds its own hearings on the bill, potentially also including testifying witnesses.
- The Senate committee makes its own markups and amendments to the version of the bill sent from the House.
- The Senate committee issues a report based on its hearings and the bill markup.
- The bill is referred out of committee to the floor of the Senate.

---

1. One way to see the Congresses by year (such as the 116th Congress sitting from 2019–2020) is to use the advanced search feature on Congress.gov.

- The Senate holds its own floor debate on the bill.
- The bill is passed by the Senate.
- If the versions passed in each chamber are different, then a conference committee from both chambers reconciles them into one version.
- Both the House and the Senate potentially hold further floor debate on the conference-committee version of the bill.
- Both the House and the Senate vote on the conference committee's version of the bill.
- After the bill passes the House and Senate, The bill is then sent to the executive (president or governor) for consideration. In this example involving a federal bill, it would go to the U.S. President.
- The President then either signs the bill (sometimes also issuing a signing statement) or vetoes the bill, sending it back to Congress.
- If the President vetoed the bill, then Congress can override the veto with both a two-thirds majority in the House and a two-thirds majority in the Senate.

Whew! At almost any stage of the above process, a bill could be rejected and die, never becoming a law. Steps to passage vary widely among the U.S. Congress and all of the states, but the above example is fairly typical. When a bill passes both chambers and is signed by the governor or president, the result is the text of a new law.

Let us turn our attention to where you can find laws that have been successfully enacted. The text of a new law exists in several specific places:

- A pamphlet or PDF of the law itself (often called a slip copy)

    The slip copy is the segment of law just passed. In the federal system, this is called a public law. Each new law has a new separate number. For example, Public Law 114-187 was the work of the 114th Congress, and was the 187th law passed by that Congress.

- A chronological compilation of laws passed (often called session laws)

    The session laws are the laws passed by the legislature, compiled in order. In the federal system, the session laws are called the Statutes at Large. They collect the public laws into chronological volumes.

- The code, where laws currently in force are organized and compiled by topic

    The code is all the collected laws, organized by topic with an index. The code is where people start when they want to find current statutory law on a topic. In the federal system, the code is called the United States Code.

Thus, the law first exists by itself, next it is compiled in a chronological form, and then it finally is placed in a topical form in the code. When a bill offers significant new law or a major amendment to existing law, legislators typically give it a "popular name."

Popular names you may recognize include the Americans with Disabilities Act, the Foreign Corrupt Practices Act, and the No Child Left Behind Act. Searching by popular name is another way to find statutory law. Popular Name Tables such as the one offered by the Office of the Law Revision Counsel[2] provide corresponding citations to the code. Researching statutory codes and reading statutes are the most useful legal literacy skills for working with statutes. We focus on those skills, with some notes on how to find legislative history.

II. The Organization of Statutory Codes

Imagine a shelf full of almost identical-looking books in a law library. They are the code for a jurisdiction. Pick one off the shelf and open it. At the front of any of these books, you should find what looks like a table of contents. It's a list of the "titles" in the code. The titles are the topical framework of a code, with each title corresponding to a topic of legislation. The actual topics and titles are different in each state and in the federal code, but the basic idea — all the statutory law organized by topic — is the same. Here are the first 10 titles in the federal code, and an example of the first 10 titles in a selected state code:

Example of Federal Code Titles (United States Code)	Example of State Code Titles (Colorado Revised Statutes)
Title 1 — General Provisions	Title 1. Elections
Title 2 — The Congress	Title 2. Legislative
Title 3 — The President	Title 3. United States
Title 4 — Flag and Seal, Seat of Government, and the States	Title 4. Uniform commercial code
Title 5 — Government Organization and Employees	Title 5. Consumer credit code
Title 6 — Domestic Security	Title 6. Consumer and commercial affairs
Title 7 — Agriculture	Title 7. Corporations and associations
Title 8 — Aliens and Nationality	Title 8. Labor and industry
Title 9 — Arbitration	Title 9. Safety — industrial and commercial
Title 10 — Armed Forces	Title 10. Insurance
The United States Code continues through Title 53. You can see the whole title structure at the Office of the Law Revision Counsel, http://uscode.house.gov/ and many other sites.	The Colorado Revised Statutes continue through Title 44. The whole title structure of the C.R.S. can be found on Lexis's open-access "Colorado Legal Resources" page.

As noted above, each title corresponds to a topic, and each topic is further broken down into sub-topics. Ultimately and most importantly, the code is broken down into individual code sections. Here is a statutory citation for one section of the United States Code:

$$29 \text{ U.S.C. } \S 202$$

---

2. https://uscode.house.gov/popularnames/popularnames.htm (downloadable PDF recommended).

The "U.S.C." in the middle identifies this citation as a statute in the United States Code. Within the code, this citation comes from Title 29, the title for Labor. And the specific section of Title 29 in this code is section 202. With this information, a researcher could find this section of the code quickly and easily in any book or online version of the code.

Here is a statutory citation for one section of the Colorado Revised Statutes:

C.R.S. § 8-12-107

The "C.R.S." identifies the citation as being from the Colorado Revised Statutes. Within the code, this citation comes from Title 8, Colorado's title for Labor and Industry. The numbers after the initial "8" further identify the citation's article and section: Title 8, Article 12, Section 107. With this information, a researcher could find this section of the code quickly and easily in any book or online version of the code. From just these two examples, you can see that code numbering conventions vary at the federal and state levels. But once you have a code citation, you should be able to locate that code section almost instantly.

III. Researching State Codes and Legislative History Online

To research statutes online, the first step is to find the relevant code—either the federal code or a particular state's code. Here are a few selected websites where you can find the text of the United States Code:

Office of the Law Revision Counsel	http://uscode.house.gov/
United States Government Printing Office, www.govinfo.gov	https://www.govinfo.gov/app/collection/uscode/
Cornell Legal Information Institute (LII)	United States Code https://www.law.cornell.edu/uscode/text

Here are a few selected websites where you can find the text of state codes or collected links to state codes:

Library of Congress	U.S. States and Territories http://www.loc.gov/law/help/guide/states.php
Cornell Legal Information Institute (LII)	Constitutions, Statutes, and Codes https://www.law.cornell.edu/statutes.html
Wikipedia	External links: https://en.wikipedia.org/wiki/List_of_U.S._state_statutory_codes
FindLaw	Findlaw cases and codes, https://caselaw.findlaw.com/

Once you have chosen an updated, credible source, then you are ready to start exploring how to find statutes using the source. In general, you have two basic options from which to choose:

- Searching the full text of the code when you already know the key word or phrase
- Browsing through the code titles using menu options when you are researching a general topic

Free online codes typically provide the text of the statute and a brief list of citations to the legislative history of the statute, including its initial passage and amendment history. Figure 8-1 shows an example of a federal statute drawn from the Office of the Law Revision Counsel's website:

Figure 8-1

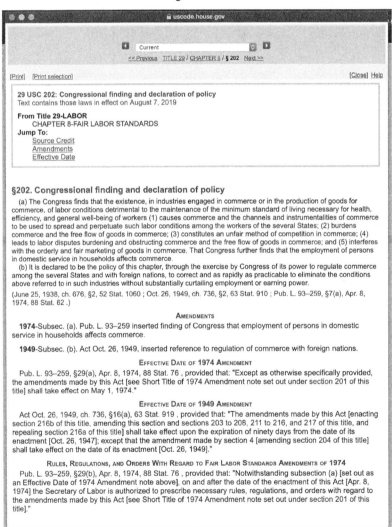

Let us explore the wealth of legal information provided in this resource. The top of the screenshot shows a menu set to the "current" version of the U.S. Code. If you needed to do historical research, that menu allows searching of prior versions as well. Most legal research, however, tends to be about understanding the current law.

This specific statute is up to date through August 7, 2019, as shown by the text stating "[t]ext contains those laws in effect on August 7, 2019." The screen shot was taken on August 8, 2019, so that's pretty up-to-date information.

The text of the statute is then laid out in its original outlined format. This statute has two subsections: 29 U.S.C. § 202(a) and 29 U.S.C. § 202(b). Section (a) further contains a list of five numbered items. Legal communications that refer to this statute should be as specific as possible in pinpointing the relevant subsection.

Beneath the text, the legislative history shows the original enactment of the statute on June 25, 1938. The statute was amended on October 26, 1949, and April 8, 1974. Using these references to legislative history, it is possible to trace the historical versions of this section if we need to know how this law has changed over time.

Note that this legislative history includes a reference to Pub. L. 93-259 in 1974. The reference to "Pub. L." means *public law*, which is the title for a bill that has actually been passed into law. Public Law 93-259 was the work of the 93rd Congress (the Congress that sat in 1973–74) and was the 259th act passed into law by that Congress. Knowing the Public Law number is crucial for more detailed legislative history research.

The congressional findings and purpose for the Fair Labor Standards Act in 29 U.S.C. § 202 have not been changed much at all, other than in 1974 when domestic workers were specifically included. To see a contrasting section in the Fair Labor Standards Act, you can find and study the national minimum wage law (29 U.S.C. § 206), which has been amended 12 times. The most recent change to section 206 was as a part of Public Law 114-187, titled the Puerto Rico Oversight, Management, and Economic Stability Act.

The Office of the Law Revision Counsel's website provides an unannotated code. It contains the text and notes on legislative history, but nothing else. Legal publishers also compile "annotated codes," which are an excellent research tool if you can gain access to them. An annotated code is organized in exactly the same way as the code itself, but it adds more information to the text of each statute. Beyond the text of the statute, and a brief reference to its legislative history, an annotated statute will provide cross-references to other legal information, particularly judicial opinions (i.e., cases) that interpret each provision. These annotated codes are extremely useful for researching how a statute is interpreted in the case law. Most annotated codes are copyrighted intellectual property and available in print in law libraries and behind paywalls at legal research platforms such as Lexis, Westlaw, and Fastcase.

If you do not have access to an annotated code, you can still conduct statutory and case research, but it will have to be in separate steps. First, you will need to read the text of the statute in an online source as shown in this chapter. Second, you will need to research cases with relevant key words or citations to that statute, as shown in chapter 10.

IV. Understanding and Using the Structure of a Code

The statutory example above was 29 U.S.C. § 202, a portion of the Fair Labor Standards Act of 1938. This was a significant act establishing numerous sections of the United States Code. Although it was passed in 1938 and the statutory scheme it created has been amended many times since then, the Fair Labor Standards Act remains vibrant today. It is the statutory authority for the Department of Labor to issue guidance on when student interns can be unpaid, an issue of administrative law used in several chapters of this book. We will use the Fair Labor Standards Act and section 202 specifically to explore some techniques for statutory research.

As noted above, a good place to research the United States Code is the Office of the Law Revision Counsel at http://uscode.house.gov/. Labor is addressed in Title 29 of the United States Code, and the Fair Labor Standards Act is found in Chapter 8 of that title:

Figure 8-2

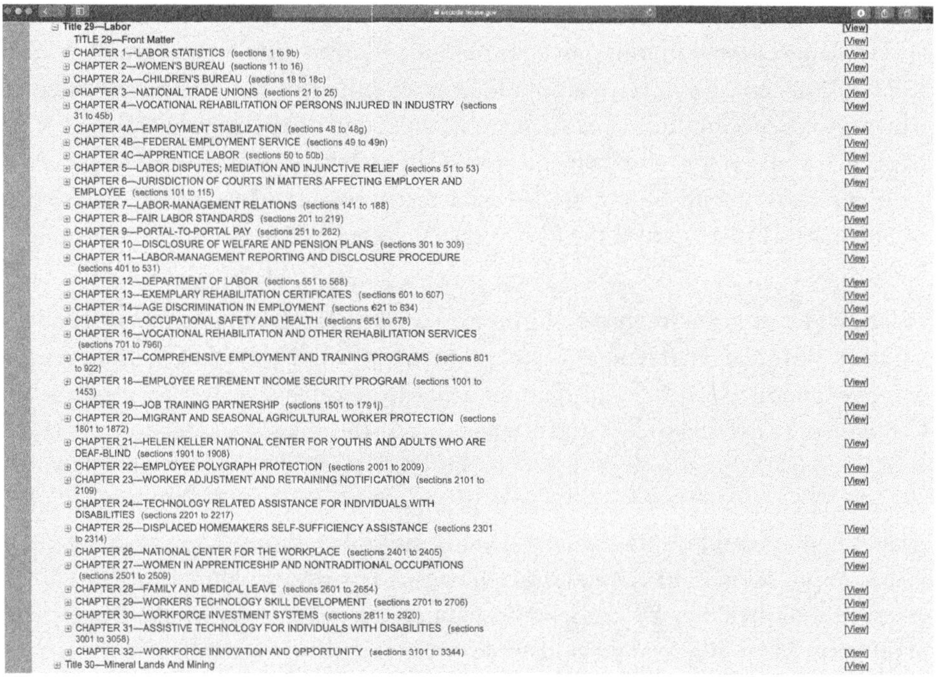

The chapter on Fair Labor Standards can be unfolded to show the whole organization of the Fair Labor Standards Act:

Figure 8-3

uscode.house.gov/browse/prelim@title29/chapter8&edition=prelim

CHAPTER 7—LABOR-MANAGEMENT RELATIONS (sections 141 to 188)	[View]
CHAPTER 8—FAIR LABOR STANDARDS (sections 201 to 219)	**[View]**
CHAPTER 8—Front Matter	[View]
Sec. 201. Short title	[View]
Sec. 202. Congressional finding and declaration of policy	[View]
Sec. 203. Definitions	[View]
Sec. 204. Administration	[View]
Sec. 205. Repealed. Pub. L. 110-28, title VIII, §8103(c)(1)(A), May 25, 2007, 121 Stat. 189	[View]
Sec. 206. Minimum wage	[View]
Sec. 207. Maximum hours	[View]
Sec. 208. Repealed. Pub. L. 110-28, title VIII, §8103(c)(1)(A), May 25, 2007, 121 Stat. 189	[View]
Sec. 209. Attendance of witnesses	[View]
Sec. 210. Court review of wage orders in Puerto Rico and the Virgin Islands	[View]
Sec. 211. Collection of data	[View]
Sec. 212. Child labor provisions	[View]
Sec. 213. Exemptions	[View]
Sec. 214. Employment under special certificates	[View]
Sec. 215. Prohibited acts; prima facie evidence	[View]
Sec. 216. Penalties	[View]
Sec. 216a. Repealed. Oct. 26, 1949, ch. 736, §16(f), 63 Stat. 920	[View]
Sec. 216b. Liability for overtime work performed prior to July 20, 1949	[View]
Sec. 217. Injunction proceedings	[View]
Sec. 218. Relation to other laws	[View]
Sec. 218a. Repealed. Pub. L. 114-74, title VI, §604, Nov. 2, 2015, 129 Stat. 599	[View]
Sec. 218b. Notice to employees	[View]
Sec. 218c. Protections for employees	[View]
Sec. 219. Separability	[View]

From here, it is possible to go to the text of any code section.

To find legislative history, you can also use a search engine to see if another legal researcher has already compiled a history, which often happens for significant legislation. For example, the early and foundational legislative history of the Fair Labor Standards Act has been compiled in a posting at the Department of Labor's website.[3]

V. When Research Comes Up Empty

One of a legal researcher's most challenging situations is researching and finding absolutely nothing. This situation is especially difficult with statutory research. As stated at the very beginning of this chapter, if there is a statute on point, you've got to find it.

To ensure your statutory research is complete, try these steps:

- Research in secondary sources, such as those described in chapter 7, to ensure you have context and the right search terms.
- Try to full-text search the official code at a government website.
- Browse the official code to find the area of the code where your research topic is addressed, then open the folders or menus and investigate the subsections to search for relevant statutes.
- Try to full-text search the unofficial code at a legal research portal such as FindLaw or Justia.
- Research the relevant key words in recent cases, and read the cases in context to discover if a statute governs the issue. Researching cases is addressed in chapter 10.

---

3. Jonathan Grossman, *Fair Labor Standards Act: Maximum Struggle for a Minimum Wage*, Department of Labor, https://www.dol.gov/oasam/programs/history/flsa1938.htm (originally printed in the Monthly Labor Review, June 1978).

VI. Reading Statutes

Once you have found a relevant section or sections of the code, you are ready to read and interpret the statutory law. Reading statutory law can mean different tasks: reading a single statute, a few statutes situated next to each other in the code, a scattered group of statutes in several different titles, or an entire act. Whether you are focusing on one section or a comprehensive act, reading statutes can be like putting a puzzle together. You need both a big-picture understanding and to focus on small details and how they fit together.

The skills discussed in chapter 4 on reading legal information are very useful for reading statutory language. Gain context by using the structure of the legal information itself. Note where in the code this section is located—what title is it in? What subdivision within the title? Can you find an outline of how this title is organized? Are there any defined terms at the beginning of this portion of the code? Where does the relevant segment of related code sections begin and end? Skim the code around the section you found. The process of legal research can help with reading and interpreting the statute.

Beyond using the structure of this information, use your knowledge of the law itself. Is the statute civil or criminal or regulatory in nature? What conduct does the statute cover? Does the statute provide rights flowing out of that definition, or does it give penalties or consequences because of some act or omission related to that definition?

Critical reading skills are invaluable when reading statutes. Beyond critical reading in general, legal experts use specific methodologies for reading statutes and arguing about what they mean. These methodologies are known as statutory interpretation and are introduced in the next section.

A. A Brief Introduction to Statutory Interpretation

Legal experts agree that the text of the law itself is very important. Courts must follow and apply statutory language that is clear, unless they are using judicial review to declare it unconstitutional. For example, key language such as "must" or "may" separates legal requirements from legal possibilities. Key language such as "and" or "or" separates conjunctive rules using "and," in which *all* the elements must be satisfied from disjunctive rules using "or," in which several different options could satisfy a rule.

Where legal experts start to disagree is whether the text of the law is the *only* thing that is important—especially when the language is unclear. For example, section 207(a)(1) of the Fair Labor Standards Act forbids an employer from requiring an employee to work more than 40 hours per week "unless such employee receives compensation for his employment in excess of the hours above specified at a rate not less than one and one-half times the regular rate at which he is employed." Section 207(o) of the statute applies it to public employers such as state government, and allows substitution of compensatory time—in other words, comp time off—for paid overtime. Because certain circumstances trigger the payment of all comp time in cash compensation, the City of Houston implemented a policy requiring employees to take comp time, to cut down on large amounts of accrued time. The question in *Christensen v. Harris County*, 529 U.S. 576 (2000) was whether this practice violated the Fair Labor Standards Act. The explicit text of the statute did not forbid the practice, and the case thus involved a complex application of statutory interpretation principles to decide whether it implicitly forbade the practice. Section II of the Supreme Court opinion provides a detailed example of how the Court interprets statutory sections together and applies well-known techniques for statutory interpretation known as "canons of construction" to resolve statutory questions. (Use your case research skills to find this case and skim section II if you'd like to see more detail with this example.)

B. Differing Approaches to Statutory Interpretation

Statutory interpretation has distinct schools of thought, and law professors representing these schools of thought are constantly battling it out in books and law review articles. These debates affect the results of cases too, such as the *Christensen* case dictating overtime policy for thousands of City of Houston employees.

The "textualist" approach to statutory interpretation focuses solely on the text of the law. Text analysis may include approaches such as dictionary definitions and grammatical analysis. One vivid example of textual interpretation can be found in the United States Court of Appeals for the Tenth Circuit's decision in *United States v. Rentz*, 777 F.3d 1105, 1106–07 (10th Cir. 2015) (en banc). The issue in that case was the meaning of 18 U.S.C. § 924(c)(1)(A):

> [A]ny person who, during and in relation to any crime of violence or drug trafficking crime…uses or carries a firearm, or who, in furtherance of any such crime, possesses a firearm, shall, in addition to the punishment provided for such crime…be sentenced to a term of imprisonment of not less than 5 years.

In the case, the defendant fired "a single shot" that "hit and injured one victim but then managed to strike and kill another." The legal question under § 924(c)(1)(A) was "in circumstances like these, does the statute permit the government to charge one violation or two?" The Tenth Circuit reversed the panel's decision and held that a single use of a firearm could give rise to a single charge under 18 U.S.C. § 924(c)(1)(A)). The "en banc" opinion (meaning all the judges, not just a panel of three) was written by then-Circuit Judge Neil Gorsuch, now a Justice of the United States Supreme Court. Judge Gorsuch described the statute as "enigmatic" and a "bramble of prepositional phrases" and thus resorted to sentence diagramming to interpret the statute:[4]

---

4. *Rentz*, 777 F.3d at 1106, 1110. Please note that this case is unusual because the diagram appears as an image in the opinion's text, and unfortunately several of the free online caselaw sources do not show embedded graphics. The diagram is not apparent in the Google Scholar version of this case, as of early 2019, for

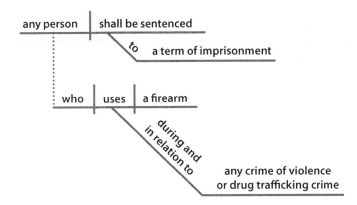

Literally diagramming a sentence is an unusual illustration of text-based interpretation, but it shows the importance of law's precise language, including the relationship of words to one another as part of that text.

Textualists may also use an "originalist" approach where they research the meaning of words in the text and grammatical practices at the time the language was originally drafted and passed. The late United States Supreme Court Justice Antonin Scalia was famously passionate in advocating for textualism and originalism, and railing against legislative history as a possible source of intent. He pointed out that legislators and different committees may have had different intents and they may have even changed their own intent within the process, or their intent may be very different from what they stated in the legislative history.[5]

Beyond textualism and originalism, other approaches take the plain language into account, but also inquire into the legislature's intent in drafting that language. "Intentionalists" delve into what the legislature actually intended to do. "Purposivists" focus on the purpose of the law in light of what a reasonable legislature would have objectively intended to do. This inquiry helps the court interpreting the statute to reach a more meaningful interpretation of the law's text, even if individual legislators had different subjective intent or their intent is not knowable.[6]

These are some key judicial philosophies in interpreting statutory text and applying it to new factual situations.

---

example. The diagram can be seen in the official opinion posted on the Tenth Circuit's website at https://www.ca10.uscourts.gov/opinions/12/12-4169.pdf.

5. *See, e.g.,* Bradley Karkkainen, *Plain Meaning: Justice Scalia's Jurisprudence of Strict Statutory Construction,* 17 Harv. J. L. & Pub. Pol'y 401 (1994).

6. *Legal Theory Lexicon 078: Theories of Statutory Interpretation and Construction,* Legal Theory Lexicon (May 21, 2017), http://lsolum.typepad.com/legal_theory_lexicon/2017/05/theories-of-statutory-interpretation.html; *see, e.g., Thunder Basin Coal Co. v. Reich,* 510 U.S. 200 (1994) (rejecting a mine operator's pre-enforcement challenge to a new mine safety law, in part because "[t]he legislative history of the Mine Act confirms this interpretation. At the time of the Act's passage, at least 1 worker was killed and 66 miners were disabled every working day in the Nation's mines.") (citing S. Rep. No. 95-181, p. 4 (1977) and other legislative-history sources).

C. Canons of Construction

Beyond these broad philosophies, judges interpreting statutes also use a toolkit of ideas for interpreting statutes called the "canons of construction." The canons are specific ideas about how to interpret statutory language in predictable situations. They are frequently (and perhaps unfortunately) best known by their Latin names.

Here are a few well-known canons of construction:

- Including a list of items means excluding other items not on the list. This canon is sometimes referred to as *Expressio unius est exclusio alterius*.

- Statutes should be interpreted to give effect to every word and phrase; courts should avoid interpreting a statute to render any word or phrase meaningless or duplicative. This canon is sometimes described as *the rule against surplusage*.

- A list of specific items followed by a more general catch-all means that the catch-all at the end should be interpreted to include items similar to the list of specific items. This canon is sometimes described as *ejusdem generis*.

- When a statute is ambiguous, the court can look to other statutes on the same topic to help determine the ambiguous statute's intended meaning. This canon is sometimes referred to as interpreting a statute *in pari materia*.

- Similarly, when a word in a statute is ambiguous, the court can interpret it consistently with the rest of the statute. This canon is sometimes referred to as *noscitur a sociis*.

Let us consider how some of the canons might function in a real-world example. Suppose a statute defines breakfast fruits as "blueberries, strawberries, and bananas." We presumably then know that breakfast fruits do *not* include oranges. This reading is because the canon of *expressio unius est exclusion alterius*, which means that to expressly include one thing on a list is to exclude other things not present on that list. But what if the statute says that breakfast fruits "include blueberries, strawberries, bananas, and other fruits"? Then we have to analyze what "other fruits" might include. Does it include oranges? An important question here is whether oranges are like blueberries, strawberries, and bananas. The relevant canon here is *ejusdem generis*, meaning "of the same kind." Under *ejusdem generis*, the general catch-all "other fruits" must be interpreted to include fruits that are *of the same kind* as blueberries, strawberries, and bananas. So does it include oranges or not? Oranges are like these fruits because they are all top-selling popular fruits. Oranges are not like these fruits because oranges are citrus and the others are not. As you can see, canons of construction support specific arguments of what a statute means, but they are not necessarily definitive.

Put differently, canons of construction are often helpful, but they are also capable of contradicting themselves. In 1950, renowned law professor Karl Llewelyn wrote an article that itself became famous because it showed 28 situations where the canons of construction could contradict each other.[7] One thing is certain: debates over statutory construction have generated reams of pages of legal scholarship and theory. One in-depth public source on statutory construction is Larry Eig, *Statutory Interpretation: General Principles and Recent Trends*, Congressional Research Service (Sept. 24, 2014), https://fas.org/sgp/crs/misc/97-589.pdf. This section was a quick introduction to the basic legislative process and the debate over how to proceed when statutory language leaves any room for interpretation. Law is a process, and these debates continue in scholarly and practical ways everywhere law affects people and organizations.

VII. Conclusion

Strong legal literacy requires skills at finding and reading statutes. For some legal and policy-making roles, it is especially important to understand and be able to find documents from the lawmaking process as well. Statutory and legislative research is heavily influenced by government publications and websites, with commercial services offering enhanced versions for supplemental research. Online statutory research requires skill and resilience at navigating menus, browsing tables of contents, and utilizing search bars. After finding the relevant statute or statutes, the researcher must become a skilled legal reader, parsing through the statutory language with not only a dictionary but also an understanding of the canons of construction used for statutory interpretation. The next step beyond finding and reading statutes is placing them in context, adding research into regulations and cases as needed for complete legal research.

Having studied this chapter, you should be able to:

- Explain generally how legislation is proposed, passed into law, and then organized into a statutory code
- Use the structural logic of a statutory code as an entry into multiple ways to research statutes
- Find and use free and reliable online legal research sites to locate statutes
- Recognize the role of canons of statutory construction as concepts for interpreting statutory language

---

7. Karl N. Llewellyn, *Remarks on the Theory of Appellate Decision and the Rules or Canons About How Statutes Are to Be Construed*, 3 Vand. L. Rev. 395, 401–06 (1950).

Case Study

Olivia Ralston is interested in incorporating her new business as a *public benefit corporation*. She has done some preliminary internet research and talked with others in the social justice entrepreneurial community. Two states of particular interest are Massachusetts and Texas.

She wants to find and study the statute or statutes allowing the incorporation of a public benefit corporation in each state, understand the text of these statutes, and compare and contrast them.

Traditions and Trends

One major tradition in statutes is the distinction between unannotated and annotated codes. Unannotated codes are simply the text of the statutes and factual material about each statute's legislative history. Annotated codes are expanded, enhanced, supplementary versions of the code, which are a much more powerful research tool and highly recommended for statutory research when available.

The text of the statutory law is not copyrighted material and can be freely reproduced, under the obvious policy argument that the law belongs to the public and cannot be a private entity's intellectual property. Annotated codes are typically private intellectual property of commercial legal publishers. Thus the United States Code Annotated is available on Westlaw, and the United States Code Service is available on Lexis. The policy of open access to the law itself comes into tension with intellectual property rights around annotated codes, when the annotated code produced by a legal publisher *is* the official code of a state. That is the subject of a legal dispute over the Official Code of Georgia Annotated that, as of this book's publication, was set to be argued before the United States Supreme Court in December 2019. The case is *Georgia v. Public Resource.org Inc.* The Supreme Court filings are available on the SCOTUSblog website's page for this case. Another example of this tension between free and fee-based access to legal information is the debate over costs to use the "PACER" system for federal court filings such as complaints, answers, motions, briefs, and judicial orders.[8]

Another trend with legislative information—and all primary legal information—is the spread of information via social media. Social media has allowed instant sharing of public documents; thus, the legislative process on hot-button issues may be shared widely and in real-time via screen shots of legislative information generated from the legislative process. Notices of proposed regulations as well as final regulations can be shared and discussed on social media. Screen shots of snippets from new Supreme Court cases are regularly shared, highlighted, and

---

8. *See* Adam Liptak, *Attacking a Paywall That Hides Public Court Filings*, New York Times (Feb. 4, 2019).

discussed online among lawyers activists, journalists, and many others. And the transcripts of oral arguments in Supreme Court cases are shared and discussed immediately when they become available, which is months before the Court actually issues the opinion deciding the case. This trend is not necessarily an influence on the law itself; for example, tweeting about a proposed regulation is a far cry from filing a comment on Regulations.gov. But this trend does show the expanding dissemination of legal information and the wider role for comments informed by legal literacy among the general public.

Chapter 9

Finding and Reading Regulations and Other Administrative Sources

From a rule of law perspective, the big advantage of federal agencies is that they have the capacity, and often the legislative mandate, to generate a lot of detailed rules expeditiously and to publicize those rules as binding upon the entire nation. Case-by-case adjudication, which is the characteristic mode for courts, takes longer to generate rules, especially national rules binding on everyone. In contrast, agencies have a variety of mechanisms that allow them to generate national rules relatively quickly: administrative rulemaking, published guidances, handbooks, and even online websites. These are more accessible to the general public than judicial precedents are, they have immediate national application, and they are more detailed (sometimes much more detailed) than precedents usually are or can aspire to be.[1]

— William N. Eskridge Jr.

Regulations grow at the same rate as weeds.

— Norman Ralph Augustine

Administrative law means rules and regulations, but it can mean other forms of law and legal information too. Administrative law influences almost every aspect of modern life. Although you may never actually read the product safety rules for microwaves, you may be influenced by them when you accidentally enter "33 minutes" for the cook

---

1. William N. Eskridge Jr., *Expanding Chevron's Domain: A Comparative Institutional Analysis of the Relative Competence of Courts and Agencies to Interpret Statutes*, 2013 Wis. L. Rev. 411, 419 (2013) (citations omitted).

time to pop some popcorn when you meant "3 minutes," creating a fire within your microwave that remains self-contained.[2]

At the federal level, to give just a few examples, federal agencies regulate agricultural waste,[3] food labeling,[4] credit card transactions,[5] and signs posted on interstate highways showing nearby gas stations and restaurants.[6] At the state level, for further examples, state agencies regulate hair braiding and barber shops, hearing aids, x-rays, dry cleaning, and certain aspects of coastal wetlands (in concert with federal environmental regulations).

Administrative agencies do important work because Congress cannot efficiently make all the laws at the level of detail needed for modern government to continue functioning effectively. Well-known political and practical arguments weigh both for and against the scope and detail of the administrative state, and legal literacy can help inform arguments on both sides of this debate. Is government too big, or should it be doing more? Regardless of your position, this chapter focuses on the basic framework of the current system and how it operates.

I. Overview of the Federal Administrative State

The so-called administrative state exists within the executive branch, which is headed by the President. The 15 executive agencies are Cabinet-level appointments, meaning their lead administrator attends Cabinet meetings with the president. These executive agencies sit at the top of a pyramid of sub-agencies. For example, the Department of Health and Human Services is the executive agency that contains the Food and Drug Administration. The executive branch also includes a number of "independent" agencies, deemed independent because they are designed to allow for less influence by the President in their regular operations. For example, members of the Federal Reserve Board are appointed by the President, but they have staggered terms (perhaps covering multiple presidential administrations) and cannot freely be removed during their terms.

There are a few legislative agencies — "legislative" because they are under the direct control of Congress — such as the Congressional Budget Office and, importantly for legal information, the Government Publishing Office, which is responsible for govinfo.gov, where much federal government information can be found. And there are also "judicial" agencies, such as the United States Sentencing Commission. There is even a small administrative agency that studies the functioning of the administrative state:

---

2. 21 C.F.R. § 1030.10. (setting performance standards for microwave ovens).

3. *E.g.,* 40 C.F.R. § 125.10(a).

4. 21 C.F.R. § 101.

5. 12 C.F.R. § 226.

6. 23 C.F.R. § 750.

the Administrative Conference of the United States, which we will revisit a little later in this chapter.

Agencies are not allowed to do whatever they wish. They cannot roam around freely to adjudicate administrative cases and promulgate regulations. Agencies must have specific authority that is delegated to them by Congress, and Congress must oversee each agency's authority in certain ways. The *nondelegation doctrine* prevents Congress from completely delegating its lawmaking responsibilities. When Congress wants an agency to regulate a specific area, it must give an agency an "intelligible principle" to work from.[7] But Congress delegates all kinds of functions to agencies, and the Supreme Court has not used nondelegation to strike down an agency's congressional authorization since the New Deal cases of the 1930s. For each agency, the statute that delegates the particular authority from Congress to the agency provides a key framework for the agency's action, and is commonly called the *organic statute* for that agency. In general, if an agency acts outside its statutory mandate, its actions can be struck down under section 706 of the Administrative Procedure Act, which functions as a sort of constitution controlling certain aspects of agencies' work. Judicial review for agency action is a check on agencies to ensure they act within their statutory mandates and avoid actions that are rightfully within the realm of the legislature. How much deference courts must or should give to agency regulations and other actions, however, is a continuing debate — one where the Supreme Court plays an important role interpreting the Administrative Procedure Act.

The main functions of agencies in general are *adjudication* and *rulemaking*. First, some agencies adjudicate (i.e., they decide) case-like matters that are delegated to them. For example, the Board of Veterans' Appeals ("BVA") decides appeals about veterans' benefits. This adjudicatory authority has been granted by Congress to the Department of Veterans Affairs, which in turn created the BVA to handle these cases. BVA decisions can be appealed in the federal court system through the United States Court of Appeals for Veterans Claims, the United States Court of Appeals for the Federal Circuit, and (if it is willing to accept the case) the United States Supreme Court.

Second, agencies make regulations, which are sets of rules that, in structure, look an awful lot like statutes. In the rulemaking process, agencies must satisfy the requirements for due process that are provided in the Administrative Procedure Act. In one version of rulemaking, agencies make regulations after holding formal hearings with live witnesses. This *formal rulemaking* is quasi-judicial in nature, meaning it works almost like a trial in court before a judge, with witnesses and evidence and a record of the proceedings, except that the judges are the commissioners or other officials of that agency.

---

7. *Whitman v. American Trucking Associations, Inc.*, 531 U.S. 457, 472 (2001).

But there is an alternative that agencies almost universally use: *informal rulemaking*, also known as *notice-and-comment rulemaking*. At the federal level, informal rulemaking takes place every day as shown in the voluminous notices published via the Federal Register and on Regulations.gov. Informal rulemaking is conducted in writing, via information and communication, with no live hearings or witnesses. The agency first gives public notice of proposed rules and solicits public comments on those proposed rules.[8] Comments submitted by the public are posted on Regulations.gov throughout the comment period; commenters can review what others have said if they wish, before crafting and submitting their own comments. (Chapter 16 uses this process to explore and give examples of persuasive writing on legal issues.)

After "consideration of the relevant matter presented,"[9] the agency then adopts and publishes its *final rule* in the Federal Register, along with a "concise general statement of [the] basis and purpose" for the final rule.[10] The final rule is then incorporated into the Code of Federal Regulations (CFR). The CFR is an organized subject-matter compilation of federal regulations that in form acts much as the United States Code does for federal statutes.

Here is a review of the informal rulemaking process, cross-referenced to the information it generates:

Steps in the informal rulemaking process	Information generated at this step
Agency proposes a regulation	Federal Register and Regulations.gov publish the proposed regulation
Agency takes comments	Comments collected by the agency and available on Regulations.gov
Agency publishes final regulation with explanation addressing the material comments it received	Federal Register and Regulations.gov publish the final regulation and explanation
Regulation needs to be easier to find than solely by chronologically searching the Federal Register	Regulations collected into a monthly hard-copy publication, the List of Sections Affected
Regulation needs to be incorporated into the Code of Federal Regulations	Regulations incorporated into the published hard-copy Code of Federal Regulations on a quarterly basis on a daily basis on the unofficial but widely used eCFR at www.ecfr.gov

The process also builds on itself in a way: a final regulation may be amended, replaced, or deleted through the same process. Apart from the statutory requirements of the Administrative Procedure Act, which can be enforced in the judicial branch, administrative agencies are checked in a number of ways, from congressional control over

---

8. 5 U.S.C. § 553(c).

9. *Id.*

10. *Id.*

the budget, to judicial review, to presidential removal powers over top officials in executive agencies. Administrative law is a complex procedural topic with far-reaching consequences at the state and federal levels. If you are interested in investigating this topic further, consult a guide to administrative law, such as the ABA's helpful publication *A Blackletter Statement of Administrative Law* (2d ed. 2014).

II. Agencies and Their Statutory Mandates

An administrative agency gets its authority, and the limits on its authority, from the applicable legislature (federal or state). The legislature must first create an agency and then provide it with authorization to act within its delegated authority. For example, Congress has charged the National Park Service with overseeing the nation's national parks:

> The Secretary, acting through the Director of the National Park Service, shall promote and regulate the use of the National Park System by means and measures that conform to the fundamental purpose of the System units, which purpose is to conserve the scenery, natural and historic objects, and wild life in the System units and to provide for the enjoyment of the scenery, natural and historic objects, and wild life in such manner and by such means as will leave them unimpaired for the enjoyment of future generations.[11]

The example above shows that statutory research can reveal the legislature's mandate to an agency. You will also often find an agency's statutory mandate recited in the agency's own regulations. For example, at the state (and quasi-state, in the case of the District of Columbia) level, the District of Columbia has legalized marijuana, and it has a number of regulations regarding marijuana and controlled substances. Here is the introduction to its regulations on point:

> 1000.1 The rules in this chapter contain the procedures governing the registration and regulation of manufacturers, distributors, and dispensers of controlled substances pursuant to Title III of the District of Columbia Uniform Controlled Substances Act of 1981 (D.C. Law 4-29, effective August 5, 1981, §§ 48-901.02 et seq.)(2001), hereinafter referred to as the "Act."
>
> 1000.2 To the extent consistent with the Act, regulations promulgated by the Federal Government pursuant to Title 21, Chapter II, of the Code of Federal Regulations (21 C.F.R. Part 1300 to End), and in effect as of the effective date of this chapter, shall be used as a guide in administering the Act.[12]

---

11. 54 U.S.C. § 100101.
12. D.C. Mun. Regs. Subt. 22-B, § 1000

Most, if not all, federal and state agencies also maintain websites where they communicate with the public about their activities and authority. For example, the Food and Drug Administration is a sprawling federal agency with an expansive regulatory jurisdiction. The FDA's website sets out its various congressional mandates on a separate page.[13] The website is further divided into tabs for the major regulated areas such as "food" and "drugs" and "medical devices" and so on. These tabs allow visitors to the webpage to focus on regulations, guidance documents, and other information relevant to one regulated area.

Depending on your goals as a researcher, you may want to find the statutory mandate as part of your legal research. For example, to comment on a proposed regulation, a researcher should find the statutory mandate because it could provide important arguments about what the agency should or should not do. The statutory mandate may also be useful in informing the public about an agency's activities. Many people seem to be suspicious of regulations, but they might not understand that state and federal regulatory regimes originated as a product of the democratic process through the legislature. Authority that Congress delegates can, after all, be taken back if Congress so wishes, and it has done precisely that on a few occasions.

You may not need to find the statutory mandate if your research is more detail-oriented. To find a specific regulation and then parse that regulation to understand it, you may not need to engage with the broader question of its statutory mandate.

III. Researching Administrative Law

Researching administrative law can be challenging, but in many ways it has been the greatest beneficiary of the internet revolution. Government sources once considered obscure or tucked away in special depository libraries are now available at the click of a mouse. In this section, we will consider some important administrative law sources and their websites.

A. The Federal Register (and State Counterparts)

Federal and state agencies do a lot of work, and thus they generate a vast amount of information each business day. The daily business of the administrative state is recorded in a "register." At the federal level, the Federal Register collects and publishes the administrative information that is required to be published. For example, notices of proposed rulemaking and final rulemakings must be published in the Federal Register. The Federal Register is published in physical form as a notebook-sized paperback with newsprint pages, also available in PDF. You can recognize a page of the printed Federal Register by its distinctive column format:

---

13. *Law Enforced by the FDA,* U.S. Food & Drug Administration (Mar 29, 2018), https://www.fda.gov/RegulatoryInformation/LawsEnforcedbyFDA/default.htm

Figure 9-1

23804 Federal Register / Vol. 83, No. 100 / Wednesday, May 23, 2018 / Rules and Regulations

Richmond, VA, Richmond Intl, RNAV (GPS) Z RWY 34, Amdt 1D
Richmond, VA, Richmond Intl, RNAV (RNP) Y RWY 2, Orig-B
Richmond, VA, Richmond Intl, RNAV (RNP) Y RWY 16, Orig-C
Richmond, VA, Richmond Intl, RNAV (RNP) Y RWY 20, Orig-B
Richmond, VA, Richmond Intl, RNAV (RNP) Y RWY 34, Orig-C
Highgate, VT, Franklin County State, VOR RWY 19, Amdt 5B
Burlington, WI, Burlington Muni, VOR RWY 29, Amdt 8B, CANCELED
Milwaukee, WI, Lawrence J Timmerman, LOC RWY 15L, Amdt 6D

Rescinded: On April 9, 2018 (83 FR 15052), the FAA published an Amendment in Docket No. 31186, Amdt No. 3793, to Part 97 of the Federal Aviation Regulations under section 97.33. The following entry for Kailua/Kona, HI, effective April 26, 2018, is hereby rescinded in its entirety:

Kailua/Kona, HI, Ellison Onizuka Kona Intl at Keahole, RNAV (RNP) Z RWY 17, Orig-B

[FR Doc. 2018–10818 Filed 5–22–18; 8:45 am]
BILLING CODE 4910–13–P

DEPARTMENT OF TRANSPORTATION

Office of the Secretary

14 CFR Part 382

[Docket No. DOT–OST–2018–0067]

Nondiscrimination on the Basis of Disability in Air Travel

AGENCY: Office of the Secretary (OST), U.S. Department of Transportation (DOT).

ACTION: Interim statement of enforcement priorities.

SUMMARY: The U.S. Department of Transportation (DOT or the Department) is issuing a statement of enforcement priorities to apprise the public of its intended enforcement focus with respect to transportation of service animals in the cabin of aircraft. The Department regulates the transportation of service animals under the Air Carrier Access Act (ACAA) and its implementing regulation. The Department seeks comment on this interim statement, and intends to issue a final statement after the close of the comment period.

DATES: The interim statement of enforcement proprieties is applicable May 23, 2018. Comments should be filed by June 7, 2018. Late-filed comments will be considered to the extent practicable.

ADDRESSES: You may file comments identified by the docket number DOT–OST–2018–0067 by any of the following methods:

• *Federal eRulemaking Portal:* Go to *https://www.regulations.gov* and follow the online instructions for submitting comments.
• *Mail:* Docket Management Facility, U.S. Department of Transportation, 1200 New Jersey Ave. SE, West Building Ground Floor, Room W12–140, Washington, DC 20590–0001.
• *Hand Delivery or Courier:* West Building Ground Floor, Room W12–140, 1200 New Jersey Ave. SE, between 9:00 a.m. and 5:00 p.m. ET, Monday through Friday, except Federal holidays.
• *Fax:* 202–493–2251.

Instructions: You must include the agency name and docket number DOT–OST–2018–0067 at the beginning of your comment. All comments received will be posted without change to *https://www.regulations.gov*, including any personal information provided.

Privacy Act: Anyone can search the electronic form of all comments received in any of our dockets by the name of the individual submitting the comment (or signing the comment, if submitted on behalf of an association, business, labor union, etc.). You may review DOT's complete Privacy Act statement in the **Federal Register** published on April 11, 2000 (65 FR 19477–78), or you may visit *https://www.transportation.gov/privacy*.

Docket: For access to the docket to read background documents and comments received, go to *https://www.regulations.gov* or to the street address listed above. Follow the online instructions for accessing the docket.

FOR FURTHER INFORMATION CONTACT: Robert Gorman, Senior Trial Attorney, or Blane A. Workie, Assistant General Counsel, Office of Aviation Enforcement and Proceedings, U.S. Department of Transportation, 1200 New Jersey Ave. SE, Washington, DC 20590, 202–366–9342, 202–366–7152 (fax), *robert.gorman@dot.gov* or *blane.workie@dot.gov* (email).

SUPPLEMENTARY INFORMATION:

Background

The Air Carrier Access Act (ACAA) prohibits discrimination in airline service on the basis of disability. 49 U.S.C. 41705. DOT's rule implementing the ACAA generally requires that airlines permit an individual with a disability to travel with his or her service animal in the cabin at no additional charge. 14 CFR 382.31(a). Service animals play a vital role in the lives of many individuals with disabilities. For example, service animals serve as guides for persons with visual impairments, notify persons who are deaf or hard of hearing of public

announcements and/or possible hazards, warn persons with post-traumatic stress disorder or other mental or emotional disabilities at the onset of an emotional crisis, and retrieve items for passengers with mobility impairments. At the same time, the Department recognizes that airlines have a responsibility to ensure the health, safety, and welfare of all of its passengers and employees. In enforcing the requirements of Federal law, the Department is committed to ensuring that our air transportation system is safe and accessible for everyone.

DOT requires airlines to allow a wide variety of service animals in the cabin of aircraft flying to, from, and within the United States. Under the ACAA, the Department considers a service animal to be any animal that is individually trained to assist a person with a disability, or an animal that is necessary for the emotional well-being of a passenger. 14 CFR 382.117(e) and Guidance Concerning Service Animals in Air Transportation, 73 FR 27614, 27658 (May 13, 2008). However, airlines are never required to accept snakes, reptiles, ferrets, rodents, sugar gliders, and spiders. Airlines may also exclude animals that are too large or heavy to be accommodated in the cabin, pose a direct threat to the health or safety of others, cause a significant disruption of cabin service, or are prohibited from entering a foreign country. 14 CFR 382.117(f). In addition, airlines may deny transport to a service animal that is not well-behaved, suggesting a lack of proper training. 14 CFR 382.117(i) and Guidance Concerning Service Animals in Air Transportation, 73 FR 27614, 27659 (May 13, 2008). Foreign air carriers are required to only transport dogs. 14 CFR 382.117(f).

Under DOT rules, airlines determine whether an animal is a service animal or pet by the credible verbal assurance of an individual with a disability using the animal, or by looking for physical indicators such as the presence of a harness or tags. 14 CFR 382.117(d). If the animal is a psychiatric service animal (PSA) or an emotional support animal (ESA), airlines may also require documentation by a licensed mental health professional stating that the passenger has a mental or emotional disability recognized in the Diagnostic and Statistical Manual of Mental Disorders IV (DSM–IV) and that the passenger needs the animal for air travel or activity at the passenger's destination. 14 CFR 382.117(e). Airlines may also require 48 hours' advance notice and check-in one hour before the check-in time for the general public as a condition for travel with an ESA or

---

The same information for each day's issue of the Federal Register is also available in a web version at https://www.federalregister.gov/. Figure 9-2 shows the top of the first page in that version:

Figure 9-2

Each day's issue of the Federal Register begins with a Table of Contents listing every agency with an entry in that day's issue. The Federal Register for May 23, 2018, has three pages just for its Table of Contents; the full issue runs 237 pages.

State administrative law generally functions in much the same way. State legislatures can and often do enact a state statute at least somewhat similar to the federal Administrative Procedure Act; a Model State Administrative Procedure Act[14] is available for states wishing to adopt legislation "off the shelf," so to speak. Colorado, for example has an Administrative Organization Act[15] setting up state agencies and a State Administrative Procedure Act[16] providing their authority and procedures for rulemaking and administrative adjudication.

Similar to the federal system, the states also publish registers but in slightly different formats from state to state. For example, the state of New Jersey publishes the New Jersey

---

14. Uniform Law Commission, Model State Administrative Procedure Act, Revised (2010).

15. Colo. Rev. Stat. § 24-1-101–137 (2019).

16. Colo. Rev. Stat. § 24-4-101–24-4-108 (2019).

Register and Administrative Code via Lexis (no fee or password required for this portion of the information). The state of Texas publishes the Texas Register on its own official state website. In Florida, the Administrative Code (with regulations in force) and the Administrative Register (with pending regulations and other activity) are combined into one website, the Florida Administrative Code and Florida Administrative Register. In New York, the New York Code, Rules, and Regulations are found under one tab on the Secretary of State's website, and the New York Register is found under another tab.[17]

The Federal Register publishes a great deal of information, but not *all* administrative information. Administrative documents that *must* be published in the Federal Register include the following:

- Rules created through formal rulemaking with quasi-adjudicatory process
- Rules created through informal rulemaking with notice to the public of proposed rulemaking, a period in which the agency accepts public comments, and then a final rulemaking with explanation of how the agency addressed the public comments
- Executive Orders of the President

Administrative documents that need not be published in the Federal Register include the following:

- Agency opinion letters in response to queries
- Agency policy statements and interpretive guidelines
- Agency manuals and internal directives
- Administrative adjudications of individual cases decided by administrative judges (discussed later in this chapter)

To sum up this overview, agencies cannot just declare their regulations by fiat. The process of rulemaking — that is, the process of promulgating regulations — is highly managed and controlled by statute at both the federal and state levels. State administrative procedure acts are similar in their structure and function. Informal rulemaking is by far the more popular procedure for promulgating administrative rules. And despite its name, "informal" rulemaking has quite a bit of formality to it, as a perusal of a typical day's Federal Register reveals.

B. Regulations.gov

Regulations.gov publishes a broad variety of federal regulations and related information: rules, proposed rules, comments, and other forms of administrative law information. Some of the features on the Regulations.gov website include:

---

17. Each of these state-specific administrative-law resources are easily locatable using a state-government portal or search engine; thus we do not provide the unwieldy URL citations here.

- A search box that searches broadly for rules, comments, adjudications, or supporting documents
- An advanced search feature that allows more precise searching
- Lists of "trending" notice-and-comment opportunities
- A calendar of "comments due soon" and "newly posted" opportunities to comment
- A tab for browsing "featured" regulations by alphabetical topic from aerospace to technology
- A tab for learning about the regulatory process

C. The New Govinfo.gov

A key site for federal administrative law research is www.govinfo.gov. On the Govinfo site, you can search and browse many types of administrative documents:

- General regulatory collection (https://www.govinfo.gov/app/browse/category/regulatory-info)
- The Federal Register as of the date you open the site (https://www.govinfo.gov/app/frtoc/today) and historically day-by-day (https://www.govinfo.gov/app/collection/fr)
- The Code of Federal Regulations for the current year, in official form and updated quarterly, as well as past years (https://www.govinfo.gov/app/collection/cfr)
- The electronic CFR, which is updated daily although it is not the official Code of Federal Regulations (www.ecfr.gov).
- The Unified Agenda, which is the semiannual posting of what federal agencies have done and are planning to do (https://www.govinfo.gov/collection/unified-agenda?path=/GPO/Unified%20Agenda)

As of December 2018, Govinfo.gov is replacing the well-known FDsys.gov site, which in turn replaced www.GPOAccess.gov. These changes reflect the fact that both public and privately maintained websites with official and unofficial information are always changing. Links to FDsys and GPOAcess should still work, but those connections may erode over time as systems are maintained and updated differently. A legally literate researcher should always be curious about new updates in how the state and federal governments are publishing information, and should not expect that well-established, useful sites will stay the same. Whether on publicly accessible government-sponsored sites or on commercial fee-based research platforms, the only constant is change.

D. Agency Websites

If you know which agency regulates the area you are researching, an alternative to these powerful but extremely broad websites is to go directly to the agency website for your legal information needs. Federal agencies are listed, with links, on USA.gov. States may have a single page collecting links for all of that state's agencies.

Determining which agency regulates the area you are researching may be easy or not so easy. For example, it is commonly known that the Food and Drug Administration regulates medical devices.[18] In contrast, which agency defines what a "farm" is? The FDA regulates food, and the Department of Agriculture regulates agriculture, but agricultural farms produce food—so who controls the regulatory definition of "farm"—the FDA or the Department of Agriculture? The answer turns out to be "both," and with different definitions.[19]

The point here is that going to an agency website for regulations could be the most precise way to do targeted research, but it could also be too narrow. A law librarian, lawyer, compliance professional, or other expert in the field will likely have useful advice about how to select and use an agency website alongside other resources for administrative law research.

E. State-Specific Administrative Law Sites

State administrative law is different in each state, but generally follows the broad framework in the federal Administrative Procedure Act: agencies must follow a statutory mandate and must give notice and the opportunity to comment on proposed regulations before finalizing them.

Selected resources that collect links to each state's official sources of administrative law include:

- Cornell Legal Information Institute, state listing with administrative codes of many states, https://www.law.cornell.edu/states/listing
- Findlaw for Legal Professionals, state listing with administrative codes of many states, https://caselaw.findlaw.com/
- States should have a single official page for public access to government services with links to all of that state's agencies, such as California (CA.gov) and Texas (Texas.gov)

---

18. *Medical Devices,* U.S. Food & Drug Administration, (June 16, 2018) https://www.fda.gov/Medical-Devices/default.htm.

19. Compare 7 C.F.R. § 4284.902 (one definition of farm or ranch promulgated by the Department of Agriculture) with 21 C.F.R. § 1.227 (one definition of farm by the Food and Drug Administration). These are just representative examples from each agency; in fact, each agency has created multiple definitions of "farm" for different legal contexts. One way to manage this complexity and find the right definition in context is to browse within the relevant segment of the C.F.R., which is organized by titles, which are broken into chapters, which are broken into parts, which are broken into sections.

F. Agency Guidance

Beyond the informal and formal rulemaking processes, agencies issue interpretive rules, policy statements, and other guidance. The Administrative Conference of the United States (ACUS) is an independent federal agency with the statutory mandate to study problems with the administrative state and develop recommendations, promote public participation and efficiency in rulemaking, reduce litigation, improve the use of science in the regulatory process, and improve the laws that apply to the regulatory process.[20] In 2017, the ACUS issued a report, *Federal Agency Guidance: An Institutional Perspective*,[21] and a set of recommendations[22] advocating reforms such as limits on the use of policy statements and more public participation in the content of policy statements. As an example of seeking public participation on the role of guidance itself, from February to July 2018, the Consumer Financial Protection Bureau sought comments on how it uses guidance materials in carrying out its activities.[23] The Supreme Court, in assessing agency guidance, gives it less deference than the Court gives to regulations promulgated pursuant to notice and comment.[24] Notice-and-comment rulemaking is, after all, a much more deliberative and public process than most issuances of agency guidance.

Because policy statements and other guidance can be influential even though they should not create new rights and obligations, legal researchers working on regulatory research should consider searching for agency guidance as well as regulations. Guidance is published in the Federal Register, but the best source of agency guidance is likely going to be the agency website. Secondary research may also help uncover the way guidance is being used—for example, are judicial opinions citing and relying on agency guidance as an influential source?

Legal researchers should of course use information literacy and critical reading to assess the information they may find. For example, a search for "FAA service animal guidance" returned near the top of search results a link to a Power Point presentation

---

20. 5 U.S.C. § 591 (2018).

21. Nicholas Parrillo, *Federal Agency Guidance: An Institutional Perspective*, Administrative Conference of the United States (October 12, 2017).

22. Administrative Conference of the United States, *Agency Guidance through Policy Statements*, Recommendation No. 2017-5 (December 22, 2017).

23. Consumer Financial Protection Bureau, Requests for Information: Bureau Guidance and Support, 83 Fed. Reg. 13959 (April 2, 2018).

24. *See Christensen v. Harris County*, 529 U.S. 576 (2000) (concluding that Department of Labor's opinion letter was entitled lesser deference under the test in *Skidmore v. Swift & Co.*, 323 U.S. 134 (1944), contrasted with the more deferential treatment of agency regulations under *Chevron U.S.A., Inc. v. Natural Resources Defense Council, Inc.*, 467 U.S. 836 (1984)).

titled "Service Animal Relief Areas: Guidance and Best Practices."[25] This title may suggest the document is itself agency guidance, but on closer inspection, this Power Point is a presentation made *to* the FAA on guidance and best practices for "relief areas" for service animals. Just because this Power Point was found on a .gov website and contains the word "guidance" in the title does not make it official agency guidance.

IV. Reading and Interpreting Agency Rules and Guidance

Reading rules and rule-like information is like reading statutes—except on steroids. Administrative agencies' specialized expertise is why they are needed, but also why their primary information can be highly detailed and thus challenging to read and understand. Agencies also publish helpful consumer-oriented material to explain their regulations in simpler language. As a legally literate researcher, you will want to distinguish between the primary rules and guidance, and the explanatory material that presents the law to the general public.

The reading skills already discussed in this book will help you with reading regulations and other primary administrative sources:

- Read for key terms
- Read for structure
- Read for connections with other regulations

Particularly with regulations, it can be helpful to look at a regulation within the larger regulatory scheme around it. For example, the regulation governing service animals on commercial airlines is 14 C.F.R. § 382.117. Figure 9-3 shows a screenshot of that regulation from the eCFR, showing that it is part of a larger Subpart H for "Services on Aircraft":

---

25. Laurel Van Horn, Open Doors Organization, *Service Animal Relief Areas: Guidance and Best Practices*, Presentation to FAA National Civil Rights Training Conference for Airports (September 7–9, 2016).

Figure 9-3

Home
gpo.gov
govinfo.gov

Browse / Search Previous

e-CFR Navigation Aids
Browse
Simple Search

Advanced Search
— Boolean
— Proximity

Search History
Search Tips
Corrections
Latest Updates
User Info
FAQs
Agency List
Incorporation By Reference

Electronic Code of Federal Regulations
e-CFR

Related Resources
The Code of Federal Regulations (CFR) annual edition is the codification of the general and permanent rules published in the FEDERAL REGISTER by the departments and agencies of the Federal Government produced by the Office of the Federal Register (OFR) and the Government Publishing Office.

Download the Code of Federal Regulations in XML.

Download the Electronic Code of Federal Regulations in XML.

Monthly Title and Part user viewing data for the e-CFR is available for download in CSV format.

Parallel Table of Authorities and Rules for the Code of Federal Regulations and the United States Code
Text | PDF

Find, review, and submit comments on Federal rules that are open for comment and published in the FEDERAL REGISTER using Regulations.gov.

Purchase individual CFR titles from the U.S. Government Online Bookstore.

Find issues of the CFR (including issues prior to 1996) at a local Federal depository library.

[A2]

Electronic Code of Federal Regulations

e-CFR data is current as of August 13, 2019

Title 14 → Chapter II → Subchapter D → Part 382 → Subpart H → §382.117

Browse Previous | Browse Next

Title 14: Aeronautics and Space
PART 382—NONDISCRIMINATION ON THE BASIS OF DISABILITY IN AIR TRAVEL
Subpart H—Services on Aircraft

§382.117   Must carriers permit passengers with a disability to travel with service animals?

(a) As a carrier, you must permit a service animal to accompany a passenger with a disability.

(1) You must not deny transportation to a service animal on the basis that its carriage may offend or annoy carrier personnel or persons traveling on the aircraft.

(2) On a flight segment scheduled to take 8 hours or more, you may, as a condition of permitting a service animal to travel in the cabin, require the passenger using the service animal to provide documentation that the animal will not need to relieve itself on the flight or that the animal can relieve itself in a way that does not create a health or sanitation issue on the flight.

(b) You must permit the service animal to accompany the passenger with a disability at any seat in which the passenger sits, unless the animal obstructs an aisle or other area that must remain unobstructed to facilitate an emergency evacuation.

(c) If a service animal cannot be accommodated at the seat location of the passenger with a disability who is using the animal, you must offer the passenger the opportunity to move with the animal to another seat location, if present on the aircraft, where the animal can be accommodated.

(d) As evidence that an animal is a service animal, you must accept identification cards, other written documentation, presence of harnesses, tags, or the credible verbal assurances of a qualified individual with a disability using the animal.

(e) If a passenger seeks to travel with an animal that is used as an emotional support or psychiatric service animal, you are not required to accept the animal for transportation in the cabin unless the passenger provides you current documentation (*i.e.*, no older than one year from the date of the passenger's scheduled initial flight) on the letterhead of a licensed mental health professional (*e.g.*, psychiatrist, psychologist, licensed clinical social worker, including a medical doctor specifically treating the passenger's mental or emotional disability) stating the following:

(1) The passenger has a mental or emotional disability recognized in the Diagnostic and Statistical Manual of Mental Disorders—Fourth Edition (DSM IV);

(2) The passenger needs the emotional support or psychiatric service animal as an accommodation for air travel and/or for activity at the passenger's destination;

(3) The individual providing the assessment is a licensed mental health professional, and the passenger is under his or her professional care; and

(4) The date and type of the mental health professional's license and the state or other jurisdiction in which it was issued.

(f) You are never required to accommodate certain unusual service animals (*e.g.*, snakes, other reptiles, ferrets, rodents, and spiders) as service animals in the cabin. With respect to all other animals, including unusual or exotic animals that are presented as service animals (*e.g.*, miniature horses, pigs, monkeys), as a carrier you

By clicking on the link to Subpart H, a researcher can unfold it and see the surrounding sections, a helpful step to gain more context for 14 C.F.R. § 382.117:

Figure 9-4

Electronic Code of Federal Regulations

e-CFR data is current as of August 13, 2019

Home
gpo.gov
govinfo.gov

Browse / Search Previous

e-CFR Navigation Aids
Browse
Simple Search

Advanced Search
— Boolean
— Proximity

Search History
Search Tips
Corrections
Latest Updates
User Info
FAQs
Agency List
Incorporation By Reference

Electronic Code of Federal Regulations
e-CFR

Related Resources

The Code of Federal Regulations (CFR) annual edition is the codification of the general and permanent rules published in the Federal Register by the departments and agencies of the Federal Government produced by the Office of the Federal Register (OFR) and the Government Publishing Office.

Download the Code of Federal Regulations in XML.

Download the Electronic Code of Federal Regulations in XML.

Monthly Title and Part user viewing data for the e-CFR is available for download in CSV format.

Parallel Table of Authorities and Rules for the Code of Federal Regulations and the United States Code
Text | PDF

Find, review, and submit comments on Federal rules that are open for comment and published in the Federal Register using Regulations.gov.

Purchase individual CFR titles from the U.S. Government Online Bookstore.

Find issues of the CFR (including issues prior to 1996) at a local Federal depository library.

[A1]

Title 14 → Chapter II → Subchapter D → Part 382 → Subpart H

Browse Previous | Browse Next

Title 14: Aeronautics and Space
PART 382—NONDISCRIMINATION ON THE BASIS OF DISABILITY IN AIR TRAVEL

Subpart H—Services on Aircraft

Contents
§382.111 What services must carriers provide to passengers with a disability on board the aircraft?
§382.113 What services are carriers not required to provide to passengers with a disability on board the aircraft?
§382.115 What requirements apply to on-board safety briefings?
§382.117 Must carriers permit passengers with a disability to travel with service animals?
§382.119 What information must carriers give individuals with vision or hearing impairment on aircraft?

↰ Back to Top

§382.111 What services must carriers provide to passengers with a disability on board the aircraft?

As a carrier, you must provide services within the aircraft cabin as requested by or on behalf of passengers with a disability, or when offered by carrier personnel and accepted by passengers with a disability, as follows:

(a) Assistance in moving to and from seats, as part of the enplaning and deplaning processes;

(b) Assistance in preparation for eating, such as opening packages and identifying food;

(c) If there is an on-board wheelchair on the aircraft, assistance with the use of the on-board wheelchair to enable the person to move to and from a lavatory;

(d) Assistance to a semi-ambulatory person in moving to and from the lavatory, not involving lifting or carrying the person; or

(e) Assistance in stowing and retrieving carry-on items, including mobility aids and other assistive devices stowed in the cabin (*see also* 382.91(d)). To receive such assistance, the passenger must self-identify as being an individual with a disability needing the assistance.

(f) Effective communication with passengers who have vision impairments or who are deaf or hard-of-hearing, so that these passengers have prompt access to information the carrier provides to other passengers (*e.g.* weather, on-board services, flight delays, connecting gates at the next airport).

[Doc. No. DOT-OST-2004-19482, 73 FR 27665, May 13, 2008, as amended at 75 FR 44887, July 30, 2010]

↰ Back to Top

§382.113 What services are carriers not required to provide to passengers with a disability on board the aircraft?

As a carrier, you are not required to provide extensive special assistance to qualified individuals with a disability. For purposes of this section, extensive special assistance includes the following activities:

And Subpart H on "Services on Aircraft" is part of an even larger topic, Part 382, which covers "Nondiscrimination on the Basis of Disability in Air Travel." The same steps can be followed to unfold Part 382 and see the table of contents for each section in that Part. This example reinforces, yet again, the importance of flexibility and curiosity in conducting legal research and interpreting legal information. Other research websites, such as the Cornell Legal Information Institute's site, provide similar structural context.

V. Administrative Adjudicatory Decisions

In many regulated areas, disputes can or must first be handled through the administrative process. An agency with adjudicatory powers may publish its decisions on its website. For example, federal contractors can use the administrative process to file bid protests. Two key sites for finding bid-protest decisions are the Civilian Board of Contract Appeals' website or Government Accountability office website.

In general, decisions by administrative courts do not create formal precedent or stare decisis that the same decision-maker must later follow, even when the decisions are expressed in detailed written opinions. However, administrative decisions may provide important information about the agency's approach. Academic law library websites may be a good resource for finding general updates and collected research guidance on how to find administrative decisions.[26]

VI. Conclusion

Finding and interpreting administrative law materials requires a structural understanding of the administrative state plus careful research skills. Research into administrative law, as with legislative research, typically requires the use of government publications drawn from free official sites. Administrative research may also benefit from secondary and other contextual research when available, but some administrative questions are so specific and arcane that the researcher must be able to handle the task independently. Whether you believe the administrative state is necessary, expert, and even beneficial, or unruly and captive to special interests and not so beneficial, researching administrative law will reveal numerous examples of administrative agencies going about their work.

Having studied this chapter, you should be able to:

- Summarize what administrative agencies do and what information they produce
- Find regulations and agency guidance in free online government sources
- Explain the connection between an agency's regulatory activity and its statutory mandate
- Research and identify administrative adjudications

---

26. E.g., University of Virginia Law Library Guide to Administrative Decisions, https://guides.lib.virginia.edu/administrative_decisions

Case Study

Olivia Ralston is preparing to open her new coffee shop. She is determined to offer both dairy cream and dairy alternatives as creamers. She has secured a supply of oat milk from a local distributor, and wishes to relabel it with her own branding: "Oat Milk from Olivia's Beans." She will check any federal and Colorado state regulations on food labeling and identification rules for milk and milk alternatives such as oat milk and almond milk. She is documenting her findings for her own files in deciding how to proceed.

Traditions and Trends

Since the original 1946 enactment by Congress of the Administrative Procedure Act, administrative agencies have promulgated rules through two channels: formal rulemaking in a court-like hearing format that produces a written transcript (rarely used); and informal rulemaking (heavily used). Informal rulemaking relies exclusively on written information, with the agency publishing its notice of a proposed rulemaking in the Federal Register, then taking comments from the public, then publishing the final rule in the Federal Register. Once finalized, a rule was collated in the monthly pamphlet called the List of Sections Affected, and then integrated into hard copy of the Code of Federal Regulations. Traditionally, the mechanism for filing a comment was to mail it to the address listed in the notice. Interest groups sometimes shared a template comment with their members to consider reproducing and submitting as a sign of support. The mechanism to access comments already on file during a pending comment period was through a request to the agency; comments were shared with the public via photocopies or scanned files. Agencies also published interpretive guidance documents in the Federal Register, although guidance is not law in the same way as a rule made through notice and comment.

As with so many areas of legal information and legal research, the movement of legal information to the internet drives the trends in regulations and administrative information generally. Agencies publish their guiding statutes, regulations, guidance documents, and other resources for public use. Courts relying on regulatory information in their judicial opinions may cite websites and PDFs by hyperlinks, which may end up being removed (the dead-link problem) or changed (thus reflecting different information than what the opinion intended to cite).

General websites managed by umbrella agencies such as the Library of Congress are periodically overhauled or replaced, generally with more flexible options for research and online tasks. The Regulations.gov site now offers an online form for submitting comments. It also offers updated monitoring and access to comments filed in open comment periods. These capabilities are connected to the trend of "robo-comments" in which a similar comment is reproduced and uploaded hundreds if not thousands of times. The trend of online commenting is thus a positive for public participation in the administrative rulemaking process, but also a potential negative for the possibility of digital-comment overload from groups with sophisticated resources including—worst-case scenario—hackers seeking to influence and distort United States law.

Chapter 10

Finding and Reading Cases

"[T]here was a time when there were no rules … guid[ing] courts in making their decisions. With the development of the concept of equality and justice, the similarity of essential facts was observed in the earlier cases and made the basis of a formulated rule to serve as a guide for future cases. This process has extended over the whole field of litigated questions, so that a modern court called upon to decide a case will most frequently find, laid down in earlier cases, the rules needed for the determination of this particular controversy.… But as society developed from the simple to the complex, cases constantly arose, touching which no rule had as yet been formulated by the courts."

— Charles E. Carpenter, *Court Decisions and the Common Law*,
17 Colum. L. Rev. 593, 596 (1917).

Courts decide disputes between parties. Disputes can progress through the court system for months or even years before any court issues a written order concluding the case. Most orders are not appealed, but when a dispute does result in an appeal, the appellate court will decide the appeal in the form of a judicial opinion. And that opinion will likely be published as a "case" in a book and online. That case will be read and studied by people in the future trying to glean what the law is. That case becomes part of the "precedent," at least for some future disputes in its own jurisdiction.

Thus, legal literacy requires an understanding of the court system that produces judicial opinions, and the ability to find and interpret relevant judicial opinions. Interpreting judicial opinions means not just reading a single case but also placing cases into context with other cases. What if you find ten cases, none of which overrules any other, but each has a slightly different description of the law and various outcomes that may or may not be consistent with one another?

Chapter 4 of this text gave an overview of techniques for reading one case in isolation. This chapter focuses on researching cases in context on the internet, and interpreting them together. Cases build upon one another, with the courts following previously decided cases in their same jurisdiction—the famous principle of *stare decisis,* Latin for "to stand by things decided,"[1] which underlies the U.S. court system at both the federal and state levels. Thus, courts in the United States must follow the relevant constitution (federal or state) and statutory law, and must give some deference to regulations with the force of law, and they also follow their own binding precedents. But each case has slightly different facts, so courts have some flexibility in applying binding legal precedent to a new factual situation. Thus, legal literacy requires familiarity with how to find relevant cases and read them together with one another and in conjunction with other sources of law. We begin with an overview of the court structure in the federal and state systems.

I. The Structure of the Court System in the United States

Federal and state courts have a common structure with three layers. Cases start in a trial court, then get a first appeal to an intermediate appellate court, and then may have the opportunity for another appellate review by the highest court in the jurisdiction. Here is the court system, organized from left to right by where the case starts (at trial) to where it may finish (in the jurisdiction's highest court):

First: The trial court decides whether a case goes to trial, then holds a trial (before a jury or before the bench).

Second: The intermediate appellate court decides most appeals from trial.

Last: The high court in the jurisdiction generally has discretion on which appeals to take.

There are exceptions to this basic structure, of course. For example, many jurisdictions have specialized trial courts such as probate court, magistrate court (or small

---

1. Cornell Legal Information Institute, Legal Dictionary, *Stare Decisis,* https://www.law.cornell.edu/wex/stare_decisis

claims court), family court, juvenile court, and so on. Some jurisdictions have regional intermediate appellate courts that hear appeals from trial courts within their region, and others have just one intermediate appellate court for the whole state. And some cases go directly from trial to the highest court in the jurisdiction. But the basic three-step structure is still a useful way to picture both federal and state court systems.

These courts work together, but they do not all do exactly the same thing. Each has its own particular strengths and weaknesses, and the way a case progresses through the court system shows each court's role.

A. Trial Courts

The trial court is most interested in the facts. A case begins with a document alleging facts and one or more legal claims—namely a complaint in a civil case, or an indictment or other form of criminal charge. After that, the defendant responds to the initial complaint or charges, and the case continues on a path to trial. Trial courts are a hectic place both behind the scenes and in court; lawyers file briefs with attached affidavits and deposition transcripts to establish the facts leading up to trial. The trial court has to decide if the party bringing a complaint has enough facts to justify the cost and time of a trial. If not, the trial court will grant a motion for summary judgment (if the defendant files one, as is commonly done). The idea is to imagine whether a hypothetical reasonable jury—not *every* jury, but a reasonable jury out there in the world—could rule for the plaintiff on each required part of the plaintiff's claim. If not, then the case should not go any further. A motion that, if granted, would end a case before trial is known in litigation as a "dispositive motion." When granting a dispositive motion, trial courts write orders that explain their decisions to the parties.

If the case is not resolved by dispositive motions, that means the facts contain enough of a dispute to justify a trial. The trial may be a bench trial, which means the judge is the fact finder, or a jury trial, which means a jury selected from the pool of voters is the fact finder. That depends on what the plaintiff or prosecutor has demanded from the beginning of the case and whether the parties have agreed to a bench trial even though one has a right to demand a jury trial.

Throughout the case from the motions all the way through trial, the trial court is generating a "record" that is a collection of pages of everything it considered, from attorney filings and witness affidavits to the transcript of exactly what was said at trial. At trial, the judge works with the lawyers to create a list of jury instructions that tell the jury what the law is. In a way the judge is like a project manager for everyone involved in the case.[2] The jury fills in the blanks (sometimes literally) to decide the case.

At the trial level, much of the case takes place in public, in open courtrooms, with a court reporter transcribing all verbal exchanges. But in practical terms, most trials are

---

2. The pros and cons of judges as managers has been discussed for decades in legal scholarship. *See, e.g.*, Judith Resnik, *Managerial Judges: The Potential Costs*, 96 Harv. L. Rev. 374 (1982).

semi-private. Unless reporters or others are present, the decision-making process is apparent to the parties and their lawyers, but not many others.

A case ends in a final order at the trial level. Then the losing party decides whether to appeal. Before delving into that process, let us say a word about what the trial court's decision means. The trial court's decision is binding on the parties before it, unless reversed on appeal. But a trial court's decision is not binding precedent on future cases. If a case is decided in a state trial court in Denver, Colorado, today, and a factually similar case comes up next week, the trial court next week *does not have to* follow the holding from today because today's holding does not function as binding precedent. The trial court next week may choose to reach a conclusion consistent with the holding from today if lawyers or others make that trial court aware of that decision. But trying to find and alert trial courts to what previous trial courts have done is not part of trial lawyers' typical practice because trial-level decisions are merely persuasive, not binding. What a trial court *must* do is to follow state statutes and decisions of the state's highest court plus binding intermediate appellate decisions. That body of law (statutes and binding cases of higher appellate courts) is what the lawyers and the court refer to in pretrial motions, jury instructions, and other decisions at trial.

The merely persuasive nature of trial-court decisions does not mean, however, that these decisions have zero informational value. Some legal scholars and businesses specializing in "legal analytics" are very interested in empirical data about how trial courts decide cases. If most cases are decided at trial and never see an appeal, then data about what trial courts do could be informative and valuable. Scholars might want to study the patterns and statistics about a whole category of cases, to make a larger scholarly point about how the law works. And commercial research platforms and other businesses want to sell that information because they recognize a market for data-based prediction to supplement traditional predictive legal analysis and risk assessment.[3]

B. Appellate Courts

If the losing party does appeal, it will file a notice of appeal with the trial court and then take the case up to the intermediate appellate court. The appellate courts have a more limited role. They decide whether an error was made in the trial court below. They generally have two choices: "reverse" (change the result below) or "affirm" (agree with the result below). No new evidence can come into the record on appeal. What the appellate courts have before them — and *all* the appellate courts have before them — is the "record." The record means a record of all that happened at trial, in documentary form: typically, the parties' pleadings starting the case, the parties' motions at the trial level, the transcripts of depositions and trial proceedings, and orders by the trial court deciding

---

3. *See generally* Mark Osbeck, *Lawyer as Soothsayer: Exploring the Important Role of Outcome Prediction in the Practice of Law*, 123 Penn. St. L. Rev. 41 (2018).

various preliminary and final issues. While the appellate court can see the paper-based record of everything that happened at trial, what the appellate court never sees is an actual "live witness" giving testimony. Even if the record happens to include video testimony as part of the record, the appellate court does not evaluate whether any of the witnesses at trial were credible and truthful.

The appellate court also will consider the lawyers' written arguments on appeal, which are called "appellate briefs." The appellate court may allow the lawyers to argue the case in person at an oral argument. There, the lawyers each outline their strongest points, answer a barrage of questions from the appellate judges, and respond to weaknesses in their arguments.

Because the appellate court's role is limited in these ways, its decisions are also constrained by a procedural principle known as "the standard of review." The standard of review literally refers to the *standard* the appellate court applies in *reviewing* what the trial court did, and specifically how much *deference* the appellate court gives to what happened in the trial court. Should the appellate court defer to what happened below, meaning it respects the trial court's decision and hesitates to change it? That would be a more deferential standard of review. On the other hand, should the appellate court take a fresh look at what the trial court did, deciding for itself what the right answer is, without regard to what the trial court decided the first time? Reviewing something all over again from scratch like this is known as a "de novo" or "plenary" standard of review. This means the appellate court decides the question anew, without deferring whatsoever to what happened below.

What standard of review applies on appeal is itself a legal question, but there are well-established categories that depend on who decided the issue below at trial and when. Appellate courts are extraordinarily deferential to jury verdicts. Appellate courts are moderately deferential to decisions the trial court had to make in managing a trial, such as deciding whether to admit evidence presented by one of the parties. Appellate courts are not deferential to trial courts' decisions on preliminary motions to end the case before trial, such as motions to dismiss and motions for summary judgment. These motions are decided "on paper" without assessing the credibility of live witnesses, so appellate courts are in just as good a position to decide as the trial court. Appellate courts are also not deferential to trial courts' decisions on pure questions of law—for example, the interpretation of a statutory term.

Appellate courts' decisions are constrained by the way the appellate process works as described above, but their decisions have far-reaching consequences for future cases. In deciding the appeal, the appellate court will generally write a judicial opinion explaining its decision. "With very few exceptions, when appellate courts decide a case, they relay their outcome and the justification for it in the form of a written opinion. This written opinion serves a number of functions including constraining and guiding the behavior of other courts and judges, administrative agencies, litigants, and members of the broader public."[4] The written decisions of appellate courts are typically what is meant by the shorthand term "cases." Because appellate case law serves as the binding precedent constraining and guiding various actors in the legal system, being able to find and read those opinions is crucial.

The structure of the appellate review system typically involves not one but two layers of possible review. There is a first appeal to the intermediate court of appeal, described above. The first appeal is an appeal as of right, meaning the losing party has a right to that appeal simply by filing the required paperwork and fees for the appeal. That first appeal will be heard by the appropriate appellate court because the losing party has the right to it. The first appeal is heard by an "intermediate" appellate court of appeal, so-called because it is intermediate between the trial court and the highest court of that jurisdiction.

After the first review to that intermediate court of appeal, the losing party at the intermediate level may attempt to appeal to the highest court in the jurisdiction. The highest court in the jurisdiction is also known as the "court of last resort." You might assume the highest court in a jurisdiction is the "supreme court" of that jurisdiction, and often it is literally named as such: The high court in the federal system is the United States Supreme Court, and the high court in the state of Georgia is the Supreme Court of Georgia. But in some states, the state supreme court is not actually called "the Supreme Court." New York is the most famous example of this; its highest state court is the New York State Court of Appeals. In New York, the "Supreme Court" is the trial court, i.e., the lowest court in the court system.

It may seem inefficient to have two layers of review, but this system allows the high court to review the various decisions of the intermediate appellate courts and clarify possible inconsistencies. A jurisdiction's high court is not required to take every appeal; it generally has discretion to accept cases upon petition for further review.[5] In the United States Supreme Court, these are "petitions for certiorari" or "cert petitions." If the high court grants the petition, then the parties may go on to file another set of briefs on the merits of the case and the court may also grant oral argument. Then the court decides the case by issuing a judicial opinion. These opinions are where courts interpret the law, evaluate precedent, and apply law to facts under the governing standard of review. In their judicial opinions, appellate courts must explain what they are doing and why.

C. Federal and State Courts

The structure described above exists at both the federal and state level. The terminology is somewhat different in the federal and state systems; and as you can imagine, each state has its own terminology as well. This section gives a broad overview of the

---

4. Christina Boyd, *Opinion Writing in the Federal District Courts*, 36 Just. Sys. J. 254, 254 (2015).

5. Supreme courts often have a few select areas of mandatory appellate jurisdiction, but generally take appeals only upon using their discretion to grant a petition for certiorari.

structure and terminology for both. If you find yourself researching federal cases or cases in a particular state, you will want to dive even deeper into the court system and terminology of that particular jurisdiction.

1. Federal Courts

Federal courts are a product of the United States Constitution, Article III. Here is a basic diagram of the courts of the United States, i.e., the federal courts:

First: District courts are the trial level of the federal system. The district courts also hear appeals from the federal bankruptcy courts and magistrate courts.

Second: Circuit courts are the intermediate appellate level of the federal system. There are 12 regional circuit courts plus the Federal Circuit for specialized cases such as patent appeals.

Last: The United States Supreme Court grants petitions for certiorari in about 80 cases every year.

The district courts and circuit courts are arranged not only in this hierarchy, but also by geography. Although this is a *federal* court system, it uses state borders for certain purposes, as shown in this map from the United States Courts website:[6]

Figure 10-1

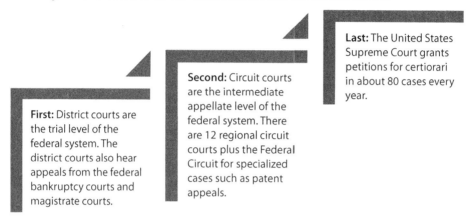

Geographic Boundaries
of United States Courts of Appeals and United States District Courts

6. United States Courts, *Geographical Boundaries of United States Courts of Appeals and United States District Courts*, https://www.uscourts.gov/sites/default/files/u.s._federal_courts_circuit_map_1.pdf

This map shows two important geographical aspects of the federal courts. They are divided into circuits—those are the large groups of states, such as the Ninth Circuit, which covers Washington, Montana, Oregon, Idaho, California, Nevada, and Arizona. Each circuit is divided into districts. Some district courts cover an entire state: the state of Nevada is one federal district—the District of Nevada. But some district courts cover just part of a state: the state of California has the Northern District, Eastern District, Central District, and Southern District.

Where can you sue someone in federal court? The federal courts use state boundaries in part because of jurisdiction. Federal jurisdiction is a complex question that has to do with where the defendant is physically located or does business, and whether the parties to a case are citizens of different states. A lawyer representing a plaintiff with a federal claim against someone located in Colorado would file the lawsuit in the District of Colorado because the plaintiff can assert jurisdiction over the defendant there. It bears repeating that jurisdiction is complicated, and relates not just to where the defendant is, but also what the nature of the claim is. For example, a party from California might sue a party from Arizona over a contract governed by Colorado law. There is no federal claim here at all, but the parties are "diverse," meaning they are from different states, and thus they may be able to have their case heard in federal court under the court's "diversity jurisdiction."[7]

Although the federal courts' jurisdiction relates to state boundaries, federal courts do not follow state law just because they are located in a particular state. The federal district court in the District of Colorado does not give any special deference to Colorado state law. If the federal district court is deciding a case with some aspect governed by Colorado state law, then it would apply Colorado law. But the applicable state law comes from the case itself, not from where the court is located. And the converse is also true: state courts in Colorado do not have to follow what the federal courts say about Colorado state law. If a federal court interprets Colorado law in a certain way, the Colorado courts can consider that interpretation as a persuasive authority, but they are not bound to follow it. The only exception would be if the federal court is declaring Colorado law unconstitutional under the U.S. Constitution; then, under the Supremacy Clause, the Colorado courts must follow. But for general interpretations of law, such as what a a Colorado statute means, Colorado state courts are bound by the Colorado Supreme Court, not by any federal court—up to and including the United States Supreme Court.

After a case is decided in a federal district court, the losing party may decide to appeal. Figure 10-1 shows the boundaries of the intermediate appellate courts in the federal system—what are referred to as the "circuit courts." There are eleven circuits

---

7. 28 U.S.C. § 1332 (2018). Beyond personal jurisdiction and subject matter jurisdiction, the case's location in federal court also depends on the procedural concepts of "venue" under 28 U.S.C. § 1391 and the court's discretionary authority to grant a motion for "forum non conveniens," meaning the case should be heard in a different location.

spread out over various regions in the United States plus the U.S. Circuit Court for the District of Columbia and the U.S. Circuit Court for the Federal Circuit. A party that loses in district court has one "appeal as of right" to the circuit court in the appropriate jurisdiction. For example, an appeal from the Northern District of Ohio would go to the United States Court of Appeals for the Sixth Circuit. There are some exceptions; for example, appeals of patent cases go to the United States Court of Appeals for the Federal Circuit.

The highest court in the land is the United States Supreme Court. This is what is referred to as "the court of last resort"; there is nowhere else to go once a case has been sent to the Supreme Court. Appealing to the Supreme Court means first petitioning for the right to have the appeal heard and decided. Parties must file a "petition for certiorari" to convince the Court it should hear the appeal because the Supreme Court has discretion over which cases it hears. The Supreme Court is not typically convinced by petitions that argue unfairness or mistaken application of law. "Circuit splits" are one well-known way to convince the Court to hear a case. That means one circuit court has reached a different result from another circuit court on the same question. The confusion this can sow nationally is a good reason for the Supreme Court to grant the certiorari petition and decide the law for the nation as a whole. The Supreme Court receives 7,000–8,000 certiorari petitions per year, and has, on average, granted petitions for 80 cases per year.[8]

For more information on the federal court system, we recommend exploring the United States Courts website at www.uscourts.gov and the Federal Bar Association's website at www.fedbar.org.

2. State Courts

State courts are similar in structure to the federal courts. At the lowest level, trial courts of general jurisdiction function as fact finders, holding bench and jury trials. Some states have trial courts that specialize in certain matters. Depending on the particular state, a court system may include probate court (meaning trusts and estates, which manage people's affairs after death), business court, divorce court, drug court, juvenile court, magistrate or "night" court, and other types of specialized courts.

Most states have an intermediate court of appeals for hearing the first appeal as of right from the trial court. Some of these state intermediate courts of appeals are unitary, meaning there is a single court of appeals for the whole state. Georgia is one example: it has one intermediate court of appeals, the Georgia Court of Appeals. Other state intermediate courts of appeals are divided, meaning they are organized into sub-districts, and opinions within those districts may be binding only within that dis-

---

8. SCOTUSblog.com, Supreme Court Procedure, http://www.scotusblog.com/reference/educational-resources/supreme-court-procedure/ (recommended as a readable overview of litigation from district court to Supreme Court).

trict's area of the state. Florida is one example: it has five districts for its Florida District Courts of Appeal. Texas is another example, as shown on the About Texas Courts page published by the Texas court system.[9] Anyone starting legal research in a new state should research that state court system's website to understand its structure.

The state's highest court takes certain cases by mandatory jurisdiction and most cases by discretionary jurisdiction. Thus, similar to the federal system, parties who want their case to be heard by the highest court in the state must file a petition for certiorari asking for the high court to exercise its discretion and hear the case.

State courts vary in their structures, but, whatever state you are researching, you can use online resources to learn how it works. Let's examine the state of Colorado as an example. A search engine can be used to find information about the state court system through a search such as "Colorado court system." This search reveals the result shown in Figure 10-2, a result that is promising because it appears to be the official site of the Colorado courts:

Figure 10-2

---

9. Texas Judicial Branch, About Texas Courts, http://www.txcourts.gov/about-texas-courts/

The Colorado State Court System's website reveals that the Colorado court has three levels: a trial court, an intermediate court of appeals (the Colorado Court of Appeals), and a state supreme court named the Colorado Supreme Court. At the trial level, the Colorado court system has a typical trial court of general jurisdiction, the District Court. There are 22 different districts. There are two specialized courts: Water Courts, which are organized into jurisdictions corresponding to river basins in Colorado and which handle disputes under the Water Rights Determination and Administration Act; and the County Courts in the various 22 districts, which handle smaller cases.

State court systems have many common features, but also many small variations. Thus, it bears repeating: Anyone starting legal research in a new state should research that state court system's website to understand its structure.

II. Researching Cases

Many cases are freely available online. Here are some of the free online resources for finding cases. These resources vary in scope.

- Google Scholar (check the "Cases" radio button), www.scholar.google.com
- Cornell Legal Information Institute (federal resources), https://www.law.cornell.edu/federal
- Cornell Legal Information Institute (state resources), https://www.law.cornell.edu/states/listing
- FindLaw, FindLaw for Legal Professionals, https://lp.findlaw.com/
- Justia, U.S. Law, https://law.justia.com/
- Administrative Office of the United States Courts, http://www.uscourts.gov/about-federal-courts/federal-courts-public/court-website-links

These sources make the law much more widely available for free. At the same time, precisely because they are free, these online websites may require some persistence and patience on the user's part. The links aren't always perfect; a broken link does not mean the entire site cannot be trusted. In terms of how to search case law, these sites vary widely. Many open-access databases have useful sorting mechanisms, discussed in more detail below.

Here are two resources that, as of late 2018, allow some degree of case research free with an email registration:

- Casetext: https://casetext.com/ (allowing case law to be searched and read, but separately offering a free trial of additional fee-based capabilities)
- Fastcase Mobile App (Apple App Store): https://itunes.apple.com/us/app/fastcase/id352470511

These sites could be described as "freemium" because they offer some content for free, but then encourage a fee-based sign-up for the full scope of premium services. Commercial legal research businesses constantly compete and upgrade to attempt to capture research accounts and user loyalty. They negotiate large contracts with big law firms, accounting firms, and other well-resourced users, while also selling to government and, on a very different scale, to small law firms and solo practitioners.

The subsections below address some key filtering skills for efficient case research. A key point to keep in mind is that legal-research platforms change all the time. Any screen shots of any website or platform, free or fee based, could become outdated before this book is even printed. The best advice we can give is to be an active and alert user of any research tool:

- Try the search box, but do not rely solely on default search settings.
- Find the research tool's "advanced search" or other filtering capabilities.
- Filter by jurisdiction and key term to find the cases you need.
- Use the research tool's capabilities to sort the results in the most effective way for your research.

With these big goals in mind, the subsections below cover filtering by jurisdiction and level of the court, key term, and date. Legal research is interesting partly because it is so flexible. Keep your own research goals in mind and make any website's search capabilities work for you.

A. Searching and Filtering for Jurisdiction

As shown by the first half of this chapter, judicial opinions — even appellate opinions — are not all of equal weight and importance. A federal case is not binding on a state court unless it's about the U.S. Constitution. A state case is not binding on a federal court unless it's about a state question being decided in the federal court. Here are some guidelines for selecting the jurisdiction to research cases. If you're not sure about whether your issue is state or federal or neither or both, go back to the basics and consult a secondary source for more context. (See chapter 7.)

1. Researching State Law

To research cases on a question of state law, focus on that state's own courts. In particular, focus on the appellate courts in that state — the state supreme court and the intermediate court of appeals. If your research is about Colorado law, you should research cases from Colorado, namely the Colorado Supreme Court and Colorado Court of Appeals.

Here are some examples of prototypical state-law research issues:

➡ Finding the state's precedent on intentional infliction of emotional distress
➡ Finding the state's definition of adverse possession in property law

➡ Finding the state's approach to covenants not to compete: are they permitted, are they void against public policy, or do they fall somewhere in between?

Researchers should be interested in state supreme court opinions and intermediate appellate opinions. The state supreme court would be authoritative and better authority than the intermediate appellate court. And both the state supreme court and intermediate appellate court are more authoritative on state law than federal courts interpreting state law. Federal courts sometimes encounter questions of state law because they hear cases involving both federal and state claims and they do have some jurisdiction over claims between citizens of different states. When that happens, they apply state law to the state issues in the case, but their opinions do not bind state courts. Thus to come full circle, the right place to look for questions of state law is that state's own appellate courts.

2. Researching Federal Law

If you are researching a question of federal law, the most obvious and correct answer is to research United States Supreme Court cases. Here are some examples where the Supreme Court research is the answer:

➡ Finding the most recent big case on whether police searches of cellphone site location data are constitutional under the Fourth Amendment

➡ Finding out how the Supreme Court applies fair use as a defense to copyright infringement in the United States

➡ Finding out whether mandatory union fees for government workers are constitutional under the First Amendment

The Supreme Court decides only about 80 cases a year, and it often allows issues to percolate through the circuit courts before granting certiorari. The two main reasons the Supreme Court will grant certiorari and decide a case are constitutional questions and disagreement—known as a split—among the circuit courts over a question of federal law, even if it is merely statutory or regulatory and does not rise to the level of a constitutional challenge. Research into federal cases may need to include circuit-level cases, especially when clarifying the law in a particular area—for example, in Denver, Colorado, how do the federal courts decide whether a student intern can be unpaid?

In the federal system, published opinions of the district courts are not binding precedent. Thus, a researcher might want to filter those out, selecting just the courts whose opinions could bind: the Supreme Court and the relevant circuit courts of appeals. Figure 10-3 provides an example from Google Scholar of how to do that, filtering to search binding cases in the Supreme Court and the Tenth Circuit:

First, use the tool to "select courts":

Figure 10-3

Use the option to "select courts" and further select a more specific court or jurisdiction. For researching federal law that would apply to the case study in this book (set mostly in the state of Colorado), the U.S. Supreme Court and the Tenth Circuit would be the best options. District-level cases are not binding on future courts and should not be treated as of equal weight with Tenth Circuit cases.

3. Not Sure If State or Federal Law, or Both

If you are researching an area of law that may be state or federal or both, use secondary research to gain context and narrow your approach. Searching all cases in all jurisdictions is rarely an efficient way to conduct legal research. It will return too many results, and the results will likely be too specific to provide helpful context.

B. Searching and Filtering for a Key Term

After selecting a jurisdiction, the next step is to execute a search. Online case research is excellent for full-text searching. But searching will only be as good as your search terms. In the rest of this chapter we use italics for a search without quotation marks around it, and italics plus quotation marks to show a search with quotation marks around it. Thus, the search *unpaid intern* would show the step of typing those words into the box with no quotation marks, and *"unpaid intern"* would show typing the words enclosed in actual quotation marks in the box. Search engines generally will lean toward exact matches when you use quotation marks, but some algorithms may include frequently cited cases that do not.

For example, a search for *"unpaid intern"* in the Supreme Court and Tenth Circuit (Court of Appeals) reveals several key cases:

Figure 10-4

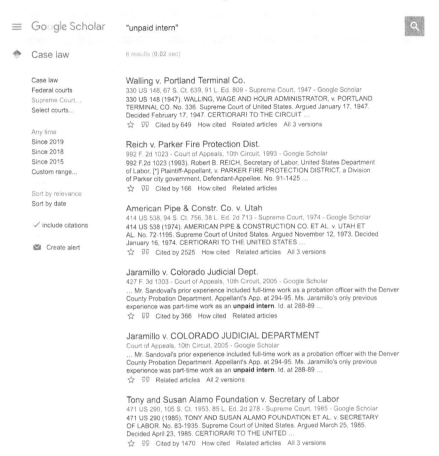

Using quotation marks around the search term such as *"unpaid intern"* helps narrow the search. But quoted phrases can turn out to be too narrow. In the example above, searching the words *"unpaid internship"* would exclude the relevant Tenth Circuit case of *Reich v. Parker Fire Protection District.* That case is absolutely crucial to understanding the current law of unpaid internships anywhere in the Tenth Circuit. This example shows why multiple searches may be necessary. It also shows why some search engines allow you to use symbols that allow searching for terms with different endings (e.g., *intern!* to find both *intern* and *internship*).

C. Sorting Results

Many research sites, including Google Scholar, give the option to sort cases by date or by relevance:

→ Date sorting will order the cases from newest to oldest or, on some platforms, oldest to newest.

→ Relevance sorting will bring to the top the cases that use the key term the most, and that seem to have the most influence over the case law.

Date sorting allows you to focus first on the most recent cases. That can be helpful to find current law, but when you sort by date from newest to oldest, the sorting will ignore everything else and give you the most recent case, even if it only mentions the key term once. Sorting by date is still useful, however, for skimming through results from top to bottom and finding the most recent cases that do have a substantive analysis of the issue.

Sorting by relevance allows you to focus first on the cases with the most important analysis of the issue. What is the most "relevant" case? The factors that contribute to a relevance rating are determined by the research platform or website's programming and algorithms. It may have the most frequent use of the key term you entered. It may be frequently cited by subsequent cases. Keep in mind that an important older case — *which has been limited or even overruled* — could theoretically rise to the top of a relevance search.

You may also be surprised to learn that not every judicial opinion you can find is actually "published." It is published in the sense of being available to the public in print. But there is a technical legal aspect to a court's decision to "publish" a case for precedential purposes. Some courts decide the dispute and write an opinion explaining their result and reasoning, but withholding the opinion from becoming part of the published precedent of that jurisdiction. The opinion is still "published" in the sense it is available to the public. But these opinions are non-precedential, meaning a later court will not rely on them as part of the precedent of that jurisdiction.

Often the top of the case itself will generally show whether it is unpublished, such as with a designation in capital letters, "THIS CASE IS NOT FOR PUBLICATION." When researching federal cases, you may discover a case is unpublished because of what it does *not* have, namely a legal citation to a case reporter. Citations to the Federal Reporter (F.2d or F.3d) indicate published circuit authority. Citations to the Federal Supplement (F. Supp. 2d or F. Supp. 3d) indicate a published district court case. Lacking either of these citations and/or having a citation to the Federal Appendix (F. App'x or Fed. Appx.) would indicate an unpublished case.

Be aware that very recently decided cases may not yet have a case reporter citation because the publisher simply hasn't assigned it yet. And when you find a judicial opinion published on a court's own website, it probably will not have a case reporter citation. Case reporter citations fall into place when the publisher designates them, and eventually are reflected on free research sites such as Google Scholar.

Scanning for case reporters seems technical and unfamiliar at first, but becomes more intuitive with more experience. Figure 10-5 shows some sample case research on Google Scholar.

Figure 10-5

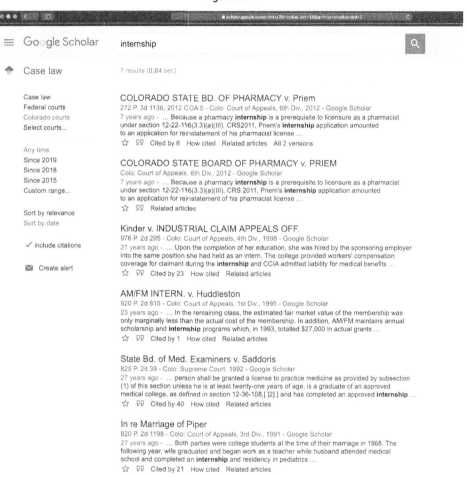

Note that the search in Colorado state cases reveals all published cases, which is indicated by the fact they all have a citation to P.2d or P.3d reporter, indicating they were published in the Pacific Reporter Second Series (P.2d) or Pacific Reporter Third Series (P.3d).

In contrast, Figure 10-6 shows a search in the Tenth Circuit including both circuit-level and district-level cases. You can see here that some cases have a citation to F.3d or F.2d (for circuit appellate cases) or F. Supp. 2d (for district-court orders), and some have no citation:

Figure 10-6

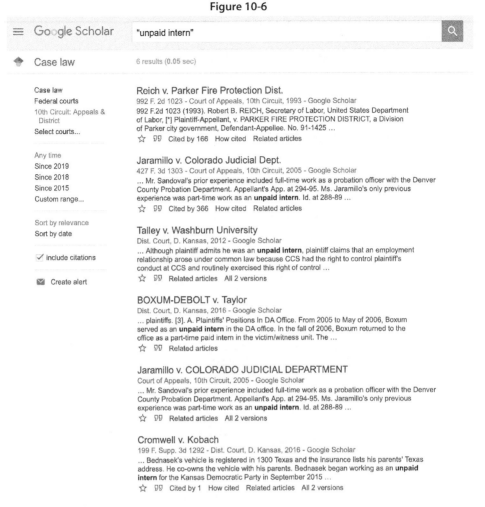

As noted above, reporter citations are a reasonable proxy that a case is published, but they are not perfect. Very new cases (just recently decided) do not immediately get assigned a citation. Legal researchers should be aware that very new cases may lack a case reporter citation but may still be published. Also read the top of cases themselves to see if they indicate they are unpublished.

D. Validating and Updating Case Research: Is It "Good Law"?

Free and open-access case research tools are excellent at showing the *text* of judicial opinions—which are public documents and should be free to everyone—but generally do not have comprehensive capabilities at showing the network of later cases that cite a case found in research. This capability is called a "citator service." Competent legal research must reflect an effort to find out if a case has been overruled, reversed, or otherwise weakened through later cases. In free, open-source legal research into cases, finding later cases that cite the case you are reading can be a difficult challenge. It is a large-scale data project, and the premium services add an element of human discretion such as deciding whether a later case is positive, negative, or neutral toward the case it is citing. Commercial legal research platforms provide excellent citator services. Free and open-access case research tools have—understandably—not made the same investment.

The "How Cited" feature on Google Scholar is one way to attempt to find subsequent citations. It can be very helpful. Figure 10-7 provides an example showing subsequent citations to a Tenth Circuit case on firefighter trainees as unpaid workers, *Reich v. Parker Fire Protection District*, 992 F.2d 1023 (10th Cir. 1993):

Figure 10-7

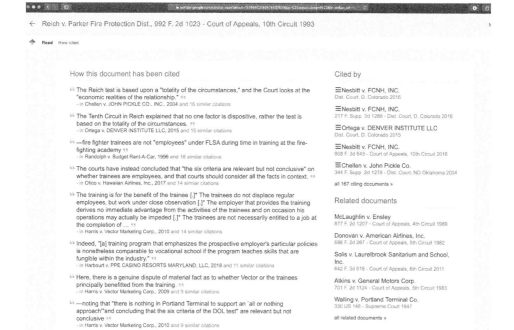

This example of Google Scholar's "How Cited" feature reveals a crucial piece of additional information: the Tenth Circuit's 2018 decision of *Nesbitt v. FCNH, Inc.* The *Nesbitt* case extensively discusses current developments in unpaid internship law, and extensively analyzes the *Reich* case. Competent legal research on unpaid internships in the Tenth Circuit conducted in late 2018 needs to include the most recent Tenth Circuit case on point.

In this case, Google Scholar's "How Cited" feature shows how validation works and reveals the most recent binding case on point. However, legal researchers should be cautious in how much—if at all—they rely on free online sources for validation. Google Scholar's "How Cited" feature may not be comprehensive and should not be relied on for high-stakes decisions. It is the authors' opinion that a lawyer does not meet the ethical standard for competent legal research by relying on Google Scholar's "How Cited" feature to validate case research. We believe the standard for competent legal research by a licensed attorney requires using a reliable validating service such as Shepard's on Lexis, KeyCite on Westlaw, BCITE on Bloomberg Law, or Authority Check on Fastcase. Still, free online networks are helpful in providing informal access to the network of subsequent citing cases.

E. Tracking Pending Cases

The court websites that publish judicial opinions may also maintain public dockets of pending cases. Pending cases are cases in process but not yet decided. State court websites vary widely on how their dockets are available, if at all. An old-fashioned phone call to the clerk of court's office may be necessary.

In the federal system, the most prevalent way to track pending cases is through the PACER system of online filings. PACER stands for Public Access to Court Electronic Records and is found at https://www.pacer.gov/cmecf/. Advocates and court reformers often critique PACER for being expensive and difficult to use, and it is the subject of continued public discussion. State courts vary widely in providing public access to pending cases. The National Center for State Courts collects links to state-court record systems on a page titled "Privacy/Public Access to Court Records."[10] Whether searching for federal or state cases, and whether online or by phone, the docket number of the case will be a significant help.

It is relatively easy to find a search engine for cases, enter a key term, and receive a list of results. It is slightly more advanced to use the search tools and sort by either date or relevance, as shown above. The next step is in what you do after that: confronting the search results and skimming, then reading the cases.

III. Reading and Synthesizing Cases

It is rare that a single case is the only relevant and binding case on point. More commonly, researching cases means finding a group of cases that are all slightly different. Some may be binding; some may be merely persuasive. Some may be recent; some may be old. Some may be cited a lot in subsequent cases; some may never be cited again. In those citations, some may be treated with respect and relied on heavily throughout later cases; others may in fact be reversed or criticized or limited to their specific facts. Some may be appellate opinions; some may be orders entered by a trial-level court. Some may be very well-reasoned and clear and focused on the issue you

---

10. https://www.ncsc.org/topics/access-and-fairness/privacy-public-access-to-court-records/state-links.aspx

are actually researching; some may be confusing, intertwining other facts and legal issues with what you are researching.

The goal is to find out what the cases mean, together. The challenge to achieving this goal is that the network of cases can seem to go on forever. This section sets out some guidelines about focusing on what is most important.

Once you have a collection of cases produced by your search, you need a strategy for organizing, skimming, and focusing on the key cases to study in depth. Synthesis is an exercise in critical thinking that cannot be reduced to a simple formula. Imagine this scenario for a group of cases all analyzing the same issue in the same jurisdiction:

- Researcher finds Case 4.
- Case 4 explains its reasoning and decision, citing Case 1, plus additional Cases 2 and 3.
- Case 5 is decided, citing Case 4.
- Case 6 is decided, citing Cases 4 and 5.
- Case 7 is decided, citing Case 5.

So, after this scenario, what is the law?

Is it just Case 7 because 7 is the most recent? Is it just Case 1 because 1 is the original case on point? You might say the law is all of these cases. That is sort of correct, because all of these cases appear to be "good law"—that is, none of them overrules or criticizes any of the previous cases.

What if Case 6 says something a little different from Case 4 or Case 5 even though it cites them? What if Case 7 uses different phrasing from Case 4, which it does not cite, but it also does not overrule? This scenario is extremely common in case research.

One answer here is to hire a lawyer to conduct a complete analysis of these cases, along the lines of the research memo discussed in Chapter 5. Another answer is to find the most recent case on point as a loose proxy for the current state of the law, but to understand that the most recent case may represent only a fragment of the law that may affect a future situation. We delve into legal analysis of cases again here to reiterate that cases must be read together.

Each case cites previous cases. In writing a judicial opinion, a court can cite previous cases for any number of reasons: to review the precedent and continue it, or to say what the law used to be but is *not* now. Thus, cases cited within a case are not uniformly *more* or *less* valid as a result of being cited. Critical reading skills are crucial here to understand what the opinion is saying about the case it is citing.

If you find a case that relies on many prior cases and continues the line of precedent, you may or may not need to read those older cases. Legal reasoning is not the same as historical reasoning, where a historian would want to retrace the primary sources back to the original source of a statement. In contrast, the practical goal of reading cases in most professional settings is to identify the basic legal standard that applies *right now*. So if you are researching an area of law and you find a solid recent case with a lot of very old, ancient cases cited in it, you probably do not need to exhaustively read those ancient cases. But if you are researching an area of law and you find a recent case citing other recent cases on highly relevant points, you should probably skim them for relevance.

In addition, unless you are reading an opinion decided very recently (in the last few weeks or months), that case is probably cited by later cases. One way to help understand what a case means is to look at how later cases talk about and use that case. The key in using later cases is to focus on the ones that matter and skim or skip the ones that do not. More authoritative sources, such as a Supreme Court case, are going to be more important. Nonbinding sources that cite the case you are looking at may be a distraction and waste of time.

Thus, in reading a group of cases, you are reaching backward to an extent (to the cases cited within cases) and forward (to the cases that cite the cases you are looking at). Being legally literate with case law means grasping that cases work together and often must be read in a group for a full picture of the law.

Here are the basic steps of synthesis when you have various cases all analyzing the same legal issue:

- Identify the key cases and read the key portions of all of them. Key portions include the beginning, the relevant facts and reasoning, and the results. Experienced legal readers learn to quickly skim irrelevant parts of judicial opinions by using headings, key words, and other cues.

- From the key parts of the key cases, focus on finding the legal rule for the issue. What is the test — in other words the legal standard — for the legal issue? The legal test or legal standard may also be referred to as the rule; these all mean basically the same thing. When you read each case, what test does it use? Recall chapter 5's coverage of rules and how they operate in legal analysis.

- Assess and balance various factors in deciding what the law is now. The strategy will vary in each situation, but a number of key factors should be considered:
  - ➡ Consider the hierarchy of courts. A supreme court case is more authoritative than an intermediate court of appeals case.
  - ➡ Consider the date of the opinions. A more recent case is often more influential than an older case, even if the more recent case is from an intermediate court of appeals rather than the highest court.
  - ➡ Consider the facts and holding of each case. Holdings are far more important than dicta. In addition, the facts may lead a court to emphasize one part

of a legal test; the fact that the court is silent on other parts of the test does not mean those other parts are no longer the law, just that they are not relevant to that case. Recall chapter 4's coverage of reading cases.

- ➡ Consider the amount of support in the opinion. A detailed opinion may be more influential than a terse opinion.

- ➡ Consider the quoted language in the opinion. When a later court quotes an earlier court and relies on that language, the language may be more influential.

• Determine what you think all of this information means: for the issue you are researching, what do you think the law is? What is the test?

Students studying for a J.D. spend a great deal of time and effort reading cases individually and collectively. Lawyers read cases together to find tension points and gaps that leave room for future results to evolve and change, even as precedent is followed. Lawyers also use case analysis to proceed to the next step, applying the law to the facts. They assess the facts of a client's case and compare and contrast them to the facts of relevant precedent cases. By applying the law to the facts, the lawyers arrive at a cautious prediction of what a future court (following binding precedent) would do when presented with the client's specific facts. As noted earlier in chapter 3, those without a law license should not advise others on what they predict the law will be as applied to a set of facts. But anyone can use their own legal literacy skills to assess their own situation and proceed accordingly.

As to the hypothesis above about Cases 1 through 7, Cases 7 and 5 look particularly valuable because they are the most recent and most heavily cited in this group. Case 4 does not seem particularly important even though it is the first case the researcher found. But any one of Cases 4–7 may be the most important if it goes into the most depth, or if its specific facts and holding are most analogous to the matter being researched. So the true answer is, "It depends."

IV. Conclusion

Reading cases together and synthesizing them is not a formula, but more of a skill. On the one hand, you need persistence. Your search might reveal ten or more cases that need to be skimmed. On the other hand, you need judgment. Your search might reveal 100 cases, which is too many to handle even by skimming. In working with cases, legal literacy means paying close attention to the factors that make case law dynamic yet reliable, such as the date, the level of authority, and — most importantly — the content of each opinion's analysis.

Having studied this chapter, you should be able to:

- Provide an overview of federal and state court systems in the United States
- Perform online research of case law by jurisdiction and key term
- Recognize the limits of free online research in validating case law
- Read cases not just individually, but together with other cases and other sources of law such as statutes and regulations

Case Study

Olivia Ralston wants to start an unpaid internship in her new business in Denver, Colorado. She has found several legal authorities and is trying to understand what they mean, together, about how unpaid internships are analyzed under the Fair Labor Standards Act.

She has found the following cases in the Tenth Circuit:

- *Nesbitt v. FCMH Inc.*, 908 F.3d 643 (10th Cir. 2018).
- *Reich v. Parker Fire Protection District*, 992 F.2d 1023 (10th Cir. 1993).

She has also found the most important Supreme Court case in the area of unpaid internships:

- *Walling v. Portland Terminal*, 330 U.S. 148 (1947).

And she has found a Ninth Circuit case that she knows is influential in the Department of Labor's recent revision to Fact Sheet #71 on the unpaid internship rules:

- *Benjamin v. B&H Education*, 877 F.3d 1139 (9th Cir. 2017).

She is reading and considering each of these authorities as to how it will affect her own decision-making in setting up an unpaid internship program for her business. She also is considering whether she should seek legal advice about how she intends to set up her unpaid internship program.

Traditions and Trends

Historically, judicial opinions were organized into chronological order and published in "case reporters." Two major sources of case reporters were: (1) official state case reports published by the state government's official publisher and (2) the National Reporter System, developed by West Publishing. West provided these regional sets of case reporters that collected not just opinion text, but also a collection of "headnotes" added by West at the top of each opinion. Headnotes are short points of law that represent the main points in the opinion; they are collected separately in a database of all related headnotes, known as the West Digest System. For legal research, the West system made it possible to search cases by topic. Market competition arose from legal publishers such as LexisNexis and Bloomberg, and these premium legal research services also developed headnote systems as a supplemental research tool. Alongside these database-inspired ways to research cases by topic, full-text searching of opinion text has been available since the 1990s.

A crucial tradition for comprehensive case research is validating—often referred to as "Shepardizing." The validation process means starting with a case citation, and using that citation to check for any subsequent cases and other authorities that cite that case. The most important goal is to ensure the case is still "good law"—in other words, that it is valid because it has not been reversed or overruled or otherwise called into question. The term "Shepardizing" actually comes from the brand-name validation service built into LexisNexis's research platform. Other fee-based legal research platforms provide similar services. These services can be used for broader research purposes, not just to find out if the case is still good law, but to find any and all later citations to the case so as to understand how it is interpreted and how the law stands currently. The ability to check cases (and other primary authorities) to ensure they are still good law is a crucial part of these fee-based services' value proposition for legal-research consumers.

A significant trend in judicial opinions is their publication on courts' own websites and on other open-access platforms. The opinions themselves are increasingly available, although without any of the editorial enhancements such as the headnote systems of commercial legal publishers. Thus, researchers working with open-access cases need strong text-searching and skimming skills. Free research tools do not provide validation services like Shepard's and therefore are not an option for high-stakes case research. They may, however, provide a rudimentary network of cases, allowing the reader to see subsequent cases citing a particular case. The possibilities of open-access case law extend beyond resources for individual researchers. Harvard Law School has created a dataset of cases available to the public for use in their own innovative projects, through its Caselaw Access Project and Caselaw Access Project Application Programming Interface (CAPA-PI). It is not a direct user interface for researching cases, but rather a resource for software programmers to draw from.

A trend in the style of judicial opinions is a less formal writing style using increasingly accessible language, even including references to popular culture in some opinions. The Plain Language movement is a tradition (not just a current trend), and thus readable judicial opinions have always been lauded. Yet the legal community is not united in praising opinions that use humor and pop culture, especially in cases with somber and difficult facts. Lawyers writing to persuade courts are taking more latitude to include these references, sometimes resulting in public critique that their risky writing decisions may not truly serve their clients.

Chapter 11

Reading and Writing
Legal Citations

> [A]s a system of communication that is built upon precedent, legal writing in the
> Anglo-American legal system depends on citation in ways that other fields do
> not and never will. *Citation is integral to how our meaning gets made.*
> — Alexa Z. Chew and Katie Rose Guest Pryal, *Ziff on* The Bluebook, *and a
> Little Bit About Citation Literacy*, The Complete Legal Writer Blog (Dec. 28, 2016).

Legal citations provide crucial information about what a source is, who created it,
how recent it is, and where to find it. Reading legal citations is itself a specialized form
of literacy—coined "citation literacy" by Professor Alexa Chew.[1] Reading with cita-

---

1. Alexa Z. Chew, *Citation Literacy*, 70 Ark. L. Rev. 869, 869 (2018) (coining the term "citation literacy" to refer to the ability to read and write citations).

tion literacy means recognizing a legal citation and quickly understanding not only what the source is, but also how it relates to the rest of the writer's statements. Expert readers of legal citations can quickly extract key information from a densely cited passage of text.

Reading citations is a useful part of overall legal literacy because legal communication must be reliable. Citations are an obvious indicator of reliability because they suggest that the writer has carefully vetted and chosen legal sources. In particular, legal writing by lawyers often features an abundance of citations. Such frequent citations help to address the concerns of skeptical, risk-averse readers who wonder, "Is this really the law?"[2] Legal writing with frequent, heavy citations can still be "stylish"[3] and smooth in how the citations are incorporated. Writing about law for the general public must adopt a different style for readable, accessible legal information.[4]

Thus, another aspect of citation literacy is not only reading legal citations but writing them. Legal citation guides show thousands of rules for citing almost any type of information, from a federal statute to a tweet. Legal citation is not necessarily difficult because it is a series of small mechanical decisions, but it is very technical. Beyond writing standard legal citations, an even more advanced skill is to be able to generate citations that are tailored for the intended audience. A group of consumers may be interested to know something about the legal support for an information sheet, but they do not want, need, or appreciate formal legal citations. This chapter addresses all three goals: reading citations, writing standard citations, and tailoring citations to the audience.

I. Basic Functions of Citations

Learning to read citations unlocks the potential to understand and verify legal information. A legal citation provides a lot of useful information about the authority it describes:

- The type of authority
- Its date
- Its source
- How to find it

For example, imagine Ms. Ralston is working on her website and wants to create an email list from visitors to the website, but she knows there are some legal restrictions on privacy and online data collection. She finds the following citations and now is

---

2. Michael Higdon, *The Legal Reader: An Expose*, 43 N.M. L. Rev. 77, 106 (2013).

3. Alexa Chew, *Stylish Legal Citations*, 71 Ark. L. Rev. 823 (2019).

4. Jennifer Murphy Romig, *Legal Blogging and the Rhetorical Genre of Public Legal Writing*, 12 Legal Comm. & Rhetoric: JALWD 29, 50 (2015) (discussing links and citations in public legal writing on legal blogs).

using her legal literacy (broadly) and citation literacy (more specifically) to determine what each of them communicates:

A. Sample Citations

Cal. Bus. & Prof. Code §§ 22575–22579 (2019).
Children's Online Privacy Protection Act of 1998, 15 U.S.C. §§ 6501–6506 (2018).
16 C.F.R. Part 316 (2019).
Mainstream Marketing Servs., Inc. v. FTC, 358 F.3d 1228 (10th Cir. 2004).
Holcomb v. Jan-Pro Cleaning Sys., 172 P.3d 888 (Colo. 2007).

B. What Each Citation Communicates

Cal. Bus. & Prof. Code §§ 22575–22579 (2019).
This is the California Online Privacy Protection Act. It can be found at subsections 22575 through 22579 of the California Business and Professions Code. It was actually passed into law in 2004, but the original year of passage is never part of the citation. The 2019 in the citation indicates that the law is current as of 2019.

Children's Online Privacy Protection Act of 1998, 15 U.S.C. §§ 6501–6506 (2018).
This is a federal law passed by Congress, which can be found in the United States Code at Title 15 and, specifically, subsections 6501 through 6506 of that Title. This citation is current through the 2018 edition of the United States Code.

16 C.F.R. Part 316 (2019).
This is a portion of the Code of Federal Regulations, specifically from Title 16. Title 16 deals with Commercial Practices and contains regulations of the Federal Trade Commission and Consumer Product Safety Commission. Part 316 is the specific portion of this citation. This part contains the regulations for the federal CAN-SPAM Act on email data collection.

Mainstream Marketing Servs., Inc. v. FTC, 358 F.3d 1228 (10th Cir. 2004).
This is a federal case decided at the Circuit Court level, which is the intermediate appellate court between the trial courts (known as district courts) and the Supreme Court. Specifically, this case was decided by the Tenth Circuit, which reviews appeals from the federal district courts in Colorado, Kansas, New Mexico, Oklahoma, Utah, and Wyoming. This case can be found in volume 358 of the Federal Reporter, Third Series. The Federal Reporter collects cases decided by all the circuit courts, and places them in chronological order. This case is found at page 1228 of that volume. It was decided in 2004.

Holcomb v. Jan-Pro Cleaning Sys., 172 P.3d 888 (Colo. 2007).
This is a case from state court, specifically the Colorado Supreme Court. It was decided in 2007. It can be found at volume 173 of the Pacific Reporter, Third Series, which collects state court opinions from various western states. This case is found at page 888 of that volume.

These are just a few examples of legal citation formats and what they convey. Note that none of them contain a hyperlink to a webpage, although each one of them is available freely and openly, online. Traditional legal citation does not emphasize use of hyperlinks, which may look like a weakness since legal sources are widely available online. But the information in a traditional legal citation will remain constant even if the hyperlinks change or stop working, so the traditional format of legal citations is also a strength.

II. A Quick History of Legal Citation

Legal citation is rooted in several traditions: the format of books themselves, the history of legal publishing, and the hierarchies within legal education.

First, the format of legal books is a huge influence on legal citations. Many citation formats are a text-and-numerical representation of the actual book where the source is found. Take the citation format for a statute:

20 U.S.C. § 6301 (2012 & Supp. V 2017).

This citation format could be translated as "Title 20 of the United States Code at Section 6301, which is found in hard copy in the 2012 version of the Code and the fifth paperback supplement to the 2012 version." Here is more detail on each part of the citation and how it relates to the hard copy of the United States Code:

- **The first number is the title, which is a topical subdivision of the United States Code. The title number can be found on the spine of the book.** The United States Code is divided into titles from title 1 to title 54. Some titles are longer than others, so some take up several volumes (meaning, books) of the code. The citation above comes from title 20 of the United States Code, which covers education. Read more about title and topical codification in chapter 8 on statutes.

- **The "U.S.C." indicates the actual source at the core of the statutory citation — here, the U.S.C. itself, which is the official United States Code.** The key point in this example is that U.S.C. refers to the United States Code, which is the compilation of U.S. statutory law. The U.S.C. is available online at the Office of Law Revision Counsel website, as discussed in chapter 8 on statutes. Other sources, such as the Cornell Legal Information Institute provide the text of the United States Code and designate it as "U.S.C." but their publication of the code is not actually the official code. If, for some reason, it became necessary to prove the actual text of the statute in an information form not subject to dispute, the official code published directly by the U.S. government would be needed. For federal statutes, sometimes the citation refers to U.S.C.A. or

U.S.C.S. These are unofficial versions of the United States Code produced by Thomson Reuters (the parent of Westlaw) and Reed Elsevier (the parent of LexisNexis), respectively. These commercial publications are unofficial "annotated" versions of the statute. Their extensive annotations provide relevant case citations and summaries, research cross-references, and much other helpful information about each statute. Although it is extraordinarily unlikely that the statutory language reprinted in a commercial annotated code would be inaccurate, the words of the statute reprinted in U.S.C.A. and U.S.C.S. are not actually the official code of the United States. In the example above, the citation to "U.S.C." indicates a citation to the official United States Code itself.

- **The § number refers to the statutory section.** A crucial part of any statutory citation is the section number. The section number indicates the subdivision in the title. Here, the researcher could go to the books, select the book for title 20, and then flip through the book to turn to § 6301. If title 20 is big enough to span across multiple books, then the section number indicates which one to pull off the shelf, since the side of the book might say something like "Title 20 Education § 6000 – § 6400." That would indicate to a researcher that § 6301 could be found in that particular book. Some sections are short and simple; others are long, with many subparts. The section number is indicated on the top of the page, similar to the guide words at the top of a dictionary page. The title and section provide all the information needed to find the right volume of the U.S.C. and turn to that section of the code.

- **The year in a statutory citation indicates the publication date of the whole code set.** The entire United States Code is re-published in whole every six years, with 2006, 2012, and 2018 being the most recent publication dates. But new statutes are being enacted almost immediately upon the date the new Code volumes arrive on the shelves. To cover the numerous interim updates, the Code receives periodic supplemental volumes. They are softback pamphlet-style books that sit on the shelf next to the most current United States Code volumes. The statutory citation above indicates that the reader should look in both the 2012 version of the Code and "Supplement V" on the shelf next to it. This system is rather cumbersome! It shows the advantage of a constantly updated online version, and in fact the United States Code is available in updated online format through the Office of the Law Revision Counsel. Less formal legal citations often omit the date. Any citation that does not include a date will be assumed by readers to be current, so make sure your statutory citation is as up-to-date as possible.

That is the long version of what "20 U.S.C. § 6301 (2012 & Supp. V 2017)" means. Our point with this example was to show how the physical form of books influences the citation form for legal sources.

A second major point about legal citations is how the history of legal publishing has influenced them. West Publishing was founded in Minnesota in the late nineteenth century and began the practice of systematically publishing cases in chronological collections called "reporters." The examples above showed cases published in the Federal Reporter, Third Series; and the Pacific Reporter, Third Series. LexisNexis entered the legal market in the 1970s. Throughout the 1980s and 1990s, West and LexisNexis were involved in lawsuits about the copyright to the citation paging and the content of judicial opinions. The end result now is that the content and pagination of judicial opinions are not copyrighted; thus, judicial opinions are available on free online sources. At the same time, publishers and fee-based providers have fought to protect editorial enhancements such as "headnotes," which are a type of outline of the legal points in each case and which enable researchers to find other cases on similar headnotes. Thus, the history of legal publishing has influenced the current state of legal citations because in most jurisdictions, cases are still cited using the conventions developed by West in the nineteenth century. Free online legal research has disrupted the market to an extent, but has not changed the fact that editorial enhancements and many influential treatises are still available primarily in law libraries (the ones with budget to purchase hard copies) and behind expensive paywalls on fee-based legal-research platforms.

Third, hierarchy in legal education has played a role in citation format. The "rules" of legal citation have evolved from a short pamphlet published by the student editors of the Harvard Law Review to a series of highly detailed rules collected in a 300-plus-page manual. The citation manual most commonly discussed and critiqued and bemoaned is *The Bluebook: A Uniform System of Citation*. This book is now in its twentieth edition and was, for many years, essentially the only nationally accepted source for legal citations, assigned to generations of law students. Leading law professors in the field of legal writing created a competing book conveying citation formats in an accessible way for law students — the *ALWD Guide to Legal Citations*, now in its sixth edition. But it is also hundreds of pages long. Open-source advocate Public Resource, along with law professor Christopher Sprigman, created an open-source citation manual called *The Indigo Book: A Manual of Legal Citation* (2016). Still, many lawyers use the term "Bluebooking" to mean checking a citation carefully to ensure it complies with common conventions of legal citation. The extreme level of detail in these citation "rules" has led to criticisms that legal citation is a form of unnecessary, fetishistic perfectionism, and citations should be simpler and more practical.

III. Basic Primer on Citation Formats

The more legal citations you read, more you will get out of them and the easier it will become. Here is a basic primer to several types of citations:

A. Primary Sources

United States Constitution	U.S. Const. amend. XIII, § 1.
Federal statutes	29 U.S.C. § 202 (2018).
Federal legislative history	American Clean Energy and Security Act, H.R. 2454, 111th Cong. (2009).
Federal regulations	20 C.F.R. § 681.100.
Federal Register of agency activity	81 Fed. Reg. 56071 (Aug. 18, 2016).
Supreme Court cases	*Walling v. Portland Terminal Co.*, 330 U.S. 148 (1947).
Circuit Court cases	*Glatt v. Fox Searchlight Pictures, Inc.*, 811 F.3d 528 (2d Cir. 2016).
District Court cases (published)	*Daugherty v. Encana Oil & Gas (USA), Inc.*, 838 F. Supp. 2d 1127 (D. Colo. 2011).
District Court cases (unpublished — most likely available only on a commercial database)	*Coldwell v. RiteCorp Envtl. Prop. Sols.*, No. 16-cv-01998-NYW, 2017 WL 1737715 (D. Colo. May 4, 2017). Or *Coldwell v. RiteCorp Envtl. Prop. Sols.*, No. 16-cv-01998-NYW, 2017 U.S. Dist. LEXIS 68252 (D. Colo. May 4, 2017).
State statutes	C.R.S. § 8-12-107 (2018).
State legislative history (citations vary widely)	2018 Colorado Senate Bill 174. Colorado Senate Journal, 2018 Reg. Sess. 93rd Day page 752 (April 12, 2018), available at https://leg.colorado. gov/sites/default/files/2018_Senate_Journal.pdf.
State regulations (citations vary widely)	8 Colo. Code Regs. § 1202-1 (2019). Or, following state-specific citation practices in Colorado: 8 CCR 1201-2 (2019).
State Supreme Court cases (traditional citation format using a West regional reporter)	*Hernandez v. Ray Domenico Farms, Inc.*, 414 P.3d 700 (Colo. 2018).
State Supreme Court cases (online open-access citation format plus traditional citation format)	*Hernandez v. Ray Domenico Farms, Inc.*, 2018 CO 15, 414 P.3d 700 (2018).
State cases from the intermediate court of appeals	*Redmond v. Chains, Inc.*, 996 P.2d 759 (Colo. App. 2000).

B. Secondary Sources

Treatise	Colorado Employment Law (Lexis 2014).
Law review article	Bradley Karkkainen, *Plain Meaning: Justice Scalia's Jurisprudence of Strict Statutory Construction*, 17 Harv. J. L. & Pub. Pol'y 401 (1994).
Magazine article	Peter Cole, *The Law That Changed the American Workplace*, Time, Jun. 24, 2016.
Restatement of Law	Restatement (Second) of Contracts § 261 (1981).
Web page	*Legal Theory Lexicon 078: Theories of Statutory Interpretation and Construction*, Legal Theory Lexicon (May 21, 2017), http://lsolum.typepad.com/legal_theory_lexicon/2017/05/theories-of-statutory-interpretation.html.

IV. Reading Citations in Text

Here's a passage of legal writing from a judicial opinion, *Clark v. Colbert*, 895 F.3d 1258 (10th Cir. 2018). This case deals with a plaintiff's civil rights claim against police officers. The plaintiff was suffering from schizophrenia, and his brother called the police for help. When the police officers arrived, the plaintiff charged at them with a knife, and they shot him. He survived but did not fully recover, and brought this suit alleging constitutional violations as well as violations of the Americans with Disabilities Act.

First, read the passage below in unannotated form just as it appears in the opinion. Then you will see the identical text with annotations interpreting each citation.

> Clark claims the Wagoner County Board violated the Americans with Disabilities Act by not properly training its police officers to handle mentally ill arrestees like himself. According to Clark, this failure-to-train predictably led the officers to forgo reasonable accommodation of Clark's mental illness while arresting him. As a result, Clark argues, he suffered "greater injury or indignity," during his arrest than other arrestees would have. *Gohier v. Enright,* 186 F.3d 1216, 1221 (10th Cir. 1999).
>
> * * *
>
> The ADA mandates that "no qualified individual with a disability shall, by reason of such disability,… be subjected to discrimination by any [public] entity." 42 U.S.C. § 12132. To enforce this directive, Congress incorporated the remedies of the Civil Rights Act. *See id.* at § 12133. Accordingly, when a public entity discriminates on the basis of disability, the ADA provides a right of action to any victim of such discrimination. *See Barnes v. Gorman,* 536 U.S. 181, 185 (2002). But the Wagoner County Board clearly did not discrimi-

nate against Clark *directly*. Instead, if it discriminated against Clark at all, it did so through the actions of the Broken Arrow officers who formulated the arrest strategy and fired the pepperballs.

To be sure, federal regulations specify that the ADA's terms still apply when a municipality discriminates "through contractual, licensing, or other arrangements." 28 C.F.R. § 35.130(b)(1). Even still — as Clark himself recognizes, *see* Aplt. Br. at 16 — an invocation of this provision requires proof that those who actually discriminated acted as *agents of* the defendant public entity. *See Mason v. Stallings*, 82 F.3d 1007, 1009 (11th Cir. 1996). Of course, there is no federal body of agency law readily applicable to ADA claims. To fill this interstitial gap in the regulation, we must therefore incorporate state law to the extent it does not frustrate the ADA's "specific objectives." *Kamen v. Kemper Fin. Servs., Inc.*, 500 U.S. 90, 98 (1991); *see United States v. Kimbrell Foods, Inc.*, 440 U.S. 715, 727–729 (1979).

A reader with strong legal literacy skills will understand what each of these sources is, how up-to-date it is, and where to find it. Now we want to provide you with details about each source. Here is an annotated version of the same text with more information about each source cited.

Clark claims the Wagoner County Board violated the Americans with Disabilities Act by not properly training its police officers to handle mentally ill arrestees like himself. According to Clark, this failure-to-train predictably led the officers to forgo reasonable accommodation of Clark's mental illness while arresting him. As a result, Clark argues, he suffered "greater injury or indignity," during his arrest than other arrestees would have. *Gohier v. Enright*, 186 F.3d 1216, 1221 (10th Cir. 1999).

| Federal appellate case decided by the 10th Circuit in 1999 |

* * * * *

The ADA mandates that "no qualified individual with a disability shall, by reason of such disability, ... be subjected to discrimination by any [public] entity." 42 U.S.C. § 12132. To enforce this directive, Congress incorporated the remedies of the Civil Rights Act. *See id.* at § 12133. Accordingly, when a public entity discriminates on the basis of disability, the ADA provides a right of action to any victim of such discrimination. *See Barnes v. Gorman*, 536 U.S. 181, 185 (2002). But the Wagoner County Board clearly did not discriminate against Clark *directly*. Instead, if it discriminated against Clark at all, it did so through the actions of the Broken Arrow

| Some portion of the original quote is omitted here |

| Federal statutory code |

| Same title of federal statutory code cited immediately above, with a different section |

| United States Supreme Court opinion from 2002 |

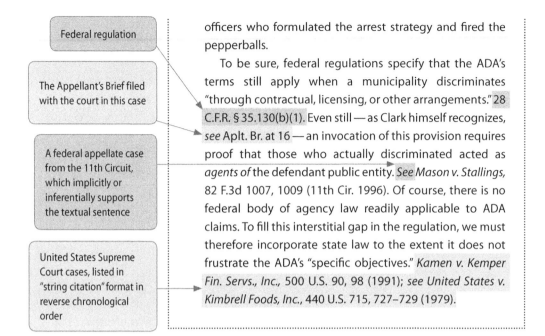

Federal regulation

The Appellant's Brief filed with the court in this case

A federal appellate case from the 11th Circuit, which implicitly or inferentially supports the textual sentence

United States Supreme Court cases, listed in "string citation" format in reverse chronological order

officers who formulated the arrest strategy and fired the pepperballs.

To be sure, federal regulations specify that the ADA's terms still apply when a municipality discriminates "through contractual, licensing, or other arrangements." 28 C.F.R. § 35.130(b)(1). Even still — as Clark himself recognizes, *see* Aplt. Br. at 16 — an invocation of this provision requires proof that those who actually discriminated acted as *agents of* the defendant public entity. *See Mason v. Stallings,* 82 F.3d 1007, 1009 (11th Cir. 1996). Of course, there is no federal body of agency law readily applicable to ADA claims. To fill this interstitial gap in the regulation, we must therefore incorporate state law to the extent it does not frustrate the ADA's "specific objectives." *Kamen v. Kemper Fin. Servs., Inc.,* 500 U.S. 90, 98 (1991); *see United States v. Kimbrell Foods, Inc.,* 440 U.S. 715, 727–729 (1979).

So, as you can see, the citations provide lots of detailed information about what the source is, how recent it is, and how to find it. By reading legal citations with ease, you can read legal information faster and judge whether to rely on it.

V. Citations as Part of Legal Literacy and Problem-Solving

At this point, you have read about what citations are for, what they look like in the abstract, and what they look like in a passage of legal text. The next step is to incorporate your knowledge of citations with more practical questions. Reading citations is *not* just about recognizing esoteric technical forms. As shown in the short examples below, reading citations can help with making efficient, reliable, practical decisions about whether to rely on legal information.

A. Judging the Reliability of a Secondary Source

Imagine you are interested in opening a food truck in Tacoma, Washington. You use a search engine to look for "how to open a food truck in Washington State." This search turns up a blog post that contains the following passage:

This post was first published in 2017 but has since been updated.

Food trucks have become increasingly popular in recent years. They are also complicated from a regulatory standpoint because they are both vehicles and food service establishments. As a result, food truck operators typically must obtain several state and local authorizations to do business in a given location. This blog post will sort through applicable food truck laws and regulations and cite examples of approaches taken by Washington municipalities that regulate food trucks in their jurisdictions....

Local Food Truck Regulations

Cities have a broad amount of discretion with respect to issuing permits for food truck locations. Cities often require prior approval for a food truck operator to operate in a specific location. For example, the City of Lacey (Municipal Code Chs. 16.70.050 and .060) designates certain areas in the right-of-way for food truck use and also provides that food trucks may operate in certain zones with the prior authorization of the city. In addition, some cities, such a Everett (Municipal Code Ch. 5.84.090), specify locations at which a food truck may not operate.

In Tacoma, a partnership between the City of Tacoma and the Tacoma Pierce County Health Department has resulted in a regulatory license that allows mobile food trucks or trailers to legally operate curbside at select zones in the city. A Food Truck Vendor Checklist helps to guide applicants through the process. In addition, the City of Vancouver offers a helpful matrix that describes various approval requirements depending on whether the food truck will be on public or private property and whether it will be temporary or permanent. For a smaller city example, please see the City of Ridgefield mobile food vending webpage, which contains a concise description of the applicable regulatory requirements.[5]

Question:

Should you rely on this blog post?

Answer:

Yes, with additional investigation and careful reading of the sources it cites. This post is a strong example of readable, reliable, useful, updated legal writing for the public. It uses some formal legal citations to the city ordinances. These citations help the reader cross-reference these city ordinances if needed. But this post also provides useful links in a readable form. And it begins by giving a date of publication as well as informing the reader the post has been updated since 2017, further demonstrating its reliability. This post is a good exemplar because it uses formal legal citations when they are useful, but it does not worship at the altar of legal citation to the point that the citations obscure the actual informational content.

B. Assessing a Legal Source Found by Typing a Question into a Search Engine

Imagine you are a North Carolina resident and have a business idea for a new product. You want to start up a company in the Charlotte area because you are becoming more and more confident your idea fills a gap in the market, particularly the Charlotte

---

5. Oskar Rey, *Food Truck Laws and Regulations,* Municipal Research and Services Center of Washington (June 26, 2018), http://mrsc.org/Home/Stay-Informed/MRSC-Insight/June-2018/Food-Truck-Laws-and-Regulations.aspx

market. Your product also is relatively easy to produce because it can be combined from commercially available components. That is your biggest concern — can you still have a protected business idea if it relies on off-the-shelf components? You do some quick searching on the Internet with questions like "Can a proprietary business idea rely on commercially available components?" That leads you to understand that the key term for what you want to establish is a "trade secret." You experiment with more Internet searches, including in Google Scholar for cases. Your search produces a case that quotes the following language:

> [A] trade secret can exist in a combination of characteristics and components, each of which, by itself, is in the public domain, but the unified process, design and operation of which, in unique combination, affords a competitive advantage and is a protectable secret.

The case with this language is *Act II Jewelry, LLC v. Wooten*, 318 F. Supp. 3d 1073, 1090 (N.D. Ill. 2018). The passage itself is a block quote from another case: *Syntex Opthalmics, Inc. v. Novicky*, 745 F.2d 1423, 1434 (Fed. Cir. 1984), *judgment vacated on other grounds*, 470 U.S. 1047, 105 S. Ct. 1740, 84 L. Ed. 2d 804 (1985).

Question:

This language answers the exact question you asked and is from a very recently decided federal case. Should you rely on it?

Answer:

No. This language is from an opinion by the United States District Court for the Northern District of Illinois. You are trying to determine your legal situation under North Carolina law. This case is deciding an issue under the Illinois Trade Secrets Act.

Moreover, the actual quote in the case is from a 1984 case decided by the Federal Circuit. The Federal Circuit is a specialized federal appellate circuit that hears patent appeals, appeals from the Federal Court of Claims, and other specific appeals. Its decisions are not binding on any state court. Yet another difficulty with the quoted passage is that the quoted opinion was "vacated on other grounds." You can see that information in the citation; it is called "subsequent history." The concept itself is actually a correct and reliable statement of trade secret law nationwide. This particular source, however, is not a good source to rely upon and cite as support for this concept in a current analysis of North Carolina law.

C. Evaluating Primary Sources Contained within Another Primary Source

Imagine you are working on a compliance issue with the Social Security Administration and you come across this case, *Sims v. Apfel*, 530 U.S. 103 (2000). Page 108 of the case states the following:

It is common for an agency's regulations to require issue exhaustion in administrative appeals. See, *e.g.,* 20 CFR § 802.211(a) (1999) (petition for review to Benefits Review Board must "lis[t] the specific issues to be considered on appeal"). And when regulations do so, courts reviewing agency action regularly ensure against the bypassing of that requirement by refusing to consider unexhausted issues. See, *e. g., South Carolina* v. *United States Dept. of Labor,* 795 F. 2d 375, 378 (CA4 1986); *Sears, Roebuck and Co.* v. *FTC,* 676 F. 2d 385, 398, n. 26 (CA9 1982). Yet, SSA regulations do not require issue exhaustion. (Although the question is not before us, we think it likely that the Commissioner could adopt a regulation that did require issue exhaustion.)

Question:

   If you wanted to write a report and claim "it is common for an agency's regulations to require issue exhaustion in administrative appeals," would you want to cite 20 C.F.R. § 802.211(a) (1999)"?

Answer:

   No. That version of the C.F.R. was up to date as of the *Sims* decision, but because *Sims* was decided in 2000 the version of the C.F.R. used in *Sims* is almost 20 years old as of the printing of this book. Thus, citing it as if you know it is "good law" would be a mistake — at least if you intend to rely on law that is valid *as of today.* You would need to verify 20 C.F.R. § 802.211(a) in the current version of the Code of Federal Regulations.

VI. Writing Legal Citations

   Citation literacy means not only reading legal citations with a critical eye, but also being able to write them. To work on skills in writing citations, begin by studying what a "full citation" is — similar to the complete citation you would list in a bibliography to a research paper. After creating a basic full citation, the next steps include adding more precise information and also subtracting by using "short citation" formats to refer to a source that was fully cited the first time. Variations on these skills are discussed below.

A. Creating a Full Citation

   One basic principle of legal citations is that the first time a source is cited, the citation should be a "full" citation. That means giving all the standard information about the source. The full citation should allow the reader to understand what the source is, precisely where it can be found, its jurisdiction if applicable, and its year. The examples in Section III's basic primer above are all examples of full citations.

Full citations—of statutes, cases, or anything else—can be incorporated into the text of a sentence or placed after a sentence. Here are two examples:

Citation in text
Under the CAN-SPAM Act of 2003, 15 U.S.C. §§ 7701–7713 (2018), certain email practices are prohibited.

Citation after textual sentence
The CAN-SPAM Act of 2003 prohibits certain email practices. 15 U.S.C. §§ 7701–7713 (2018).

B. Adding a Pinpoint Page Citation (Pincite)

Legal citations seek to help the reader as much as possible; they direct the reader not only to the legal source, but also to the specific subsection or page of that source.

Here is one paragraph from the *Clark* case excerpted above. It is reprinted here with boldface and underlined type highlighting the specific sections and pages incorporated within each citation:

> To be sure, federal regulations specify that the ADA's terms still apply when a municipality discriminates "through contractual, licensing, or other arrangements." 28 C.F.R. § 35.130**(b)(1)**. Even still—as Clark himself recognizes, *see* Aplt. Br. **at 16**—an invocation of this provision requires proof that those who actually discriminated acted as *agents of* the defendant public entity. *See Mason v. Stallings,* 82 F.3d 1007, **1009** (11th Cir. 1996). Of course, there is no federal body of agency law readily applicable to ADA claims. To fill this interstitial gap in the regulation, we must therefore incorporate state law to the extent it does not frustrate the ADA's "specific objectives." *Kamen v. Kemper Fin. Servs., Inc.,* 500 U.S. 90, **98** (1991); *see United States v. Kimbrell Foods, Inc.,* 440 U.S. 715, **727–729** (1979).

As shown here, it is not enough to simply refer to a source generally. Very broad citations can be inaccurate and unhelpful because they make the reader do the work of looking for more specific support. Effective legal citations are very precise, and using pincites to specific subsections and pages is the way to be precise.

C. Incorporating Legal Citations into the Text

Academic legal writing, such as in law review publications, makes heavy use of footnotes, but in practical legal writing today, the majority preference is to incorporate citations into the text. This is why much legal writing contains textual sentences and citations embedded together, as in this example:

> The ADA mandates that "no qualified individual with a disability shall, by reason of such disability,... be subjected to discrimination by any [public] entity." 42 U.S.C. § 12132.

When a citation follows a sentence, it is communicating to the reader that it serves as direct support for that sentence. In the example above, the textual sentence is a direct quote from the Americans with Disabilities Act. The citation immediately following supports the text by providing the source of the quote. It is inserted right after the sentence, with no parenthesis or bracket or textual signal to integrate it or set it off. The fact that the citation is inserted plainly like that shows that it is a direct citation. It directly supports the textual sentence before it. This is always the right choice when you are supporting a quotation. You can also use a direct citation for a very close paraphrase.

The next most common relationship of a citation to the text is to support it by inference. The following citation begins with "See":

> Reproduction is a major life activity for purposes of the Americans with Disabilities Act, even in cases where the plaintiff who does not view reproduction as an important part of his or her life. *See Bragdon*, 118 S. Ct. at 2204–05.[6]

In this example, the citation begins with the *See* signal. The use of *See* shows that the citation provides inferential support for the text. That means the page of the cited source (here, the *Bragdon* case) does not explicitly say everything in the textual sentence. But the meaning of the cited source does support the textual sentence. A citation with *see* allows the writer to use legal information to draw inferences—and communicate to the reader that an inference is being drawn. This signal allows legal writing to do more than just quote and paraphrase exact text. This signal adds flexibility and legal reasoning to the mechanical citation process. Professionals interpreting the law must be able to go beyond what it literally says and interpret what it implies—in other words, not just what it says but the broader universe of what it means. Far from diminishing the reader's confidence in the statement, the careful use of a signal indicates the writer's care and concern for accurately informing the reader how the citation relates to the text.

One more signal may be practically useful, and that is the signal *E.g.*, which is shown in the following example:

> The ADA does not define "major life activities" or "substantial limit[ation]." However, the regulations promulgated by the EEOC under the ADA explain these terms. While these regulations are not binding, they provide us with guidance in interpreting the ADA. *See, e.g., Francis v. City of Meriden,* 129 F.3d 281, 283 n. 1 (2d Cir.1997) (great deference owed EEOC regulations interpreting ADA).[7]

In the example above, the writer uses *See, e.g.,* to indicate these are a few examples but there are more not listed. The purpose of *e.g.* is to save space and avoid adding unnecessary repetitive detail.

---

6. This passage is adapted from *Colwell v. Suffolk Cty. Police Dep't*, 158 F.3d 635, 642 (2d Cir. 1998).

7. *Ryan v. Grae & Rybicki*, 135 F.3d 867, 870 (2d Cir. 1988).

The examples above focus on three specific signals: no signal, *See*, and *e.g.*, For most practical legal writing, these three signals are likely to provide all the necessary flexibility. But you might run into other citation signals:

See generally indicates general background material, such as a key secondary source.

Cf. indicates support by analogy, such as showing that state law runs parallel to federal law on a certain point where they both apply.

Compare ___ with ___ indicates that two sources contrast with one another in a relevant way, such as where you are showing what would satisfy a legal test and what would not, or showing an area of law that protects personal privacy with another area of law that does not protect personal privacy.

Academic legal citation also envisions negative citations. Citations beginning with *Contra* or *But see* identify sources that say the opposite of what the text is saying—in other words, authorities that contradict the text. In practical legal writing, you are unlikely to use these signals. If you find legal authority that says the opposite of your point, you should conduct further analysis and resolve the contradiction, then explain relevant ideas in text. Complicated citations will not help to clear up unresolved questions in practical legal writing.

D. Using Short Citations

Legal citations come in two varieties: full citations and short citations. Full citations are used the first time the source is mentioned. The full citation provides complete information about the citation—all the information needed about how to find the source and its date.

Short citations are used after the full citation. Short citations still provide key information necessary to support the text, but they cut out some information from the full citation. Short citations have different formats depending on how they are used. Most are a shortened version of the full citation, as in these examples:

Full citation	Short citations
29 U.S.C. § 202 (2018).	29 U.S.C. § 202. § 202.
29 C.F.R. § 500.1.	29 C.F.R. § 500.1. § 500.1.
Utility Workers Union of America Local 464 v. Federal Energy Regulatory Commission, 896 F.3d 573 (D.C. Cir. 2018).	*Utilities Workers Union of America*, 896 F.3d at 574. 896 F.3d at 574.

Sometimes a passage of legal writing is drawing from the same exact source in several sentences in a row. When this happens, legal writers use the short citation *Id.*, which is a very short citation that indicates a citation to *the exact same source cited immediately before this one.*

Id. can be used by itself—literally just *id.* and nothing more—which means the exact same page of that same source. Or it can be used with a page or section number like this: *Id.* at 123. This use of *id.* indicates the following: *The exact same source as before, but a different page.* Thus, *id.* at 123 would be page 123 of same source just cited. *Id.* at § 203 would indicate Section 203 of the same statute or regulation just cited.

The important point with *id.* is that it applies only when the same source is cited two or more times in a row, with no interruptions. If you cite case X, and then you cite case Y, you cannot then use *id.* to refer to case X. *Id.* only works for what was cited immediately prior, not something cited several sources ago. Here is an example:

> The Union asserts associational standing on behalf of its members who are retail electricity customers in the relevant market. *See Hunt v. Wash. State Apple Adver. Comm'n*, 432 U.S. 333, 342-43 (1977). Petitioners must establish that either Clark or at least one Union member meets all three requirements for individual standing. *Id.*[8]

So far, this chapter has provided a lot of details and information about the theory, history, function, and details of legal citation. Reading and writing legal citations can seem intimidating at first, but gaining experience as a legal reader will make the citations much easier to read and process.

VII. Alternatives to Formal Legal Citations: Attributions and Links

Knowing how to read and write formal legal citations does not mean they are appropriate in every piece of legal information. In particular, using formal legal citations is probably inappropriate when writing to readers who do not care about or want that type of detail. And using formal legal citations is certainly inappropriate and probably unethical when writing to readers who probably cannot understand them at all.

A writer with legal and citation literacy should be flexible when choosing a less formal option.

A. Choosing and Incorporating Hyperlinked Sources

For online reading, a link to the source can be much more useful than a traditional citation. It can also make the sentence itself more readable by leaving out the technical text necessary for a precise legal citation. Here is a simple example, with underlined text representing a hyperlink to another source:

---

8. *Util. Workers Union of Am. Local 464 v. Fed. Energy Regulatory Comm'n*, 896 F.3d 573, 577 (D.C. Cir. 2018)

The <u>CAN-SPAM Act</u> prohibits certain data collection practices.

The writer would have several reliable and useful choices on what to use for the link.

- The relevant portions of the CAN-SPAM Act on the United States Code on the Office of the Law Revision Counsel's website (and we apologize in advance for this URL, which is an example of why traditional legal citation can be more readable than a URL): http://uscode.house.gov/view.xhtml?req= granuleid%3AUSC-prelim-title15-chapter103&saved=%7CKHRpdGx lOjE1IHNlY3Rpb246NzcwMSBlZGl0aW9uOnByZWxpbSkgT1IgKGdy YW51bGVpZDpVU0MtcHJlbGltLXRpdGxlMTUtc2VjdGlvbjc3MDEp% 7CdHJlZXNvcnQ%3D%7C%7C0%7Cfalse%7Cprelim&edition=prelim
- An overview of the CAN-SPAM Act found on a reputable website such as Cornell's Legal Information Institute: https://www.law.cornell.edu/wex/ inbox/what_is_can-spam
- The Federal Trade Commission's web publication *The CAN-SPAM Act: Compliance Guide for Business*: https://www.ftc.gov/tips-advice/business -center/guidance/can-spam-act-compliance-guide-business
- Wikipedia's page on the CAN-SPAM Act: https://en.wikipedia.org/wiki/ CAN-SPAM_Act_of_2003

In the list above, which of the sources are primary and which are secondary? What do you think about linking to the primary source (the statute) versus a secondary source about the statute? What types of readers would appreciate a primary link? Who would appreciate a secondary link?

Using a search engine to find "The CAN-SPAM Act" would generate many other possibilities as well. Deciding which source to cite is a matter of discretion, especially when there are many possible sources to choose from:

- For example, this article is from an attorney at a prestigious law firm, but it is dated April 2016: https://www.lexisnexis.com/lexis-practice-advisor/the -journal/b/lpa/archive/2016/11/08/complying-with-the-can-spam-act.aspx Do you think this article would be a good source to link to?
- Here is an article from *Forbes* magazine dated April 2018: https://www. forbes.com/sites/forbesagencycouncil/2018/06/06/is-your-email-marketing -compliant-with-the-can-spam-act/

Do you think either of the above options would be a good source to link to? Try using a search engine for "The CAN-SPAM Act" and see what options your search reveals.

B. Journalistic Attributions in Text

In a print publication, or another setting where linking may not be the best solution, legal sources can be described in a more journalistic style. Using journalistic style for citations means building the source information into sentences with or without full citation information. Here are three examples:

> The California Online Privacy Protection Act, known as CalOPPA, governs online privacy in several ways. For example, websites must state how they respond to "do not track" browser signals, under the most recent amendment to CalOPPA found at the California Business & Professional Code § 22575(b)(5)–(6).

> In *Holcomb v. Jan-Pro Cleaning Systems* decided in 2007, the Colorado Supreme Court considered whether a residential consumer on the Colorado No-Call List was, in fact, outside the protection of the List where that consumer's phone number was also listed in Dun & Bradstreet's public business records.

> When interpreting a statute, courts aim to determine the legislature's intent through the words of the statute itself. The Colorado Supreme Court has reaffirmed this principle of statutory construction many times, such as in the 2007 case of *Holcomb v. Jan-Pro Cleaning Systems of Southern Colorado*, 172 P.3d 888 (Colo. 2007) (en banc).

The examples above show that some detail is sacrificed in these attributions. It is difficult to include pinpoint page citations in these kind of citations. But pinpoint page citations may be unnecessary in some contexts.

C. Footnotes

Another option for providing simple, readable text while also providing full formal citations is using footnotes. Arguably, footnotes allow the main text to do what it does best—that is, provide clear, connected sentences, with all the number- and abbreviation-heavy citations collected below in the footnotes. Legal writing expert Bryan Garner has strongly advocated that footnotes should not be limited to academic legal writing, but should be used by practicing attorneys in their practical legal writing. Others have argued that citations in the text are preferable, especially for anything read on a computer screen or smartphone, because footnotes require the reader's eyes to "bounce" between the main text and footnotes elsewhere.[9]

Whether to use footnotes is therefore, like many other citation decisions, a matter of discretion and judgment. In a legal document addressed to the general public, even the mere presence of a footnote number in the main text may send an intimidating or

---

9. Wayne Schiess and Elana Einhorn, *Bouncing and E-Bouncing: The End of the Citational Footnote?*, 26 Appellate Advocate 409 (Summer 2014).

overly academic message. On the other hand, footnotes may permit the writer to focus the main text on clear writing that is easy to follow, with legal citations collected unobtrusively elsewhere for readers who are interested. A good example of consumer-friendly legal writing with footnotes can be found in the California Attorney General's report available online, *Making Your Privacy Practices Public: Recommendations on Developing a Meaningful Privacy Policy* (May 2014).

VIII. Conclusion

Legal citation manuals are lengthy and detailed, and passages of legal text filled with legal citations can look impenetrable. But legal citations are actually very readable and useful once you understand how they are structured and what they communicate. Perhaps counter-intuitively, being "perfect" at formal citation form is a fairly basic skill. What is more advanced is being able to incorporate legal citations that are readable and accessible as well as accurate and reliable, *and* tailored to the needs and interests of the audience. Legal writers can develop this advanced skill by finding and studying examples of legal writing tailored to the type of audience that they hope to reach.

Having studied this chapter, you should be able to:

- Recognize the purpose and parts of legal citations
- Read legal citations for the major types of legal sources (primary and secondary)
- Evaluate the credibility and reliability of online legal information based in part on its legal citations
- Write formal legal citations for statutes, regulations, and cases
- Recognize and understand short citations in cases and other detailed legal writing
- Use flexible citations and links to online sources for your intended audience

....

Case Study: Legal Citations

This is a list of the sources to be used in an article about Olivia Ralston's internship program at Olivia's Beans. The article will be in a magazine for entrepreneurs both inside and outside of Colorado. How should the following sources be cited? What if the magazine was a color glossy magazine for new and aspiring entrepreneurs? What if the magazine was a text-heavy and technical source with a lot of detail about finance, accounting, and legal issues?

- The Fair Labor Standards Act (include the full span of sections that comprise this Act)
- Department of Labor Fact Sheet #71 (as found on the internet, with URL included in the citation)
- Colorado Revised Statutes § 7-101-503 (2019)
- Nesbitt v. FCNH Inc. in the Tenth Circuit, printed in volume 908 of the Federal Reporter, Third Series, at page 643 (dated November 9, 2018)
- 1 Colorado Code of Regulations 3.01(1)(c)(iii)

As another step in this case study, the following draft attempts to incorporate legal citations into a readable essay. The draft comes across as too formal and too legalistic, especially for the online format where it will be published. This draft needs to be edited for more readable legal citations. Some of them may be unnecessary, and links to websites might be more helpful in certain places.

Please note also that Olivia Ralston might decide not to publish this essay sharing her deliberations on legal compliance with federal labor standards. It is possible that publishing this essay could draw unwanted scrutiny. Whether to share this type of essay in writing is a separate question you may want to discuss. The immediate focus here is practicing incorporating legal citations in a readable way.

Starting an Educational Internship Program: Not Easy, but Worth It
By Olivia Ralston, as told to Arjun Navuluri

The State of Colorado motto is *Nil sine numine*, which is Latin for "Nothing without providence." The journey to launch Olivia's Beans has seen its share of providence, but a few moments have been more about the grind than any luck. Starting an internship program is the most memorable example.

The main federal law we ran into with the internship idea was the Fair Labor Standards Act. It requires a minimum wage, 29 U.S.C. § 206, but the Department of Labor (which enforces the Act) allows unpaid internships in some limited and kind of murky circumstances. The DOL has a "fact sheet" on its guidelines for unpaid internships. Wage and Hour Division, Department of Labor Fact Sheet #71: Internship Programs Under the Fair Labor Standards Act (January 2018), https://www.dol.gov/whd/regs/compliance/whdfs71.htm. In that Fact Sheet, the DOL opens the door for unpaid internships at non-profits: "Unpaid internships for public sector and non-profit charitable organizations, where the intern volunteers without expectation of compensation, are generally permissible." *Id.* at fn. 1. On the other hand, "for profit" employers have to pay minimum wage unless they have an appropriate unpaid internship under the factors laid out in Fact Sheet #71, which we will get to in a moment.

Before that, the first question we faced was: what exactly are we? Olivia's Beans is a public benefit corporation. (Check out the Secretary of State's website, https://www.sos.state.co.us/pubs/business/FAQs/pbc.html, and the Public Benefit Corporation of Colorado Act, Colo. Rev. Stat. § 7-101-503, for more information on these new corporate forms.) Our corporate charter explicitly states our profit motive but also our public mission, which is creating a healthy and safe space for anyone with dairy or other food allergies. We found that the answer here was pretty clear-cut because under Colo. Rev. Stat. § 7-101-503, a public benefit corporation is still a "for profit" corporation in Colorado.

The issue then was how to structure the internship to meet the DOL's own guidelines, and—we hoped—to minimize the possibility of anyone successfully suing us for minimum wage. The last thing a startup needs is a case like that. So the first thing we looked at was the DOL's own Fact Sheet #71. It states seven factors for considering who is the "primary beneficiary" of the internship.

That seemed clear-cut until we looked up federal cases to see whether interns were suing for this kind of thing around the Denver area. We found a November 2018 case from the 10th Circuit—that's one step short of the Supreme Court. That case, *Nesbitt v. FCNH Inc.*, 908 F.3d 643 (2018), did something different from the DOL test. In *Nesbitt*, the 10th Circuit explicitly rejected the primary beneficiary test and stuck with the old six-factor test:

> (1) whether the training received is similar to that which would be given in a vocational school; (2) whether the training is for the benefit of the trainee or the employer; (3) whether the trainees displace regular employees, or rather work under close observation or supervision; (4) whether the employer that provides the training derives an immediate advantage from the activities of the trainees; (5) whether the trainees are necessarily entitled to a job at the completion of their training period; and (6) whether the employer and trainees understand that the trainees are not entitled to wages for the time they spend in training.

Id. at 646–647. What we decided to do was to try to satisfy *both* tests. We wrote down the requirements of all these factors next to each other and designed our internship program to give us a really strong argument on each factor. The DOL's seven-factor test and the six factors in *Nesbitt* overlap substantially so this process looks more difficult than it actually was.

We were confident our program complies with federal law, but we know that employment and wage law operates at both the federal and state level. We started researching the minimum wage provisions and found that minimum wage laws define an employee as someone who works "for the benefit" of an employer. Colo. Rev. Stat. § 8-4-101. So long as the intern is serving for educational purposes, the benefit flows to the intern rather than Olivia's Beans. We give them meaningful experiences that do help our company, but the interns definitely do reap the benefit of their time at Olivia's Beans. There are lots of internships and practicums for other professions like teachers. *See, e.g.*, 1 Col. Code Reg. 3.01(1)(c)(iii) (2018). But for the business and food-science crowd, there aren't as many offerings, and we think we have something pretty special.

Given all the considerations we went through to set up this internship program, it is only fitting that we train our interns on compliance issues. We want them to leave their internship with Olivia's Beans not only smarter about the coffee business and more caring about allergy and anaphylaxis issues, but also more alert to state and federal rules and regulations, and more knowledgeable on when to consult with legal counsel in problem-solving for the business.

Traditions and Trends

A combination of factors in the late nineteenth and early twentieth centuries led to increasing standardization of federal and state citations. West Publishing began producing case reporters organized into regions, with a standard format, and a related set of "digests" which were a sort of print-based database of cases by topic. (Before full-text searching in computer databases, digests were an essential method for locating cases by topic.) Legal education became somewhat less parochial and more national in scope, with a corresponding need for common resources on legal citation. Students at Ivy League law schools sought to standardize the citation practices for academic legal writing in the academic journals known as law reviews. *The Bluebook: A Uniform System of Citation* came to dominate legal citation practices not just in academic legal writing but also in practical client-based legal writing. Thus, under the influence of legal publishing and legal education, a common understanding of legal citations developed. This common understanding was the exclusive domain of law-school-trained, bar-licensed attorneys, although in some law offices, legal paraprofessionals (paralegals) learned citation formats. But beyond the domain of law practice, laypeople and others did not have much access to legal information and did not have the knowledge needed to understand and write citations to share precise legal information with others.

Web-based legal research and the growth of open-access legal information have had a moderate influence on formal legal citation. Fee-based legal research platforms largely reproduced the information so as to maintain traditional print-based citation forms. Some reforms have originated with state court systems, such as Ohio and Colorado, which have adopted "neutral citations," also known as vendor-neutral citations. A neutral citation is a citation format that can be generated from the court's own website; no law-library access or subscription to Westlaw or Lexis is necessary. These citation forms allow researchers to find and cite cases in compliance with that jurisdiction's rules even without access to the information for a traditionally formatted citation. Traditional citation formats are still widely used in licensed attorneys' legal writing, but in jurisdictions with neutral citations, the traditional citations are often supplemented with the neutral citation.

As websites have become more widely accessible, the issue of website accessibility for people with disabilities has become more important. Federal and state-government websites must provide accessible content, as required by Section 508 of the federal Rehabilitation Act. Website accessibility is playing a more prominent and pressing role in the public and private delivery of legal information.

Chapter 12

Reviewing Contracts — Form and Organization

> Contract law is essentially a defensive scorched-earth battleground where the constant question is, "if my business partner was possessed by a brain-eating monster from beyond space-time tomorrow, what is the worst thing they could do to me?"
>
> — Charles Stross, Science Fiction Writer

Like many humorous exaggerations, the above quote is built around a kernel of truth. Parties prepare and execute written contracts because they want to create some degree of legal certainty in a future full of unknown and uncertain events. The negative unknowns in a business deal can range from minor annoyance to financial calamity. Contracting parties want to address those possibilities—even if they fall short of intervention by a brain-eating monster from outer space. Despite the potential worst-case scenarios, most contracts arise in an atmosphere of great optimism because the parties have decided that they are better off with a deal than they were without it.

Reaching and managing a business deal and memorializing it by a written contract is inherently a multi-person effort. At a minimum, two parties are negotiating their deal, but those parties may well involve lawyers and business advisors as well. In some organizations, employees even hold the title of "contracting officer" because their jobs consistently involve managing or negotiating contacts.

The purpose of this chapter and the next is to help prepare you to be an integral part of teams that deal with contracts, whether in the front-end process of document preparation, in the heart of the contract negotiation as the parties seek agreement on terms, or in the back-end management of executed, binding contracts. Because the skill of reading contracts is integral to all parts of the contracting process, that is our starting point.

I. What Do We Mean by the Term "Contract"?

The word *contract*, even as used in this book, has at least two different meanings—its legal meaning and its broader meaning as commonly understood.

The first meaning is a legal definition. A contract is a promise or group of promises that the law will enforce.[1] Enforceable promises do not necessarily have to be in writing. Some contracts can be completely oral, although others cannot be because of a doctrine called the *statute of frauds*. Under the statute of frauds, particular contracts must be evidenced by a writing, such as contracts for the sale of land.

Even where contracts are founded on a writing, the writing may not be a formal contract. In the famous case of *Lucy v. Zehmer*, 84 S.E.2d 516 (Va. 1954), the disputing parties wrote and signed an agreement for sale of a piece of real estate on the back of a restaurant receipt. The Virginia Supreme Court held that writing to be proof that the parties had entered an enforceable contract. Thus, an agreement meeting the legal definition of a contract can, in fact, be unexpectedly informal.

Most business professionals and lawyers involved in making significant deals, however, do not rely on a person's spoken word as his or her bond or on scribbled terms on the backside of a receipt. The second meaning of *contract*, and the one more important for present purposes, is its common understanding: that is, a document containing the agreement of the parties. Here, a contract is the formal writing by which the parties have agreed to be bound, usually by placing their signatures on the document. When lawyers and laypeople speak of "drafting a contract," they are referring to the creation of a formal written contract.

Whether using a technical legal definition or the common understanding of a formal written contract, people who say "contract" really mean "binding contract." What makes it binding?

A contract is a foundational building block of *private law*. Recall from chapter 2 that *public law* is law that applies to members of the public regardless of whether they agree to it. You and a group of friends cannot get together and choose to opt out of laws against robbery, as you would quickly learn from your capture and prosecution following a bank heist. The public law against robbery applies to you regardless of any individual intent or group agreement. But when parties enter into enforceable contracts, they create private law—legal duties and obligations that apply only to specific persons

---

1. Restatement (Second) of Contracts § 1 (1981).

or entities. In the case of contract law, these are people or entities who have given their assent to be bound by a contract.

Private law is a form of law because it creates a set of obligations that are ultimately enforceable by resort to the legal system. Every contract places some sort of limitation on a party's legal future in the event of a broken promise — in other words, "breach of contract." Consider a simple example of a real estate contract. If Olivia Ralston has contracted to sell a parcel of land to Arthur Dent next year for $100,000, then Olivia has given up the legal right to sell that same land to Tricia McMillan three months from now, even if Tricia is offering to pay $200,000. If Olivia breaches the contract with Arthur by selling the land to Tricia at a higher price, and if Olivia does not have a legal excuse for doing so, she can be held liable to pay damages to Arthur or face other legal consequences. The legal consequences are faced only by Olivia, and only because she chose to limit her legal future by entering into a contract with Arthur.

If contracts ultimately serve to limit the options and impose potential liability on contracting parties, then why does anyone enter into a contract? Typically, at the time of contracting, the parties each believe that they will benefit by trading their legal flexibility in exchange for a benefit from the other side. The limitations and liabilities that one contracting party imposes on itself generally do benefit the other side and vice-versa. A legal obligation that one assumes in a contract is known as a *duty*, while the flip side of a duty is a *right* that benefits the other side.[2] When Olivia agreed to sell the land to Arthur, she accepted a duty to transfer that land to him, and she received the right to enforce Arthur's promise to pay $100,000 at the agreed-upon time. Arthur, in turn, secured the right to obtain the property at a time and price he found acceptable as reflected in the contract, and he accepted he accepted the duty to provide the agreed-upon payment at the agreed-upon time.

Both parties to a contract secure for themselves access to the legal system to enforce their rights against one another. This reality is the key to why private law is actually "law." Parties can and do conduct business based on trust, but the availability of a reliable legal system with well-understood methods of enforcement reduces the risk of placing (or, misplacing) that trust. Having a strong legal system built on the rule of law thereby encourages parties to bind their futures together in beneficial ways they might otherwise not do. Olivia and Arthur may have no reason to trust one another if they never have met before their negotiations for the sale of the land, but both still can be sure that the legal system is backing up their agreement.

That is the awesome power of contracts as private law. Parties who enter into valid contracts set the rules by which they bind each other, and those rules will be enforced. There are exceptions, of course, such as contracts that are void due to public policy. For

---

2. *See generally* Tina Stark, *Drafting Contracts: How and Why Lawyers Do What They Do* 22–27 (2d ed. 2014). We will again address the presence of legal duties and legal rights in our discussion of covenants in Chapter 13.

example, it is generally illegal to contract for the private sale of a human organ in the United States; the only legal way to give and receive human organs is through the United Network for Organ Sharing, which manages the U.S. network of human organ procurement and distribution. Despite some exceptions, U.S. law generally does provide wide latitude for freedom of contract. As a participant in the contract preparation and contract management process, you will frequently need to access and understand the private rules contained in a professionally drafted contract.

II. Contract Drafting Style

In theory at least, formal contracts can take as many forms as contracting parties wish to imagine. Some contracts are brief and minimalist, like terms printed on the back of a concert ticket. Other contracts run for hundreds of pages, containing elaborate detail, complex what-if scenarios, and voluminous exhibits, like a contract for the merger of two publicly traded corporations. Thus, any discussion of the parts of a contract requires a significant caveat: Not every contract will necessarily conform to the parts, style, and ordering discussed here.

Despite the many variations in contract style, professionally drafted contracts actually do share many features. Our evaluation of contracts focuses on a writing style that Tina Stark, an influential leader in contract-drafting theory and education, has identified as *contemporary commercial drafting*.[3] These contracts are professionally drafted in a modern writing style, yet they maintain some degree of formality. Contemporary commercial contracts are a useful baseline for our study because a reader can then recognize their features in a broad array of documents.

What other styles of contract documents might you encounter in your professional life? Some form contracts involving consumers are drafted in an almost conversational version of plain language. For example, the parties may be identified as "we" and "you," and the language may include contractions. For example: "We won't cancel your homeowner's policy due to late payment if you make the payment no more than 30 days after its due date." Some contracts remain in a musty and archaic style largely unchanged from a century ago. If you see a contract referring to "the party of the first part" and "the party of the second part," you know you are looking at an "antiquated"[4] contract that would probably benefit from more modern style. Certain fill-in-the-blank retail contracts err on the side of minimalism, even eschewing complete sentenc-

---

3. Tina L. Stark, *Drafting Contracts: How and Why Lawyers Do What They Do* 5 (2d ed.2014). Professor Stark's work is an enormous influence and inspiration for much of the material covered in Chapters 12 and 13, and the authors owe her an enormous debt for her pioneering work in transactional legal education. Readers who wish to explore the realm of contract drafting in far more depth than this book permits should consult the excellent *Drafting Contracts* text.

4. Cornell Legal Information Institute, Wex Legal Dictionary, *"Party of the first part"* definition (quoting Nolo's Plain English Law Dictionary).

es on the apparent theory that people will figure out what the drafter meant based entirely on context (a practice we do not advise in any circumstance, incidentally). With this nod to the diverse contract styles out there, let us now turn our attention to the business of reading contemporary commercial contracts.

III. Parts of a Formal Contract

A skilled reader of contracts should be able to identify the typical sections of a commercial contract. Here, we will walk through and identify these parts in an order that is fairly representative of well-drafted contracts. Our vehicle for the walk-through is a contract arising from Olivia Ralston's employment with Braggadocio, Inc. We will excerpt and discuss relevant parts of the document one at a time, but the provisions of a formally drafted agreement are often interrelated. Thus, the contract reader's first job is to consider the complete document. Take several minutes to skim the Noncompetition Agreement between Olivia Ralston and Braggadocio, Inc.:

Title

preamble

NONCOMPETITION AGREEMENT

THIS NONCOMPETITION AGREEMENT (the "Agreement") is made and entered into as of the 1st day of February, 20XX, by and between Braggadocio, Inc., a Delaware corporation with its principal place of business in Boulder, Colorado ("Braggadocio"), and Olivia Ralston (the "Employee"), a resident of the State of Colorado.

Recitals

Recitals

A. Braggadocio is in the business of acquiring, producing, and retailing coffee, tea, and related products and services (the "Business") throughout the United States.

B. Employee is, as of February 1, 20XX, Braggadocio's Associate Director of Human Resources for the company region of Colorado (the "Position") and has executed an Employment Agreement of the same date providing the principal terms and conditions of Employee's employment with Braggadocio.

C. Braggadocio and Employee wish to provide for the orderly succession of Employee's replacement, when Employee's employment with Braggadocio ends, regardless of when such end will occur, by providing a fixed period of time during which Employee will not compete with Braggadocio and will be available to provide counsel to Employee's successor.

Words of Agmt

Employee and Braggadocio accordingly agree as follows:

Agreement

Def.

1. **Definitions.** The terms defined in the preamble and recitals have their assigned meanings and each of the following terms has the meaning assigned to it:

Def.

"**Annualized Base Salary**" means twelve times the monthly salary paid to Employee under the Employment Agreement in such amount as may be adjusted from time to time during the employment of Employee.

"**Benefits**" means the non-cash consideration that Braggadocio provides its employees, including health insurance and retirement account contributions, but not including the use of company vehicles.

"**Just Cause**" means fault on the part of Employee that is detrimental or potentially detrimental to Braggadocio, including but not limited to the indictment or arrest of Employee for any felony offense, credible allegations of fraud, conversion, or embezzlement by Employee against Braggadocio, and any public statement by Employee that may reasonably constitute libel or slander against any Person.

"**Person**" includes a business entity, such as a corporation, partnership, limited liability company, or professional corporation.

"**Services**" has the meaning assigned to it in section 5.

working prov.

2. **Non-Competition.** In consideration of the provisions of this Agreement and in consideration of the provisions of Employee's Employment Agreement with Braggadocio, Employee shall not, for a period of eighteen months immediately following her last day of employment:

(a) directly or indirectly own, manage, operate, participate in, consult with, or work for any person, partnership, or business that is engaged in the Business anywhere in the state of Colorado; or

(b) either alone or in conjunction with any other Person, directly or indirectly, solicit or divert or attempt to solicit or divert any of the employees or agents of Braggadocio or its affiliates or successors to work for or represent any competitor of Braggadocio or its affiliates or successors or to call upon any of the customers of Braggadocio or its affiliates or successors where such customers of Braggadocio are located in the state of Colorado.

3. **Non-Compete Compensation.** In consideration of the covenants contained in this Agreement, including the eighteen-month period of non-competition following Employee's last day of employment, Braggadocio agrees that if Employee is terminated by Braggadocio without Just Cause, then Braggadocio shall compensate Employee with

(a) a payment of one-sixth of Employee's Annualized Base Salary as of her last day of employment, with such payment being due Employee by no later than 45 days after Employee's last day of employment; and

(b) 60 days of Benefits.

4. **Just Cause Termination or Voluntary Separation.** If Employee is terminated by Braggadocio for Just Cause, or if Employee voluntarily resigns the Position of her own accord, then Employee will remain bound by this Agreement, but Braggadocio will have no obligation to make any of the payments or provide any of the other benefits to be made to Employee under this Agreement.

5. **Consultation with New Associate Director of Human Resources for Colorado.** Upon request by Braggadocio, Employee shall provide consultation services (the "Services") to the person replacing Employee in the Position as is reasonably needed to effect a smooth transition.

6. **Program Ineligibility Acknowledged.** Employee acknowledges that, following the last date of her employment with Braggadocio, she will not receive any vacation pay or sick pay, and she will no longer be eligible to participate in Braggadocio's bonus programs and stock option plans.

7. **No Conflicting Agreements.** Employee represents and warrants to Braggadocio that Employee has the legal right to enter into this Agreement and that Employee has no contractual or other impediments to the performance of Employee's obligations.

8. **Independent Covenants.** The covenants on the part of the Employee contained in this Agreement are to be construed as agreements independent of any other provision in this Agreement. Without limitation of the generality of the preceding sentence, Employee's specific obligation to provide the Services is not dependent upon any other provision in this Agreement. The relief for any claim or cause of action of the Employee against Braggadocio, whether predicated on this Agreement or otherwise, will be measured in damages and does not constitute a defense to enforcement by Braggadocio of these covenants.

9. **Relationship to Employment Contract.** The parties intend that this Agreement and the Employment Contract of the same date between the parties both be effective and enforceable. In the event, however, of any conflict between the terms of the Employment Contract and the terms of this Agreement, this Agreement controls, and the Employment Contract is fully subject to this Agreement.

10. **Injunctive Relief; Attorney's Fees.** In recognition of the irreparable harm that a violation by Employee of any of the covenants contained herein would cause Braggadocio, the Employee agrees that, in addition to any other relief afforded by law, an injunction (both temporary and permanent) against such violation or violations may be issued against the Employee and every other person and entity concerned thereby, it being the understanding of the parties that both damages and an injunction are proper modes of relief and are not to be considered alternative remedies. Employee consents to the issuance of such injunction relief without the posting of a bond or other security. In the event of any such violation, THE EMPLOYEE AGREES TO PAY THE COSTS, EXPENSES AND REASONABLE ATTORNEY'S FEES IN-

Working Prov.

CURRED BY BRAGGADOCIO IN PURSUING ANY OF ITS RIGHTS WITH RESPECT TO SUCH VIOLATIONS, IN ADDITION TO THE ACTUAL DAMAGES SUSTAINED BY BRAGGADOCIO AS A RESULT OF THE VIOLATION.

11. **Notice.** Any notice sent by registered mail to the last known address of the party to whom such notice is to be given will satisfy the requirements of notice in this Agreement.

12. **Severability.** If any provision of this Agreement is determined by a court to be unenforceable in whole or in part, the Agreement will be deemed modified to the minimum extent necessary to make it reasonable and enforceable under the circumstances.

13. **Entire Agreement.** This Agreement is the final and exclusive agreement between the parties as to the matters contained in this Agreement. Earlier and contemporaneous negotiations and agreements between the parties on the matters covered by this Agreement are expressly merged into and superseded by this Agreement.

14. **Counterparts.** The parties may execute this Agreement in one or more counterparts, each of which is an original, and all of which constitute only one agreement between the parties.

15. **Governing Law.** This Agreement is governed by the substantive laws of the State of Colorado, without giving effect to its principles of conflict of laws.

16. **Heirs, Successors, and Assigns.** The terms, conditions, and covenants of this Agreement extend to, are binding upon, and inure to the benefit of the parties and their respective heirs, personal representatives, successors, and assigns.

General Prov.

By their signatures below, the parties have executed this Agreement to be effective as of the day, month, and year first above written.

Braggadocio, Inc.   **Olivia Ralston**

By: *Charles Howard*   *Olivia Ralston*

Its: Senior Vice President   Olivia Ralston, individually

....

The divisions of this sample contract that are plainly visible to the reader are the headings and section numbers—and those are definitely helpful enhancements to the text. As chapter 4 points out, initially skimming a document for structure is an effective reading strategy. That strategy is just as important for reading a contract as it is for reading narrative text.

An experienced contract reader will notice that the Noncompetition Agreement has a particular ordering; this is the logical "flow" of many contracts. These parts of a contract are not necessarily labeled or numbered, but they are present all the same. Let us consider the structure of this contract in eight parts, as follows:

Eight Parts of a (Typical) Professionally Drafted Business Contract
Title ✓
Preamble ✓
Recitals ✓
Words of Agreement ✓
Definitions ✓
Working Provisions ✓
General Provisions ✓
Signature Blocks ✓

A. Title

The contract between Olivia and Braggadocio is titled "Noncompetition Agreement," which is usefully descriptive of what the contract seeks to accomplish—preventing Olivia from later competing against her employer. Most formal contracts have a title, even if the title is nothing more than "Contract" or "Agreement." Some titles are more descriptive, such as "Contract for the Sale of Goods" or "Limited One-Year Warranty." A more specific title is often more useful—especially if a businessperson has a lot of contracts on her desk, but it should not be too long and should not just repeat all of the information in the preamble. Notice that all of these examples of titles are capitalized. This capitalization is a common legal drafting convention by which a common descriptive noun in converted into a specific proper noun. A general noncompetition agreement (not capitalized) becomes a particular Noncompetition Agreement (capitalized) of a specific date and between two specific parties. Note that some contracts do not state their title separately at the top of a document, but the title still exists as part of the next section naming the contract.

B. Preamble

After its title, Olivia's contract begins with the following one-sentence paragraph:

> **THIS NONCOMPETITION AGREEMENT** (the "Agreement") is made and entered into as of the 1st day of February, 20XX, by and between Braggadocio, Inc., a Delaware corporation with its principal place of business in Boulder, Colorado ("Braggadocio"), and Olivia Ralston (the "Employee"), a resident of the State of Colorado.

A statement like this at the beginning of a contract is known as a *preamble*. A preamble serves a number of contextual functions for the entire document. It repeats the contract's title but also assigns to it a shorter defined term. Here, the contract itself has a long-form title "Noncompetition Agreement" and now also a short-form title (just "Agreement.") There are billions of agreements in this world, but for anyone reading this particular document, the words "the Agreement" mean only one thing—this particular agreement. Even though we have not reached the Definitions section of the contract, the preamble has provided short-form references for the agreement itself along with the parties to the contract—namely, the corporate entity of Braggadocio and Olivia Ralston as the specific employee bound by this agreement. We will say more on the importance of identifying the contracting parties below.

A preamble will often state the date on which the parties entered into the contract. The date is important to distinguish this contract from any other contracts signed on other dates between the parties, as is often the case in long-term business relationships. The date can be the date on which the parties actually sign the contract, but contracts can also name a date before or after the signing date (the "as of" date) on which the parties have agreed to consider themselves bound. For this contract, Olivia may have started working for Braggadocio on February 1, but the parties did not get around to fully documenting their agreement until February 15. In the first 14 days, the parties operated on trust and oral understandings of what at least some parts of their agreement would be. In an employment setting, the parties have probably agreed on the amount of the employee's salary, title, and the rough starting benefits. Other matters are not actually agreed to until the contract is put in writing and signed. This convention for dating contracts reflects the reality that parties often—and at their own risk—begin performing their contracts before they have finished "papering" their deal.

The preamble also formally identifies the specific contracting parties. This identification is arguably the most important information in the preamble. Clear identification is important for several reasons. Several people or entities may have the same name, for instance. The identification of Olivia Ralston narrows down this contract to the one in Colorado, not another Olivia Ralston in Florida or anywhere else. For corporations or other organizations entering contracts, the entity identification in the preamble is also important because it identifies the precise legal entity bound by the contract. It also shows that the actual contracting party is the entity, not the human being who signs the contract on the entity's behalf. We will revisit this concept when we review the signature blocks at the end of the document.

Mentioning residence or incorporation locations helps ensure that the contracting parties are sufficiently identified. Some preambles go further than our example does and include physical addresses, tax ID numbers, or other identifying information. Here, both Olivia Ralston and Braggadocio, Inc. are identified by name and state of residence: In our document, both parties are physically located in Colorado. A corporation or other business entity (such as a limited liability company or a limited partnership) is usually also identified by the jurisdiction in which it is incorporated, and that jurisdiction is not necessarily the same state where the company has its principal place of business. In the United States, as you might have gathered, business entities are typically chartered by states. Braggadocio, Inc. has its corporate headquarters in Colorado, but its state of incorporation is Delaware—a small state that has established itself as a giant in the area of corporate law. Braggadocio may have no business operations in Delaware, despite its corporate charter being issued there. It is nonetheless a "Delaware corporation."

The preamble of a contract has a great deal of information packed into a single sentence. For a contract reader, information identifying the contract name, parties, and the effective date of the contract can serve a valuable context-setting function for a future reader who is unfamiliar with the document.

C. Recitals (Background)

After its preamble, the Noncompetition Agreement contains a collection of background factual statements, each of which is known as a recital. In a contract drafted in an older style, these recitals are sometimes called "Whereas" clauses, so named because the first word of each recital was always "Whereas." The Loan and Guarantee Agreement at the end of Chapter 13 uses this style. Regardless of the writing style, contractual recitals are statements that set up the factual setting for the parties' agreement.

Recitals can be a place where both parties stake out a position on the story behind a contract. That story must be one that is relatively palatable to both sides. But a note of realism is in order at this point: the story of a contract may be controlled by the contracting party with more economic or other power, and so can the contract's substantive terms. Here, even though Olivia signed and assented to the Noncompetition Agreement, it was drafted by Braggadocio and largely serves the company's interest. The idea that Olivia would be prohibited from competing with her employer after leaving that job originated with the employer, not Olivia. The brief story in the recitals is stated in objective terms, but it is the story that Braggadocio wants told. This story, although subtly favorable to Braggadocio, is stated in terms that, on balance, would not offend or bother Olivia—at least not so much that she would object or walk away from her new job.

In that context, consider the recitals in Olivia Ralston's agreement:

A. Braggadocio is in the business of acquiring, producing, and retailing coffee, tea, and related products and services (the "Business") throughout the United States.

B. Employee is, as of February 1, 20XX, Braggadocio's Associate Director of Human Resources for the company region of Colorado (the "Position") and has executed an Employment Agreement of the same date providing the principal terms and conditions of Employee's employment with Braggadocio.

C. Braggadocio and Employee wish to provide for the orderly succession of Employee's replacement, when Employee's employment with Braggadocio ends, regardless of when such end will occur, by providing a fixed period of time during which Employee will not compete with Braggadocio and will be available to provide counsel to Employee's successor.

Another characteristic of contractual recitals is that they do not do any of the formal work of the contract, meaning that they do not create any rights or obligations in any of the parties. No one makes a promise in the recitals, and there is no claim for "breach of recital" if a statement is false. (Recitals known by one side to be false could, however, provide evidence for a fraud claim by the other side.) Put differently, these provisions are *non-operative*. The operative or "working" provisions of the contract come later. One reason why recitals are not operative provisions is that they precede the *words of agreement*, the next part of the contract. These recitals are a thumbnail story explaining why the contract exists. Why did the parties enter into the agreement? What did they intend to accomplish? More to the point, what do the parties want a future reader of the contract — such as a judge hearing a breach of contract suit — to know about the parties, their intentions, and their plans? Contract drafting, as students are often surprised to learn, has room for use of some of the persuasion skills covered in Chapter 16. The advocacy is fairly subtle, however.

D. Words of Agreement

The words of agreement are where the parties state that they are agreeing to the terms of the contract. Without the words of agreement, the contract is arguably mere text on a page that does not do anything. In a contract written in contemporary commercial contract-drafting style, the words of agreement in a contract tend to be plain. They are crucial nonetheless. The words of agreement in our sample contract are:

Employee and Braggadocio accordingly agree as follows:

In this example, the word "accordingly" shows the logical connection between the background recitals and the operative provisions of the agreement. Because of the story just told in the recitals, the parties usually think they are better off entering into this contract than their alternative of not doing so.

Older contract forms might have a longer words of agreement section, perhaps something like this:

WHEREFORE, in consideration of the mutual promises contained herein, the sufficiency of which is expressly acknowledged, the Parties hereto agree as follows:

The second example accomplishes the same thing as the first, though it takes three times as many words to do it. Some attorneys are more comfortable with the older form, especially with its express acknowledgement that the parties' mutual promises suffice as "consideration," which is a requirement for an enforceable contract.[5] Using either format, the goals for the drafter are to connect the recitals to the operative

---

5. An extended discussion of the legal doctrine of consideration is beyond the scope of this chapter. The essential point is that contract law requires both sides to exchange something of value for a contract to be enforceable. That is the contract's consideration. A mere promise to give a gift, in contrast, is not supported by consideration and is not a contract.

provisions and affirmatively state that the operative provisions are, in fact, what the parties have agreed upon. Whether the words of agreement are plain or more formalistic, everything that follows these words is the substance of that contract.

E. Definitions

The first thing to notice about our example definitions section is its prefatory language (which means language that prefaces or precedes the main content to follow):

> 1. **Definitions.** The terms defined in the preamble and recitals have their assigned meanings and each of the following terms has the meaning assigned to it:

The definitions section of a contract is not a dictionary. Rather, it is a storehouse for the specialized vocabulary belonging to a specific contract. These specialized vocabulary words are capitalized to show their specific meaning in this contract. Capitalization of defined terms is a well-recognized convention of contract drafting, signaling to the reader that a term is being used in its specialized meaning rather than an ordinary one.

The Definitions section in this contract states not only that it contains defined terms, but it also references other terms that were already *defined in context* in the preamble and recitals. This language prevents the (unlikely) argument that only the terms explicitly listed below in the definitions section have a binding meaning. If no terms were defined in the preamble and recitals, then the prefatory language might be shorter or even nonexistent. After the heading for "Definitions," the rest of the section would go on to list all applicable definitions in the contract.

Contract definitions generally fall into two categories. The first is a definition representing the parties' agreement about what a term should mean. The second is a shorthand form of a long phrase, used so the parties do not have to repeat the long phrase each time they refer to it. Contract drafters often find that their document reads more smoothly when the parties can agree to use certain words in ways that are either: (1) more precise than the ordinary meaning or (2) more efficient than a lengthy phrase, especially one that must be repeated multiple times in the document. Not all words in a contract need to be defined; if a word is merely to be used in its ordinary meaning, then there is no need to put a definition in the contract. But once a term is defined, it must be used accurately and consistently as defined. Using synonyms or other references to the same general idea will not suffice if what the drafter really intends to do is refer to what that term itself means.

Skim through this contract's list of definitions. In some contracts, the defined terms are numbered in a list, but in this example, the terms are listed in alphabetical order without numbers. The drafting practice of alphabetizing a list of definitions makes the document more efficient and friendly for readers seeking to locate a definition:

"Annualized Base Salary" means twelve times the monthly salary paid to Employee under the Employment Agreement in such amount as may be adjusted from time to time during the employment of Employee.

"Benefits" means the non-cash consideration that Braggadocio provides its employees, including health insurance, retirement account contributions, but not including the use of company vehicles.

"Just Cause" means fault on the part of Employee that is detrimental or potentially detrimental to Braggadocio, including but not limited to the indictment or arrest of Employee for any felony offense, credible allegations of fraud, conversion, or embezzlement by Employee against Braggadocio, and any public statement by Employee that may reasonably constitute libel or slander against any Person.

The first three definitions are good examples of specialized terminology within a contract. The definition of "Annualized Base Salary" seems not that different from the ordinary understanding of that term, so why might it be included here? In this case, the definition serves a clarifying function by preventing an ambiguity. Suppose Olivia gets a raise after working 12 months for Braggadocio. What is her annualized base salary in month 14? It could plausibly be the total of her monthly salary of the past 12 months, which varied, but the definition of Annualized Base Salary assures a different — though equally plausible — understanding. It means 12 times what Olivia earns *now*, at the time of computing the number. By including a specific definition, the contract prevents a later dispute over how to compute the figure.

The definition of "Benefits" clarifies matters, but also allows for continuation of a potential ambiguity. The term specifies that "Benefits" are those benefits that Braggadocio provides to its employees. The "including" phrase at the end ensures that references to Benefits must cover, at a minimum, Olivia's health insurance and employer-sponsored retirement plan. In contrast, the use of a company vehicle is specifically excluded. Other possible benefits, like a flexible spending account or disability insurance, are neither precluded nor promised based on this definition. Some contract-drafting experts discourage this use of "includes/does not include," but the agreement to disagree is sometimes a necessary evil that parties are willing to live with in order to reach a deal. Parties have a variety of reasons why they do not nail down every factual detail in a contract, such as a failure to reach agreement on some less important terms or perhaps an "agreement to disagree" on some matter that the parties do not believe will be a problem later.

"Just Cause" is an important definition in the Noncompetition Agreement because it might be a triggering event — what contract law often calls a *condition*. Here, the term appears to be intentionally broad, encompassing many reasons why the company might want to fire Olivia in the future. The specific examples, however, are all events representing some risk of harm to the company that is at least arguably under Olivia's control. Here is another note about the balance of economic power reflected in this agreement: The "including but not limited to" language in this definition is, from an employee's perspective, overbroad and pretty scary stuff. An employee in Olivia's position often has little bargaining power over such phrasing.

Following these three direct declarations, the remaining two definitions are examples of two other types of definitions: exemplary definitions and cross-referenced definitions.

> **"Person"** includes a business entity, such as a corporation, partnership, limited liability company, or professional corporation.
>
> **"Services"** has the meaning assigned to it in section 5.

The definition of "Person" is a helpful definition because it lists several examples. The examples, however, are intentionally nonexhaustive, which means other examples beyond the specific ones listed here could also meet the definition of "Person." For example, this definition of Person does not *exclude* human beings even though it also does not list them. By starting a definition with "includes" rather than "means," the drafter is intentionally seeking to add specialized meaning without excluding ordinary meaning. For this contract, as in much of law, "Person" explicitly includes business entities also, which is a meaning not necessarily included within common understandings of the word "person."

The term "Services" is *defined in context*, just like the terms defined in context in the preamble and recitals. The difference here is that the contextual definition comes after the definitions section rather than before it, referring the reader to section 5. "Services" is included here as a cross-reference so that the Definitions section can serve as a one-stop clearinghouse for a contract reader to locate all of the defined terms in the document. Why, you might wonder, is the "Services" definition not stated here rather than in section 5? Contract drafters have a variety of reasons for this practice, but the most common one is to deal with *localized* defined terms—terms that are not spread throughout the document but are just used a few times in proximity to each other. In that situation, a definition that is near the localized use tends to be more helpful for the reader, especially if the contract is long. Note, however, that a contract reader usually sees the Definitions article early in the document. If there are too many cross-referenced definitions in the text, the reader may get annoyed, and the drafter has missed the opportunity to educate the reader about the deal. There often is no "right" decision on whether a definition should be provided in context rather than spelled out in the definitions section. In reading numerous contracts, you are likely to see both practices a great deal and should know that both are widely accepted.

F. Working Provisions

Following the definitions, we come to the operative provisions that form the bulk of the contract. Here, we will call this large middle of the contract the *working provisions*, because this is where the substance of the parties' deal is actually done. The declarative definitions are called into action to do their actual work. While there can be a great deal of variety in the ordering of these working provisions, the provisions fulfilling the main purpose of the contract usually come first, while matters that are less central to the agreement tend to come later in the document.

1. Principal Working Provisions

In the Noncompetition Agreement, the main purposes of the contract are carried out in sections 2 and 3. Consider those here:

2. **Non-competition.** In consideration of the provisions of this Agreement, Employee shall not, for a period of eighteen months immediately following her last day of employment:

   (a) directly or indirectly own, manage, operate, participate in, consult with, or work for any person, partnership, or business that is engaged in the Business anywhere in the state of Colorado; or

   (b) either alone or in conjunction with any other Person, directly or indirectly, solicit or divert or attempt to solicit or divert any of the employees or agents of Braggadocio or its affiliates or successors to work for or represent any competitor of Braggadocio or its affiliates or successors or to call upon any of the customers of Braggadocio or its affiliates or successors where such customers of Braggadocio are located in the state of Colorado.

3. **Non-Compete Compensation.** In consideration of the covenants contained in this Agreement, including the eighteen-month period of non-competition following Employee's last day of employment, Braggadocio agrees that if Employee is terminated by Braggadocio without Just Cause, then Braggadocio shall compensate Employee with

   (a) a payment of one-sixth of Employee's Annualized Base Salary as of her last day of employment, with such payment being due Employee by no later than 45 days after Employee's last day of employment; and

   (b) 60 days of Benefits.

In this instance, the main purpose of the agreement is to prevent Olivia Ralston from competing against Braggadocio after leaving the company's employment. A brief sidebar on employee contracts is appropriate at this point.

Where employment is "at will" rather than for a specified term, employers have a wide latitude in changing the terms of employment. Salary, benefits, job responsibilities, titles, and other key elements of the job can change at the employer's insistence because the employee always has the legal right to quit the job if she dislikes the changed terms. In a sense, every day (or at least every pay period) is potentially a new deal.

What Braggadocio seeks from Olivia in this contract is different, however, because it involves restrictions on her *post*-employment life. You may recall from chapter 2 that our legal system will not enforce certain agreements based on policy grounds. While the common law of contracts would conceivably allow an employee to bargain away her future employment freedom in exchange for present employment, most courts and legislatures have determined that unlimited enforcement of such agreements would be problematic and bad public policy—and therefore unenforceable. The question for lawmakers was where to draw the line between legitimate employer interests in protecting a business and undue restrictions on individuals' freedom to work in their chosen field. The line is not always entirely clear, and it is certainly not the same in every state. As we will discuss later in this chapter, the substance of the law governing a contract is key to understanding many of its provisions.

For the moment, you should know that, roughly speaking, a post-employment non-competition agreement is more *likely* to be enforceable if the employee is paid separate consideration—something apart from her regular job compensation—in exchange for the promise not to compete. This separate exchange of consideration is what is happening in sections 2 and 3. In section 2, Olivia is promising not to compete against Braggadocio for 18 months after leaving the company's employ. In section 3, Braggadocio is promising to pay something to Olivia in exchange for her promise in section 2 (at least if certain conditions are met). The main purpose of the Noncompetition Agreement is thus largely contained in sections 2 and 3.

2. Secondary Working Provisions

The secondary working provisions are important, but they only support or are subsidiary to the main deal in sections 2 and 3. Such provisions might deal with specific possible scenarios that may (or may not) occur. Consider sections 4 through 6:

4. **Just Cause Termination or Voluntary Separation.** If Employee is terminated by Braggadocio for Just Cause, or if Employee voluntarily resigns, the Position of her own accord, then Employee will remain bound by this Agreement, but Braggadocio will have no obligation to make any of the payments or provide any of the other benefits to be made to Employee under this Agreement.

5. **Consultation with New Associate Director of Human Resources for Colorado.** Upon request by Braggadocio, Employee shall provide consultation services (the "Services") to the person replacing Employee in the Position as is reasonably needed to effect a smooth transition.

6. **Program Ineligibility Acknowledged.** Employee acknowledges that, following the last date of her employment with Braggadocio, she will not receive any vacation pay or sick pay, and she will no longer be eligible to participate in Braggadocio's bonus programs and stock option plans.

Section 4 implements the earlier definition for "Just Cause," making it the standard under which Braggadocio can terminate Olivia, yet not have to make the payments under section 3. Notice that voluntary separation—which is not defined—is treated the same way. Although section 3 is part of the main deal, we cannot fully understand what it will and will not do without considering section 4. Likewise, section 5 is a tack-on to Olivia's noncompetition promise contained in section 2. Her principal obligation in section 2 is one of *forbearance*—a promise to *not* do something. The promise in section 5 requires an affirmative *act*, actual consultation with her replacement when such is sought by Braggadocio.

3. Representations and Warranties

Section 7 illustrates two types of provisions that frequently, but not always, appear as a secondary working provision in a contract. A *representation* is a statement that a past or present fact is true. A *warranty* is related to a representation, but has some important differences. It is a promise that stated facts are true, and it is also a promise to pay damages if the facts are not true. Note that section 7 has wording ("represents and warrants") that invokes both types of provisions:

> **7. No Conflicting Agreements.** Employee represents and warrants to Braggadocio that Employee has the legal right to enter into this Agreement and that Employee has no contractual or other impediments to the performance of Employee's obligations.

Representations and warranties are placed into contracts as two different means of creating liability in the statement-making party if facts contained in the statements are false. Here, the facts at issue are in the statement that Olivia "has the legal right to enter into this Agreement and that [she] has no contractual or other impediments to the performance" of her obligations.

We will explore representations and warranties in more detail in our discussion of contract concepts in Chapter 13. For present purposes, suffice it to say that Olivia could face liability to Braggadocio if any of the facts represented or warranted in section 7 turn out to be false.

4. Construction Terms

Sections 8 and 9 are *construction terms*, meaning that they provide special guidance as to how this contract should be construed and understood by future readers, especially by a judge or an arbitrator.

> **8. Independent Covenants.** The covenants on the part of the Employee contained in this Agreement are to be construed as agreements independent of any other provision in this Agreement. Without limitation of the generality preceding sentence,

Employee's specific obligation to provide the Services is not dependent upon any other provision in this Agreement. The relief for any claim or cause of action of the Employee against Braggadocio, whether predicated on this Agreement or otherwise, will be measured in damages and does not constitute a defense to enforcement by Braggadocio of these covenants.

9. **Relationship to Employment Contract.** The parties intend that this Agreement and the Employment Contract of the same date between the parties both be effective and enforceable. In the event, however, of any conflict between the terms of the Employment Contract and the terms of this Agreement, this Agreement controls, and the Employment Contract is fully subject to this Agreement.

Section 8 is intended to ensure that a breach of a promise (also known in contract-drafting lingo as a *covenant*, a contract concept we will discuss in more detail in chapter 13) by one of the parties does not excuse the other party from fulfilling its promises. Here, the intent is for both sides to continue fulfilling their obligations, recognizing that they might choose to sue even as they continue to perform, because each breach gives rise to potential liability to the other party.

Returning to the specific working provisions of the contract, section 9 addresses the specific fact that the Noncompetition Agreement is not the only contract between Braggadocio and Olivia. How do those agreements relate to one another? The parties may assume that there is no conflict in the two separate agreements, but careful contract drafters will account for the possibility of inadvertent error. Here, it appears that Braggadocio wants the noncompetition obligation to be controlling in the event of conflict with Olivia's general employment agreement.

5. Endgame Provisions

Not even the best and most carefully drafted contract will create a contractual relationship that lasts forever. Often, the latter or final provisions of the customized working sections of a written agreement will address the future ending of the parties' contractual relationship. These provisions are sometimes referred to as *endgame provisions* because, chronologically, they deal with some phase of the agreement where the main deal is done. In an apartment lease, for instance, the contract may provide for when the tenant must hand over the keys and when the landlord must refund any unused portion of the security deposit. Endings can be friendly or hostile, and when a hostile ending is possible, the parties may agree to provisions on how their dispute will be handled.

In Olivia's Noncompetition Agreement, Section 10 addresses an ending where Olivia violates the agreement. As with other provisions mentioned above, this provision shows Braggadocio's strategic advocacy for contract terms that would work to its advantage. The language reflects the sort of drafting advocacy that we previously saw in the contractual recitals.

10. Injunctive Relief; Attorney's Fees. In recognition of the irreparable harm that a violation by Employee of any of the covenants contained herein would cause Braggadocio, the Employee agrees that, in addition to any other relief afforded by law, an injunction (both temporary and permanent) against such violation or violations may be issued against the Employee and every other person and entity concerned thereby, it being the understanding of the parties that both damages and an injunction are proper modes of relief and are not to be considered alternative remedies. Employee consents to the issuance of such injunction relief without the posting of a bond or other security. In the event of any such violation, THE EMPLOYEE AGREES TO PAY THE COSTS, EXPENSES AND REASONABLE ATTORNEY'S FEES INCURRED BY BRAGGADOCIO IN PURSUING ANY OF ITS RIGHTS WITH RESPECT TO SUCH VIOLATIONS, IN ADDITION TO THE ACTUAL DAMAGES SUSTAINED BY BRAGGADOCIO AS A RESULT OF THE VIOLATION.

Braggadocio is thinking ahead to Olivia's potential breach. In addition to the normal contract remedy of monetary damages, Braggadocio has secured Olivia's consent to the extraordinary equitable remedy of an *injunction*. An injunction is a court order requiring a party to do or refrain from doing a specified act. If the subject of a valid injunction violates it, the court can enforce the injunction with its contempt powers, which include the authority to have the violator imprisoned until she complies with the order. The violator, it is said, holds the keys to the jail cell in her pocket because she will be released as soon as she commits to stop violating the order. You can see why an injunction is an extraordinary remedy reserved only for certain types of disputes. American courts tend to be very sparing in their exercise of contempt power.

Notice that the final sentence of section 10 is written in all capital letters, LIKE THIS. When you come across text in a contract that differs in style from its surroundings—such as all-capitals, bold typeface, larger size, or even a distinctive color—the drafters are trying to make that provision *conspicuous*. The most common reason that contracts contain conspicuous terms is because they contain a term required by law to be conspicuous in order to be enforceable. Have you ever been asked to place your initials next to certain provisions of a contract? A similar principle is at work there, as the document drafter wants to prove that your attention was specially drawn toward the initialed term.

G. General Provisions (Boilerplate)

Having reached the end of the working provisions, we are near the end of the contract, which is the usual grouping place for *general provisions*, sometimes referred to as "standard terms" or "boilerplate." The popular slang term *boilerplate* derives from sheets of metal used in the manufacture of steam boilers utilized in factories or steam locomotives. The same plates came to be used in the newspaper industry. The stories and headlines in a newspaper varied from day to day and would thus be set with blocks of moveable type. Other parts—like the newspaper's masthead and certain repeat advertisements—would be engraved in boilerplate metal because that repeated content did not change. Today, the word "boilerplate" is used to describe any text that is frequently repeated and seldom revised.

These provisions are rarely drafted from scratch, and in some settings they are pasted into the document as almost an afterthought. Do not be deceived, however, because boilerplate provisions actually deal with important matters and are no less enforceable just because they are less customized. Despite the "boilerplate" nickname, general provisions can actually be customized in particular contracts. And the general provisions that are common in one business context may not be the same as those in another setting.

The Noncompetition Agreement contains six general provisions that are classic boilerplate content:

11. **Notice.** Any notice sent by registered mail to the last known address of the party to whom such notice is to be given will satisfy the requirements of notice in this Agreement.

12. **Severability.** If any provision of this Agreement is determined by a court to be unenforceable in whole or in part, the Agreement will be deemed modified to the minimum extent necessary to make it reasonable and enforceable under the circumstances.

13. **Entire Agreement.** This Agreement is the final and exclusive agreement between the parties as to the matters contained in this Agreement. Earlier and contemporaneous negotiations and agreements between the parties on the matters covered by this Agreement are expressly merged into and superseded by this Agreement.

14. **Counterparts.** The parties may execute this Agreement in one or more counterparts, each of which is an original, and all of which constitute only one agreement between the parties.

15. **Governing Law.** This Agreement is governed by the substantive laws of the State of Colorado, without giving effect to its principles of conflict of laws.

16. **Heirs, Successors, and Assigns.** The terms, conditions, and covenants of this Agreement extend to, are binding upon, and inure to the benefit of the parties and their respective heirs, personal representatives, successors, and assigns.

Notice that sections 11 through 16 cover issues that, though important to the Noncompetition Agreement, could apply to a wide variety of other agreements. We will explore other common general provisions in the next chapter, but these six are a solid starting point to understand the function of boilerplate.

Notice Provision: Section 11 specifies how the parties can contact each other when they must do so formally. The parties certainly can and will have normal conversations with each other, but when they want to document a communication and ensure that the other side is responsible for having received it, the parties here require a writing placed in the mail to a known address.

Severability Clause: Section 12 addresses what the parties want done with this contract in the event that any part of it is held by a court to be unenforceable. In some contracts, that possibility might be remote, but in others the potential is quite real. In that circumstance, the court could conceivably void the entire agreement, an outcome that the parties may or may not want. This severability clause states that the parties' intent in such a situation is to save as much of the contract as possible rather than eliminate it.

Merger Clause (Integration Clause): The "Entire Agreement" provision in section 13 is known in drafting parlance as either a *merger clause* or an *integration clause.* A merger clause is added to a contract as evidence that the parties want their final written agreement to be their exclusive deal. Suppose one of the parties later wants to argue, "Wait! That isn't what you told me you meant when we were negotiating." The merger clause instructs the court to ignore prior or contemporaneous evidence of party negotiations or agreements when determining the legal meaning of the contract.

Counterparts Provision: Section 14 is a straightforward piece of boilerplate dealing with a very common issue: What happens when both parties sign the agreement, but they do not sign the same piece of paper or same copy of an electronic document? Contracting parties are sometimes hundreds of miles away from each other, after all, or they may simply not have reason to get together into a room for some sort of signing ceremony. A counterparts provision effectively blesses the practice of signing separate documents so long as all the documents say the exact same thing.

Choice of Law Clause: Section 15 identifies the state law that will govern this contract. Such provisions are quite common and usually serve to resolve any uncertainty over what jurisdiction's law will apply to a contract when there are several with a plausible claim. Here the substantive governing law for this contract will be the law of the State of Colorado. The choice of law is important enough that we will explore its role separately below.

Heirs, Successors, and Assigns: The final general provision appears here and in other contracts in recognition of the fact that English common law was quite reluctant to grant contractual rights to a non-party to the contract. Non-parties, in this setting, are said to lack contractual *privity,* which means a direct legal connection. Section 16 seeks to get around the common law tendency by showing that the original parties anticipated future substitute parties and are fine with them. Suppose, for example, that after entering into this contract, Braggadocio is acquired by and merged into Fivebucks, an international coffee conglomerate. Section 16 would expressly allow Fivebucks, as the successor entity, to assume the rights and responsibilities of Braggadocio, the original contracting party.

H. Signature Blocks

We have now reached the final part of our review of the Noncompetition Agreement, the signature blocks. That section also includes some important prefatory language:

> By their signatures below, the parties have executed this Agreement to be effective as of the day, month, and year first above written.

This prefatory language shows that the function of the signature is to assent to the contract by executing it. The signature on this document is not a receipt, an acknowledgement, or a doodle; it is a legal act by the parties with legal consequences. Some contract documents omit this or a similar statement and then simply add the signature blocks after the last substantive term. Such an omission is not wise because it leaves open the question of why the parties are signing their contract and what those signatures mean. Even though contract documents will lack the preface, if the contract were litigated, a reviewing court would *probably* determine that the signatures show contractual assent. If you have a choice, however, certainty and clarity are better than ambiguity and vagueness.

The block for Olivia's signature is fairly straightforward. Her signature as an individual binds her as an individual. Entity signatures, like that of Braggadocio, require a bit more care.

Braggadocio, Inc.

By: *Charles Howard*

Its: Senior Vice President

Here, the signature first identifies the employer by the nickname to which it is referred in the contract, "Braggadocio," just like Olivia is identified as the "Employee." For the actual signature, we return to the employer's full legal name "Braggadocio, Inc.," a corporation. Corporations and other entities cannot actually sign anything without the interaction of a human being. Here while the signing party is Braggadocio, Inc., the signing action is by its authorized human agent, Charles Howard, an officer of the company. Charles Howard's name in the signature block is preceded by the term "By:," which helps indicate that he is not signing the contract in his individual capacity where he might be individually liable. Rather, he is solely signing as the Senior Vice President of Braggadocio, Inc.

And with that, our review of the contract is done! Your goal in this chapter should be to understand the basic structure and content of a contract. Many of the provisions we have walked through above have additional layers of depth and hint at the goals and motivations of the parties. In the next chapter, we will consider some of the finer points of contract provisions, with an eye toward you adding value as a client or employee engaged in the contracting process.

IV. The Role of Governing Law

Let us conclude this chapter by making something explicit that you may have picked up in the course of reviewing the Noncompetition Agreement. The substantive law that applies to a contract is enormously important. Under the substantive law that applies to the contract, the contract provisions may be enforceable as written, enforceable but with limitations imposed by law, unenforceable in part but leaving the rest of the contract intact, or completely unenforceable.

The parties have some freedom to choose the governing law through a choice of law clause as shown above in Section 15. But parties do not have complete freedom to choose any jurisdiction's law. Although contract law is *similar* in its broad outlines throughout the United States,[6] contract law is not *the same*. A provision enforceable under one state's law might be unenforceable if the law of another state applies. For example, a noncompetition agreement entered into in California between a California company and an employee located in California probably could not specify that Georgia law governs, since the contract bears no relationship to the state of Georgia or Georgia law, and such agreements are unenforceable under California employment law but at least somewhat enforceable under Georgia employment law. One size does not fit all, and contracting parties must be very careful in assuming that a deal that works well in one state is equally viable elsewhere.

The Noncompetition Agreement between Olivia Ralston and Braggadocio, Inc. is a stark example of this fact. American states have very different approaches to these types of agreement, ranging from broad unenforceability to broad enforceability, with many nuanced approaches in between. You have now carefully read a contract between Olivia and Braggadocio. It is written in contemporary commercial drafting style; it is logical; it is customized to the situation. So it must be enforceable, right?

Without more information or guidance, you still don't actually know whether the contract is enforceable. A lawyer advising you or your company on the enforceability issue must have a strong working knowledge of the applicable law to be able to answer that question. As an informed contract reader, you are a better partner in that effort, because you can bring your understanding of business goals and concerns into the process of reaching a better result. Always remember that a written contract is only one piece of a complete business and legal situation. What is written within the "four corners" of the document must be read against the backdrop of governing law.

---

6. Louisiana is an exception to many general statements about how similar contract law is throughout the United States. The legal system in Louisiana has its origins in French civil law rather than English

Having studied this chapter, you should be able to:

- Provide a legal definition of a contract and how it differs from common understanding of the term
- Identify generally how the private law of contracts fits into and often changes the default rules of the U.S. legal system
- Distinguish professionally drafted formal contracts from informal contracts
- Identify the typical parts of a formal contract, including both formal provisions and working provisions
- Define types of boilerplate language and the role such language plays in formal contracts
- Recognize the impact of governing law on the scope, meaning, and enforcement of contracts

....

Case Study

Two weeks ago, Olivia Ralston received a notice from the City Code Compliance Office that the roasting facility for Olivia's Beans did not have an adequate fire alarm system. The company was given 90 days from the date of notice to get the facility into compliance or else be shut down until it can prove that it has a compliant system.

As a result of this unexpected crisis, Olivia has spent parts of the last two weeks shopping for industrial fire alarm systems and is leaning toward the Warn2000 System manufactured by Alarm Experts, Inc. ("AEI"), a Dallas, Texas-based company with a major branch office in Denver, Colorado. AEI has offered to sell and install the system at the roasting facility for $12,000, which appears to be the lowest price available for a code-compliant system. Olivia has specifically asked whether the $12,000 cost will cover everything, and AEI's Colorado District Manager, Reyna D'Ignazio, has assured Olivia that it would.

AEI has now sent Olivia the contract form shown below. Review the contract and answer the following questions:

1. Recall this chapter's discussion of eight parts of a professionally drafted contract (**Title, Preamble, Recitals, Words of Agreement, Definitions, Working Provisions, General Provisions, Signature Blocks**). Where—if at all—do each of those eight parts appear in the contract below?

---

common law, and the civil law of "obligations" fills the role occupied by the common law of contracts in the other 49 states. Louisiana is also the only state that has not adopted Article 2 (Sales of Goods) and Article 2A (Leases of Goods) of the Uniform Commercial Code, a major source of statutory contract law in the United States. *See* Uniform Law Commission, https://www.uniformlaws.org/home.

2. The next chapter contains a more extensive discussion of contract content and risks. We have found in teaching, however, that many professionals have already faced both personal and work situations where they must evaluate contracts quickly and intuitively. What concerns might you have about this contract if you were in Olivia's position? Be prepared to share at least three concerns with your professor and your classmates.

3. Assume that Olivia will be meeting with her company's outside counsel later today regarding another matter. What questions do you think she should ask the lawyer about this contract? Try to list at least three specific questions.

Contract for Sale and Installation

This Contract for Sale and Installation ("Agreement") is made this 15th day of January, 20XX between Alarm Experts, Inc., a Texas corporation ("Seller") and Olivia's Beans, Inc., a Colorado corporation ("Buyer").

Background

- Buyer wishes to acquire an industrial-quality fire alarm system sufficient to satisfy the building code and other regulatory requirements applicable to Buyer's facility; and
- Seller has substantial experience with the goods and services sought by Buyer; and
- Buyer and Seller are desirous to conduct business with each other under the terms and conditions specified in this Agreement.

Accordingly, in consideration of the mutual promises stated in this Agreement, the parties agree as follows:

Definitions

The terms defined in the preamble have their assigned meanings, and each of the following terms has the meaning assigned to it:

"Effective Date" means the date stated in the preamble of this Agreement.

"Force Majeure" means events or other circumstances beyond the control of Seller, including, but not limited to, strikes, acts of God, political unrest, embargo, failure of source of supply, or casualty.

"Goods" means a Warn2000 Fire Alarm System.

"Parties" means Buyer and Seller, collectively.

"Purchase Price" means $12,000.00.

<u>Terms</u>

1. **Sale.** Subject to the terms and conditions of this Agreement, Seller shall sell the Goods to Buyer, and Buyer shall pay the Purchase Price to Seller.

2. **Payment.** Buyer shall pay the Purchase Price in four equal monthly installments, the first of which is due on the Effective Date, and the remaining payments of which are due on the first day of each month following until payment in full. Buyer shall pay the Seller each installment of the Purchase Price no more than fourteen days before the scheduled delivery date of the shipment of Goods. Buyer shall pay Seller on time. Despite the preceding sentence, if Buyer has an unpaid balance the day after a due date, Buyer shall pay 18% per annum interest on the unpaid balance.

3. **Delivery.** Seller will arrange for delivery through a carrier chosen by Seller. Buyer shall pay any costs of delivery of the Goods in addition to the Purchase Price.

4. **Risk of Loss.** The risk of loss from any casualty to the Goods, regardless of the cause, will be the responsibility of the Seller until the Goods have been received by the Buyer.

5. **Acceptance.** Buyer will have the right to inspect the Goods upon receipt, and within 3 business days after delivery, Buyer must give notice to Seller of any claim for damages on account of condition, quality, or grade of the Goods, and Buyer must specify the basis of the claim in detail. Failure of Buyer to comply with these conditions will constitute irrevocable acceptance of the Goods by Buyer.

6. **Installation**. Seller shall install Goods using sound construction practices on a date agreed to by both Buyer and Seller, but in no event will such date be later than the due date of the final installment payment.

7. **Warranty.** Seller warrants that the goods sold hereunder are new and free from substantive defects in workmanship and materials. Seller's liability under the foregoing warranty is limited to one year's replacement of goods or repair of defects or refund of the purchase price at Seller's sole option. No other warranty, express or implied, including the warranty of merchantability, is made by Seller, and none shall be imputed or presumed.

8. **Taxes.** All sales taxes, tariffs, and other governmental charges shall be paid by Buyer and are Buyer's responsibility except as limited by law.

9. **Governing Law.** This Agreement is governed by the laws of the State of Texas.

10. **Force Majeure.** Seller may, without liability, delay performance or cancel this Agreement on account of Force Majeure.

11. **Notice.** All notices between the parties must be in writing and delivered by courier or by certified mail, return receipt requested.

12. **Arbitration of Disputes.** Any controversy or claim arising out of, in connection with, or relating to this Agreement or a breach thereof, will be settled by arbitra-

tion administered by the American Arbitration Association under its Commercial Arbitration Rules, and judgment on the award rendered by the arbitrator(s) may be entered in any court having jurisdiction. The arbitration proceeding will be held in the city and state where Seller's principal office is located.

13. **Assignment and Delegation.** The parties may not assign rights or delegate duties under this Agreement unless both parties consent prior to the assignment or delegation. A purported assignment or delegation in contravention of this section is void.

14. **Severability.** If any provision of this Agreement is determined to be illegal or unenforceable, the remaining provisions remain in full force, so long as the essential provisions for each party remain legal and enforceable.

15. **Merger.** This Agreement is the final and exclusive statement of the parties' agreement as to all matters contained in this Agreement. It supersedes all previous negotiations and agreements.

16. **Amendments in Writing.** The parties may amend this Agreement only by an agreement in writing that both parties execute.

To evidence the Parties' agreement to this Agreement, they have executed and delivered it as of the date set forth in the preamble.

Alarm Experts, Inc.

By: _____
Its: Reyna D'Ignazio, District Manager

Olivia's Beans, Inc.

By: _____
Its: Olivia Ralston, President

Traditions and Trends

Lawyers and other professionals who are drafting contracts typically do not start their work from a blank piece of paper. They consult prior contracts, perhaps from matters on which they or a colleague had worked previously. Such existing documents are known as *precedent documents*. Precedent documents should not be confused with precedent cases, which we have learned are binding on courts under the principle of *stare decisis*. Nonetheless, the concepts are related. In both contract drafting and in case law, someone is following in the footsteps of legal work that has been done in the past. From the pre-digital age to today, contract-drafting lawyers have found ways to save and re-use contractual language, both individually and within law firms and organizations.

When lawyers are faced with a novel legal or business concept that they must translate into contract terms, they have traditionally turned to *formbooks*. In twentieth-century law offices, formbooks were almost always printed volumes, often in a multivolume set, that are full of sample contract clauses and documents, organized according to subject matter. One formbook might cover sales contracts, another might address construction contracts, and still another might cover intellectual property licenses. This very specialized content was exclusively the province of a brick-and-mortar law library.

Technology has greatly changed the use of precedent documents and formbooks in contemporary contract drafting—and not always for the better. Internet legal research and modern word processing software have tremendously improved ease of access to existing contract clauses, and that has been a great timesaver for contract drafters. The problem with current and emerging technology is that it can make the replication of mistaken, irrelevant, or even harmful provisions much too easy.

Amazon famously has section 57.10 in its lengthy terms of service,[7] requiring the safe use of one of its developer tools. The section concludes with the following clause:

> However, this restriction will not apply in the event of the occurrence (certified by the United States Centers for Disease Control or successor body) of a widespread viral infection transmitted via bites or contact with bodily fluids that causes human corpses to reanimate and seek to consume living human flesh, blood, brain or nerve tissue and is likely to result in the fall of organized civilization.

Contracting around a Zombie Apocalypse may seem amusing, but what happens when someone decides to cut and paste Amazon's contract provisions into its own deal? You can imagine the result: Once a contract is out on the internet or an organization's document cloud, it can act like a computer virus (albeit not a zombie virus). Harmful contract language can essentially replicate itself over and over again. Form provisions that might be correct in one state can be copied off the internet and transplanted to another state where they are unenforceable.

Contract drafting has not resisted the trend toward automation, but in the immediate future there is still an important role for expert human beings who can recognize and eradicate unintended legal problems in transactional documents.

---

7. https://aws.amazon.com/service-terms/

Chapter 13

Reviewing
Contracts — Content

> "The first part of the party of the first part shall be known in this contract as
> the first part of the party of the first part shall be known in this contract...."
> Look, why should we quarrel about a thing like this? We'll take it right out, eh?
>
> — Groucho Marx, *A Night at the Opera*

The focus of chapter 12 was on the "big picture" of a professionally drafted contract—recognizing the document format and its major components. This chapter now turns to the finer points. What do individual contract provisions within the big picture actually mean? While the potential for creative contract drafting is nearly infinite in variety, certain types of provisions should be recognizable to legally literate professionals. Our goal for this chapter is that you would ultimately (1) have a working understanding of these contract provisions, and (2) be prepared, in appropriate cases, to negotiate changing the provisions. Access to the services of a skilled transactional lawyer is invaluable in these situations, but even having such access does not change the fact that *you* will quite possibly be the person who knows your company's situation or personal situation the best of all. You should be prepared to play an informed role as one of the creators of the legal obligations that will govern your or your employer's interests.

The language that could appear in contract documents can—and does—fill hundreds of volumes on the shelves of a law library. This chapter focuses on two types of information that will aid you in understanding a contract. The first of these is a set of tools that contract-drafting expert Tina Stark has labeled "contract concepts."[1] The contract concepts show up in every properly drafted agreement. They relate to style and language that professionals use to accomplish certain conceptual goals, such as how to make an enforceable promise into a documented obligation. The contract concepts are abstract, transcending particular substance. But once you can identify them, your skill and potential in the art of reviewing and revising contracts will significantly increase.

The second type of information we will consider here is tied to specific substance — commonly used and disputed "standard" terms. These are the types of terms that are tossed about so frequently that they have earned names from lawyers, such as "a forum-selection clause" or a "liquidated damages clause." For these terms, half the battle is sometimes learning the vocabulary, yet these terms are so prominent because they can be enormously consequential, both in monetary terms and in dictating important legal rights. Chapter 12 briefly touched on standard terms, and those plus the common examples discussed here should give you enough understanding of common provisions that you will be better equipped to recognize when something might be amiss or worth further investigation.

I. Identifying the "Contract Concepts"

When reviewing a complete, professionally drafted contract, most all of the business accomplished in the contract can be tied back to contract concepts. These concepts are the foundational building blocks by which the substance of parties' deal is translated into language memorializing it for purposes of later enforcement. In her excellent materials for lawyers who draft contracts, Professor Stark identifies seven discernible contract concepts:

The Seven "Contract Concepts"

(1) Declarations
(2) Covenants
(3) Rights
(4) Discretionary Authority
(5) Representations
(6) Warranties
(7) Conditions

In the sections that follow, we will consider each of these concepts along with one or more examples of how each one is implemented in a contract. For our abbreviated

---

1. Tina L. Stark, *Drafting Contracts: How and Why Lawyers Do What They Do* 9 (2d ed. 2014). The sections in this chapter on contract concepts are informed by Professor Stark's pioneering textbook.

discussion, we will consider some closely related concepts in tandem: Covenants and rights are closely related, as are representations and warranties. Let us begin with perhaps the most straightforward concept—declarations.

A. Declarations

A declaration is a factual statement that both parties agree is true for purposes of the contract. One common form of declaration is a definition. For instance:

> **"Distribution Territory"** means Canada, Mexico, and the United States of America except for the states of Alaska and Hawaii.

Here the declaration is a definition—a statement that the parties agree to a specialized meaning of "Distribution Territory" whenever that term is used in the contract. Declarations show up outside of the definitions section, however, such as in the following examples:

> **14.4 Governing Law.** The laws of the State of New York govern all matters, including torts, arising under or relating to this Agreement.
>
> **3.1.4 Term.** The term of this Lease begins on January 1, 20XX and ends on December 31, 20XY.
>
> **5(c) Down Payment.** The down payment is $5,000 or five percent of the Estimated Total Purchase, whichever is greater.

All of these declarations state policies or terms of engagement under which the parties will carry out their agreement. Certain law will govern the agreement, and the lease in question will have a specified beginning and ending date. A characteristic trait of declarations that will help you identify them is that, *standing alone*, declarations do not obligate the parties to do anything. Instead, declarations only cause legal events to occur[2] by the declaration's use within active contract concepts—such as a covenant or a representation—that creates specific obligations of the parties. As you read the "Down Payment" provision above, for example, notice that it does not by itself state that anyone is obligated to pay the down payment. That comes elsewhere—likely in a covenant provision.

B. Covenants (and Corresponding Rights)

A *covenant* is a promise that a party will do something or will refrain from doing something. In well-drafted contracts, a covenant is usually signaled by use of the words *shall* or *shall not*. A contract reviewer cannot count on every contract being well drafted, however, and thus must be on the lookout for variations. In any format, a covenant

---

2. Professor Stark uses the more memorable phrase that declarations are "kicked into action" by the other contract concepts. *Id.* at 39.

will be in the nature of a promise to act or abstain from acting in the future, such as in the following examples:

C. Payment. Tenant shall pay Landlord the Rent by no later than the first day of each month of the Term of this Lease.

2.7 Services. During the term of this Agreement, Agent shall use commercially reasonable efforts to procure acting roles for Talent in the film and television industries.

7.2(b) Noncompetition. For three years following the Closing of the sale of Pizza Paradise, Inc. to HoldingCorp, Seller shall not engage in any restaurant business, whether as owner, manager, or employee.

3. Subject to the terms and conditions of this Contract, Seller agrees to sell and Buyer agrees to buy all of Buyer's requirements for tires over a three-year period beginning on April 1, 20XX and ending on March 31, 20XY.

Unlike the declaration examples in the previous section, these covenant provisions contain discernible promises that create obligations in identified parties, such as the Tenant and the Agent. In the first two examples, the signal verb for the covenant is "shall," with the subject of the verb being the party who is making a promise to perform. In the third example, the verb signaling the covenant is "shall not," because the promise is one of forbearance — to *not* do something that the party would otherwise have a legal right to do.

The fourth example contains reciprocal covenants by the Buyer and Seller using, as sometimes happens, the phrase "agrees to" rather than "shall." While this style is not the preferred drafting practice (the *entire* document is an agreement, after all), the provision read as a whole still indicates a promise. This example of a covenant is a special type that is the main or overarching promise of the contract, a covenant for which Professor Stark has coined the immensely useful term *subject-matter performance provision*.[3] Such a provision contains the promises that are the main objectives of the parties, but it characterizes them as "subject to" other requirements of the contract. Parties will often place their main, overarching obligation near the beginning of their contract, but with an understanding that later contract provisions will elaborate on the specific details and limits of the main obligation.

Covenants frequently use defined terms drafted as declarations that are located elsewhere in the contract. Such covenants are the mechanism for converting the declarations into an obligation. The obligation of the Tenant in the first example is to pay the capital-R "Rent," so we should expect to see "Rent" as a declaration elsewhere in the lease, such as:

---

3. *See, e.g., id.* at 49.

> **"Rent"** means $4,800 per month during the first six months of this Lease, and $6,000 per month thereafter for the remainder of the Lease term.

Thus, understanding the meaning of a given covenant may require reference to defined terms in other parts of the contract.

Any discussion of covenants would be incomplete without the related concept of contractual rights. In most cases, a *right* is the other party's perspective on one party's covenant. Put another way, when one contracting party has a covenant obligation to perform, the other party has a reciprocal right to obtain that performance. If the tenant has a legal obligation to pay rent, then the landlord has a right to receive such rent. Thus, where one party has the ability to require or prohibit action by another party under a contract under penalty of legal liability, that party has an enforceable right. It is also possible for a covenant to be buried beneath a statement of a right, like so:

> **C. Payment.** Landlord is entitled to payment of the Rent by Tenant no later than the first day of each month of the Term of this Lease.

The "is entitled to" language in the above example signals the statement of a right, and a contractual right requires the existence of a corresponding obligation—in this case the tenant's obligation to pay rent. When reviewing a contract or considering its implications for the parties, thinking about covenants and rights together is a helpful exercise. One party's substantive right will be intertwined with another party's substantive covenant, no matter how the provision is drafted. While most contract drafting experts would recommend stating an obligation as a covenant rather than a right, you likely will see both formulations out in the real world.

C. Discretionary Authority

Because of the broad way in which the term "right" may properly be used outside the realm of contract drafting (such as in reference to "a constitutional right," for example), you might imagine that rights cover anything that a party has the legal authority to do or not do within a particular contract. In the arena of contract concepts, however, that view would be incorrect. While a contractual right is tied to another party's covenant, express permission to act or identification of a choice whether to do something is known as *discretionary authority*. Even the most voluminous and thought-out contract will not cover every possibility for how the parties might conduct themselves in the future. Some possibilities, however, are so foreseeable that the parties will want to specify the presence or extent of discretion. Discretionary authority in a contract is often signaled by use of the word "may":

> **7.1.3. Order Placement.** The Buyer may submit purchase orders to the Seller in writing, by email, or by telephone. In the event of submission by telephone, the

purchase order will not be deemed received until Seller has confirmed the order in writing or by email.

9(a). Assignment. The Buyer shall not assign any of its rights under this Agreement, except that it may assign its rights to a wholly-owned subsidiary of the Buyer.

The first example is a straightforward identification of discretionary authority: The Buyer is specifically authorized to choose among three methods of order placement. The Seller would have no grounds to complain about any of the three, though use of the telephone has a consequence of possible delay in the sending of a confirmation. The second example shows discretionary authority identified as an exception to an otherwise blanket covenant. In an anti-assignment clause, the Buyer promises not to assign its contractual rights to another party. Within that promise, however, is a discretionary exception: If the Buyer decides to assign its rights to a company that it wholly owns, then that assignment would be permissible.

Notice from these examples that the party granted discretionary authority is not obligated to exercise it in a particular manner, and that is rather the point of these provisions—creating options. These options are not necessarily available at all times. Consider an example where discretionary authority has been paired with a condition (a contract concept we will explore in more detail shortly):

11.9 Early Termination. If, by 11:59 p.m. on December 31, 20XX, Author's weekly online column has not generated at least 100,000 discernable clickthroughs, then Website may, within 90 days of such date, terminate this Agreement under the procedures described in section 13.1, and Author will not be entitled to further payments from Website.

Again the existence of discretionary authority is signaled by the use of "may," but the discretion in this provision is constrained by a condition. The only situation where the Website "may" terminate its contract with the Author is if the Author's column has not been the subject of sufficient clicks by a specified date. Even if that condition is met, the discretion to terminate the contract exists only within a 90-day window.

Discretionary authority to walk away from a contract early is a powerful use of the concept. Notice how much better discretionary authority is for a party rather than a self-executing declaration that a contract terminates. The Website would have the ability to keep its contract with the Author even if she generated only 90,000 click-throughs by the deadline. The Website might, for example, have been impressed with the most recent trajectory and growth of demand for the Author's content. An automatic termination, in contrast, would end the contract even if both parties did not wish it to end.

D. Representations and Warranties

A *representation* is a statement that a past or present fact is true. If the fact is not true, then the recipient may have a claim for misrepresentation (sometimes in the form of a tort known as "negligent misrepresentation"), giving rise to recovery of damages if the other side reasonably relied upon the factual statement. If a contractual representation is intentionally false and for the purpose of inducing entry into the contract under false pretenses, then the recipient's claim could be for *fraud*, an intentional tort that sometimes also provides for the recovery of *punitive damages*—a civil penalty whose purpose is to punish the wrongdoer, and a type of damages that is almost never available for mere breach of contract. Damages for fraud also require proof of reasonable reliance upon the false information by its recipient. A representation can never properly be made about future facts (though that is not a promise that you will never see such a thing in a badly drafted contract provision). Thus, the following would be an appropriate set of representations in a loan agreement:

6. **Representations.** Borrower represents to Lender that—

  (a) Borrower's audited financial statements for the past three complete fiscal years, which are attached as Schedule 1, are correct in all material respects; and

  (b) Borrower has current supply contracts with unexpired terms of one year or more with national retailers Stuff-Mart, Bullseye, and Needless-Markup.

A *warranty*, in contrast, is a promise that stated facts are true, and it is also a promise to pay damages if the facts are not true. Unlike a claim for misrepresentation, a warranty claim does not require proof of reasonable reliance. A warranty also cannot give rise to a fraud claim. Indeed, the maker of a warranty may know that its stated facts are false but is simply willing to agree to pay damages. Finally, a warranty can, unlike a representation, be made about the truth of *future* facts. Imagine you have purchased a new car, and it came with a manufacturer's three-year limited warranty. That warranty is effectively a promise that the car will not suffer covered mechanical breakdowns, *or* (more importantly) that if it does suffer such breakdowns, the manufacturer will cover the repair costs (i.e., pay specified damages for the benefit of the buyer).

Imagine a commercial lease for a lunchtime restaurant on the first floor of a new office building. The restaurant is concerned about whether the building will have enough tenants to generate sufficient lunchtime business. The landlord desperately wants the restaurant as a ground-floor tenant because it will help attract new office tenants for the upper floors. After some negotiation, the landlord agrees to add the following warranty to the lease:

G. **Warranty.** Landlord warrants to Restaurant that, within eighteen months of the effective date of this lease, the Building will be at least 70% occupied by tenants with leases of one year or longer in duration.

By this provision, Landlord is effectively agreeing to pay damages to Restaurant for breach of warranty if Landlord falls short of its stated leasing target. Landlord cannot represent that it will make the target because the target is a future fact that is not capable of being known with certainty. A warranty, however, is entirely appropriate.

To further distinguish between representations and warranties, consider the combined provision that appeared in Olivia Ralston's Noncompetition Agreement with Braggadocio in the previous chapter. Olivia is the "Employee":

> **7. No Conflicting Agreements.** Employee represents and warrants to Braggadocio that Employee has the legal right to enter into this Agreement and that Employee has no contractual or other impediments to the performance of Employee's obligations.

Here, if Olivia had a contract with a previous employer that prevented her from entering into this agreement with Braggadocio, her factual statement to the contrary would be a misrepresentation. If the previous employer sued Braggadocio for tortious interference with that contract, any damages assessed against Braggadocio would be a result of Olivia's misrepresentation and could become her liability as well. For Braggadocio to recover from Olivia based on misrepresentation or fraud, however, it must affirmatively prove that it actually relied on Olivia's representation and that its reliance was reasonable. If Braggadocio put little thought or investigation into Olivia's representation, such reliance might be difficult to prove.

Braggadocio would have a much easier time proving a breach of warranty because such a claim typically does not require proof of reliance. In effect, the company need only show that the untruth of Olivia's factual statement caused it monetary damage. When, as here, a factual statement is made both a representation and a warranty, the recipient has a broader array of legal remedies and can choose whichever one is easiest to prove (usually warranty) or whichever one provides for greater damages recovery (often fraud, if the surrounding circumstances will support it).

Like covenants, both representations and warranties create the possibility of contractual liability. Unlike covenants, the liability for not living up to a representation or warranty does not arise from a failure to perform obligations. Instead, misrepresentation and breach of warranty exist because of the failure of certain *facts* stated in a contract to be true. Given their functionality, contracting parties have numerous reasons why they might seek—or resist—the inclusion of certain representations or warranties in a contract. A professional involved in the negotiation or review of a contract should have a grasp of the business implications for such liability-creating provisions.

E. Conditions

Last in our brief survey of contract concepts is the *condition*. The classic definition of a condition is that it is "an event, not certain to occur, which must occur, unless its non-occurrence is excused, before performance under a contract becomes due."[4] Per-

---

4. Restatement (Second) of Contracts § 224 (1981). See Chapter 7 of this book for more information on the Restatements of Law.

haps the easier way to understand conditions is by thinking of them as an electrical switch. A switch can potentially be put in the on position or the off position, and certain items will or will not function depending on the switch's position. In a contract, certain consequences will follow if a condition is satisfied, but those consequences will not follow if the condition is not satisfied. A condition is also analogous to an *if/then* statement in computer programming: The "if" provision must be true in order for the "then" section of the program to be triggered. An if/then provision is one way to form a condition:

> **19. Deadline Extension.** *If* the Contractor is unable to work due to weather conditions for more than 30 days during the term of this Agreement, *then* the Completion Deadline will be extended until September 1, 20XX.

While no particular words are always present in a well-drafted condition, some of the most common words signaling a condition are "must," "if," and "unless." Consider the following examples:

> **14. Renewal.** To renew this Lease for an additional one-year term at Landlord's then-prevailing rate, Tenant *must* notify Landlord in writing by no later than the thirtieth day before the expiration of the existing Lease term.

> **5.2 Shipment.** *Unless* Buyer, by no later than the first day of the month in which Seller's shipment of gravel is scheduled for delivery, notifies Seller that Buyer intends to cancel the shipment, Seller shall ship the gravel on the fifteenth day of the month.

III. CONDITIONS TO CLOSING

The Buyer is obligated to close the sale of the Property only *if* the following conditions have been satisfied or have been waived:

A. The Warehouse *must* have been demolished and all debris removed on or before the Closing Date.

B. Seller's board of directors *must* have authorized the sale of the Property by way of a resolution substantially in the form of Exhibit "A" to this Agreement.

C. All liens on the Property other than those listed on Schedule 3 *must* have been removed.

These examples illustrate some of the variety in drafted conditions, but they all share a commonality: A contractual event will or will not occur based on the status of the condition. In the first example, lease renewal will occur only if timely notice has been given. The second example shows when a monthly gravel delivery will or will not happen, with cancellation triggered by notice. The third example, from a real estate contract, shows just how consequential a condition provision can be. Here, the Buyer can bring an entire real estate transaction to a grinding halt unless each listed condition is satisfied. A professional reviewing a contract should keep a keen eye out for the presence—and consequences—of conditions expressed in a contract. Know when and how an event can "flip the switch."

II. Identifying Important Common Provisions

Recall from Chapter 12 our consideration of "general provisions" in a contract, also commonly known as "boilerplate." Such terms are typically (to use our newly acquired contract-concept vocabulary) stated as declarations. As a reminder, the example of Olivia Ralston's Noncompetition Agreement with Braggadocio contained six types of general provisions illustrated in the previous chapter:

"General Provisions" Previously Illustrated in Chapter 12
Notice: specifies how the parties are to provide effective notice where the contract requires notice
Severability: states that the parties intend the rest of the contract to remain in force even if parts are determined to be unenforceable
Merger Clause/Integration Clause ("Entire Agreement"): evidences that the contracting parties want their final written agreement to be their exclusive deal, to the exclusion of any terms outside of the writing
Counterparts: expressly provides discretionary authority to the parties to sign or otherwise execute separate but identical copies of a contract
Choice of Law ("Governing Law"): states which jurisdiction's law will govern the contract, including its interpretation and remedies for its breach
Heirs, Successors, and Assigns: affirms that the parties intend for the contract to bind any legal successors to the original contracting parties

Many other contract provisions are common enough to be considered boilerplate. These terms often—but not always—also appear in the general provisions sections of a contract. Here, we will cover six other common provisions about which any professional negotiating or reviewing a contract should be aware, at least at the level of knowing whether to explore with a lawyer the use and consequences of such provisions.

A. Arbitration Clause

An arbitration clause obligates parties to a contract to resolve contract disputes before a private arbitrator (or panel of arbitrators) instead of by litigation in either a state or federal court. You have likely agreed to dozens of arbitration clauses in your life as they have become ubiquitous in daily consumer contracts. Arbitration can offer many benefits to disputing parties, including expedited procedures and more control over their process than a one-size-fits-all courtroom litigation might provide. The arbitrator's final decision—called an "award"—can be filed with an actual court and enforced like any other judgment, such as by the pursuit of collection efforts. Downsides usually include the lack of any appeal of the arbitrator's award and an obligation for the parties to pay for the arbitrator's services (as opposed to judges, who receive a public salary). Still, arbitration in the United States, especially since the 1980s, has come into increasingly widespread use. In some fields, such as construction and securities dealing, arbitration is so dominant that litigation is extremely rare. The standard form contracts in those fields all include arbitration clauses.

Once parties have agreed by contract to arbitrate, the agreement is exceedingly difficult to avoid. The United States Supreme Court has held that the Federal Arbitration Act of 1925 [5] established a broad policy in favor of arbitration, and the federal mandate to enforce arbitration clauses applies in state courts as well as in federal courts. A dispute will only be excluded from the mandate to arbitrate if it is clearly outside the scope of the agreement. When an arbitration clause is challenged, most doubts will be resolved in favor of arbitration.

Here is a typical arbitration clause, based on a language recommended by the American Arbitration Association,[6] one of the nation's largest providers of private dispute resolution services:

Any controversy or claim arising out of or relating to this contract, or the breach thereof, shall be settled by arbitration administered by the American Arbitration Association in accordance with its Commercial Arbitration Rules [or other AAA Rules], and judgment on the award rendered by the arbitrator[s] may be entered in any court having jurisdiction thereof.

Another of the largest dispute resolution service providers, JAMS,[7] suggests language contained in the following arbitration clause:[8]

Any dispute, claim or controversy arising out of or relating to this Agreement or the breach, termination, enforcement, interpretation or validity thereof, including the determination of the scope or applicability of this agreement to arbitrate, shall be determined by arbitration in [insert the desired place of arbitration] before [one/three] arbi-

---

5. 9 U.S.C. §§ 1–16.

6. American Arbitration Association, https://www.adr.org/Clauses.

7. JAMS originally was an acronym that stood for Judicial Arbitration and Mediation Services, due to the significant role retired judges played in founding the company. The name is no longer an acronym today. JAMS, https://jamsadr.com/about-the-jams-name/.

8. JAMS, https://www.jamsadr.com/clauses/#Standard.

trator(s). The arbitration shall be administered by JAMS pursuant to its Comprehensive Arbitration Rules and Procedures [and in accordance with the Expedited Procedures in those Rules] [or pursuant to JAMS' Streamlined Arbitration Rules and Procedures]. Judgment on the Award may be entered in any court having jurisdiction. This clause shall not preclude parties from seeking provisional remedies in aid of arbitration from a court of appropriate jurisdiction.

These arbitration clauses are illustrative of the variety appearing in many contracts. They are both in the form of a declaration of a policy governing the parties. Both clauses refer to particular service providers and specific sets of rules. As a result, the parties have agreed to a litany of procedures—largely tried and tested—for how the arbitration process will occur, addressing such matters as how to initiate the process, how to select an arbitrator, and the extent of discovery. The JAMS example also specifies the location in which the arbitration is to take place. Take a few minutes to browse the websites for the AAA (www.adr.org) and for JAMS (www.jamsadr.com). The ready-made rules available from either organization are far more voluminous than the one-paragraph arbitration clause, yet these rules become a vital part of the parties' contract once a dispute arises.

Because arbitration is a creation of contract, however, clauses need not follow specific forms. Within the limits of contract law, parties can dream up almost any dispute resolution process that they find mutually acceptable and incorporate it into their agreement. When reviewing or negotiating a contract, pay close attention to the specific requirements stated in an arbitration clause. If the clause refers to special rules, look up those rules—they are probably on the internet. Similarly, if preserving the right to courtroom litigation is important to your side of the deal, you may want to strike the arbitration clause entirely. If your side is comfortable with particular arbitration providers or processes, you may want to add an arbitration clause to a contract that lacks one. At the dealmaking phase, these are all open questions. By the time a dispute arises, the parties will be locked into their prior agreement on dispute resolution. Be thoughtful and careful while you still have choices.

B. Forum-Selection Clause

Where a contract does not contain an arbitration clause, or where it contains only a limited-purpose arbitration clause, parties will sometimes try to dictate where a lawsuit must be brought by use of a *forum-selection clause*. The forum is the court (identified by location, not by judge) that would hear any litigation arising from a contract dispute amongst the parties. Although such clauses are often enforceable, they present more tricky issues than does an arbitration clause. First, the parties cannot select just any court. The court must be one that would have *jurisdiction* over the parties and their case. While the subject of the extent of American courts' jurisdiction over contracting parties is well beyond the scope of this chapter, suffice it to say, for present purposes, that the parties and their deal must usually have some notable connection to the state in which their chosen court is located. If the chosen court has no jurisdiction over the case, then the forum-selection clause is effectively unenforceable.

Jurisdictional questions aside, however, most courts will enforce a forum-selection clause where there is a legal basis for doing so. If a case is filed somewhere other than the contractually chosen location, the filing court can transfer *venue* of the case to a new location. Such a transfer can be significant, providing one side with the convenience of a home court and the other with complicated logistics and higher costs.

The following example of a forum-selection clause is drawn from an insurance contract and is paired with a choice-of-law clause (a reasonably common occurrence):

> **Choice of Law and Forum** — In the event that the Insured and the Company dispute the validity or formation of this policy or the meaning, interpretation or operation of any term, condition, definition, or provision of this policy resulting in litigation, the Insured and the Company agree that the law of the State of New York will apply and that all litigation or other form of dispute resolution will take place in the State of New York.

Where at least one of the parties is located in New York, there is little question in most states that this clause would be enforced and that a breach of contract suit filed in Texas, for example, would (from a Texas state court) be dismissed with instruction for the plaintiff to refile in New York or would (from a Texas federal court) be transferred to a federal court sitting in New York.

Notice what this provision does *not* do. It does not specify that the lawsuit must be brought in any *particular* "state court" or "federal court" in New York. Such an omission is wise. Demanding specific courts beyond the basic geography of a city or state greatly increases the risk that the clause will not be enforced because it seeks to require use of a court that does not have jurisdictional authority to hear the case, even though it is situated in the proper state pursuant to the contract. A contract provision specifying a particular judge (rather than following the normal case assignment procedures of the state or district) is unlikely to be enforced, even where the court would have jurisdiction. As a whole, the United States legal system frowns upon such pinpoint "forum shopping" as being against public policy. The safest approach is to identify a jurisdiction with a fairly high level of generality.

Forum selection clauses seem innocuous at the time of contracting, but they loom large once a dispute arises. Where contracting parties have sufficient bargaining power, most insist on a court in their own city or state.

C. Recovery of Attorney's Fees

The so-called "American Rule" on legal fees generally does not allow a party bringing a lawsuit to recover from the other party sums paid to its own attorney, regardless of who wins or loses the case. The American Rule got its name by being different from the law in England, where the loser of a lawsuit pays both parties' fees incurred in that lawsuit.

Two major exceptions to the American Rule exist. First, statutes have been enacted that allow a litigant to recover "reasonable" legal fees incurred in the pursuit of certain specific claims (e.g., certain civil rights violations, certain consumer protection claims). The second exception, and the one that concerns us here, is contractual. If parties to a contract agree that the prevailing party in a contract dispute is entitled to recover its attorney's fees,[9] then courts (or arbitrators, for that matter) will generally allow such a recovery.

Here are some typical fee recovery clauses that a court (or arbitrator) would tend to enforce:

L. **Attorney's Fees.** If any suit or action is instituted to enforce or interpret this Agreement, the prevailing party will be entitled, in addition to the cost of disbursements otherwise allowed by law, such sum as the court or arbitrator may adjudge as reasonable attorney's fees in such suit or action.

12.1 **Fee Recovery.** If any attorney is employed by either party with regard to any legal or equitable action, arbitration or other proceeding brought by such party for enforcement of this Note or because of an alleged dispute, breach, default or misrepresentation in connection with any of the provisions of this Note, the prevailing party will be entitled to recover from the other party reasonable attorney's fees and other costs and expenses incurred, in addition to any other relief to which the prevailing party may be entitled.

In contract litigation, an attorney's fee recovery provision is only half the battle. The prevailing party must typically prove: (1) the amount of the fees and the tasks for which they specifically were incurred, and (2) that the fees are reasonable. Realize that the losing party is probably not going to hand over its credit card for whatever the winner claims. Like most other claims, attorney's fees must be supported by sufficient evidence.

D. Liquidated Damages Clause

A liquidated damages clause seeks to specify in advance what a party's damages will be in the event of a later breach of contract. Can parties contractually do that? The answer to that question is, "sometimes." Damages agreed to in advance are known as

---

9. As a legally literate professional, you should be aware of a quirk of written grammar and usage. Statutes, contracts, and many legal writers have divergent terminology for the fees charged by lawyers. In even a casual perusal of sources, you will find support for the terms *attorney fees*, *attorney's fees*, and *attorneys' fees*. The terms are all used to mean the same thing—the money that lawyers charge for rendition of their services. For consistency's sake, we use the term "attorney's fees" in this book, but do not be at all surprised to find its counterparts lurking around on documents that you see out in the real world.

liquidated damages. The term "liquidated" does not mean that the party is awarded water, of course. Instead, liquidated refers to a claim being reduced to a specific amount, as opposed to a claim that is "unliquidated" and the total amount not yet known.

The well-established rules on when liquidated damages provisions are enforceable require that the amount chosen by the parties be a reasonable estimate of anticipated or difficult-to-prove losses.[10] If a contract term provides for liquidated damages that function as a "penalty" imposed on the breaching party, American courts will refuse to enforce the clause. What is a penalty? A provision that generally makes the breaching party liable for more than it would be in actual damages for breaching a contract is considered a penalty. It functions to compel a party into performing a contract even where a breach and payment of damages would be more financially beneficial.

The best liquidated damages clauses frequently contain a list of recitations of why the stated damages are a reasonable estimate of damages in light of future unknown facts surrounding a breach. Consider the following example:

> **17. Liquidated Damages.** If the Seller fails to deliver the Products by the Delivery Date (the "Seller Breach"), the Seller shall pay to the Customer an amount equal to 15% of the Purchase Price of the Products (the "Liquidated Damages"). The parties intend that the Liquidated Damages constitute compensation, and not a penalty. The parties acknowledge and agree that the Customer's harm caused by a Seller Breach would be impossible or very difficult to accurately estimate at the time of this Contract, and that the Liquidated Damages are a reasonable estimate of the anticipated or actual harm that might arise from a Seller Breach. The Seller's payment of the Liquidated Damages is the Seller's sole liability and entire obligation and the Customer's exclusive remedy for any Seller Breach.

The contract drafter made it a point in this provision to disclaim any attempt to impose a "penalty." This liquidated damages clause also recites the important point that the stated damages are a reasonable estimate of harm that is inherently difficult to estimate. The final sentence of this particular liquidated damages clause probably seals the deal on its enforceability. It specifies that *both* Seller and Customer are stuck with the liquidated damages, regardless of whether they overcompensate or undercompensate the Customer. In other words, both sides are taking a risk. If a liquidated damages clause sets up a situation where the non-breaching party will (or almost always will) be overcompensated as compared to its actual harm, that creates an unenforceable penalty.

As with many other provisions, a liquidated damages clause demands careful thought about its consequences. Is the certainty worth the possibility of paying more (or receiving less)? How great is the risk of the clause being an unenforceable penalty?

---

10. *See, e.g.*, Restatement (Second) of Contracts § 356 (1981).

These and other questions are often areas where professionals and the lawyers with whom they work can make a most effective problem-preventing team.

E. Force Majeure Clause

Failure to perform obligations under a contract is usually a breach of contract, but parties do not always want this to be the case. When events outside the reasonable control of the parties prevent performance, then performance may be temporarily or permanently excused based on a *force majeure* clause. The term "force majeure" is French for "superior force," and that phrase captures the magnitude of the kinds of things that will excuse a party from doing what it agreed to do.

The following clause is typical:

Force Majeure. No failure or omission by the Parties in the performance of any obligation of this Agreement will be deemed a breach of this Agreement or create any liability if the same will arise from any cause or causes beyond the control of the Parties, including, but not limited to, the following: acts of God; acts or omissions of any government; any rules, regulations or orders issued by any governmental authority or by any officer, department, agency or instrumentality thereof; fire; flood; storm; earthquake; accident; war; rebellion; insurrection; riot; and invasion. The affected Party shall notify the other Party of such force majeure circumstances as soon as reasonably practical, and shall promptly undertake all reasonable efforts necessary to cure such force majeure circumstances.

Many force majeure clauses are catch-all descriptions of large-scale disruptions: natural disasters, governmental action, or even war. Notice that this example clause contains the "including but not limited to" expansion. While such open-ended phrasing is sometimes ill-advised, it often has a place in a force majeure provision. The idea is that the parties probably cannot imagine or list *every* large-scale disruptive event, but those that are listed are representative of the type of occurrence that would preclude a breach.

Professionals who are negotiating or reviewing contracts should consider the presence or absence of a generalized force majeure clause in the greater context of the complete deal. What sorts of matters should (or should not) get a party off the hook for otherwise breaching a contract? Where an industry is susceptible to specific events, a party would be wise to ensure that those events are specified in a force majeure clause. Think, for example, of a farmer who might face hail, drought, or other sources of crop failure and would want a contract provision to help manage risk for such events.

F. Indemnity Clause

An *indemnity clause* is a provision in which a party agrees to reimburse another party for some specified loss or harm. These clauses often have clear reasons for being. Imagine, a high-profile corporate executive who is concerned about the very real possibility that she could be sued in her individual capacity, for example, by a disgruntled former employee or by someone who feels wronged by one of her public statements on behalf of the company. She might insist on the following indemnity provision as part of the employment agreement:

> **7.2 Indemnity.** To the fullest extent permitted by law, the Corporation shall indemnify Executive and hold her harmless for any acts or decisions made by her in good faith while performing services for the Corporation. In addition, to the fullest extent permitted by law, the Corporation shall pay all expenses, including attorney's fees, actually and necessarily incurred by Executive in connection with the defense of any action, suit or proceeding challenging such acts of decisions and in connection with any appeal thereon including the costs of settlement. This indemnification obligation shall survive the termination of the Executive's employment hereunder.

On the other hand, indemnity clauses can also sneak into contracts with no notice or reason. Perhaps the prior contract form had such a provision in it and it was copied over, like a computer virus. Lack of attention to such a provision can prove costly. Consider the following provision, for example:

> **K.7 Indemnity.** Each party shall indemnify and hold harmless the other party, and its shareholders, directors, officers, employees, and agents, from and against all damages, costs, expenses, liabilities, claims, demands, and judgments of whatever kind or nature, including reasonable attorney's fees and costs, for which either party might liable, in whole or in part, arising out of or related to the acts and/or omissions of the indemnifying party and its shareholders, directors, officers employees, and agents.

What does that provision mean? What will it or will it not cover? This clause creates the possibility of liability, but the reasons are dangerously unclear. Any professional reviewing or negotiating a contract should be able to articulate clearly: (1) why an indemnity clause is present and (2) what specific interest it protects. If both of these inquiries have clear and acceptable answers, and if the provision is clearly drafted to address the specific interests it protects, then the clause can stay put. If these inquiries do not have clear answers, or if the risk your side is being asked to assume is unacceptable, remove the indemnity clause. Failing the ability to remove it, try narrowing the scope of what it covers to minimize the potential risk.

III. Balancing Legal Advantages with Business Issues

The chapters in this books that explore the form and function of professionally drafted contracts have only scratched the surface of the subject. This discussion of contract provisions and illustrative examples has shown you both the pitfalls and the possibilities that exist when two sides seek to draft a legally enforceable agreement. The main purpose of negotiating such an agreement should be to reach a workable business deal, so it's important to keep that objective in mind while parsing through the contract provisions. Wise negotiators avoid becoming so enamored with getting "the upper hand" in the review and revision process that they lose sight of the overall objective. Sometimes, in the heat of negotiation or batting alternative terms back and forth, a party focused on the legal aspects of the agreement (including lawyers who are involved) can forget that *law* is only one part of the equation. Two other business issues that are commonly intertwined with the law are *money* and *risk*.

If your background is in business, software development, or project management, you may have heard the saying, "Fast. Good. Cheap. Pick two." A project can be done quickly and excellently, but it will be expensive. It can be done excellently and at a reasonable price, but it will be done slowly, perhaps squeezed in between other time-sensitive premium jobs. Or it can be done quickly and cheaply, but it will not be very good. The magical combination of fast *and* good *and* cheap is practically unattainable because every choice requires a trade-off. The unstated corollary to "Pick two" is that a project cannot have all three. That is why this triangle is sometimes referred to as the "Triple Constraint."

Similarly, in the diagram here, a deal's money position, business risk, and legal position are all interrelated. A party could focus on reaching the best possible term as to money, whether receiving the most (e.g., a seller) or paying the least (e.g., a buyer). The other party may be willing to improve the price point if it can reduce its business risk, such as by reducing or eliminating its future warranty liability. It may also be willing to deal more favorably on price for better legal rights, such as a longer-term license on a valuable item of intellectual property. But there are tradeoffs within this triangle. The negotiating party might envision an excellent business idea at low cost, which can be documented in a contract the counter-party is willing to accept and will likely carry out. That all sounds great until you realize this deal is an illegal anticompetitive arrangement—in other words, an antitrust violation creating significant legal risk. Or a negotiating party might come up with an airtight contract and low financing risks, but the business value of doing such a deal is unclear. With these interrelationships, a person thinking about a contracting matter might imagine reaching a deal point at a position somewhere in the triangle pictured in this section. This triangular graphic helps conceptualize some of the *possible* tradeoffs in reaching an agreement.[11]

Some deal points may relate to two sides of the triangle. A more expansive set of excuses in a force majeure clause for non-performance of a contract both improves the legal position of a seller and reduces the business risk if something goes wrong with the

---

11. Of course, contracting can be far more complex than this simplified representation. Professor Stark, for example, teaches a five-pronged approach to understanding business issues, encompassing categories of money, risk, control, standards, and endgame. Tina Stark, *Drafting Contracts: How and Why Lawyers Do What They Do* 369 (2d ed. 2014).

contract. Terms and timing of payment obligations will affect both a party's money position and its business risk. Working on credit is often necessary, but it is inherently riskier than working on a pre-paid basis. The possible tradeoffs are nearly endless. A less advantageous legal position might be worth a more favorable payment structure. A party concerned with the potential for excessive costs in arbitration could negotiate a term capping the cost of dispute resolution processes.

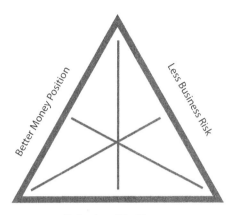

Better Legal Position

None of these situations are inherently the "right" way to shape a contract. Every deal involves different circumstances and different parties who will value different sides of the triangle for a variety of reasons. Any professional working in the contracting process can be more effective, however, by being more informed about the situation on her side. Don't get so lost in the weeds of any one part of the situation—like the language and terms discussed in this chapter—that you lose the big picture of reaching the *right* deal for a particular situation. As Peter Drucker famously said, "There is nothing so useless as doing efficiently that which should not be done at all." If a beautifully drafted contract describes an economically empty business deal, that contract serves no purpose. And even more problematic is the contract that actually creates unexpected risk. Contracts are like power tools: They accomplish great things when used skillfully. When used carelessly, they can also cost a metaphorical limb.

We, of course, want for you to be among the skilled users of contracts.

Having studied this chapter, you should be able to:

- Identify many key provisions in formal commercial contracts
- Use the framework of "contract concepts" to assess various types of contracts
- Survey common types of contract provisions to understand their uses and potential misuses
- Analyze and flag proposed contract terms that may benefit from further evaluation

Case Study

Olivia's Beans has had some promising same-location sales volume growth, so Oliva Ralston has put together a business plan to open three coffee shops in the next year—in Castle Rock, Colorado Springs, and Pueblo. Getting these shops up and running will cost roughly $250,000 more than the money Olivia's Beans has on hand. When Olivia was investigating possible ways to raise the money, she came across an interesting possibility in Green Ventures, LLC.

Green Ventures seeks to finance sustainable and environmentally friendly companies, but does so through a combination of traditional lending and purchasing of equity (i.e., an ownership interest) in its Borrowers. Green Ventures has provided Olivia the proposed "Loan and Guaranty Agreement" reproduced below. You, the erstwhile Risk Manager for Olivia's Beans, are reviewing the agreement.

1. Recall the seven contract concepts described in this chapter:
    1. Declarations
    2. Covenants
    3. Rights
    4. Discretionary Authority
    5. Representations
    6. Warranties
    7. Conditions

    Can you locate at least one example of each of these concepts in the Loan and Guaranty Agreement?

2. Should Olivia's Beans be concerned about any provisions of this contract? If so, which ones? What about Olivia, individually?

3. Olivia will be meeting with her company's lawyer tomorrow regarding another matter. Are there any questions that you think she should ask the lawyer? If so, what?

Loan and Guaranty Agreement

This Loan and Guaranty Agreement (this "Agreement"), dated April 24, 20XX, is by and between Green Ventures, LLC, a Colorado limited liability company (the "Lender"), Olivia's Beans, Inc., a Colorado corporation (the "Borrower"), and Olivia Ralston, an individual (the "Guarantor").

Recitals

WHEREAS, the Lender desires to provide the Borrower with a loan to meet its capital needs with respect to opening certain retail establishments in Colorado; and

WHEREAS, the Borrower has indicated that it wishes to borrow an aggregate of up to $250,000.00 (U.S.); and

WHEREAS, the Borrower and the Guarantor desire that the Lender will loan the Borrower money to be used to meet its capital needs for the aforementioned Colorado projects;

NOW THEREFORE, in consideration of the foregoing recitals, mutual covenants contained herein, and other good and valuable consideration, the receipt and sufficiency of which are hereby acknowledged, the Parties hereby agree as follows:

Definitions

The terms defined in the preamble have their assigned meanings, and each of the following terms has the meaning assigned to it:

"Covered Matters" has the meaning assigned to it in Section 20.

"Effective Date" means the date on which Lender releases the Loan Amount to Borrower.

"Loan Amount" means the aggregate principal amount of $250,000.00.

"Note" has the meaning assigned to it in Section 1.

"Parties" means the Lender, the Borrower, and the Guarantor collectively.

"Purchase Option" has the meaning assigned to it in Section 5.

"Section" means a section of this Agreement, and the plural "Sections" means more than one section of this Agreement.

1. **Principal.** Upon receipt of funds, the Borrower promises to unconditionally pay to the order of the Lender the Loan Amount as set forth in the associated promissory note, together with interest pursuant to this Agreement and the corresponding promissory note documenting the Loan Amount. Repayment of the Loan Amount is subject to the terms and conditions of this Agreement and the promissory note attached hereto as Exhibit A (the "Note"), to be issued to the Lender upon receipt of funds.

2. **Interest Rate.** The rate of simple interest for the Loan Amount is TWELVE PERCENT (12%) per annum and will be due as provided herein.

3. **Installments.** All payments, including interest payments, will be deferred until such time as the first of the three retail facilities to be opened by Borrower using the proceeds of this agreement has been conducting product sales for sixty calendar days, but in no event will payments start later than September 1, 20XX. Borrower shall pay interest and principal on the Loan Amount amortized over sixty monthly payments, with the first such payment commencing as provided in this section.

4. **Guaranty; Pledge.** Funding of the Loan Amount is conditioned upon receipt of the personal guaranty of the Guarantor and a UCC-1 pledge on all equipment, fixtures, and inventory of Borrower. Lender acknowledges and understands that in the event of default of the Note, which is not cured as addressed in the Note, the Lender may elect to apply any or all unpaid Note payments toward the Purchase Option described in Section 5.

5. **Purchase Option.** As inducement to entering into this Agreement, Lender has the option to purchase from Guarantor up to twenty-five percent ownership of Borrower at a price of $20,000 per each one-percent of the total outstanding shares of stock (the "Purchase Option"). The Purchase Option is valid for three years from the Effective Date of this Agreement.

6. **Representations and Warranties.**

   Lender and Borrower each represents and warrants to the other as follows:

   6.1 **Powers and Authority.** It has all necessary power to carry on its present business and has full right, power and authority to enter into this Agreement, to make the loans or borrowings, as applicable, herein provided for, and otherwise perform and to consummate the transactions contemplated hereby.

   6.2 **No Conflicts.** This Agreement does not, and the performance or observance by the party of any of the matters and things herein provided for will not, constitute an Event of Default, as defined in the Note, or event which with the lapse of time, the giving of notice or both, would constitute an event of default under any other agreement to which it is a party or by which it is bound.

   6.3 **Corporate Organization.** It is a duly organized and validly existing corporation under its jurisdiction of organization.

   6.4 **Corporate Authorization.** The board of directors or other governing body of the party has authorized the execution and performance of this Agreement.

7. **Fees and Expenses.** Except as expressly set forth in this Agreement to the contrary, each party shall pay the fees and expenses of its advisers, counsel, accountants and other experts, if any, and all other expenses incurred by such party incident to the negotiation, preparation, execution, delivery and performance of this Agreement. The Borrower shall pay up to $5,000.00 of the Lender's reasonable, documented attorney's fees incurred in connection with the negotiation of this Agreement and the issuance of the Note, and such fees will be added to the principal of the Note.

8. **Successors and Assigns: Assignment.** Except as otherwise expressly provided herein, the provisions hereof inure to the benefit of, and are binding upon, the successors, assigns, heirs, executors and administrators of the parties hereto. Nothing in this Agreement, express or implied, is intended to confer upon any party, other than the parties hereto and their successors and assigns, any rights, remedies, obligations or liabilities under or by reason of this Agreement, except as expressly provided herein. The Borrower may not assign or delegate this Agreement or any of the rights or obligations referenced herein without the prior written consent of the Lender. The Lend-

er may assign and delegate this Agreement, in whole or in part, without the prior consent of the Borrower, and any assignee of this Agreement will inure to all of the rights of the Lender hereunder.

9. **Notices.** Any notice, demand, request, waiver or other communication required or permitted to be given pursuant to this Agreement must be in writing (including electronic format) and will be deemed by the parties to have been received (i) upon delivery in person (including by reputable express courier service) at the address set forth below; (ii) upon delivery by electronic mail (as verified by a printout showing satisfactory transmission) at the electronic mail address set forth below (if sent on a business day during normal business hours where such notice is to be received and if not, on the first business day following such delivery where such notice is to be received); or (iii) upon three business days after mailing with the United States Postal Service if mailed from and to a location within the continental United States by registered or certified mail, return receipt requested, addressed to the address set forth below. Any party hereto may from time to time change its physical or electronic address or facsimile number for notices by giving notice of such changed address or number to the other party in accordance with this section.

If to the Lender at:
Green Ventures, LLC
301 Rocky Heights
Monument, CO 80132
Attention: Ariana Capaldi
Email Address: acapaldi@greenventures.net

If to the Borrower or Guarantor at:
Olivia's Beans, Inc.
2200 Central Parkway
Denver, CO 80201
Attention: Olivia Ralston
Email Address: olivia@oliviasbeans.com

10. **Heading; References.** All headings used herein are used for convenience only and may not be used to construe or interpret this Agreement.

11. **Binding Agreement: Survival.** This Agreement binds and inures to the benefit of both parties, and except as otherwise expressly provided to the contrary herein, each of their respective heirs, successors and assigns.

12. **Delays or Omissions.** No delay or omission to exercise any right, power, or remedy accruing to the Lender, upon any breach or default of the Borrower under this Agreement, will impair any such right, power, or remedy of the

Lender nor will it be construed to be a waiver of any such breach or default, or an acquiescence therein, to in any similar breach or default thereafter occurring; nor will any waiver of any single breach or default be a waiver of any other breach or default therefore or thereafter occurring. All remedies, either under this Agreement or by law or otherwise afforded to the Lender, are cumulative and not alternative.

13. **Construction.** The Parties acknowledge that the Parties and their counsel have reviewed and revised this Agreement and that the language used in this Agreement has been chosen by the parties to express their mutual intent. Accordingly, no rules of strict construction will be applied against any party with respect to this Agreement.

14. **Cumulative Rights.** No delay on the part of the Lender in the exercise of any power or right under this Agreement or under any other instrument executed pursuant to this Agreement will operate as a waiver of any such power or right, nor will a single or partial exercise of any power or right preclude other or further exercise of such power or right or the exercise of any other power or right.

15. **Payments Free of Taxes, Etc.** All payments made by the Borrower under this Agreement will be made by the Borrower free and clear of and without deduction for any and all present and future taxes, levies, charges, deductions, and withholdings. In addition, the Borrower shall pay upon demand any stamp or other taxes, levies or charges of any jurisdiction with respect to the execution, delivery, registration, performance, and enforcement of this Agreement. Upon request by the Lender, the Borrower shall furnish evidence satisfactory to the Lender that all requisite authorizations and approvals by, and notices to and filings with, governmental authorities and regulatory bodies have been obtained and made and that all requisite taxes, levies, and charges have been paid.

16. **Severability.** If one or more provisions of this Agreement are held to be unenforceable under applicable law, such provision(s) will be excluded from this Agreement and the balance of this Agreement is to be interpreted as if such provision(s) were so excluded and will be enforceable in accordance with its terms.

17. **Other Interpretive Provisions.** References in this Agreement to any document, instrument or agreement (a) includes all exhibits, schedules, and other attachments thereto, (b) includes all documents, instruments or agreements issued or executed in replacement thereof, and (c) means such document, instrument or agreement, or replacement or predecessor thereto, as amended, modified and supplemented from time to time and in effect at any given time.

18. **No Oral Modification or Waivers.** The terms herein may not be modified or waived orally, but only by an instrument in writing signed by the party against which enforcement of the modification or waiver is sought.

19. **Attorney's Fees.** In the event of any suit or action to enforce or interpret any provision of this Agreement or otherwise arising out of this Agreement, the prevailing party is entitled to recover, in addition to other direct incremental costs, reasonable attorney's fees in connection with the suit, action, or arbitration, and in any appeals.

20. **Governing Law: Jurisdiction; Venue.** This Agreement, and all matters arising directly and indirectly from it (the "Covered Matters"), are governed in all respects by the laws of the State of Colorado as such laws are applied to agreements between parties in Colorado. The Borrower irrevocably submits to the personal jurisdiction of the courts of the State of Colorado and the United States District Court for the District of Colorado for the purpose of any suit, action, proceeding or judgment relating to or arising out of the Covered Matters. Service of process on the Borrower in connection with any such suit, action or proceeding may be served on the Borrower anywhere in the world by the same methods as are specified for the giving of notices under this Agreement. The Borrower irrevocably consents to the jurisdiction of any such court in any such suit, action or proceeding and to the laying of venue in such court. The Borrower irrevocably waives any objection to the laying of venue of any such suit, action or proceeding brought in such courts and irrevocably waives any claim that any such suit, action or proceeding brought in any such court has been brought in an inconvenient forum.

22. **Entire Agreement Integration Clause.** This Agreement sets forth the entire agreement and understandings of the parties hereto with respect to this transaction, and this Agreement supersedes and nullifies all other agreements made between the Parties as to the subject matter of this Agreement. The Note is part of this Agreement.

23. **Counterparts.** This Agreement may be executed in as many counterpart copies as may be required. All counterparts collectively constitute a single agreement.

IN WITNESS WHEREOF, the parties have executed this Agreement as of the date first written above.

BORROWER
Olivia's Beans, Inc., a Colorado corporation

By: _____

      Olivia Ralston,
      President and CEO

LENDER
Green Ventures, LLC, a Colorado limited liability company
By: Lowercase Capital, Inc., Manager

By: _____
         Ariana Capaldi
         Chief Lending Officer

GUARANTOR

_____
         Olivia Ralston,
         Individually

[Assume that the Exhibit "A" Promissory Note is attached after the signature page. In the interest of brevity, the promissory note is not reproduced here.]

Traditions and Trends

"Legalese"—the pejorative term used to describe dense and stilted language in legal texts—is an unfortunate tradition in legal drafting. Legalese in contract term provisions did not begin with bad intentions, but rather arose from repeated attempts by individual lawyers to make their documents more precise and certain in directing a particular outcome. In many situations, the excess verbiage gave only the illusion of precision. By the text becoming more twisted and confusing over time, the seeds of new interpretive arguments were unintentionally sown into various contract forms.

Such excess verbiage is unfortunate because "more" is not necessarily "better" in contract language; indeed, more can be distinctly worse. When a contract is needlessly difficult to read, it increases the *transaction costs* of the deal it is attempting to accomplish. Think of transaction costs as the expense required to get a deal done, an expense that funnels into a business's overall costs along with interest, maintenance expenses, and other costs.

Difficult contracts increase transaction costs because they take more time to read and understand than do clear ones, resulting in lost time for businesses and their employees who must carry out the contract terms. Twisted and ill-fitting contract terms create unintended risks that may take time and money to avoid, minimize, renegotiate, or (perhaps worst of all) litigate. Unlike maintenance costs—which reduce downtime and increase safety, thereby contributing to profit and social benefit—an unintentionally convoluted contract does not save time or reduce risk. In that sense, contract legalese is a net loss. On a more positive note, every well-written contract is—even if only in a small sense—saving money by avoiding legalese. One General Electric subsidiary reportedly reduced its negotiation costs by 60 percent after a plain-language initiative.[12] Adobe Systems took the unusual step of creating and publishing the *Adobe Legal Department Style Guide* to encourage clarity, conciseness, and a "common voice" in its agreements as well as policy and training materials.[13]

What does the future hold for contract drafting as both lawyers and businesses recognize the inherent financial benefits of avoiding legalese? A recent article by William Pitt in the *Harvard Business Review* suggests that a significant advantage of emerging technology is its ability "to personalize and present contracts," such that "businesses can dramatically cut their length and their abstract complexity, making it easier for customers to understand their rights and responsibilities—all without diminishing legal certainty."[14] The examples recounted by Pitt are impressive:

> A pioneer in this field is Creative Commons, the global nonprofit organization that empowers writers, artists, and other creators to build copyright licenses delineating specific approved uses for their works. The system makes available to consumers a "human-readable summary" of the license, which runs to less than a tenth of the length of the full "legal code" version. Since the publication of the first Creative Commons licenses in 2002, they have come to govern the sharing of more than a billion works via millions of websites.
>
> More recently, the insurance industry has been warming to the idea of personalized digital policies designed for humans and lawyers alike, and two insurers have begun issuing them.

This trend toward technology-aided, personalized contract drafting could have far-reaching positive consequences for consumers and the law-trained professionals who implement such contracts. Thus, legal literacy in contract language appears more and more likely to call for a strong understanding of technology. That does not necessarily mean coding skills, but it does mean understanding and evaluating the risks and benefits of new possibilities in deciding whether to purchase or develop contract drafting systems for your own organization.

---

12. Shawn Burton, *The Case for Plain-Language Contracts*, Harvard Business Review (January-February 2018).

13. Adobe Legal Department Style Guide, https://www.adobe.com/legal/legal-innovation.html (available for download).

14. William Pitt, *Fighting Legalese with Digital, Personalized Contracts*, Harvard Business Review (Feb. 27, 2019).

Chapter 14
....

Email and
Other Correspondence

> Email has been blamed for the death of the letter. We think that's unfair.
> Email is responsible for the death of the useless phone call.
> (And, by the way, it was the telephone that killed the letter.)
>
> — David Shipley and Will Schwalbe,
> *Send: The Essential Guide to Email for Office and Home* (2007).

Consistent with the subtitle of this book, "Working with Law and Lawyers," a large part of working with law and lawyers is dealing with written correspondence. Correspondence is a very broad concept, including formal letters on letterhead, as well as emails, text messages, direct messages on social media, and chat messages. The key point is that correspondence is written *from* a specific sender *to* a specific recipient or small group; it is not publishing. Correspondence regardless of form—whether it is on letterhead or in a chat box — is subject to the same legal doctrines as letters printed on letterhead, signed in blue ink, and sent via certified mail.

In particular, email is a dominant form of correspondence in professional life and work today across many industries, including law. In a recent study, law professors Ann Sinsheimer and David Herring used anthropological techniques to study lawyer behavior in the workplace to find out what they were doing at their desks all day. They found that lawyers spend an inordinate amount of time strategically crafting emails: "Email accounted for a lot of what [lawyers] read and wrote, and their composing process for email exhibited meticulousness and a high degree of concern for word choice and tone."[1] But lawyers do not have a monopoly on being meticulous with written correspondence, and meticulousness helps with all forms of correspondence, from formal letters down to text messages. This chapter reviews some basic legal doctrines that are relevant to correspondence, and it then focuses on organizing and writing effective correspondence, especially email.

I. Background Law and Terminology Affecting Legal Communications

This section is a high-level summary of key legal terms and doctrines relevant to law-related correspondence, and of course state law will vary on these issues. If you work in a company with a general counsel's office or other legal oversight, seek out their guidance on specific doctrines relevant to your work. This section's purpose is to create general awareness and combat a few common myths.

A. Attorney-Client Privilege and the Work-Product Doctrine

The attorney-client privilege protects communications between attorney and client for the purpose of getting and giving legal advice. The attorney-client privilege guards the sanctity, trust, and confidence of communications between a lawyer and client; the idea is that, within some important limits what you tell your lawyer and what your lawyer tells you is private and cannot be used against you in court or otherwise. The purpose of the attorney-client relationship is to allow the client to trust the attorney and share information to obtain legal advice, without fear that the information will be disclosed. Thus, the privilege protects attorney-client communications to promote trust and the giving and receiving of legal advice. Privileged documents do not need to be disclosed in litigation even if they are requested in discovery, and they cannot be admitted into evidence in court. A client can decide to waive the privilege by disclosing privileged information, but that decision belongs to the client and not to the attorney.

Because the privilege applies only to communications made for the purposes of giving and receiving legal advice, it does not extend to preexisting documents you give to

---

1. Ann Sinsheimer and David J. Herring, *Lawyers at Work: A Study of the Reading, Writing, and Communication Practices of Legal Professionals*, 21 Legal Writing 63, 73 (2016).

your lawyer. A document that came into existence for different reasons is not privileged simply because a client shares that document with a lawyer. Likewise, a document is not privileged just because someone writes "privileged" on that document. Such a label can be helpful if it is accurate, but it is confusing and may cause problems if it is not accurate. Similarly, if a lawyer is copied on a business conversation, the business conversation does not become privileged simply because the sender decided to include a lawyer. You should be mindful of the possibility that you might accidentally waive the attorney-client privilege if you share privileged communications with someone who is neither the lawyer or the client.

Privilege can also be impacted by the presence of a third party not subject to the privilege — for example, if a third party is present in the room during a conversation between attorney and client, or if a third party is copied on an email conversation. In addition, privilege can be waived if the client forwards the message to a third party not protected by that privilege. Thus, forwarding a privileged document to a business associate not covered by the privilege would waive the privilege over that document — again, even if a lawyer is copied on the forwarding message.

There is a related but distinct doctrine in litigation called the "work-product doctrine." It provides some additional protection from having to produce documents in discovery, even if they are not subject to privilege. Essentially, the work-product doctrine covers documents prepared in anticipation of litigation, even if they are not privileged communications between attorney and client. For example, the notes from a lawyer's interview with a third-party witness that contain the lawyer's mental impressions of the witness could be protected by the work-product doctrine and thus harder for the other side to obtain in discovery — although not impossible in all cases. Communications prepared in the normal course of business are not protected by the work-product doctrine. This is true even if the document relates to risks, compliance, accidents, and other law-related situations. Consult with a licensed attorney on attorney-client privilege and the work-product doctrine because every jurisdiction sets its own rules.

B. Discovery

The concept of "discovery" relates to what documents and information must be shared in a lawsuit. More specifically, discovery is the mechanism by which the parties to a lawsuit — the plaintiff and defendant — request documents, information, and formal testimony from each other. In federal court and many state jurisdictions, the rules require certain "mandatory disclosures" at the beginning of a lawsuit, which are standard requests in every case. Then, during the discovery period, the parties can customize their requests using the various forms of discovery. These forms include requests for documents, interrogatories requesting specific answers to questions, and requests for admissions that require an answer admitting or denying the requested statement. Discovery requests may also include depositions, where one party requests that the other party produce a witness to give testimony in response to live questioning, which is recorded by a court reporter.

These discovery requests aren't optional; once received, they create an obligation for the receiving party to either respond fully or object. The receiving party can argue that the discovery requests are irrelevant or burdensome, but the rules for discovery allow lawyers a lot of leeway to request information that can lead to relevant information. Typically, the receiving party works with a lawyer to review all documents before they are produced, removing documents that are protected by attorney-client privilege, not responsive to the specific request, or otherwise arguably exempt from production. Ignoring a discovery request or not responding to it appropriately can give the other party grounds to file a motion to compel, or a motion for sanctions including a request for legal fees. A grant of these motions would mean that the party filing the motion to compel is entitled to get the documents *and* get reimbursed for attorney fees expended on the motion.

Written correspondence is subject to discovery, and thus must be produced when requested unless an exception applies. One word people often use for this concept is "discoverable." Written correspondence is discoverable, whether it's an email or a text message or any other form of written communication.

C. Third-Party Discovery and Subpoenas

Discovery is primarily exchanged between the parties to a litigation — that is, the named plaintiff or plaintiffs, and the named defendant or defendants. But parties to a litigation can engage in discovery from others not even named in the lawsuit. Anyone who is not a party to a lawsuit is a third party for purposes of that lawsuit. The rules of procedure protect third parties from burdensome discovery but not from all discovery. Thus, written correspondence might be subject to discovery even if the sender or recipient is not directly involved in a lawsuit.

Subpoenas are another way that parties to a lawsuit use the force of law to collect evidence. In both criminal and civil cases, third parties can be compelled to produce documents or testify pursuant to a subpoena. Ignoring or not complying with a subpoena could subject the recipient of the subpoena to a contempt order and related penalties. The way to object is filing a motion with the court that issued the subpoena to "quash" the subpoena as being too burdensome or otherwise legally improper. Responding to subpoenas is an example of what corporate in-house counsel do on a regular basis on behalf of the corporation.

D. Document Retention Policies and Spoliation

A document retention policy is an organization's policy for systematically maintaining and destroying correspondence and other documents in its possession. Keeping every piece of data, forever, is not required by the law. But strategically destroying all evidence of potentially harmful facts and keeping beneficial evidence is also not appropriate, and it can lead to legal consequences for "spoliation." Written correspondence cannot be deleted or thrown away to avoid producing it. In a situation that may lead to litigation or is actively involved in litigation, destroying evidence is known as spoliation and can have severe consequences. Spoliation can lead to sanctions such as having to pay fees and fines. And it can lead to what is known as an "adverse inference," which punishes the party that destroyed the relevant evidence. In a jury trial, for example, the judge could instruct the jury that the defendant destroyed the evidence of a letter, and therefore the jury can draw an adverse inference that whatever was in that letter is adverse—meaning damaging—to the defendant's case. In the most severe consequence, spoliation can result in having a judgment entered against the responsible party, which means losing the whole case. Adopting and adhering to a reasonable document retention policy is a wise practice for any organization.

The privilege doctrines above all focus on the role of written correspondence in litigation. A document may be privileged and therefore protected. Or it may be subject to a discovery request and not privileged, and therefore "discoverable."

E. Substantive Legal Doctrines

Correspondence is, of course, subject to the rest of the law as well, not just the law of litigation procedure. For example, correspondence may create a binding contract. This can happen even if the correspondence is not a formal letter but is an email or even a text. "One of the repeated misconceptions is that businesses and consumers tend to assume that provided they haven't signed a document, there's no way they can be bound to an email or text message. Indeed, consumers and businesses are often quite surprised, and, in some cases alarmed, to learn that seemingly casual conversations, which contain relevant language, can be sufficient enough to create a legally binding contract or even a guarantee."[2] Tort law also applies to correspondence, whether formal or informal. If a piece of correspondence contains defamatory information or reveals private facts, then publishing or releasing it may create tort liability. Those are just two examples; in general, the law applies to all correspondence regardless of form, and there is no "I was just texting" defense to legal consequences for statements or actions.

On the other hand, just as labeling a document "privileged" does not make it privileged, labeling correspondence "CONFIDENTIAL" does not necessarily make it confidential in a legally binding way. A duty of confidentiality might arise from contract law if, for example, the correspondence is covered by a nondisclosure agreement. And a duty not to disclose information might arise from tort law if, for example, the information is an employer's trade secret and the person receiving it is an employee who may face liability for misappropriating it by giving it to a competitor. The larger legal

---

2. *Can Emails and Messages Constitute a Legally Binding Agreement?*, DBL Law Legal Blog, September 12, 2016, https://www.dbllaw.com/can-emails-messages-constitute-legally-binding-agreement/

issues are interesting and important, but they are beyond the scope of this chapter; all of these issues could be a reason to seek legal advice.

II. Overview of Legal Correspondence

This section introduces some key categories of correspondence on legal matters. Because the idea of correspondence is so broad, it is impossible to define every possible category of written correspondence involving legal matters. This high-level overview identifies some common categories.[3]

A. Correspondence by Attorneys

1. Client Letters and Other Attorney-Client Communication

Attorneys and their clients correspond in a variety of ways ranging from highly formal to extremely informal. The very first correspondence between an attorney and his or her client is often very formal: A retainer agreement, also called an engagement letter, often forms the initial contract between attorney and client for the attorney's services and the client's agreement to pay for those services. In some situations, attorneys may provide legal advice in the form of a detailed client-advice letter. This detailed client letter provides advice based on an attorney's in-depth legal analysis. The attorney may use a legal memorandum containing research and analysis as the basis for the client letter, but adapt the analysis for the client's needs as an audience. As discussed in chapter 5, a legal memorandum is usually written from one attorney to another attorney, providing research support with formal legal citations to statutes and cases. The same analysis customized for the client in a client letter would not provide such detailed citations, but would convey the information needed to help the client use the legal advice to decide on a course of action.

Of course, correspondence between attorney and client is not all formal letters. Attorneys and clients typically exchange emails for checking in, and giving updates, as well as for seeking and giving legal advice. There are no limits on how attorneys and clients communicate, and indeed attorneys today are adjusting to the strong desire of many clients to communicate by text.[4]

2. Demand Letters, Including Cease-and-Desist Letters

A demand letter is a formal letter from one party literally demanding that the receiving party do something, such as settle a dispute for a certain amount, take a certain

---

3. Chapter 16 on persuasive legal arguments discusses two common categories of persuasive documents: administrative comments filed by members of the public in response to a request for comments, and appellate briefs filed by lawyers in court. By studying several examples of a certain type of document, you can not only create a template but also develop the expertise and confidence to modify that template as needed for your situation. *See* Alexa Chew & Katie Rose Guest Pryal, *The Complete Legal Writer* 27 (2016).

4. *See, e.g.*, New Hampshire Bar News, Ethics Corner Article, *The Ethics of Texting: Preserving Client Files* (December 16, 2015), https://www.nhbar.org/resources/ethics/ethics-corner-practical-ethics-articles/2015-12.

action, stop taking a certain action, or otherwise act or change their conduct in some way. Demand letters may be conciliatory in tone, asking for a certain action but with language that signals the intent to be reasonable and continue working together. Or demand letters may be aggressive, suggesting that the sender is essentially an adverse party and possibly soon to become an opposing party in litigation.[5]

The law does not require that demand letters be written by attorneys and only by attorneys. But writing demand letters will, in many if not most cases, be a good task for a licensed attorney, since the demand letter itself can establish, change, or abandon one's legal rights, including possible damages and recovery of attorney's fees. A cease-and-desist letter is a specialized kind of demand letter. It demands that the recipient stop doing something. Cease-and-desist letters are common in various contexts such as trademark disputes, where one party claims its trademark rights preclude the receiving party from using a mark in connection with its goods or services.

3. Opinion Letters

In a few specific practice contexts such as real estate and patent law, attorneys write formal opinion letters. These are high-stakes correspondence because their purpose is to represent a legal opinion based on the attorney's analysis of law and fact. Such opinions draw on the skills and in-depth analysis shown in chapter 5 of this book, but the purpose of a formal opinion letter is not to advise the client as it was in chapter 5. The purpose is for the client to forward the letter to negotiating counter-parties or third parties to rely on. For example, in real estate transactions, "[t]he fundamental purpose and justification for an opinion letter from an adversary party's lawyer is to facilitate due diligence as to matters not otherwise, or not easily, accessible to the recipient and its counsel."[6] In patent law, an opinion letter can help a client establish that it is acting in good faith, which can enhance its legal position by reducing the amount of damages that patent plaintiffs might expect to gain if they later prove the client was in fact infringing a patent. Because an attorney's opinion letter must be carefully researched and drafted, following best practices for the process and common conventions for that type of letter, an opinion letter can be costly.

The express purpose of an opinion letter is to seek a non-privileged legal opinion on which others may rely, and thus it is a "practice of law" task exclusively for a licensed attorney. Other industries, such as engineering and accounting, use professional opinion letters too. For example, certified public accountants write a variety of opinion letters, such as audit opinion letters, applying professional standards that differ de-

---

5. *See* Bret Rappaport, *A Shot Across the Bow: How to Write an Effective Demand Letter*, 5 Legal Communication & Rhetoric: JALWD 32 (2008); Carrie Sperling, *Priming Legal Negotiations through Written Demands*, 60 Cath. U. L. Rev. 107 (2010).

6. Robert A. Thompson, *Real Estate Opinion Letters: Introduction*, GPSolo eReport, American Bar Association (June 28, 2017), https://www.americanbar.org/groups/gpsolo/publications/gpsolo_ereport/2012/october_2012/real_estate_opinion_letters_introduction/

pending on the nature of the situation, such as auditing a publicly traded company or a government contracting vendor. When a client company is being audited using generally accepted accounting principles, the client or its accountant may, in turn, issue a request to the client's lawyers seeking information about legal matters related to the audit. In this situation, the attorneys follow specialized procedures and conventions for responding. For example, an audit response letter could call for information about certain "loss contingencies," meaning how likely is it that the company will suffer a harmful verdict in a pending case. The challenge, and the reason for the specialized rules, is to respond appropriately without waiving attorney-client privilege as to information in the underlying case.[7]

Be aware that other types of correspondence—even a text—may in fact be relied on by negotiating partners and third parties. Depending on the legal situation, people can rely on a wide variety of statements by anyone; legal consequences that flow from others' reliance on a statement are certainly not limited to formal opinion letters drafted by attorneys for that express purpose. For example, if a text from one negotiating party to the other states, "The property is free and clear of liens," then the other party might be able to rely on that factual representation. This example is a simplification of real estate and other law, but understood that parties can later claim fraud based on a wide range of representations not involving attorneys or formal opinions at all.

B. Additional Select Categories of Correspondence with Legal Implications

Correspondence written by anyone, anywhere, at any time can potentially create legal obligations and affect legal rights and duties. The form of a communication does not exempt it from contract law or tort law or any other legal doctrine. For example, an Australian court had to consider whether a text message could count as a last will and testament.[8]

In contract law, one party may write a formal offer letter providing the terms of a job or other agreement. The offer letter may include a signature line at the bottom for the recipient to sign, signaling acceptance of the offer. Signing the letter does not necessarily make it a binding contract in all cases, depending on what the letter itself says. Nonetheless offer letters are often used to communicate a contract and to consummate that contract.

A notice letter is a type of letter that, simply by its existence and its being sent, causes a legal event. Many contracts contain provisions where parties have legal responsibilities that arise only if they are put on notice. For example, a seller of a machine may

---

7. American Bar Association Statement of Policy Regarding Lawyers' Responses to Auditors' Requests for Information, 31 Bus. Law. 1709 (1976), reprinted in ABA Bus. Law Section Audit Response Comm., Auditor's Letter Handbook 1 (2d ed. 2013).

8. *"I Bequeath U": When a Text Message Can Count as Your Will*, The Conversation, November 30, 2017, http://theconversation.com/i-bequeath-u-when-a-text-message-can-count-as-your-will-88207

have a warranty obligation to repair the machine if it breaks down, but the obligation does not come into existence unless the buyer sends the seller a notice letter describing the problem. Similarly, some consumer protection laws provide that a consumer cannot sue a merchant unless the consumer has first notified the merchant of her intent to sue and given the merchant an opportunity to fix the problem informally. Failure to send such a notice letter can result in the consumer's lawsuit being dismissed.

Different industries will have many more types of correspondence creating or affecting legal rights and obligations. A legally literate professional working in any given industry should study and stay up-to-date on the legal implications of key correspondence in that industry.

III. Selecting and Making the Most of Your Medium

The rest of this chapter turns to the writer's task in creating correspondence. An important first step is choosing how to correspond. What is the right format for corresponding: letter, email, text or chat, a personal conversation, telephone call, or video call? Each medium has its advantages and disadvantages. Effective communication in a legal setting means selecting the medium that is legally sound for its intended purpose and appropriate for the audience. These two concerns—purpose and audience—are the foundation of solid writing choices in any setting.

A. Letters

Some types of communication must be in the form of a letter because professional guidelines or well-established expectations demand it. The purpose of the communication itself may necessitate that the communication take the form of a letter. If a contract contains a notice provision stipulating that notice must be given by U.S. mail, then a letter is required. Beyond requirements arising from the letter's purpose, the audience might necessitate that the communication take the form of a letter. A recipient who avoids email may actually be easier to reach by a letter.

In situations where the writer has discretion to choose a letter or not, the writer might choose a letter when the purpose is to signal serious intent. Formal letters have gravitas. They carry a certain weight simply by the way they look, and they have the weight of tradition behind them. A letter communicating an offer suggests more serious intent than a phone call, even though many contracts can be made in writing or orally. A cease-and-desist letter suggests serious intent to consider litigation if the letter's demands are not met. In contrast, an email or phone call tends to signal a more conciliatory approach. If a cease-and-desist letter is required to establish the sender's legal rights to certain damages, but the sender actually wants to be conciliatory and resolve the matter, a phone call from client to client first, followed by a cease-and-desist letter on an attorney's letterhead, may establish the client's legal rights while taking a softer approach to settlement.

B. Email

Email is an extremely flexible medium. Depending on how it is used, it can be more like a formal letter or more like an informal text. That flexibility is both a strength and a weakness.

Email combines the immediate responsiveness of conversations with the informational advantages of writing things down. As Professor Ellie Margolis points out in an in-depth article about digital communications in law, "We can produce and deliver documents more quickly and easily than ever before in history."[9] Email creates a convenient written record that can be referred to later. And it also can allow groups to receive the same information at the same time, demonstrating transparency and collectively marking milestones so that groups function more efficiently and move forward in coordination. Being able to quickly and efficiently communicate about legal issues within a group reduces the time and money needed to address legal situations. It reduces possible barriers to communication between clients and lawyers. (The logical extension is texting between lawyers and clients, which is convenient but, as noted above, also brings ethical and practical challenges for lawyers.[10])

Email also makes it easier to communicate messages in a variety of ways, giving the reader the choice of how and when to encounter the information. The body of the email can deliver a summary, with a detailed memorandum attached. Or the body of the email can deliver the analysis in text form, with a chart attached as a PDF organizing the same information in a visual format. Email also makes it easy to support the analysis with links to sources. That's an advantage for communication generally, but in the legal setting it can be a particular strength. Legal information should be up-to-date and valid. Thus, providing a link to a source will, ideally, connect the reader to the most updated version of a legal authority or other source.

However, the immediate back-and-forth of email can waste time and money with chains of endless responses when a phone call would be more efficient. Attachments can create confusion when multiple people simultaneously provide comments and changes. The conversational intimacy of email, combined with its written permanence, can create an unnecessary paper trail of sensitive issues more wisely discussed in person or by phone. All professionals should know to avoid email for significant emotional messages. Sending an email that inadvertently uses the wrong tone, or is intended to sound one way but is not received in that same spirit, can exacerbate problems rather than helping to solve them.

Ultimately, the universe of possible email scenarios cannot be reduced to a list of appropriate and inappropriate use of email; professionals must hone their discretion

---

9. Ellie Margolis, *Is the Medium the Message: Unleashing the Power of E-Communication in the 21st Century*, 12 Legal Communication & Rhetoric: JALWD 1, 6 (2015).

10. *See, e.g.*, Dean R. Dietrich, *Handling Clients' Text Messages*, Wisconsin Lawyer (April 2016) (advising lawyers to use texts only for simple scheduling conversations because legal advice must be preserved as part of the client file).

and intuition about when email works and doesn't work. As with all professional writing, culture and policies must be supplemented by the writer's own judgment.

C. Text Messages

Texting has the benefit of being immediate, conversational, and efficient. The ability to text one person or a group adds to its flexibility. The efficiency of texting comes in part from its conciseness because texts tend to be short.

The purpose of communicating by text about legal matters best fits short, simple messages such as setting up a lunch meeting. Texting should not be used for messages that need background context or nuance. It is true that text enhancements such as emojis can convey some context and nuance, but only if the sender and recipient understand them in the same way. Texting also brings risks of confusion from the fact that it is quasi-permanent and can be saved and shared, but it also can be lost, subject to the vagaries of technology. Thus, texting on high-stakes matters can be risky not just because of lost nuance, but also because of potentially lost evidence.

Developing strong legal literacy means developing judgment to choose a communication format best suited for a legal situation. What if someone inside an organization texts with a request for a "quick answer"? Just because someone asks for a quick answer does not mean the answer can be given quickly. Professionals communicating about legal matters, including but certainly not limited to attorneys, need to select the communication format that best fits the situation. Beyond relying on individual discretion, an organization may develop a communication policy on texting that draws on legal advice, human resources expertise, and an understanding of customer or stakeholder needs.[11] Policies that directly or indirectly address texting and smartphone use generally may also include social media policies and bring-your-own-device policies.[12]

D. Phone Calls

Sometimes written correspondence is not the best answer. "Just pick up the phone" is perhaps a cliché, but doing so gives the speaker and audience a chance to communicate in real-time, hearing not just the content but also the tone of voice and nonverbal cues such as pauses. Nonverbal cues—even the much-maligned use of "um" and "uh"—actually make it *easier* to understand a spoken message.[13] And of course phone calls are an appropriate way to communicate when the purpose is more personal or sensitive, such as delivering bad news. Another cliché is "know your audience," and a

---

11. *See, e.g.*, Karla Grossenbacher, *Are Your Employees Texting? The Risks to Employers in Taking Communications Offline*, Employment Law Lookout: Insights for Management, Seyfarth Shaw LLP (April 11, 2017), https://www.laborandemploymentlawcounsel.com/2017/04/are-your-employees-texting-the-risks-to-employers-in-taking-workplace-communications-offline/

12. *See, e.g.*, Megan Berry, BYOD Policy Template, IT Manager Daily, http://www.itmanagerdaily.com/byod-policy-template/ ("Company XYZ has a zero-tolerance poicy for texting or emailing while driving….")

13. Barbara K. Gotthelf, *The Lawyer's Guide to Um*, 11 Legal Comm. & Rhetoric: JALWD 1 (2014).

phone call is best when the audience will likely understand the message better by talking and listening, rather than reading and writing.

The good news is that communicators have more choices than ever before to tailor their messages, from the traditional format of a written letter to a chat message sent with no punctuation but maybe an emoji. Choosing among these possibilities with legal literacy means balancing legal knowledge (such as privilege and the importance of standard document retention) with the purpose of the message and the human element of what the particular audience wants and needs.

IV. Writing Effective Correspondence

After choosing to write correspondence, the next step is crafting the message. This section focuses on email because email is so common and can function more like a detailed letter.

A. Providing Context

Providing context means giving the reader a framework to understand the rest of the message. It's a kind of orientation to the message that follows. Context may mean just one sentence identifying the basic issue in the message: "As requested, here is a summary of social media policies for home health care providers." It may explicitly restate what the audience asked for: "You requested research on social media policies for home health care providers." Or it may restate the assignment and issue *and* provide additional factual background: "You requested research on social media policies for home health care providers. Several of our regional providers have written asking questions about policy. We have a training session already scheduled for next month and would like to develop and train on a social media policy at that session."

Context can take many forms, as shown above. What is noticeably confusing is a message that lacks context. Have you ever received a message that lacked any context? For example:

> To: Trey Kelly
> From: Olivia Ralston
> Date: July 17, 20XX
> Re: Re: re: re: fw: re: Social media policy for home healthcare providers
>
> ———————————————————————————————
>
> See below. I look forward to the meeting and will bring copies of the sample policies and guidelines for all who attend.

The problems with such messages are multifold: they are abrupt and confusing. They make the reader do the work, potentially reviewing everything in the message chain, trying to find some context.

A writer can be much more effective by providing context at the beginning of every message. Providing context prepares the reader to understand the main message. Context is not just extra verbiage; it enables the reader to better grasp the point.

Example giving context before the main point:

 To: Trey Kelly
From: Olivia Ralston
 Date: July 17, 20XX
    Re: Social media policy for home healthcare providers

Dear Trey,

My name is Olivia Ralston. My mother, Carol Ralston, is one of your company's clients. Recently I have become very concerned and worried about the possibility of home health aides potentially taking photos of vulnerable clients and patients in nursing homes. News stories such as the link below from NPR have caused me anxiety since our family relies on help provided by home health aides when we cannot be there. https://www.npr.org/sections/health-shots/2016/07/14/485293079/social-media-abuse-of-nursing-home-residents-often-goes-unchecked...

This message begins with context. It introduces the writer and other relevant people in this situation, and it identifies the issue to be addressed. Then it begins to give more detail about why the issue is important. It has no prior messages to rely on as context, so it must create its own.

Even in the midst of a back-and-forth conversation by email, context can help either for clarity or for persuasion. Here is an example that both clarifies and attempts to persuade:

 To: Trey Kelly
From: Olivia Ralston
 Date: July 17, 20XX
    Re: Re: Re: Re: Social media policy for home healthcare providers

---

Dear Trey,

Thanks for your responses below on how carefully Colorado Home Health, Inc. vets all of its job applicants. Thank you also for the reassurance about the training on what aides are permitted to do while caring for clients. Also, I appreciated what you said about routinely evaluating aides' performance and establishing a track record for terminating the employment of aides with unsatisfactory records.

My concern goes beyond general job screening and training, and general hiring and firing concerns. The problem is that social media is so ingrained in people's thought process that they do not think of it as relevant to their job description at all; it almost becomes a part of their thought process.

Because social media use is so easy and seamless, some people — including employees of any type of company — become careless and even abusive in how they use it. The danger is especially great when the subject of their shared photos may be vulnerable populations such as home health clients....

The message clarifies by restating the topics of discussion up to this point, then moving into new material. The message attempts to persuade by showing an empathetic understanding of the ideas already in the conversation, then contrasting them with the new ideas.

As noted earlier, context can be concise or go into more depth. Choosing how much introductory context to include will depend on the speed of the back-and-forth in the conversation, the number of senders and recipients involved, and other factors.

B. Organizing the Content

After context, the message must deliver its core content. Even a two- or three-paragraph email still needs a logical organization. The message should be organized into relatively short paragraphs placed in a logical and strategic order for achieving its purpose.

For legal communication, the most famous — or infamous — logical organization is the "IRAC" method discussed at length in chapter 5. This type of deductive model can work well in a reasonably concise email, as in this example:

To: Trey Kelly
From: Olivia Ralston
Date: July 17, 20XX
Re: Home health care

Dear Mr. Kelly,

I wanted to bring to your attention a growing concern: social-media policies for home health aides. Reading news reports about painful incidents in nursing homes, hospitals, and in-home care has given me some sleepless nights thinking about vulnerable adults and the proliferation of social-media practices that could be used to harm their dignity.

Best practices for home health care include legal obligations as well as ethical and moral obligations to the vulnerable clients being served. The legal issues raised by social media abuse are many, one example being possible tort liability for public disclosure of private facts. For clients' private life activities that home health aides regularly encounter, posting on social media would meet each of the five elements for public disclosure of private facts.

I would like to learn more about Colorado Home Health's policies and protections against this new and disturbing trend. Please, could we make an appointment to speak by phone or to meet at your convenience?

Thank you,
Olivia Ralston

The email above uses a very relaxed but recognizable version of IRAC method. It states an issue, "public disclosure of private facts." This issue has rule consisting of a set of five elements, but the email does not explicitly lay them out.[14] Why do you think that is? How would the message be different if it also listed—or quoted and provided a legal citation for—the elements?

Then it applies the legal issue to the facts: "For clients' private life activities that home health aides regularly encounter, posting on social media would meet each of the five elements for public disclosure of private facts." This is the application of law to fact, although it is hypothetical about what "would" satisfy the test if it happened. Imagining how the law might apply in the future is a core aspect of planning and setting effective policies, as well as recognizing when to seek legal advice. The "A" in IRAC can include applying the law to past facts that may have legal consequences or to hypothetical future facts for purposes of planning and risk management. Thus IRAC can be used in a formal office memorandum from lawyer to lawyer, as shown in chapter 5, or in a short email as shown here.

IRAC is useful, but it is far from the only organizational structure that may be useful and effective. Indeed, using it for the message above sends the message to the recipient that the sender is interested in legal rights and remedies. Explicitly structuring the message around the law in this manner may halt communication by starting with aggressive content and causing the recipient to take the email to an attorney rather than continuing the conversation. Other approaches can be less legalistic. Along those lines, here are some more ideas for logical structures:

- General to specific
- Specific to general
- Background context leading to key point

---

14. The elements of public disclosure of private facts are: "(1) the fact or facts disclosed must be private in nature; (2) the disclosure must be made to the public; (3) the disclosure must be one which would be highly offensive to a reasonable person; (4) the fact or facts disclosed cannot be of legitimate concern to the public; and (5) the defendant acted with reckless disregard of the private nature of the fact or facts disclosed." *Robert C. Ozer, P.C. v. Borquez,* 940 P.2d 371, 377 (Colo. 1997).

- Key point followed by background context
- Most important to less important
- Similar to different
- Conclusion leading to detailed support
- Detailed support leading to conclusion
- Substantive issues to procedural concerns
- Analysis to recommendations
- Chronological order or reverse chronological order
- Major legal topics
- Major factual topics

The list above suggests general logical frameworks for the information itself. But some messages may be best organized by the strategic or social concerns of the situation and audience—in other words, design choices should sometimes be focused on the recipient rather than strictly logical emphasis on the content. Here are some ideas for organizing information by strategy or social concerns:

- Itemized issues raised in earlier communications
- Arguments, followed by counter-arguments
- What the recipient already knows followed by new ideas and information
- Positive information (good news) followed by negative information (bad news)
- Contributions of each person or team followed by an overall common issue

Any list of frameworks will necessarily be incomplete because information can be organized in so many different ways. What the frameworks above can teach, generally, is that a written message needs to be organized by logic and strategy, and the writer needs to make intentional choices about paragraphing and flow that implement the logic and strategy.

Here is an example of an informational email—read this draft and evaluate its organization. What exactly is happening in this draft? Try to label the organization in the margins. To do this, add short phrases in the margins describing what you see as the purpose of each segment of the email.

To: Trey Kelly
From: Olivia Ralston
Date: July 17, 20XX
Re: Resources on social media policies in home health care

_____

Dear Mr. Kelly,

Thank you for the opportunity to meet with you last week and discuss policies for social media usage by home health care providers. This message follows up with the resources we discussed, and some additional resources I found after our conversation.

- National Institute of Health article on Social Media and Health Care Professionals: Benefits, Risks, and Best Practices, https://www.ncbi.nlm.nih.gov/pmc/articles/PMC4103576/

- HIPAA Journal, HIPAA Social Media Rules, https://www.hipaajournal.com/hipaa-social-media/

- National Council of State Boards of Nursing, Nurse's Guide to Social Media, https://www.ncsbn.org/NCSBN_SocialMedia.pdf

- Medical Association of the State of Alabama, Social Media & HIPAA: When Sharing Is Not Caring, http://alabamamedicine.org/social-media-hipaa-sharing-not-caring/

Thank you again for the opportunity to speak about my concerns.

Olivia Ralston

This email provides a contextual introduction, a list of resources, and a conclusion. It is logically organized. But did you notice that the list of resources is not organized in any recognizable way? Maybe the internal logic of the resource list could be stronger. Can you think of ideas for headings to better organize this information? Here are several structures the writer could use for an informational email like this:

- Federal law, state law, and other resources
- Resources focused on home health aides and resources on health care professionals generally
- Reverse chronological order (from most recent to oldest)

What other headings or organizational strategies would work well in a message like this? Another organizational possibility could focus on the legal consequences:

- Civil liability
- Criminal liability

There are many possibilities for organizing the resources in a more law-specific way. As this discussion shows, a major step toward successful organization is simply to *have an organization you can articulate*, along the lines shown here. And remember that stream-of-consciousness is not an organizational method!

C. Being Persuasive

Being logical and being persuasive are not mutually exclusive; in fact, they are complementary. A persuasive message must also be logical or the reader won't be able to understand it. But one size does not fit all when selecting the way to organize a message persuasively. A persuasive message must be strategic about how much detail to include and the order of the ideas.[15]

Context is especially important in persuasive messages. By restating what has happened before, the message can suggest moving forward in some way.

Here is an example:

To: Trey Kelly
From: Olivia Ralston
Date: July 17, 20XX
Re: Concern about home health aide and social media usage at CCH

Dear Mr. Kelly,

As daughter and as legal guardian to Carol Ralston, I am dedicated to advocating for my mother and other patients in her situation.

As you know and as we discussed in our recent meeting, last month an incident occurred raising privacy and dignity concerns about Colorado Home Health's care. The day after Labor Day, I was visiting my mother's home while the aide employed by CHH was also present. I was in an adjacent room to where the aide was caring for my mother's personal needs in the bathroom. The door was open about six inches. Although I could not see their interactions, I heard a "snap" sound. It was the sound a smartphone makes when taking a photo.

I appreciate the time you spent talking with me about the incident. Upon reflection and talking with my mother, we both feel it is best if CHH replaces the current aide. Please take the current aide off her plan immediately. I will be staying home from work Monday and Tuesday next week so I can be present in my mother's home to meet the new aide.

As you know, I am evaluating the implications of this concerning incident under HIPAA and state privacy law, as well as the home health contract we signed with CHH earlier this year. I would appreciate knowing any additional steps that CHH is taking to address the specific concerns out of this incident and to make sure that patients' dignity and privacy interests are respected.

Thank you,

Olivia Ralston

---

15. Chapter 16 discusses persuasive theory in more detail, with longer and more formal documents in mind.

The example above shows how a message can use context to review what has happened up to this point, before stating the email's request or demand.

Another aspect of persuading someone to take action is to strategically consider what to ask for in a message, and when. There are two basic theories here: start small and build; or start big and take something less. Starting small is also called putting your "foot in the door." This question relates to the debate in persuasive theory about linking a "chain" of persuasive points from a small request to a larger one, or vice versa:

- "Foot-in-the-door" persuasion means requesting something *small* first, convincing the audience to grant that small request, then moving onto a bigger request. Ultimately, the message can move to the biggest "ask" at the end.

- "Door-in-the-face" persuasion means asking for something *big* first, then moving on to a smaller and more realistic request that is what you actually hope for. The idea is to request something you don't truly expect, and then ask for something more reasonable and realistic, which the audience may be more inclined to give since they already said "no" to the first big request and want to avoid saying no to a lesser request as well.[16]

Consider these two messages. Which uses the "foot in the door" strategy and which uses the "door in the face" strategy?

Example 1

To: Trey Kelly
From: Olivia Ralston
Date: July 17, 20XX
Re: Social media policy for home health care agencies and aides

---

Dear Mr. Kelly,

As you know I am very concerned about photography and social media use by home health aides. The responsibility to train and address these risks, and prevent them from occurring, belongs with the agency. 42 CFR § 484.80(a)(1)(viii) requires that home health agencies train their aides in "the physical, emotional, and developmental needs of and ways to work with the populations served by the HHA, including the need for respect for the patient, his or her privacy and his or her property."

Respect for privacy includes not photographing residents, not writing about them except in mandatory reporting to the agency, and certainly not sharing their images or any information about them on social media.

---

16. Kathryn Stanchi, *The Science of Persuasion: An Initial Exploration*, 2006 Mich. St. L. Rev. 411.

As my mother's guardian and the person charged with protecting her patient rights, I am requesting information on what Colorado Home Health, Inc. is doing to train its staff in these specific issues.

Additionally, personal narratives by patient guardians could add to this mandatory training, showing the personal impact of these issues. Please know that because this issue is so concerning and important to me, I am available to provide such a narrative as part of the mandatory training.

Sincerely,

Olivia Ralston

Example 2

To: Trey Kelly
From: Olivia Ralston
Date: July 17, 20XX
Re: Social media policy for home health care agencies and aides

---

Dear Mr. Kelly,

Thank you for meeting with me to discuss my concerns about home health aides' use of photography and social media. I am pleased to know that Colorado Home Health, Inc. takes these issues seriously.

I have been researching these issues and how they connect with home health agencies' policies and practices. For example, I found that "the physical, emotional, and developmental needs" of patients and "the need for respect for the patient, his or her privacy and his or her property" are subjects for mandatory training under 42 CFR § 484.80(a)(1)(viii).

Perhaps Colorado Home Health, Inc.'s training already covers photography and social media use. Could you share with me what the training does cover? And if it would be helpful and informative for aides, would you consider inviting me to speak at your next training session? Perhaps a personal narrative from a guardian could enhance the effectiveness of the mandatory training on respect for patients and their privacy.

Thank you, and I look forward to continued discussions.

Sincerely,

Olivia Ralston

In the examples above, Example #1 uses the bold "door in the face" strategy by beginning with the legal claim that a federal rule was violated, following up with a demand for more information. The last paragraph gives a smaller request or offer, which is the writer's willingness to help with training.

In contrast, Example #2 uses the "foot in the door" strategy to start with a paragraph of information conveying research about privacy practices—rather than an explicit statement that the rule was in fact violated. Example #2 then builds to two more persuasive inquiries: a request for information, and an offer of the writer's willingness to help with training. Thus, the organization of Example #1 is more litigious and combative than the tone of Example #2, which reads more like a helpful offer of assistance. The word choice in Example #1 is also more litigious. When do you think one or the other of these approaches might be more effective?

D. Editing for Appropriate Voice and Style

Effective writing about legal issues also requires the writer to gain control over the voice and style of the message: Does it explicitly claim a legal rule was violated—which is an aggressive and possibly litigious choice—or does it merely suggest that a rule is relevant for consideration—which is less aggressive but also possibly vague? Does it use words suggesting a litigious intent, or words suggesting a problem-solving intent? There is no right answer for every situation; what matters is determining strategy and then organizing and crafting the message accordingly.

Voice and style are also important to reaching the particular audience. A writer should often adopt a different voice and style in writing to a lawyer versus someone with no legal training. If the audience does not have the specialized knowledge in a given field such as law, the message should not use the specialized vocabulary of that field. Using legal jargon to someone with no legal training is a form of asserting superior power, and may not be well-received by the audience. Or the audience may seem to consent or submit to the demand because it seems legalistic and "scary," but not because of a real agreement or even understanding of the message itself.

Voice and style also play a role in addressing the possible emotional repercussions of the message. Is the audience for a message personally involved in the situation? Such an audience may be more defensive or worried about the implications, and therefore less open to the message. Here, language to defuse defensiveness may be helpful. In contrast, a recipient who does not believe he or she is actually personally involved may be passive and not very responsive, when in fact that person's input is crucial. It that situation, language to emphasize the message's urgency and importance may be needed. In the example woven throughout this chapter, writing to the home health agency's manager (who is arguably responsible for the alleged events) requires different editing considerations from writing to the state home health regulatory agency (which receives many complaints from different directions, constantly balancing various policy and investigatory duties).

Controlling a message's voice and style in an email involves both intuition and informal judgment. It is not possible to list all the helpful words that should be used, and all the risky words that should be avoided. A more realistic and flexible answer for any professional is to develop a strong writing process. Any message with legal implications or high professional or emotional stakes should not be dashed off quickly. Rather, such messages should be considered carefully before being sent. Here are three helpful steps, some of which you may already know but some of which may be new to you:

- Follow the classic writing advice: Write a draft, then save it and put it away for as long as possible—whether an hour or a day. Then come back to it with fresh eyes.

- Focus especially on the beginning and ending of the message, and the first sentence of each paragraph within it. These are the positions of emphasis within the message, and they will likely get more attention from your audience.

- Consider experimenting with a text analyzer that parses the language of a draft for its emotional content. IBM has a free online product (free and online in demo form as of this writing) called the Watson Tone Analyzer.[17] The Watson Tone Analyzer parses through a message and highlights the words that suggest certain emotions (anger, fear, joy, sadness). It also highlights words that suggest an analytical, confident, or tentative tone.

E. Wrapping Up

Signing off on correspondence can be controversial, especially for emails. Letters often end with formal sign-offs such as "Respectfully" or "Very truly yours." In the world of demand letters, there is a famously legalistic (and obnoxious) sign-off that attorneys may use and recipients may fear (or mock). Those words are: "Govern yourself accordingly." We do not recommend that sign-off.

To sign off effectively, make sure the last words are consistent with the tone of the message. Inconsistent, uneven tone is a sign of ineffective writing generally. It might seem like the safest route to have a standard sign-off such as "Sincerely" or no sign-off at all, just a signature. And a standard approach is a reasonable and efficient solution for day-to-day messages that do not stand out as crucial or highly emotional. For crucial or emotional messages, a custom approach is warranted.

Also make sure the last words are consistent with the professional context of the specific message and the industry. Professionals in the fields of art and publishing are likely to sign off their emails quite differently from professionals in civil and structural engineering. With the different professional backgrounds of students in legal masters

---

17. The Watson Tone Analyzer is available in demo form here: https://tone-analyzer-demo.ng.bluemix.net/

programs, you may find it interesting and even fun to discuss the variety of email sign-off practices in the professions represented in your class.

V. Email Etiquette and Legal Communications

This section focuses specifically on email. It begins with practical etiquette and then delves a bit more into the theory and technical aspects of email.

Rules of email etiquette—basically, social norms—help everyone in a workplace use email in the best interests of the group. What is your professional background and what are the social norms for using email in your field? In other words, what do the best communicators do with email, and what habits are viewed as annoying or even risky in your field? Some of these social norms may be covered explicitly in professional training, and other social norms may be unspoken. Students from various professional backgrounds may enjoy swapping stories with one another. There will likely be some common themes:

- Use the subject line to say what the message is about, specifically.
- Do not reply to all unless necessary.
- Do not use a company's email system to reach all recipients in any organization, or any large department or unit, unless absolutely necessary.
- Avoid long inspirational quotes at the end of an email signature.
- Avoid requiring a "read receipt" for each and every email.
- Avoid marking every message as "urgent." If everything seems urgent, then nothing is.

At a more theoretical level, choosing to send a message by email affects the message itself. Philosopher Marshall McLuhan famously stated, "The medium is the message."[18] Sending something by email changes the message from how it would come across in a letter or a phone call.

Consider the "to" and "from" fields of an email. An email is always sent "to" specific recipients, which excludes others. Have you ever gotten an email forwarded that should have been addressed to you in the first place? The writer's use of the "to" field to include certain recipients and exclude others is a choice with repercussions. And the "from" field has implications as well. Unless the sender can send generically from a board or organization under its generic name, an email will be from the sender's account under his or her personal name. That associates the sender with the message, and may direct future inquiries back to that person even if he or she is not the best person to handle

---

18. *See, e.g.,* Ellie Margolis, *Is the Medium the Message: Unleashing the Power of E-Communication in the 21st Century*, 12 Legal Communication & Rhetoric: JALWD 1, 5 (2015). (discussing the implications of Marshall McLuhan's work for email in a legal setting).

such inquiries. Have you ever debated in a meeting who would be the best person to send a message? Such debates show the implications of the "from" field.

The "cc" field of email is useful for informing other recipients. It also carries the risk of being vague. By addressing an email to one person and adding a cc to another, the sender is implicitly saying the cc recipient is not directly responsible but just needs to be informed about the content of the message. Email also has the "bcc" field, an additional hidden channel for sharing information. The benefit of bcc is allowing the sender to reach a recipient while hiding the fact the sender is including that recipient on the message. But using bcc can be dangerous. If a bcc recipient does not notice the fact he or she is a bcc—not just an open and obvious cc—then the bcc recipient could immediately reply to all, which defeats the purpose of the bcc decision and can cause other problems. A less risky alternative is to send the message to cc recipients, then forward it separately to anyone else who should be informed privately behind the scenes.

Another capability of email, for better or worse, is its instantaneousness: In the era of the ubiquitous smartphone and the "always-on" work environment, the email can be not only produced and delivered, but also received personally at almost any time. Professionals working with legal issues may read messages instantaneously as they are received, even during movies, at the dinner table, or in the middle of the night. Even easier than producing and sending a message is the act of forwarding a message sent by someone else. Effective professionals consider the implications of instantaneous, immediate features of receiving and replying and forwarding email when choosing that medium. Email wisdom includes developing intuition about when to respond immediately, and when to delay a response because of incomplete information, emotional context, or other reasons to reduce the intensity and speed of communication back and forth.

None of these capabilities of email make it the universal solution to communication challenges, and none of email's limitations mean it should be entirely avoided. An expert writer works within the medium, taking advantage of its strengths and minimizing its risks. In a professional setting, writers who use discretion on when to write, write well using email's capabilities, and observe social norms of email are likely to gain a reputation as good writers and good colleagues.

Having studied this chapter, you should be able to:

- Avoid common myths and mistakes about how the law applies to correspondence
- Select a communication method appropriate to a legal and social situation
- Organize and edit your written correspondence with the reader's needs in mind
- Weigh the advantages and disadvantages of email to communicate about legal issues
- Effectively use email in a legal setting

Case Study

Ms. Ralston has launched her small business, a coffee startup. She has hired a group of unpaid interns from local high schools and colleges, and will soon be wrapping up the end of her first session for interns. Six interns will be returning to their educational programs. Ms. Ralston is writing a departure email to all of them. Part of the content in that email should remind them not to reveal any trade secrets of the business in future work. Ms. Ralston has found Colorado's definition of trade secrets:

"Trade secret" means the whole or any portion or phase of any scientific or technical information, design, process, procedure, formula, improvement, confidential business or financial information, listing of names, addresses, or telephone numbers, or other information relating to any business or profession which is secret and of value. To be a "trade secret" the owner thereof must have taken measures to prevent the secret from becoming available to persons other than those selected by the owner to have access thereto for limited purposes.

Col. Rev. Stat. § 7-74-102(4)

She wants to write an email with a friendly, mentoring tone that also protects her interests in her business. You may use your imagination to create content for this email, or imagine protective measures taken in the business. The purpose of this exercise is to focus on the writing itself, for purposes of the email.

Traditions and Trends

The line between correspondence and publication has been somewhat blurred by digital capabilities. For example, "mail merge" on word-processing and publishing platforms such as MailChimp enable a sender to reach a mass audience with custom-looking correspondence. But for every action, there's an equal and opposite reaction, and email platforms can detect mass-produced correspondence and send it into a spam or "promotions" folder.

Demand letters are another traditional form of legal communication, and traditionally these letters have had a very limited audience: essentially the lawyers and client, including perhaps the board of a corporate client, plus the court and others involved in the judicial process. But now, the possibility of "going viral" is a real concern for anyone about to send a demand letter. Demand letters are routinely posted on blogs, social media, and YouTube. Some demand letters generate a positive response, typically when they use a friendly and reasonable tone. Other demand letters bring scorn upon the lawyer and client who sent them, typically when they seem to take an unreasonable position or use an aggressive and litigious tone. The point here is that written persuasion via demand letter is now not only a legal communication, but also, potentially, a public performance of one's "brand" and reputation that may not unfold in predictable or manageable ways.

Email as a communication medium is old enough to have its own traditions. Professionals who remember working in the mid-to-late 1990s will remember email as an exclusively text medium with a stripped-down, Microsoft DOS-like interface. As word-processing programs evolved alongside email, the tradition of attaching longer documents took hold. And as email interfaces became more graphical and less DOS-like, email came under pressure to resemble formal letters and memoranda. Thus, a tradition of email as legal communication is that it is caught between the pressure to be more instantaneous and informal (like online writing generally), and the pressure to be more cautious and formal, like legal writing. Apart from the function and writing style of email, there is another aspect to consider: the way the professional interacts with technology on an individual basis and as an employee of an organization. Traditionally, legal professionals were given a single email account by their employer for receiving and sending essentially all business communications. In other words, a professional's online writing for work was generated and stored in a business account owned by the employer.

In companies and organizations, email is not just an individual communication event, but is also a function of the business. Management can monitor use of company email. Management can quarantine certain messages sent or received, for example, by using a filter for spam or by rejecting messages with large attachments. In the legal and accounting industries, management commonly sets up all email accounts to include a standard disclaimer. These disclaimers may not have any legal effect, but they are extraordinarily commonplace. Management can also monitor the text of employee emails in a variety of ways, from individual text searches to flag any inappropriate content, to data-driven holistic searches that may identify patterns important to management. *See* Frank Partnoy, *What Your Boss Could Learn by Reading the Whole Company's Emails,* The Atlantic (September 2018).

Today, email's convenience and instantaneous nature have compromised its power. Email has become unmanageable for many, prompting some lawyers and other professionals to declare "email bankruptcy" and delete all messages. (Licensed attorneys have a professional duty of competence and a duty to communicate with clients, so any attempt at "email bankruptcy" must protect client information in the process.) The difficulty of keeping up with so many emails can, paradoxically, lead professionals to start *other* accounts for online communication, or to use texting and messaging apps to keep up with certain priority conversations. These proliferating accounts are often more difficult for an employer to monitor and archive.

Email with attachments can also be a very inefficient way to work in teams and store up-to-date versions. Thus, driven by experimentation and client demands, some legal teams are experimenting with shared communication platforms along the lines of Slack. These platforms have their own pros and cons, such as exposing lawyers' work processes to clients more than ever before (which is both a pro and a con). Innovation in online messaging and communication helps legal teams collaborate, but new platforms also raise important questions about security, privacy, and confidentiality—as well as whether they really do help with efficient exchange of information.

Chapter 15

Working with Facts

> The first step in the resolution of any legal problem is ascertaining the factual background and sifting through the facts with an eye to the legally relevant.
>
> — *Upjohn Co. v. United States*, 449 U.S. 383, 390–391 (1981).

In legal reasoning, it is useful to think of "law" and "fact" as two distinct categories. Law consists of primary sources setting forth the structures, prohibitions, rules, definitions, consequences, and processes running in the background of our individual and collective daily lives. Facts are what happen in our individual and collective daily lives. "What governs" and "what happens" are two separate categories, but law and fact overlap in many ways: A factual situation generates a lawsuit that leads to a holding in case, which is the law. Law is read by people deciding what to do, who then manage their situation and proactively shape what the facts will be. People in a particular industry or interest group realize that a certain law is affecting people or shaping their decisions in an unfortunate way—and thus creating bad factual situations on a large scale—so they investigate the statistical effects and individual anecdotal stories showing these facts as they push for legislative or regulatory reform. Working with facts is part of legal literacy because law affects situations, and situations are made of facts. Understanding the law's effect in the world means understanding facts.

The definition of legal literacy offered by Professor James Boyd White[1] includes several practical skills that involve facts:

- Advocating for oneself, such as in a zoning dispute.
  Advocating for oneself means collecting relevant facts, investigating additional facts, and demanding information if appropriate, challenging facts asserted by the opposing party, and distinguishing facts from arguments.

- Evaluating secondary sources, namely "news reports and periodical literature dealing with legal matters."
  Evaluating secondary sources, including newspapers and magazines, also requires differentiating among facts, opinions, characterizations, and conclusions. Perhaps unimaginable at the 1983 date of White's writing, digital content such as web pages, blogs, social media, and "robots" that write simple news reports[2] make critical thinking about facts even more challenging and important. A newer concern today is the possibility of so-called "deep fake" videos that look authentic.

- Serving as a responsible leader, such as on a school board or neighborhood association.
  Leading a board or association requires skills at recognizing and gathering relevant facts before taking action, and critically assessing facts and arguments asserted to the board or association.

Since Professor White's 1983 article on legal literacy, the scope and detail of regulation and compliance have expanded. Private investigators have been around for centuries, but now fact investigation is a widespread corporate and organizational function. Some corporate professionals' role focus almost entirely on gathering facts. For example, a human resources coordinator may conduct extensive fact investigations of workplace events, working closely with in-house legal counsel for the corporation or organization.

Working with facts, whether for a zoning dispute, a leadership role, or an internal investigation, requires creativity and curiosity. Skilled fact researchers are able to rec-

---

1. James Boyd White, *The Invisible Discourse of the Law: Reflections on Legal Literacy and General Education*, 54 U. Colo. L. Rev. 143, 144 (1983).

2. *E.g.*, Lucia Moses, *The Washington Post's Robot Reporter Has Published 850 Articles in the Past Year*, https://digiday.com/media/washington-posts-robot-reporter-published-500-articles-last-year/ (Sept. 14, 2017).

ognize relevant sources, collect factual information, interpret that information, continue the process of collecting more facts, and clearly describe their findings and their processes to others.

This chapter describes some important basics about recognizing what a fact is, as distinct from an inference, characterization, or legal conclusion. It then delves into the skill of asking good questions, followed by the skill of describing facts effectively when communicating them to others.

I. Facts, Inferences, Characterizations, and Conclusions

This section covers the distinctions among facts, inferences about facts, characterizations of facts, and legal conclusions drawn from facts. Critical thinking about these distinctions is crucial to legal literacy in working with facts. An example from the life of Olivia Ralston is used throughout. The issue in this chapter is a dispute over real estate and property boundaries—specifically, the property line behind Ms. Ralston's home, which she owns on a residential street in Colorado. Ms. Ralston's neighbor, Neil Nottingham, has sent her a letter about the fence located on the back boundary shared by their properties:

Dear Olivia,

It has come to my attention that the fence around your property is situated on my property. I would like to remain cordial neighbors with you, and therefore would like to discuss how you can remedy this situation and relocate the fence onto your rightful property.

Sincerely,
Neil N.

Upon receipt of this letter, Ms. Ralston sets out to investigate the situation using skills in working with facts.

A. What Is a Fact?

To work effectively with facts, an initial question is rather philosophical: What actually is a fact? A fact can be defined as "a reality that exists independently of its acknowledgment by the conscious mind of a perceiver."[3] In other words, a fact is something that is true in the world. Facts can be proven as true in a variety of ways, such as documentary proof, photos and videos and other recordings, and the testimony of people with knowledge.

----

3. Elizabeth Thornburg, *Law, Facts, and Power*, 114 Penn. St. L. Rev. Penn. Statim 1, 3 (2009) (quoting Gary Lawson, *Proving the Law*, 86 NW. U. L. REV. 859, 866 (1992)).

In the example with Olivia Ralston receiving the letter from her neighbor Mr. Nottingham, what would you say is a fact? The existence of the letter is a fact. Nottingham has made statements in the letter, and those statements are themselves facts—for example, "Nottingham stated that the fence is situated on his property." But just because Nottingham states something as a fact does not mean the fact itself is true. The next step is likely to investigate these statements and find out if they are true, as well as to investigate other relevant facts about this situation.

1. Subjective Beliefs and Intent as Facts

The definition of a fact above shows that a fact must exist in the world, independently of what anyone thinks. But sometimes what a person thinks or believes is, itself, a relevant fact. A person's state of mind can be legally relevant, as with criminal laws that require criminal intent, or civil laws that require "knowing" violations. Thinking critically about facts means distinguishing someone's *subjective* belief about the world (and *subjective intent* about the future) from the *objective* facts that exist and are provable in the world.

This subjective/objective distinction is important in several areas of law. For example, the Fourth Amendment prohibits unreasonable searches and seizures. The Supreme Court has interpreted a "search" to mean "official intrusion" into a "sphere" with a subjective expectation of privacy *and* objective expectation of privacy. Thus, in analyzing whether the Fourth Amendment applies to conversations in phone booths and smartphones seized pursuant to an arrest, courts examine whether the particular individuals in the case subjectively expected privacy on the facts, and whether that expectation is recognized by society as reasonable.[4]

In Ms. Ralston's property dispute with her neighbor Mr. Nottingham, the legal doctrine at issue is called "adverse possession." That is a doctrine that allows someone to "adversely possess" land as against its original owner and, eventually with the passage of time and other requirements, to gain ownership over the land. If indeed Ms. Ralston built a fence on Mr. Nottingham's property many years ago, she may have gained the property for herself through the doctrine of adverse possession. The requirements of adverse possession vary by state. In some states, adverse possession requires that the person occupying the land intend to adversely possess it.[5] When someone's intent is a requirement, that person's subjective state of mind becomes an important fact in itself.

---

4. *Carpenter v. United States*, 138 S. Ct. 2206 (June 22, 2018) (drawing on case law originating with *U.S. v. Katz*, 369 U.S. 347 (1967)).

5. *E.g.*, *Tran v. Macha*, 213 S.W.3d 913 (Tex. 2006) (stating that "there must be an intention to claim property as one's own to the exclusion of all others; '[m]ere occupancy of land without any intention to appropriate it'" is not sufficient).

2. Knowledge and Constructive Knowledge

There is one more layer to this subjective/objective distinction about facts and what people know to be facts. It has to do with human nature, incentives, and holding people responsible for being aware of the world around them. If a rule requires a person to have some level of knowledge (or a subjective intent) about something, and it is not in that person's interest to be subject to that rule, then maybe they could just deny any knowledge and thereby evade the rule entirely. As Upton Sinclair once quipped, "It is difficult to get a man to understand something when his salary depends on his not understanding it." In the legal setting, if the rule depends solely on their own statements about their subjective state of mine, then a self-interested person may be tempted to avoid the rule by simply denying that state of mind.

One solution to this problem is that subjective belief can sometimes be proven by surrounding circumstances. Another and more powerful solution to this problem is the concept of "constructive" knowledge. Constructive knowledge refers not just to what a person actually *did* know, but also what that person *reasonably should have known.* Thus, a legal rule that requires "actual or constructive knowledge" of something can be satisfied in either of two ways: First, the rule is satisfied when the person did actually know; but second, even if the person did not know or actively denies knowing, the rule can still be satisfied when the person reasonably should have known. For example, it is possible to sue the United States government on a dispute over land claimed by both the plaintiff and the United States. Property-related claims must be brought within 12 years of the date the claim arose, and this date can be established even if the person with the claim did not actually know of the claim. Under federal statutory law, property-related claims against the United States government "shall be deemed to have accrued on the date the plaintiff or his predecessor in interest knew or should have known of the claim of the United States." 28 U.S.C. § 2409a(g) (2018). In this way, a person cannot bring a property claim against the government 50 years after the claim accrued even if that person genuinely did not know about the claim until yesterday. The claim accrues on the date the person "should have known" about it. That is an example of constructive knowledge at work in a legal standard.

3. Common Sense

Common sense also plays a role in thinking about facts. For example, the Advisory Committee Note to Federal Rule of Evidence 201 provides:

Every case involves the use of hundreds or thousands of non-evidence facts. When a witness in an automobile accident case says "car," everyone, judge and jury included, furnishes from non-evidence sources within himself, the supplementing information that the "car" is an automobile, not a railroad car, that is self-propelled, probably by an internal combustion engine, that it may be assumed to have four wheels with pneumatic rubber tires, and so on.[6]

In Ralston's situation, then, what if Ralston or Nottingham somehow wanted to argue that the fence at issue was in fact a play structure — anything other than a fence? One important function of the law is to manage the range of meanings for commonly understood words. The range of meanings is managed through a variety of sources such as tradition, precedent, and textual definitions.[7] Thus, a landowner should not be able to and most likely would not be able to escape fence-related liability by calling a fence something other than a fence.

On the other hand, some words have broader meanings that might be commonly expected. Famously, in legal language, a "person" generally includes a corporation as well as a human person. Some would argue that this definition of person flies in the face of common sense, but it is deeply embedded in United States law. For legally literate individuals, it is actually just plain common sense that "persons" include corporations unless defined otherwise.

B. What Makes a Fact Relevant?

Facts are everywhere, but only some facts matter in a legal sense. A legally relevant fact is a fact that could make a difference to the legal outcome of a case. Of course, no one has to actually bring a case in court to use the concept of relevance. The Federal Rules of Evidence define relevance to emphasize each of these two concepts: Does the fact help to prove something, and does the fact help to prove something that matters in the case?

Evidence is relevant if:

(a) it has any tendency to make a fact more or less probable than it would be without the evidence; and

(b) the fact is of consequence in determining the action.[8]

The concept of relevance is used in every legal setting, from suing in court, to mediating and arbitrating disputes, to creating compliance policies and drafting contracts. For example, a compliance policy might include reader-friendly examples of what to do and what not to do; these examples must be legally relevant scenarios of permissible and impermissible actions. In drafting a contract, the drafter must understand the contracting party's strategic goals and select language that will accomplish those goals in light of background legal principles. So if a contracting party wants to deal with an

---

6. *Id.* at 3-4 (quoting Advisory Committee Note to Fed. R. Evid. 201).

7. Chapter 16 explores "five types of legal arguments," quoting Professor Wilson Huhn, in exploring what makes an argument legally persuasive. Arguments based on text, intent, precedent, tradition, and policy also serve to define and constrain the legal meaning of words.

8. Fed. R. Evid. 401.

economic consequence for breach of contract, the drafter must know what terms are available—such as "economic loss" and "consequential damages" and so on—and whether the desired consequence fits within the available terms.

1. Determining Relevance

The most direct way to assess relevance is to use legal logic: (1) understand the relevant legal rule (or rules); (2) gather the relevant facts; and (3) sort the facts according to their connection with the legal rules. Then assess what to do next. That is how a compliance officer might look at a new regulation that affects her company. One way to think of this process is "rules in search of facts." In problem-solving situations, in contrast, the process often starts with a situation—in other words, facts in search of rules. When the factual situation triggers the process, it uses more iterations: (1) collect preliminary facts; (2) understand the legal rules; (3) sort and gather more relevant facts as needed. Then assess what to do next.

These are, of course, fairly linear and simplified, even artificial, frameworks for what really happens in legal problem-solving. Fact investigation is a type of legal problem solving, and problem solving depends in part on the work styles and even personalities of the people collaborating to solve problems. If you have ever worked with someone who emails a question every five minutes throughout the workday, you will appreciate the discipline of working in stages with predetermined check-in points rather than an "open door" approach to questions. On the other hand, if you have worked with a process-oriented rule follower who moves forward and will not revisit earlier conclusions, you will appreciate the flexibility of a collaborative team that is willing to question its own conclusions and revise its work, modifying its work process as needed. Like collaborative teams in general, effective fact investigations must be organized and efficient, yet flexible and responsive.

Consider Olivia Ralston's situation with her neighbor, Neil Nottingham, regarding the fence he claims is on his property rather than hers. In addition to the email above, Ms. Ralston has typed out some of the facts she knows:

Ralston installed the fence in 1999 around the time her nephew was born, and the fence has remained standing since then. She has used the property as, essentially, a very large personal backyard. Nottingham has heavy brush and trees at the back of his property. Ralston is not sure what he can see from his own property about where the fence is. Ralston built a fence on the rear perimeter of the property. Ralston walked the rear area with the fencing company and instructed it where to build the fence, installing stakes to show the boundaries of what she thought was her property. Ralston bought her property from Sheldon Seller, who described the boundaries of the property to Ralston as being the area where she eventually built the fence. She is not sure what the title insurance says, or the property deed (which is held by the bank where she has her mortgage). Over the years, Ralston has had one trespasser climb over the fence, and she called the police, who came out to her property but did not find the trespasser. Nottingham is somewhat of a recluse although he attends the same church as Ralston, and she has seen him at church functions several times a year. They have greeted each other cordially. During all these short conversations at church, he has never mentioned any objections to the fence.

The legal issue is adverse possession. The test for adverse possession varies from state to state, but it has several elements, usually along the following lines:

A person adversely possesses land when that person's use of land is *hostile,* done in *good faith, open and notorious, exclusive,* and *continuous for the statutory period* (typically, many years).

Each separate element of the legal test is shown in italics above. Using legal literacy means parsing the test into separate elements and recognizing that they are separate and distinct. For example, *hostile* is different from *good faith,* which is different from *open and notorious.* And you may be surprised to learn that all of these can be true simultaneously! Applying concepts of legal literacy means looking beyond the general non-legal meaning of words to understand their legal meaning. "Hostile" is a very good example. Its general non-legal meaning is angry and aggressive, but in property law, "hostile" means taking action that suggests ownership over the property and does not involve anger at all.[9]

With this basic understanding of the elements of adverse possession, the preliminary facts Ms. Ralston wrote out can be charted, looking something like this:

Legal element	Example of relevant facts
Hostile	Ralston built a fence on the rear perimeter of the property. Ralston walked the rear area with the fencing company and instructed it where to build the fence, installing stakes to show what she thought were the boundaries of her property.
Good faith	Ralston bought her property from Sheldon Seller. At the time, Seller described the boundaries of the property to Ralston as being the area where she eventually built the fence. She is not sure what the title insurance says, or the property deed (which is held by the bank where she has her mortgage).
Open and notorious	Nottingham has heavy brush and trees at the back of his property. Ralston is not sure what he can see from his own property about where the fence is.

---

9. See, e.g. *Hostile Possession,* Legal Dictionary, Law.com, https://dictionary.law.com/Default.aspx?selected =883

Continued	
Legal element	**Example of relevant facts**
Exclusive	Ralston has had one trespasser climb over the fence, and she called the police, who came out to her property but did not find the trespasser. Otherwise Ralston has used the property as, essentially, a very large personal backyard.
Continuous for statutory period (for example in Colorado, 18 years)	Ralston installed the fence in 1999 around the time her nephew was born. The fence has remained standing since then.

In the situation above with adverse possession, would it matter that Nottingham is somewhat of a recluse but Ralston has seen him at local church functions and they have had brief conversations throughout the years? Probably not. Social connections do not help to show or not show any of the elements of adverse possession. Thus, Nottingham's social activities are not legally relevant. It may still be worth including, as noted below, but it is not legally relevant to the test for adverse possession.

The concept of relevance is closely related to another concept: what is "material" to a legal issue. In legal language, a "material fact" basically means a fact that matters. Black's Law Dictionary defines "material" to emphasize importance and influence on an outcome: "Having some logical connection with the consequential facts" such as with "material evidence"; or significant and essential, in other words "of such a nature that knowledge of the item would affect a person's decision-making."[10] The example in Black's Law Dictionary is "material alteration of the document." Other examples abound, such as material witnesses, material assets, material misrepresentations, material breaches, material changes, and so forth. Each of these will have its own precise definition tailored for that situation.

Because the concept of being "material" is itself a legal standard, the use of the term "material" may be an application of law to fact. In other words, a non-bar-licensed professional may want to be aware of the legal content implied in the statement that a fact is "material" to an issue. This awareness is important for several reasons. When using legal language, do not mix "relevance" and "materiality." Relevance is a broader and more all-inclusive concept; the statement that a fact is material to a legal issue is a distinctly *legal* assertion. Thus, stating that a fact is material could be viewed as a legal conclusion within the purview of an attorney. In general, the broader and less technical the context, the more appropriate and less risky it will be for a non-bar-licensed professional to draw a conclusion about whether a fact is relevant for legal purposes.

---

10. Black's Law Dictionary, *Material* (Bryan Garner, ed., 10th ed. 2014).

2. Background Facts

Some facts are not legally relevant, but they still are contextually relevant. As noted above, the relationship between Ralston and Nottingham at church is not strictly relevant to the test for adverse possession. But the fact they are friendly may make a difference to the legal strategy for resolving the dispute. It makes the possibility of amicably negotiating a settlement more likely. This consideration harkens back to the idea of legal thinking and problem-solving. Having a cordial relationship does not matter in a robotic application of law to fact, but it could matter very much in solving a real-world dispute between neighbors.

Along the same lines, would it matter if "Neil Nottingham" was instead "Nell Nottingham," a 78-year-old widow with health problems who rarely stepped outside her home at all? In this scenario, the elderly widow Nottingham does not have the physical ability to hike through brush and woods to inspect her back property. Thus, she probably did not have actual notice of the fence encroaching her property. However, the test in Colorado for "open and notorious" use is an objective test focusing on whether the use is obvious. It does not require the neighbor to actually know about the use.[11] Still, the fact that the neighbor was likely physically incapable of actually discovering the use would potentially be emotionally relevant. Nell Nottingham's inability to explore her own property line would likely be at least mentioned if not actually argued in a negotiation or litigation. Some facts could make a difference to how the whole story is told and perceived. Legal training isn't necessary to understand that some facts are particularly sympathetic or detract from sympathy. Some facts do not really relate to a core element of the legal test, but they change the way the story may be told and thus the way the situation may be perceived.

In addition to serving as a possible narrative background fact, this fact might also form the basis of a legal argument to change the law. Lawyers (and unrepresented parties) can make good-faith arguments to change the law. Thus the neighbor could argue that her subjective inability to actually discover the use would make the use not open and notorious, and thus not eligible for adverse possession. This argument is likely to fail because it goes against the established legal standard, but the law changes and evolves when parties make arguments to change it. If this were the neighbor's best argument and she had a lawyer representing her, the lawyer could make a good-faith argument to change the law.

This example shows that working with facts may mean not only gathering facts that are definitely relevant under existing law, but also gathering facts that may be relevant to negotiations and dispute resolution, facts relevant to the "story" behind the whole situation, and facts that may relate to an argument for changing the law. Effective fact

---

11. *Olson v. Hillside Cmty. Church SBC*, 124 P.3d 874, 880 (Colo. Ct. App. 2005) ("A use is open and notorious if it is 'sufficiently obvious to apprise the owner of the servient estate, in the exercise of reasonable diligence, that another is making use of the burdened land so that the owner may object. However, actual knowledge by the owner need not be proved.'") (citation omitted).

gathering means not only seeking out what is legally relevant, but also being curious and intuitive about what might make a difference.

C. Inferences

Facts are a type of data. But data is often incomplete. Thus, working with facts means understanding what to do about gaps in between known facts. The section above shows how to investigate and gather more data. In a perfect world, all the facts could be gathered to create a complete, definite, unambiguous picture of any given situation. But it's not a perfect world. Working with facts means working with gaps in the facts.

"Inferences are factual conclusions that can fairly and rationally be drawn or deduced from other facts."[12] Basically it means factual conclusions that are built on other facts. Civil procedure and evidence law use the concept of inferences in very technical ways. For example, often in litigation, one party tries to avoid a trial by filing a motion for summary judgment, meaning judgment before trial. The court will assess the motion by considering only undisputed facts and drawing all reasonable inferences in favor of the "non-movant," meaning the opposing party that did not file the motion seeking summary judgment. The idea of this standard is to make sure cases where the inferences could go either way are resolved at a full trial. In a courtroom setting, of course, these technical uses of the inference concept are generally within the province of licensed attorneys.

Other professionals working with facts need to know what an inference is in part so they can recognize when others are providing inferences rather than facts. For example, imagine an internal investigation of a factory accident, in which various employees are interviewed. One employee states that the floor manager did not see the accident happen. That statement may be a fact, if the employee was in another room with the manager. But it could also be an inference, if the employee knew that the floor manager routinely took a cigarette break at the exact time the accident occurred. Investigating facts carefully means parsing facts that are directly known via observation from factual conclusions built on other facts.

In the adverse possession situation above with Olivia Ralston and Neil Nottingham, imagine the fence is 12 feet tall and has always been painted cherry-apple red on both sides. This fact would create the inference that it is easy to see from either side. Even if Ms. Ralston cannot gain access to Nottingham's property to take a photo of the back property line from his vantage point, the size and unnatural color of the fence allows her to argue the factual inference that the fence is easy to see.

D. Characterizations

Working with facts requires careful separation of what is a fact from what is a belief or opinion about a fact. This is a form of not only legal literacy but critical thinking in

---

12. 29 Am. Jur. 2d *Evidence* § 199.

general. A characterization is a description of a fact. Characterization may add a moral or other suggested meaning to the way the fact is described. A characterization is something that a speaker or writer does when describing what happened. Familiarity with the concept will help you to understand what lawyers are doing when they describe the facts of a case.

For example, if an employee complained about a situation on two occasions, one party might characterize the employee as "repeatedly" complaining. But an opposing party might disagree with that characterization and point out that the complaints were 10 months apart and dealt with different variations on the situation. The opposing party would characterize the complaints not as repeated but as "sporadic" or "episodic."

In the property dispute between Olivia Ralston and Neil Nottingham, imagine if the fence were not cherry-apple red but rather a muted brown. Nottingham may characterize the fence as camouflaged, whereas Ralston could characterize it as tasteful. Both are opinions, not facts, about the fence.

E. Legal Conclusions

Working with facts also requires skill in differentiating facts from legal conclusions about the facts. What a fact is and what it means legally are two different things. A legal conclusion is a statement applying a legal category to a fact, as in these examples:

- Driving 30 miles per hour over the speed limit is "negligent."
- Exploiting a vulnerable person's weakness to emotionally torment that person for self-gratification is "extreme and outrageous" conduct.
- Doing one's best to satisfy a contractual standard is acting in "good faith."

Understanding legal conclusions can help with accurate, complete, objective investigations. This is especially true when a legally literate person is gathering facts from others who may not be as well trained. People who lack legal training may offer legal conclusions without a basis and without knowing they are arguing a conclusion.

For example, what if Ralston attempts to speak with Nottingham about the property line dispute. Nottingham claims to her, "Adverse possession doesn't apply here because I asked you not to install the fence where it stands, but you did it anyway." This statement contains a legal conclusion about whether a certain legal doctrine applies to certain facts. This statement also contains an embedded statement about the facts, namely that Nottingham asked Ralston not to install the fence where it stands, but she did so despite his request. If Ralston is able to separate the factual claims from the asserted legal conclusion, she can better respond to his statement.

In the example above, Ms. Ralston is hearing a legal conclusion and deciding how to proceed on her own behalf. A different situation arises if Ms. Ralston were asked to give a legal conclusion. Professionals should be aware when a question calls for a legal conclusion, so that they recognize the nature of the question and appropriately manage their response. For example, imagine Ms. Ralston is talking to a potential investor and describing her unpaid internship program. The potential investor then asks, "Do you have any exposure on minimum-wage liability?" This question calls for an assessment of the facts about her business and the possible risks of liability under the Fair Labor Standards Act or state law. A question calling for a legal conclusion may not be so explicit — for example, the investor might ask, "How are you able to structure your unpaid internships?" The response to such questions often should not be but does not always need to be, "I don't know; let me ask my lawyer." This is especially true when the parties are negotiating informally and anticipate a more formal due-diligence process later.

Not all legal conclusions are off-limits to people who aren't lawyers. A tax accountant can draw a conclusion on whether a certain expense is a "legitimate business expense" under the Internal Revenue Code. A government agency's Freedom of Information Officer can draw a conclusion about whether releasing requested documents would cause a "clearly unwarranted invasion of personal privacy" under 5 U.S.C. § 552(b)(6). But in any situation that seems like giving advice to another party, asserting a legal conclusion may verge on the unauthorized practice of law.

II. Generating Questions

One key skill in working with facts is asking good questions. This may mean directly asking questions of real people in one-on-one interviews. It may mean reading a pile of documents and sending questions by email to another team member. Or it may mean gathering information and generating questions about that information, then using those questions to gather more information. In other words, working with facts in a legal context means cultivating a sense of purposeful curiosity.

The main benchmark for the "purposeful" part of purposeful curiosity is the substance of the law. What is the legal issue (or issues), and what is the legal test for each issue? For example, in the adverse-possession scenario, imagine that Ms. Ralston has hired a lawyer to help her with the property dispute. The lawyer may decide to send a legal professional such as a paralegal to take photos, gather documents, and interview Ms. Ralston on the lawyer's behalf. Here are some of the questions the paralegal may ask:

Legal element	Questions
Hostile	How did you talk about the property to the fence contractor and others?
	Did you ever get a title survey?
	Have you enforced your property rights to the fenced land in any way?
Good faith	Did you believe the property belonged to you? What led you to that belief?
	Did you ever make any suggestion to anyone that you weren't sure it was your property?
Open and notorious	What does the fence look like?
	Have you ever been over the fence onto Neighbor B's property, and what did you find over there?
Exclusive	Does anyone else use your land within the fence?
	Have you enforced your property rights to the fenced land in any way? (similar relevance to the "hostile" element)
Continuous for statutory period (for example in Colorado, 18 years)	When did you install the fence?
	How was that border area used before you installed the fence?

The "curiosity" part of purposeful curiosity also means being curious about background facts. Asking direct questions about sensitive, ostensibly irrelevant facts may not be the best approach. The most effective curiosity has a flexible, improvisational quality to it. Mix open-ended and closed-ended questions. Alongside a list of written questions and in an appropriate context, set the tone with professional yet friendly social language, inviting full disclosure. One's personal and professional style and the culture of one's employer play a large role in crafting email language that fits the situation. What differences do you see between the following two examples?

Example 1

Dear Ms. Ralston,

This email follows up on our telephone conversation on August 24, 20XX, regarding the boundary behind your home, adjoining Neil Nottingham's property. Please review the attachment and send written responses to these questions.

Sincerely,
Carey Jones

Example 2

Dear Ms. Ralston,

Thank you for talking with me on the telephone on August 24, 20XX. You may recall the issue is the boundary between your property and the Nottingham property behind your home. It was helpful to talk with you about the history of the property, and I appreciate your time. In reviewing the files, some more questions have arisen. Rather than schedule another meeting, a list of questions is attached. We would appreciate it if you would read the questions and type or email your answers. If a phone call or interview would be more efficient for you, please let me know.

Thank you,
Carey Jones

A corollary to purposeful curiosity is persistence; sometimes in legal situations, the facts may be difficult to gather because they are complex or they could lead to problems and consequences. Asking good questions and approaching a situation from both a broad and narrow angle can help to break down some of the barriers to collecting information. Likewise, experts in working with facts develop good judgment on choosing a method of inquiry, such as written questions, a face-to-face interview, a phone call, an intermediary, or something else. Experts in working with facts also show good judgment in how to communicate concerning the facts, sometimes in writing formally, sometimes informally, sometimes face to face, sometimes by phone, or sometimes not at all until the right situation arises.

III. Timelines and Other Visual Tools

Working with facts effectively includes not just gathering them, but also communicating them effectively to others. Facts are often easier to understand when presented visually.

A common and extremely useful visual tool for presenting facts is a timeline. A timeline is a visual representation of a chronology of events. Making a timeline can be a type of note-taking just for yourself to help you understand a situation. A timeline may also be shared with others for a wide variety of purposes—for example:

- To create a common base of knowledge within a team
- To confirm what happened
- To show gaps in the known facts and seek additional information
- To persuade by suggesting an argument about what the facts mean

Timelines come in various formats. A plain but useful format is simply a typed page with columns for dates and events:

Sept. 4, 1988:	Neil Nottingham inherits property by deed from his father, Niles Nottingham
Feb. 20, 1995:	Olivia Ralston purchases property from Sheldon Seller
March 1999:	Olivia Ralston builds fence on back property line

Another format is a line or portrait-oriented chart running from left to right:

Sept. 4, 1988	Feb. 20, 1995	March 1999
Neil Nottingham inherits property by deed from his father, Niles Nottingham	Olivia Ralston purchases property from Sheldon Seller	Olivia Ralston builds fence on back property line

As shown in both examples above, even a simple timeline must use both the space on the page and typography to logically separate different types of information. Contrast the two examples below. Which is easier to read?

Example 1

- Sept. 4, 1988: Neil Nottingham inherits property by deed from his father, Niles Nottingham
- Feb. 20, 1995: Olivia Ralston purchases property from Sheldon Seller
- March 1999:   Olivia Ralston builds fence on back property line

Example 2

Sept. 4, 1988	Neil Nottingham inherits property by deed from his father, Niles Nottingham
Feb. 20, 1995	Olivia Ralston purchases property from Sheldon Seller
March 1999	Olivia Ralston builds fence on back property line

Example 2 is easier to read because it creates separate visual spaces for separate types of information. The reader's eye can easily separate the dates from the events. And the reader can quickly and easily choose to read the events in order, or to read the date column first and get a sense of the relevant chronology, then go back and understand what events happened in that chronology. Example 2 is the same information, with less work required of the reader and more options given to the reader for processing the information.

To be effective, a timeline needs to be designed to work with the dimensions of the printed page and the viewable computer screen. That does not mean a timeline must fit on one page, but it does mean a timeline must use space effectively whether it is a half-page or 10 pages. For a traditional list-style timeline on a portrait page, it should not let a random single item roll over onto the next page; the entire timeline should be adjusted to fit on one page. A left-to-right timeline may require a landscape page orientation (wider than tall) rather than a traditional portrait orientation (taller than wide).

Visuals can be analytical, meaning they not only state the facts but put them into context with the law.[13] So a timeline could convey more information than just what happened and when. For example, it could use different spaces to convey different types of information:

Ralston Property	Nottingham Property

	Sept. 4, 1988:
	  Neil Nottingham inherits property by
	  deed from his father, Niles Nottingham

February 20, 1995:
  Olivia Ralston purchases property from
  Sheldon Seller	

March 1999:
  Olivia Ralston builds fence on back
  property line	

This visual example shows facts relevant to each property. The two-column design sorts the facts to keep them in separate but parallel categories.

Beyond the black-and-white examples shown here, color-coding can make visual information even easier to understand—if it's done right. Color-coding should be as simple as possible to enhance the intended message. For example, two background colors could be used to represent two different categories of information. The color-coding should be internally consistent and easy for a reader to grasp. Avoid adding visual information that does not relate to the intended message; the purpose of color-coding and visual designs is not to grab the reader's attention but rather to help the reader understand the information. Be aware that some readers are color blind; thus, color coding should enhance but not be the only form of communication.

---

13. Ruth Anne Robbins and Steve Johansen, *Articulating the Analysis: Systematizing the Decision to Use Visuals as Legal Reasoning*, 20 Legal Writing 57 (2015).

Digital capabilities are beyond the scope of this text, but it is not difficult to imagine interactive timelines. The websites Timeglider and Prezi are two possibilities (as of 2018) for making online timelines or visual presentations with a timeline-like feel.

IV. Describing and Summarizing Facts

Another important skill in working with facts is achieving the all-important balance between describing the facts fully and summarizing them concisely. The most common format for a fact description or a fact summary is a series of prose sentences — that is, not bullet points or charts, but real sentences arranged in paragraphs. A good fact description takes a messy group of facts from documents and conversations and other sources and processes them into a useful set of paragraphs describing what happened.

Summarizing seems like a simple task, but it is more difficult than it sounds. Have you ever read a summary and thought "this is too long" or "this is so short, I know I'm missing something" or "this seems vague" or "I wonder what really happened here"? Summarizing information is a useful skill that takes careful thought and investment in writing and revising.

What makes a good fact description? Here are some criteria:

- Includes significant facts
- Organized by chronology or topic
- Designed for the reader with paragraphs and headings if appropriate
- Strategic in including detail that matters most
- Acknowledges limitations such as missing facts or sources or key unknown points
- Identifies the source of facts explicitly when important
- Tailored to include only facts, not opinion or conjecture
- Clear and concise

Each of these criteria is discussed and explored in more depth below.

A. Including Significant Facts

In crafting a fact description, the writer must choose which facts to include. The significant facts include those that are most likely to be legally relevant and those that are most important to the situation at hand.

In the Olivia Ralston property dispute with her neighbor Neil Nottingham, a summary would probably not include Nottingham's occupation and the fact he attends church activities occasionally. But if Nottingham was a well-known community activist who had frequently brought pro se actions in the local courts, that fact might be included in a summary. That context seems important in approaching the overall negotiation.

If the fact description is intended not just to describe the facts objectively, but to persuade the reader in some way, the writer must decide what to do with facts that help the persuasive purpose and facts that are "bad facts"—in other words, facts that seem to cut against the outcome sought by the writer. Lawyers who study advocacy and persuasive legal writing are taught to include the "bad facts" but minimize them. For example, a bad fact might be mentioned in the middle of paragraph rather than a topic sentence. Persuasive factual stories are covered in more detail in this book in chapter 16.

B. Organizing by Chronology and Topic

One of the most common questions about describing facts—whether in a full narrative or a condensed summary—is how to organize them. Facts are often easiest to understand when presented in chronological order. Beyond just putting them in order, the writer can group the facts into logical units and divide those units into paragraphs. Consider and compare Examples 1 and 2 below:

Example 1

Ralston installed the fence in 1999, the year her nephew was born, and the fence has remained standing since then. She has used the property as, essentially, a very large personal backyard. Nottingham has heavy brush and trees at the back of his property. Ralston is not sure what he can see from his own property concerning the location of the fence. Ralston built a fence on the rear perimeter of the property. Ralston walked the rear area with the fencing company and instructed the company where to build the fence, installing stakes to show the boundaries of what she thought was her property. Ralston bought her property from Sheldon Seller in 1995, who described the boundaries of the property to Ralston as being the area where she eventually built the fence. She is not sure what the title insurance says or the property deed (which is held by the bank where she has her mortgage). Over the years, Ralston has had one trespasser climb over the fence, and she called the police, who came out to her property but did not find the trespasser. Nottingham is somewhat of a recluse although he attends the same church as Ralston, and she has seen him at church functions several times a year. They have greeted each other cordially. During all these short conversations at church, he has never mentioned any objections to the fence.

Example 2

Ralston bought her property from Sheldon Seller in 1995. Seller described the boundaries of the property to Ralston as being the area where she eventually built the fence. She is not sure what the title insurance says or the property deed (which is held by the bank where she has her mortgage).

Ralston installed the fence in 1999, the year her nephew was born, and the fence has remained standing since then. She has used the property as, essentially, a very large personal backyard. Over the years, Ralston has had one trespasser climb over the fence, and she called the police, who came out to her property but did not find the trespasser.

Nottingham has heavy brush and trees at the back of his property. Ralston is not sure what he can see from his own property concerning the location of the fence. He is somewhat of a recluse although he attends the same church as Ralston. She has seen him at church functions several times a year. They have greeted each other cordially. During all these short conversations at church, he has never mentioned any objections to the fence.

Example 2 is much better because it is in chronological order, thus making it easier for a reader to understand the history of this property. Example 2 is also organized into short paragraphs. Each paragraph corresponds to a certain phase or stage of the property's history. Can you label each paragraph with its basic topic?

- Paragraph 1: purchase of the property
- Paragraph 2: maintenance of the property over the years (including fence and trespass)
- Paragraph 3: current state of the property and relationship with neighbor

The method shown above is known as a "reverse outline." It is an outline of topics. It is in "reverse" because it is something a writer or editor does while reviewing a draft—not like the traditional outline written before creating a full text draft. Reverse outlining is an excellent technique for editing your own writing whether you are describing facts, legal information, or any other complex material. If you cannot label a paragraph, you probably need to clarify its purpose and topic sentence. If you label a paragraph with too many topics, you probably need to break it up into smaller pieces.

For every guideline we could offer about legal communication, there is an exception. For example, it is not an absolute rule that all facts in a summary or full narrative must go in precise chronological order. Sometimes the order should begin with the current situation (where we are now), then go back and start the background on how the current situation arose (how we got here). Starting with the current situation helps the reader understand why other details matter.

Here is an example of that organization using the Ralston situation:

Example 3

Olivia Ralston received an email from her neighbor, Neil Nottingham, on September 27, 20XX, demanding that she relocate the fence at the back boundary of her property adjoining Nottingham's. The email claimed the fence is actually located on Nottingham's property.

Ralston bought her property from Sheldon Seller in 1995. Seller described the boundaries of the property to Ralston as being the area where she eventually built the fence. She is not sure what the title insurance says or the property deed (which is held by the bank where she has her mortgage).

Ralston installed the fence in 1999, the year her nephew was born, and the fence has remained standing since then. She has used the property as, essentially, a very large personal backyard. Over the years, Ralston has had one trespasser climb over the fence, and she called the police, who came out to her property but did not find the trespasser.

Nottingham has heavy brush and trees at the back of his property. Ralston is not sure what he can see from his own property concerning the location of the fence. He is somewhat of a recluse although he attends the same church as Ralston. She has seen him at church functions several times a year. They have greeted each other cordially. During all these short conversations at church, he has never mentioned any objections to the fence.

Example 3 is helpful because it starts with the current problem to solve. That problem makes the property history relevant. If the example were revised to follow a strict chronological order, the first paragraph would need to be cut and pasted to the end of the story. That would put the most important information—what the problem is—last. The reader would lack context for the facts and might not pay attention to the right things. Starting with the current situation, then tracing backward to tell a chronological narrative, provides context and provides logical structure for the detailed facts.

C. Designing for the Reader

As shown above, the paragraph is a powerful tool for organizing information. And the first sentence of a paragraph is, in turn, a powerful tool for telling the reader what to expect in that paragraph. Examine Example 3 above and note what happens in the first sentence of each paragraph. The first sentence signals the factual topic of that paragraph.

Sometimes a narrative—or even a shorter summary—may be so complex that headings are useful. Headings can be simple phrases or full sentences. Here is an example with simple phrases:

The Dispute

Olivia Ralston received an email from her neighbor, Neil Nottingham, on September 27, 20XX, demanding that she relocate the fence at the back boundary of her property adjoining Nottingham's. The email claimed the fence is actually located on Nottingham's property.

Ralston's Property

Ralston bought her property from Sheldon Seller in 1995. Seller described the boundaries of the property to Ralston as being the area where she eventually built the fence. She is not sure what the title insurance says or the property deed (which is held by the bank where she has her mortgage).

The Fence

Ralston installed the fence in 1999, the year her nephew was born, and the fence has remained standing since then. She has used the property as, essentially, a very large personal backyard. Over the years, Ralston has had one trespasser climb over the fence, and she called the police, who came out to her property but did not find the trespasser.

Nottingham's Property

Nottingham has heavy brush and trees at the back of his property. Ralston is not sure what he can see from his own property concerning the location of the fence. He is somewhat of a recluse although he attends the same church as Ralston. She has seen him at church functions several times a year. They have greeted each other cordially. During all these short conversations at church, he has never mentioned any objections to the fence.

In the example above, the paragraphs and details are so simple that these headings are not actually needed. But they could be quite useful in a more complex factual situation.

D. Being Strategic in Including Detail

"I know it when I see it." That is a famous quote from Justice Potter Stewart in a Supreme Court case defining obscenity, *Jacobellis v. Ohio*, 374 U.S. 184 (1964). Likewise, sometimes a fact is so important that you just know it when you see it. A key quote from a key person, or a key strong or weak fact, or an important fact that is missing and unknown, should be included in a summary. On the other hand, facts that are not likely to be important in their exact format should be paraphrased more concisely.

E. Acknowledging Gaps

Ideally, the fact-gatherer will go out and get all the relevant facts. An understanding of the law and of how the law works in practice will guide the fact-gatherer toward everything that does make a difference or could make a difference. But as noted earlier, gathering facts reinforces the cliché that we certainly do not live in a perfect world. Sometimes an important fact is missing. An effective fact description must reflect important gaps:

- Facts that are not currently known but should be investigated
  The metes and bounds listed on Ms. Ralston's deed and Mr. Nottingham's deed should be investigated as soon as possible.

- Facts that have been investigated, only to reveal something that did not happen, or the absence of an important fact

Ms. Ralston did not contact Mr. Nottingham before constructing the fence in 1999.

- Sources that may have relevant information that should be investigated
The fence contractor should be contacted for the original job bid and invoice.

- Sources that have been sought out but (in the case of documents) cannot be found or (in the case of people) are deceased, practically unavailable, or intentionally uncooperative
The fence contractor has gone out of business and cannot be located.

Thus, part of being effective at working with facts means recognizing gaps in the facts and communicating about them when they are important.

F. Attributing the Source of Facts

How do you "cite" a fact? Facts don't come in statutory codes and case reporters; they just happen in the world in conversations, emails, letters, personal observations, and every other type of human experience. That means facts don't have standardized citation formats in the same way as statutes and cases. Also, facts are used in so many different situations that a highly formal standardized citation approach is too strict anyway.

A broader and more appropriate way to describe this function is "attributing the source of facts." That means identifying where the fact comes from in a way the reader can understand and use. Some attributions can be informal and journalistic in style:

Ms. Ralston bought the property from Sheldon Seller on February 20, 1995. She remembers Seller telling her at the closing, "The best thing for that backyard would be a fence."

Other attributions are more formal, resembling citations in their form and placement:

Mr. Seller's deed conveying the property to Ms. Ralston used a somewhat unusual clause conveying all the property Mr. Seller himself owned in Adams County. Specifically, the deed stated, "Grantor hereby conveys all of Grantor's real property located in the County of Adams." See Deed from Grantor Sheldon Smith to Grantee Olivia Ralston, dated February 20, 1995, at ¶ 5.

Choosing whether to attribute the sources of facts—and if so, how—can be tricky. Sometimes it's important and necessary, and sometimes it's distracting and unnecessary.

The easiest situation to handle is when the rules clearly require source citations. You should include source citations in any fact description that is required to include source citations. For example, if a company faced an EEOC charge, it would likely engage counsel to help draft a position statement. Professionals in HR may work with counsel to research and prepare the required position statement responding to the charge. (Or an internal investigation may have already been completed with the EEOC process in mind, since the position statement must also include any internal investigations.) The EEOC's guidance on "Effective Position Statements"[14] lays out the importance of sources. For fact-based position statements, "[a]t a minimum, it should include **specific, factual** responses to every allegation of the charge, as well as any other facts which you deem relevant for EEOC's consideration." The response "should clearly explain the Respondent's version of the facts and identify the specific documents and witnesses supporting its position." The response also should include all documentary evidence believed to be responsive. These instructions show that factual descriptions prepared in this context need to include source citations and attached documentary support.

A more difficult situation to handle is when no real rules or requirements dictate how to prepare the fact description. (This is a far more common scenario than the strict requirements described above in the EEOC context.) In such situations, the key is to understand your audience's need for information. A factual description should identify the source of a fact when the audience needs to know the source to understand the fact, or when the audience would want to know the source. Imagine yourself as the reader; would you be curious about where a particular fact comes from? Would you want to stop reading the description and call or email the writer to ask, "How do you know this?" If so, anticipate those questions and include a source attribution.

In contrast to full fact descriptions, factual summaries often do not identify sources explicitly because the summary accompanies an underlying full narrative with support. But even in a summary, if a fact is best understood in context with the source of that fact, the source should be identified.

Deciding whether and how to identify a source requires judgment and discretion. Like any skill, practicing over time by working with various fact investigations and processes can help a professional develop experience about when the source matters.

G. Including Only Facts, not Opinion or Conjecture

As noted earlier in this chapter, working with facts means recognizing what a fact is, compared to an inference, characterization, or conclusion. Certainly, working with facts means distinguishing them from speculation and opinion. A fact description should not include such nonfactual information. There is one situation when speculation and opinion should be included: when the existence of another person's opinion or speculation is, itself, legally relevant. The fact description should attribute the opin-

---

14. Equal Employment Opportunity Commission, *Effective Position Statements,* https://www.eeoc.gov/employers/position_statements.cfm

ion or speculation to that particular person, because the source is crucial information. And the writer should carefully write and edit the fact description to differentiate between facts about the world and facts about what people have opined or speculated regarding the world.

H. Being Clear and Concise

A good fact description, and certainly a good fact summary, must be clear and concise. Clarity and conciseness are addressed more fully in this book in chapters 17 and 18. A few highlights of that chapter are especially relevant for writing about facts:

1. Minimizing Passive Verbs

Before:
A deed was executed conveying the property to Ms. Ralston.
The problem: Who executed the deed?

After:
Mr. Sheldon executed the deed conveying the property to Ms. Ralston.
Now we know who executed the deed.

2. Using Concrete Nouns and Subjects

Before:
There were many features about the fence that made it easy to see.
The subject position of the sentence is occupied with "There were," which does not inform the reader what the sentence is really about.

After:
The fence had many features that made it easy to see.
The subject position of the sentence is occupied with "The fence," which quickly clarifies what the sentence is about.

Before:
It was clear that the fence was tall and brightly colored and an artificial addition to the land, which is why the use was open and notorious.
The subject position of the sentence is occupied with "It was clear that," which does not inform the reader what the sentence is really about.

After:
The fence was noticeable because it was tall, brightly colored, and an artificial addition to the land. All of these features of the fence demonstrate why the use was open and notorious.
The subject position of the sentence is occupied with "The fence," which informs the reader what the sentence is really about.

V. Conclusion

Working with facts is important in many legal situations and can, at times, be fun or at least memorable. Skilled factual research requires a creative and thoughtful mix of curiosity, persistence, judgment, and precision. Communicating facts effectively is also crucial to law, business, and any endeavor that depends on accurate information for strategy and decision-making.

Having studied this chapter, you should be able to:

- Distinguish among a fact, an inference, a characterization, and a conclusion
- Use a legal rule to generate a list of legally relevant questions in a fact investigation
- Design a timeline of facts
- Write and edit an effective factual summary
- Recognize and emphasize important facts with detail

Case Study

Read these interview notes from the lawyer's interview with Olivia Ralston about her crisis with coffee bean supply.

1. Which of these statements are facts, which are opinions, and which are legal conclusions?
2. After reading the interview, what additional information seems important? What follow-up questions or emails would be useful?
3. At the end of this interview, you will see a brief overview of the contract doctrine of impossibility as a defense to a breach of contract. Based on this legal information, what other questions should be asked to bring out potentially relevant facts?

Hi Olivia. Please go ahead and give me a general overview of your business.

Well, I started Olivia's Beans as a way to combine my passions for coffee, social causes, and entrepreneurship. I thought I could do a lot of good by creating a business where people with life-threatening allergies can work safely and can also come in to have a cup of coffee without being exposed to nuts, dairy, or other common allergens. We usually buy un-roasted coffee beans from overseas, roast and package them at our facility here, and sell the finished products online or to local businesses. Sometimes, if we have extra capacity, we pick up contracts to roast coffee beans for other companies according to their specifications.

Now, can you tell me about how the Earth Foods deal came about?

So Raul Proteus, Earth Foods' chief logistics officer, actually approached me with the idea for this deal. He'd tried Olivia's Beans' Pure Colombian roast at a local café and he was impressed. Raul said that demand for sustainably sourced coffee was exploding (which I already knew) and that Olivia's Beans could go international. This looked like a once-in-a-lifetime opportunity to me, and maybe I let my excitement show too much. We had a preliminary talk about quantity, and Raul made it clear that Earth Foods would expect a significant bulk discount. Olivia's Beans normally operates with pretty small margins. The kind of sustainable coffee we believe in procuring can be more expensive than large commercial operations, so I knew I might have trouble finding a supplier that would offer me a corresponding bulk discount.

And just so I can keep track of the timeline, when did your preliminary talk take place?

That would've been July 29 or 30, 20XX. I'm sure I have notes with the exact date somewhere. We planned to meet again in a few weeks to work out a deal. August 12, to be exact. I was scrambling to put together our bid to Earth Foods before then, and again the biggest issue was finding the right supplier. Thankfully (or so I thought), I found the website for Federación de Cafeteros Pequeños de Colombia (FCPC). It seemed perfect — small farmers, good practices, low prices. I started corresponding with FCPC salepeople, and they were really excited to hear that I was a supplier for a nationwide retailer (or would be, anyway; I didn't think making the distinction mattered).

But it probably gave you some bargaining power, at least?

I think so. At least, their first bid to me was practically the amount I was planning to start negotiating from — right at $6.50 per pound. And that included most of the transportation! Of course I accepted, contingent on getting the Earth Foods deal. That left me in a great spot heading into the August 12 meeting. In fact, Raul and I worked everything out quickly and signed the contract that day.

About that contract — would you mind describing the key terms for me?

We agreed to ten bi-monthly shipments of 10,000 pounds of Pure Colombian starting on September 1, for a total of 100,000 pounds. Earth Foods would pay $7.05 per pound. I only had about two weeks to prepare for the first shipment, so I signed the supply contract with FCPC within a few days — on August 14, I think. Looking back, I suppose I should've done some "due diligence," but there really wasn't time after signing with Earth Foods. Raul always set tight deadlines (maybe that's why he's in charge of logistics), and I wasn't in any position to push back. If Olivia's Beans didn't "play ball," someone else would.

As I understand it, though, everything went well at first.

Well, that's getting ahead of the story. My last step was to find a third-party roaster that would follow our proprietary roasting methods. Olivia's Beans was to continue processing its normal orders in addition to the Earth Foods contract, but we didn't have the capacity to roast everything ourselves. Thankfully, rates are pretty constant and I knew what to expect—that's why I didn't arrange with a roaster beforehand. Well, that plus not wanting to give up Olivia's Beans' proprietary methods.

But to answer your question, yes: it seemed like a great deal at first. Maybe more so for Earth Foods than for us. I actually saw some of the Pure Colombian for sale at my local Earth Foods (I don't shop there anymore), and it was cheaper than any comparable brand. So I'm sure they were happy.

And that brings us to the current dilemma?

Correct. Shortly after Olivia's Beans made the second shipment, I called my FCPC rep to thank her. You know I really try to stay on good terms with suppliers. But this time, the call wouldn't go through. It turns out that the farmers had some sort of irreconcilable dispute. It must have been bad because they completely dissolved the co-op and abandoned the operation—without even warning me! I found out from the website, and I still can't get in touch with anyone who can help me.

I found some contact information for individual farmers on the FCPC website, and while they want to help me, none of them are able to offer Olivia's Beans the same discount or free shipping. I'm pretty sure they would all be on the hook for breach of contract, but that's not my most pressing concern right now. So far, the lowest price any other co-op or individual farmer has quoted will still leave Olivia's Beans in the red. On the 90,000 pounds of beans we've not yet delivered, we'd face about $8.25 per pound in costs, against a contract price of $7.05 per pound.

To put this in perspective, on the remaining 90,000 pounds of beans to be delivered on the Earth Foods contract, Olivia's Beans will suffer a loss of $108,000 instead of getting our expected profit of $49,500. I don't have money to throw around like this!

So when did Earth Foods find out about Olivia's Beans' predicament?

Within a few days, actually. Maybe I should have waited for something to happen with FCPC, but I'm trying to be very up front and prompt with Earth Foods. I emailed Raul Proteus, explaining that Olivia's Beans might be unable to make its next shipment due to problems with suppliers. I even offered to discuss a supplemental deal at a slightly higher rate. True to form, Raul responded quickly and got right to the point. He was "deeply troubled" at the news—as if Earth Foods will even feel this. Raul also made a lot of veiled threats about ruining Olivia's Beans' reputation. I'm pretty sure that would be defamation, so he's probably just blustering. More concerning for me, he threatened to sue Olivia's Beans if we stopped shipments.

And that's really why I'm here. I did some research and found out that companies don't have to follow impossible contracts. And that's exactly what's happening here. The Earth Foods contract is financially impossible for Olivia's Beans. Earth Foods has lots of resources and plenty of options for alternative suppliers. If we have to finish out that contract, we are not going to make it as a business and I'll be in here talking to you about bankruptcy protection next week.

That concludes interview notes. Now let's assess their completeness in a legal issue. The test for using "impracticability" as a defense to breach of contract is whether "performance as agreed has been made impracticable by the occurrence of a contingency the non-occurrence of which was a basic assumption on which the contract was made." New York Uniform Commercial Code § 2-615(a). What other questions should be asked to bring out relevant facts about this legal issue?

Traditions and Trends

Fact investigation can be a fascinating process, mixing the logic of law with the surprising variety inherent in finding out "what happened." Anyone who has worked in Human Resources will know how truly unexpected real-life facts can be. The fundamentals of factual investigation include a flexible collection of techniques: locating documentary proof and finding witnesses to give their recollections; distinguishing facts from inferences and speculations and conclusions; recognizing gaps to find out more; and exploring the possible meaning of a missing or negative fact (evidence that just is not there).

An important tradition for anyone doing sensitive fact investigations in an organization (such as a corporation) is the tradition of attorney-client privilege and other doctrines related to protecting internal information. Depending on the jurisdiction, the privilege *may* extend to fact investigations done by non-lawyers at the direction of a lawyer, or for the purpose of seeking legal advice for the organization. Therefore, before beginning a sensitive fact investigation, it is important to understand the organization's strategy about attorney-client privilege. This step will likely also include confirming the desired format and intended audience for a final report about the facts.

Witness interviewing skills (which, by the way, should not be confused with the trial lawyer's skill of courtroom witness interrogation) have always been valuable to factual investigations and remain so today. One well-known technique taught in clinical legal education classes and lawyer training is to begin with open-ended questions, letting a witness tell the story without much interruption or suggestion, and then to go back over each part of the story in much greater detail to nail it down. Experience and intuition in interviewing techniques such as knowing when to press for more information, when to back off, and when a witness may be uncomfortable or untruthful are classic and valuable techniques for investigating facts. Fact investigations are, in certain contexts, commonly performed by specialists such as human resource officers (for employers), police detectives (for the state), and private investigators (for attorneys and other individuals). Police have numerous legal limitations and policies including but not limited to constitutional protections for criminal suspects. Private investigators working for attorneys should follow the same ethics rules that bind lawyers, such as not contacting a person known to be represented by counsel. An attorney can face professional discipline for delegating or benefiting from investigatory tactics performed by others that the attorney is prohibited from doing.

Trends in fact investigation include — of course — the influence of computers, data, and data analytics. Computer and network forensics can help reveal financial fraud and theft of intellectual property, and can do so without revealing the investigation to its target. Software can scan and search large amounts of text to find exact matches, of course, as well as patterns such as conversations and language patterns of further interest in the investigation. Technology-enhanced investigation has become far more sophisticated — not just in backward-looking sweeps of past communication, but in real-time monitoring and data collection. Employees with smartphones are likely creating GPS data of their every move. Thus a trend in fact investigations should be the law and ethics of digital surveillance and proper uses of the information produced by such surveillance.

Chapter 16

Persuasive Writing

A policy advocate writes a detailed letter to a regulatory agency, arguing that the agency should change how it implements the law. The advocate will demonstrate that the agency's current implementation creates bad results inconsistent with the agency's statutory mandate.

A community resident attends a city council meeting where the council will consider whether to allow or prohibit rental scooters to be used in the city limits. The resident will argue in favor of the scooters because he believes they enhance urban life and reduce pollution from vehicle emissions. He plans to hand the council members a memo supporting his remarks in greater detail.

An adult child of an aging parent receives a letter that her parent is being evicted from the parent's assisted-living facility because the parent needs more care than the assisted-living facility says it can provide. The adult child is seeking to prevent the eviction and will write an argument based on the contract with the facility as well as her parent's medical records.

Each situation above is different, but each person needs to create a persuasive written argument. What should they consider, and how should they go about their tasks? This chapter discusses general theories of persuasion and then explores several well-known categories of legal arguments. The second half of the chapter gives detailed examples drawn from two situations: (1) comments filed in response to the Food and Drug Administration's call for comments on whether non-dairy beverages made from almonds, soy, and other plants should be labeled as "milk"; and (2) a Supreme Court case on whether pharmaceutical companies that comply with FDA labeling regulations are still subject to suit under state law for failure to warn consumers about risks. These examples show a broad range of legal arguments, some of which were generated by laypeople seeking to persuade the Food and Drug Administration and others by lawyers seeking to persuade the Supreme Court.

I. Introduction to Persuasion

Scholars and thinkers have put forth many different frameworks and theories for how to be persuasive. The following quote is from a health literacy article that applies equally in the legal context:

> There are almost as many different definitions of persuasion or persuasive communication as there are persuasion scholars. A common theme throughout these definitions is that "persuasion involves a conscious effort at influencing the thoughts or actions of a receiver." One [inclusive] definition of persuasive communication... is [Gerald R.] Miller's: "any message that is intended to shape, reinforce, or change the responses of another, or others."[1]

The goals with communicating about law are often to influence someone's actions and shape their response. Legal communication is practical, focusing more on what people do than on their thoughts and beliefs. But of course, some persuasion seeks to influence a person's thinking as a means to influencing their actions.

A. Persuasion through Influence

In a business or marketing class, you may have read or read about Robert Cialdini's work on "influence." Cialdini observed real-life situations such as used-car sales and concluded that persuasion is based on common principles: (1) reciprocity; (2) consistency and commitment; (3) social proof; (4) liking; (5) authority; and (6) scarcity. Under this theory, the writers would make sure they followed the audience's recommended or required formatting rules to establish a kind of reciprocity: "I care about your formatting rules; please will you now care about my argument?" They would invoke consistency and commitment to values the reader already possesses to emphasize that their argument falls in line with those values. They would point to other similar authorities and counterparts already taking the action they are seeking, to appeal to

---

1. Kenzie Cameron, *A Practitioner's Guide to Persuasion: An Overview of 15 Selected Persuasion Theories, Models and Frameworks*, 74 Patient Educ. & Counseling 309, 309 (2009) (citations omitted).

social proof. They would be respectful and formal but not too formal, to try to make the reader like them. They would include any legal rules, contractual provisions, or other relevant sources of authority. They might also emphasize that the time to act is now because further damage will continue to accrue and possibly make the reader legally responsible for the consequences. This strategy is an implied threat based on the idea of scarcity; the positive way to express this idea is that the writers might show that now is a window of opportunity for preventing further problems.

B. Classic Rhetoric and Persuasion

Going back thousands of years to the ancient Western philosophers, Aristotle outlined a tool still useful today, the "rhetorical triad." Imagine a triangle with three points: (1) the speaker; (2) the audience; and (3) the subject of the message. These three points are often represented as (1) *ethos* (the credibility of the speaker); (2) *pathos* (the emotions of the audience) and (3) *logos* (the logical content of the message):

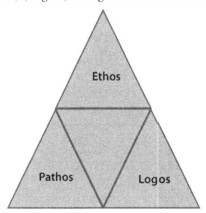

Persuasive messages must be tailored to the unique circumstances relevant to each point of this triangle. To establish ethos, or credibility, writers might emphasize their roles in the community or long-standing relationship with the reader. The speaker might also imply or openly state the intent to resolve the issue amicably (but to seek legal redress later if the issue is not resolved appropriately). To establish pathos, or an emotional appeal to their audience, the writers would consider who the audience is and what types of arguments would persuade them. They might research and then refer to the audience's background and prior decisions. They might show empathy for the audience's own situation by acknowledging that the audience has a difficult task to face. They could show how the position they advocate is actually in the audience's own best interest. They would carefully edit their message and adjust it to what they think the audience would find persuasive. And in terms of the content of the message — its logos or logical content — they would, of course, know their subject and provide accurate ideas and support, organized to emphasize the strengths of their argument.

C. Desire and Fear (Carrot and Stick)

A practical approach to persuasion suggests that persuasive reasons come in two broad categories: (1) motivating reasons—meaning the audience should *want* to take the requested action and *want* to avoid the consequences of taking the other action; and (2) justifying reasons—meaning the audience would be *right* to take the request-ed action and wrong to take the other action.[2] To motivate, persuasive writers would emphasize why the result they seek is a good result that benefits everyone. "Motivating arguments tend to be centered on facts or a combination of facts and policy."[3] Persua-sive writers might also emphasize why the result sought by others would be a bad result. Here too, facts or a combination of facts and policy support these arguments. To make a justifying argument, persuasive writers would also emphasize that the result they seek is the *right* result, meaning it is justified by authority and power—such as law and contractual obligations. "Justifying arguments are centered on legal rules or on a com-bination of rules and policy."[4]

These arguments may overlap and merge in a legal setting. An argument in favor of a certain action might assert that the requested action is low-cost and helpful, as well as legally correct. That argument could be supplemented by arguing that not taking the requested action would be costly, harmful, and wrong, and thus likely to lead to litiga-tion. The nature of the audience or decision-maker will help guide the decision to emphasize motivating fact-based arguments or justifying law-based arguments.

D. Cognitive Psychology

Even more recent work in psychology has suggested another persuasive theory. The study of cognitive psychology suggests human decision-making is a product of cogni-tive processes. Cognitive processes are always running in the human brain, as the hu-man navigates the world making an incredible number of observations and decisions every day. These cognitive processes include a wide variety of shortcuts ("cognitive heuristics") supplied by the brain to help the human make decisions. These shortcuts are the brain's practical solution to the overload of decisions humans make every day; no one can give careful thought to every single decision in life, no matter how small.

But shortcuts also take the form of various cognitive biases. One famous cognitive bias is "confirmation bias": people interpret new information to fit—and to con-firm—what they already believe. Another famous cognitive bias is the substitution effect, which basically means people base decisions about a complex topic by substitut-ing a decision on an easier topic. Under this theory, a writer would seek to polish and edit a persuasive message for flawless grammar and eloquent style because flawless grammar might be a persuasive substitute for flawless logic. Similar to Cialdini's theo-

---

2. *See* Richard K. Neumann, Jr., Ellie Margolis, and Kathryn Stanchi, *Legal Reasoning and Legal Writing* 248 (8th ed. 2017).

3. *Id.*

4. *Id.*

ry of consistency and commitment, a writer should seek to frame any argument in light of values and decisions the decision-maker has already adopted. An argument can appeal to the decision-maker's confirmation bias (as well as consistency bias) by placing the current decision within the framework of already-established values and already-decided actions.

Yet another cognitive bias is "narrative bias," which is the tendency to believe stories and to understand unrelated facts as part of a larger story. People respond to stories, and some argue that the only way to convince someone to change their ideas and opinions is through a story. A persuasive story might be true or hypothetical, and it might be drawn from the past or set in the future. The key point is to avoid directly addressing abstract ideas and direct requests for action, but instead to focus on the story of one person, one situation, or one community. Persuasive storytelling is discussed in more detail below.

E. Chains of Argument

Another persuasive theory takes the form of a debate: Should you ask for something small, get the audience to agree, then ask for something bigger? Or should you start by asking for something big, take no for an answer, then ask for what you really want?[5] This is a question about making a "chain" of arguments and about which link in the chain should come first. The first strategy, starting with a small request, is called the "foot in the door" strategy. The second strategy, starting with a large request, is called the "door in the face" strategy.

The argument for getting a "foot in the door" is that you ask someone to do something "small and easy" before you ask them to do something "large and difficult."[6] Under this approach to persuasion, a chain of arguments is "more likely to persuade readers if the first links of the chain are well-settled or widely accepted premises."[7] People want to be consistent and to affirm what they have already done; thus, convincing someone to agree to a first request (or accept a small argument) is more likely to get them to agree to a second request (or accept another, more controversial argument).

The opposite approach is the "door in the face" strategy. Here, you ask the audience to accept or do something big, expecting that they will refuse — and then you ask them for what you really want. "The research shows that the recipient, having rejected the first larger request, is thereafter somewhat more inclined to acquiesce to a second, smaller request."[8] This strategy is based on a negotiation model of requests and concessions, as well as feelings of obligation and responsibility or even guilt.[9] These two strat-

---

5. See Kathryn Stanchi, *The Science of Persuasion: An Initial Exploration*, 2006 Mich. St. L. Rev. 411, 418, 426–27 (2006).

6. *Id.*

7. *Id.* at 418.

8. *Id.* at 428.

9. *Id.*

egies are also addressed in this book in chapter 14, because they fit particularly well with decisions about how to email.

F. Bringing the Theories Together: Common Themes

The frameworks above are drawn from marketing, philosophy, and psychology, and represent just a few possible frameworks and theories about how persuasion works, not just for legal arguments but in any context. It is not possible or valuable to declare that one persuasive framework "rules them all." Knowing about different persuasive theories will help communicators select among strategies in a variety of situations.

A key common theme across the frameworks is that *persuasion depends on achieving the effect on your audience that you intend.* Trying to implement a strategy won't be persuasive if the strategy has a different effect from what you intend. For example, a persuasive strategy won't work if it is delivered in ambiguous or confusing words.

Another common theme across the frameworks is that *audiences resist persuasive efforts when they perceive the effort to persuade them.* Thus, a persuasive strategy that obviously calls attention to itself and makes the audience feel manipulated will likely not work. Balancing these two themes — having the effect you want without making your audience feel manipulated — is an advanced skill. It distinguishes communicators who are highly persuasive from those who are not.

II. Introduction to Legal Persuasion: Legal Sources and Legal Arguments

The theories above are all well and good, but you should be asking how they work in a legal setting. Are persuasive legal arguments fundamentally the same as all other types of persuasive arguments? Or are there special considerations for making an argument that is persuasive to a legal audience? The answer is "yes" to both questions. Persuasive legal arguments are a subtype of general persuasive arguments, but they are more persuasive in a legal setting if they use legal sources and law-specific arguments. This section begins with some background on who makes legal arguments and where they make them; then it explores major categories of legal arguments.

A. Background on Persuasive Legal Arguments

Persuasion using legal arguments is most frequently done by attorneys on behalf of clients. In these situations, the attorney consults with the client on the client's strategic objectives of the representation. The client sets the objectives of the representation, and the lawyer tailors the persuasive argument to make the most of the law and the facts in pursuing the client's objectives. In some of this section's examples, the key issue was whether complying with FDA labeling regulations on a pharmaceutical product exempts its manufacturer from liability under state law for failure to warn. In that situation, both sides were represented by highly experienced attorneys who helped them craft their arguments for the various stages of federal litigation. The attorneys wrote the briefs and represented the clients in court, but they had substantial guidance from the client on the objectives. Depending on the client's level of involvement and desire to do so, an attorney may provide a draft brief for the client to approve before it is filed on the client's behalf.

But courts are far from the only place where persuasion using legal arguments is useful, and this section discusses many examples not written for a court of law and not written by a lawyer. The other legal issue in the examples below involves the federal regulatory question—being debated throughout 2018 and 2019—about what can be labeled as "milk." The Food and Drug Administration's Standards of Identity, as they are actually written, allow only dairy products from cows to be labeled as milk, but the FDA has not enforced that standard as written. The current regulatory question is whether the FDA should return to the strict definition as written, or whether it should continue to permit plant-based beverages to be labeled with the term "milk," such as almond milk, soy milk, and so on. The commenting process has been open to the public in several stages of this debate; indeed, the commenting process is far more in-clusive than many people realize. It is open to all and can be easily accessed on *www. regulations.gov.*

We note that even in this setting, where representation by a licensed attorney is not required, a group or business might want to use the commenting process not just to be heard and possibly considered, but also as part of a targeted legal strategy. For example, a group might argue that a proposed regulation exceeds its statutory authority or is legally invalid because of some procedural defect.[10] For these situations, the advice of an attorney with administrative-law expertise can be invaluable. The material in this section helps with generating persuasive legal arguments, as well as evaluating those written by others.

B. Types of Legal Arguments

To create and evaluate legal arguments, it helps to know what makes an argument a *legal* argument. This section focuses on a useful framework synthesized by law professor Wilson Huhn. Huhn writes that there are five types of legal arguments; in fact, he wrote a book titled *The Five Types of Legal Argument*.[11] These five types of arguments are:

1. text
2. intent
3. precedent
4. tradition
5. policy

---

10. *See, e.g.*, Elizabeth D. Mullin, Environmental Law Institute, *The Art of Commenting: How to Influence Environmental Decisionmaking With Effective Comments* (2d ed. 2013).

11. Wilson Huhn, *The Five Types of Legal Argument* (3d ed. 2014).

These arguments derive from actual sources of law such as statutes, regulations, and cases. They loosely align with particular sources of law; for example, precedent naturally flows from judicial opinions. But the arguments overlap as well; for example, a court might write a judicial opinion interpreting a statute's text consistent with the societal traditions referenced in the statutory text. An argument about the United States Constitution might draw on tradition in the states of the United States as demonstrated by state constitutional law. The sections below explore more about each type of legal argument. For a more complete look at these arguments, Professor Huhn's book is an excellent resource.

Textual arguments are drawn from the text of statutes and regulations and the text of contracts and other legal instruments. Textual arguments may rely on well-accepted definitions of words as well as conventions of punctuation and grammar — even going so far as relying on a comma's placement, as in *O'Connor v. Oakhurst Dairy*, 851 F.3d 69 (1st Cir. 2017), discussed in chapter 4 on reading legal language; or diagramming a statute's grammar as in *United States v. Rentz*, 777 F.3d 1105 (10th Cir. 2015), discussed in chapter 8. Close reading skills are essential in interpreting the text of legal sources and finding arguments based on the text. Textual arguments are useful in interpreting and arguing about contract terms as well as statutes enacted by the legislature.

Arguments based on **intent** may also be based on the text itself. For example, if two provisions of a statute seem to be inconsistent, then the tools of statutory interpretation may help read the text of both provisions together to find the approach most consistent with the legislature's intent. Intent-based arguments might also look to the actual documentation created by the legislature — in other words, the legislative history, such as legislative committee reports and transcripts of legislators' statements. In Supreme Court jurisprudence, several justices have derided arguments based on legislative history because the legislators voted to enact the text, not the speeches and committee reports. The late Justice Antonin Scalia was the most famous critic of legislative-history arguments.

Arguments from **precedent** rely on the role of judicial opinions in the United States legal system. Precedent-based arguments can be based on the language of judicial opinions — in other words, what a court has *said* about the law in a judicial opinion. In this way, precedent-based arguments require close reading skills to find relevant statements. Another type of precedent-based argument is based not only on what judicial opinions say, but on what they *do* — in other words, the results deciding cases. Under the doctrine of *stare decisis*, courts in the future will base their results on what courts have done in similar cases in the past. Thus, a classic argument based on precedent would be that a new situation is exactly like a case previously decided on that exact same issue (in the same jurisdiction). Thus, with the exact same facts, the next case should be decided in the exact same way. This is legal reasoning by analogy; analogical reasoning can be very creative and flexible because — not surprisingly — it is rare for two situations to be exactly alike. As noted in chapter 2 on the foundations of U.S. law, new situations arise and circumstances change such that courts sometimes decide to overrule precedent. In addition, the legislature can intervene and change the law prospectively, except to change a court ruling about what is unconstitutional.

Arguments from **tradition** are most common and most appropriate where a legal standard itself incorporates community standards or traditions. The source may explicitly refer to and incorporate tradition. For example, the National Registry, maintained by the National Park Service, uses a list of criteria deeply connected with tradition, such as whether the place embodies "the distinctive characteristics of a type, period, or method of construction, or that represent the work of a master, or that possess high artistic values...."[12] Likewise, under the Public Health Service Act, the Department of Health and Human Services must designate and notify states about geographical areas with a shortage of health professionals. In designating areas with shortages, a threshold question, considered before assessing the ratio of healthcare professionals to population, is whether it is a "rational area."[13] One definition of a rational area draws on traditions:

> Established neighborhoods and communities within metropolitan areas which display a strong self-identity (as indicated by a homogeneous socioeconomic or demographic structure and/or a tradition of interaction or interdependency), have limited interaction with contiguous areas, and which, in general, have a minimum population of 20,000.[14]

Other references to tradition are implicit. In tort law, for example, the claim of "intentional infliction of emotional distress" depends in part on what society would find "extreme and outrageous." In constitutional law, the Eighth Amendment prohibits "cruel and unusual punishments." In *Roper v. Simmons*, 543 U.S. 551 (2005), the Supreme Court considered whether the death penalty violated the Eighth Amendment when applied to juvenile defendants between the ages of 15 and 17 when they committed the crime. Justice Anthony Kennedy, writing for the majority, described how the Court interprets cruel and unusual punishment:

> The prohibition against "cruel and unusual punishments," like other expansive language in the Constitution, must be interpreted according to its text, by considering history, tradition, and precedent, and with due regard for its purpose and function in the constitutional design.[15]

In *Roper*, the Supreme Court turned away from its precedent just 16 years earlier in *Stanford v. Kentucky*, 482 U.S. 361 (1989), which had held that the death penalty was

---

12. 36 C.F.R. § 60.4.

13. 42 C.F.R. Part 5, Appendix A to Part 5, (I)(A)(1).

14. *Id.* at (I)(B)(1)(A)(3).

15. *Roper v. Simmons*, 543 U.S. 551, 560–561 (2005).

not unconstitutional when applied to juvenile offenders. The Court cited an evolving national consensus since *Stanford* that the majority of states barred execution of juveniles (or execution altogether) to find that "today our society views juveniles … as 'categorically less culpable than the average criminal.'"[16] The standard for "cruel and unusual" punishment is just one example of legal standards that explicitly incorporate and invite arguments based on history and traditions.

Even when a legal source does not explicitly mention or invite a tradition-based argument, such an argument may still be persuasive. For example, one way to *oppose* a possible extension of law is by arguing that the legal institution considering that extension (legislature or agency or court or any other source of law) has *never* involved itself in that extended area. The opposite argument can be made in other circumstances advocating *for* action: the legal institution considering some action has *never hesitated* to involve itself in that area.

Policy arguments focus on the effect of an interpretation—the consequences in the real world. Professor Huhn suggests that a policy argument in a legal setting consists of two steps: evaluating what will happen if a court decides a case a certain way, and whether that result is "acceptable or unacceptable," which requires comparing the result to the purposes of the underlying law.[17]

Here it is important to distinguish general policy arguments from policy arguments in a legal context. General policy arguments focus on achieving the best result or avoiding a bad result—however that is defined. General policy arguments do not have to be tied to legal sources, although a policy argument might involve analysis of which aspect of law or government is best suited to implement that policy. In this way, a policy argument for new legislation is not a *legal* policy argument. A legislative policy argument is advocating the reasons the legislature should choose, within its discretion, to make a certain law embodying that policy.

In contrast, *legal* arguments from policy must be connected to and grounded in legal sources. A legal policy argument cannot argue that a court should reach the best result in a case despite what the statute says. That may be a type of policy argument, but it is an invalid legal argument because it is not consistent with what courts do. Courts must follow the law as expressed in statutes of their jurisdiction unless they are using their power to strike down a statute as unconstitutional. By contrast, an example of a valid legal policy argument would be that *within* the range of reasonable interpretations of a statute, the court should choose the interpretation that achieves the result in this case and in future cases that is most consistent with the statute's text and purpose—or the result that does the least harm.

---

16. *Id.* at 567 (quoting *Atkins v. Virginia*, 536 U.S. 316 (2002)).
17. Huhn, *The Five Types of Legal Argument, supra* note 11, at 67.

This brief introduction to the "five types of legal argument" should help you to recognize legal arguments in persuasion made by others and begin to add legal arguments to your own persuasion and advocacy.

III. Persuasion in Context

Now that you've read about some general persuasive theories and an overview of legal arguments, it is time to see how persuasion works in writing. The examples below draw from two types of legal documents: (1) persuasive arguments filed by consumers, lobbyists, politicians, and others on their own behalf in an administrative law (also known as regulatory) setting; and (2) appellate briefs filed by attorneys in court on behalf of clients.[18]

As to the first category, administrative comments can be and are submitted by people with a wide range of interests and credentials: lobbyists, policy experts, licensed attorneys, professionals in specialized technical fields, and laypeople. Many of the examples below are comments or excerpts of comments actually filed with the Food and Drug Administration on a regulatory question about food labeling. The question the FDA is considering as of late 2018 is whether the word "milk" on food labeling must be restricted only to milk from lactating cows—that is, "the lacteal secretion, practically free from colostrum, obtained by the complete milking of one or more healthy cows." That is the current definition in the Food and Drug Administration's "Standards of Identity" for a long list of foods, but the FDA has not been enforcing this definition against labeling practices for "almond milk" and "soy milk" and "cashew milk" and so on. The question the FDA is considering, which has generated strong interest and many persuasive administrative comments, is whether it should return to strictly enforcing the standards of identity as written.[19] The dairy industry, unsurprisingly, strongly advocates that it should. Vegan consumers and others strongly argue that there is no consumer confusion in a term such as "soy milk."

As to the second category, a few of the examples below are drawn from attorneys' Supreme Court briefs on a technical legal issue. That issue is whether a pharmaceutical drug that complies with FDA labeling rules can still be the subject of lawsuits under state tort law for inadequate labeling. That Supreme Court case is an example of arguments made by lawyers advocating for their clients on opposing sides of a lawsuit. The plaintiff

---

18. Law professors and former English majors may refer to this approach as "genre study." Studying a "genre" simply means examining sample documents of a certain type. A genre is "a recurring document type that has certain predictable conventions." Alexa Chew & Katie Rose Guest Pryal, *The Complete Legal Writer* 27 (2016). If you've ever used a template, you have used a genre. For effective professionals, the goal is not just to replicate a template but to tailor it to the situation and even change it if appropriate.

19. The Food and Drug Administration's Comprehensive, Multi-Year Nutrition Innovation Strategy; Public Meeting; Request for Comments, 83 Fed. Reg. 30180 (June 27, 2018); Use of the Names of Dairy Foods in the Labeling of Plant-Based Products, 83 Fed. Reg. 49103 (Sep. 28, 2018).

was Diane Levine, a Vermont woman who was injected with the drug Phenergan to prevent allergies and motion sickness, and who later had to have her arm amputated due to complications. The defendant was Wyeth Laboratories, which produced Phenergan and labeled it in compliance with FDA regulations.[20]

It is our hope that the persuasive lessons drawn from this example will transfer to other contexts such as legislative and policy advocacy, individual self-advocacy, and negotiation.

A. Text

A statute, regulation, or contract's precise language can be very persuasive in a legal argument. The language is the most powerful aspect of the statute itself: Its precise language governs how agencies must implement a statute and how courts interpret it. If two people are negotiating over the relative strength of their respective legal positions in an area where the statute governs, the person with the text on her side will have a significant, sometimes insurmountable, advantage.

Here is an example of an administrative comment emphasizing a regulation's precise language:

Dockets Management Staff (HFA-305)
Food and Drug Administration
5630 Fishers Lane, Room 1061
Rockville, MD 20852

RE: Docket No. FDA-2018-N-2381; FDA's Comprehensive, Multi-Year Nutrition Innovation Strategy (83 Fed. Reg. 30, 180 June 27, 2018).

The Wisconsin Farm Bureau Federation (WFBF) appreciates the opportunity to provide comments concerning the Food and Drug Administration's (FDA) proposal to update standards of identity to ensure consumers have the appropriate information about the food they purchase and consume. WFBF respectfully requests FDA to enforce existing law regarding the labeling of dairy products. Specifically, nut and plant-based beverage products should not contain the term "milk."

Under 21 CFR 131.110, milk is defined as "the lacteal secretion, practically free from colostrum, obtained by the complete milking of one or more healthy cows." Nut and plant-based beverages do not meet this definition, but use the term "milk." This is misleading to consumers and undermines the dairy industry. Dairy products are an [important] part of a healthy diet.

The 2015 Dietary Guidelines for Americans found that most people are not consuming the recommended amount of dairy products. Dairy products provide important

---

20. *Wyeth v. Levine*, 555 U.S. 555 (2009).

nutrients, such as calcium and protein, which are important for the development of children as well as adult health. Nut and plant-based beverages do not meet the nutritional value of dairy products.

Again, WFBF requests FDA to enforce existing standards of identity for dairy products to ensure consumers have accurate information regarding product labeling. Thank you for your time and consideration. [21]

In paragraph one of this comment, the writer provides some introductory context and a quick summary of the letter's overall position. Then, in paragraph two, he quotes the relevant text in a position of emphasis—namely, the very first sentence of the paragraph:

Under 21 CFR 131.110, milk is defined as "the lacteal secretion, practically free from colostrum, obtained by the complete milking of one or more healthy cows."

As an example of writing, this comment shows that quotation skills are very useful when highlighting the exact text of a legal source. The original language above at the beginning of the sentence is tailored for the writer's purposes in the comment, until it selectively quotes the narrow snippet of language that it wants to emphasize. Quoting more than necessary would dilute the point of focusing on the language. Quoting snippets of language is a good technique for emphasizing what is in the snippets; just make sure that the material around the snippet is accurate in context as well. Quoting out of context is just as bad (if not worse) in legal writing as in any other form of professional writing. Using a minimalistic quoting style—focusing on just what is needed to make a point vividly with the original language—is often very effective in legal writing, as it is in other forms of professional writing.

You might wonder why the example above does not argue *more* vehemently that the C.F.R. language itself controls the outcome. The problem with that approach is that the FDA is asking the public what the C.F.R. definition should say. The entire question being asked here is whether that language should change or stay the same. Still, the text features prominently in the comment: the writer quotes the language in a position of emphasis. Thus the writer highlights the fact the FDA already has an effective and clear definition—one that limits the scope of the term "milk" to milk produced by cows.

Arguments about the meaning and common understanding of language can take many forms. The following comment concisely connects food descriptions to the concept of consumer confusion:

---

21. Wisconsin Farm Bureau Federation, Comment Letter on The Food and Drug Administration's Comprehensive, Multi-Year Nutrition Innovation Strategy; Public Meeting; Request for Comments, ID No. FDA-2018-N-2381-0886 (Aug. 27, 2018) (available at regulations.gov).

> As a consumer of plant-based milk products, I submit this comment to ask the agency not to restrict these products from using the terms milk, cheese, yogurt, cultured yogurt, or other dairy food terms on the labels. Consumers are not confused by the content or nutritional profiles of these products. Terms like almond milk or cashew yogurt already make it abundantly clear that these are not products made with cows milk. Current labeling allows consumers like me to quickly differentiate between products and easily seek out plant-based dairy foods and beverages. New labeling regulations are unnecessary, and instead would create significant consumer confusion and inaccurate labeling information. I respectfully request that FDA refrain from making any change in its enforcement policy with regards to labeling of plant-based dairy products.[22]

One final point about text-based arguments. Referring to a dictionary may or may not be effective, depending on the situation. If an authoritative legal source has already begun using the dictionary to define the text, such as a case that interprets a statutory term according to its dictionary meaning, then legal arguments based on the dictionary may work. If the issue calls for evidence of common understanding, such as in the FDA's analysis of what consumers understand "milk" to be, dictionary definitions may be relevant and helpful. In contrast, the concept of what is "reasonable" has a vast development in many legal doctrines, so arguing the dictionary definition of the word "reasonable" is unlikely to be persuasive. Using legal literacy skills to advocate means including dictionary-based arguments when they are likely to be persuasive.

B. Intent

What was the legislature trying to do when it passed this statute? What were the contracting parties trying to do when they both signed the contract with these provisions?

The intent of the legislature is often closely related to the purpose of the law. In the excerpted comment below, the writer invokes the reason federal standards of identity were created:

> I am writing regarding docket FDA-2018-N-2381-0317, specifically concerning modernizing standards of identity related to dairy products and the labeling of these products....
>
> Federal standards of identity have been created to promote honest and fair dealing to help consumers, but it has been frustrating to see the retail dairy case contain a growing number of plant-based products with false and misleading labels. These products are competing with — and being labeled as a substitute for — fluid milk and traditional dairy products. We understand that consumers may want to choose an imitation

---

22. Comment from Helen Wong, NA, ID No. FDA-2018-N-3522-11872 (February 11, 2019) (available at regulations.gov).

product for a variety of reasons, but they should not be misled into thinking the imitation product is nutritionally similar to milk or dairy products.[23]

The following excerpt opens with more direct and pointed references to what Congress intended to happen:

Dear Commissioner Gottlieb:

We are pleased that your agency plans to take action to enforce FDA regulations defining what may be labeled a dairy product, to combat the proliferation of imitation and substitute dairy products in the marketplace that violate FDA regulations by employing standardized dairy terms on non-dairy products. We appreciate that you are following the direction provided to your agency by Congress in the recently-enacted Fiscal Year 2018 Consolidated Appropriations Act (H.R. 1625).

We are greatly concerned about the lack of enforcement of existing dairy terms that are described in 21 Code of Federal Regulations parts 131, 133, and 135, which pertain to milk and cultured milk products, cheeses, and frozen dairy desserts, respectively. These standards were written with the express purpose of promoting honesty and fair dealing in the interest of consumers by promulgating regulations that fix and establish, under their common or usual names, reasonable definitions or standards of identity for foods.[24]

An unusual fact about the excerpt above is that its authors are 48 members of Congress—each of whom signed individually in blue ink at the end of the letter. (These signatures are a kind of visual persuasion in themselves.) But the authorship of this comment letter is not what makes it a legal argument based on intent. The letter's references to "direction provided to your agency" by Congress is an example of an argument from intent. The letter also refers to the "express purpose" for why the standards of identity were written.

In their most classic and technical form, arguments based on intent may draw on the legislative history or other background of how the law was made. The most traditional form of such an argument would be to actually cite the legislative history leading up to Congress's passing the law and the President signing it. It is difficult to find an explicit reference to legislative history in the regulatory comments partly because the FDA's notice requesting comments did not include that as a topic. The notice did begin—as agency notices typically do—by stating its statutory authority in food and drug statutes. Thus, the focus of this persuasive situation is much more on the general

---

23. See, e.g., Daren Brubaker, ID No. FDA-2018-N-2381-1348 (Oct. 22, 2018) (example of identical comment submitted by numerous individual commenters at regulations.gov).

24. Peter Welch et al., Comment letter on Use of the Names of Dairy Foods in the Labeling of Plant-Based Products, ID No. FDA-2018-N-3522-0518 (Oct. 5, 2018) (available at regulations.gov).

purpose of the law and policy effects of the FDA's enforcement decisions. The FDA's notice requesting comments is consistent with the overall administrative setting, in which citizen commenters offer their expertise and opinions to guide the administrative agency's informal rulemaking decisions within its statutory mandate.

To examine an explicit intent-based argument, we must digress for a moment from the administrative comments on standards of identity for milk. Intent-based arguments are sometimes made to the United States Supreme Court as it grapples with how to interpret statutes. Justice Antonin Scalia was a famous critic of intent-based arguments, arguing that legislative history can justify almost any argument and does not provide a limiting principle. Justice Scalia's school of thought focuses on text and the original meaning of words at the time Congress enacted them. Still, intent-based arguments may help to show that a particular result is consistent with what the legislature intended — or not.[25]

To explore what an intent-based argument looks like, the Supreme Court case of *Wyeth v. Levine*, 555 U.S. 555 (2009) is instructive. There, the Supreme Court addressed whether a plaintiff can sue a drug manufacturer under state law for failure to warn about risks of the drug, even where the federal Food and Drug Administration has approved the label. In other words, if a pharmaceutical company seeks and receives FDA approval of its label, is it thereby insulated from a claim based on state law that it inadequately warned consumers of the drug's danger? In the Supreme Court briefs, the drug manufacturer made an explicit intent-based argument. The excerpt below begins with the first drug-related legislation in 1906; the rest of this section in the brief builds up to the current statutory regime:

> The statutory regime under which FDA regulates prescription drugs reflects a pervasive and particularized federal role in regulating the safety and effectiveness of their labeled uses. Drug labeling has been subject to federal control since the 1906 enactment of the Pure Food and Drugs Act. Pub. L. No. 59-384, 34 Stat. 768 (1906). The 1906 Act authorized the federal government to seize drugs that were adulterated or misbranded and to prosecute their manufacturers. Id. §§ 1, 2, 5, 10. "Misbranded" drugs included drugs with labeling that was "false or misleading in any particular." Id. § 8. The Act did not require premarketing approval, but even during this limited early stage of federal supervision, Congress showed concern about disparate state-law labeling standards and an intent to bring about uniform national labeling. See H.R. Rep. No. 59-2118, at 4 (1906) (expressing concern regarding "the varying requirements as to standards and labels in different States" for food products); 40 Cong. Rec. 1217 (1906) (statement of Sen. Nelson) ("[T]he bill will, whenever there is a conflict between the State law and this law, leave this law controlling and be the means of equalizing and

---

25. We discussed statutory language and legislative intent in more detail in Chapter 8 on statutes.

doing justice to all parts of the country, instead of having the difficulties we now encounter in many of the States.").[26]

The Supreme Court ultimately rejected this argument, elaborating on legislative intent in its opinion:[27]

Wyeth contends that the FDCA establishes both a floor and a ceiling for drug regulation: Once the FDA has approved a drug's label, a state-law verdict may not deem the label inadequate, regardless of whether there is any evidence that the FDA has considered the stronger warning at issue. The most glaring problem with this argument is that all evidence of Congress' purposes is to the contrary. Building on its 1906 Act, Congress enacted the FDCA to bolster consumer protection against harmful products. See *Kordel v. United States,* 335 U.S. 345, 349, 69 S.Ct. 106, 93 L.Ed. 52 (1948); *United States v. Sullivan,* 332 U.S. 689, 696, 68 S.Ct. 331, 92 L.Ed. 297 (1948). Congress did not provide a federal remedy for consumers harmed by unsafe or ineffective drugs in the 1938 statute or in any subsequent amendment. Evidently, it determined that widely available state rights of action provided appropriate relief for injured consumers. It may also have recognized that state-law remedies further consumer protection by motivating manufacturers to produce safe and effective drugs and to give adequate warnings.

If Congress thought state-law suits posed an obstacle to its objectives, it surely would have enacted an express pre-emption provision at some point during the FDCA's 70-year history. But despite its 1976 enactment of an express pre-emption provision for medical devices, see § 2, 90 Stat. 574 (codified at 21 U.S.C. § 360k(a)), Congress has not enacted such a provision for prescription drugs. See *Riegel,* 552 U.S., at 327, 128 S.Ct., at 1009 ("Congress could have applied the pre-emption clause to the entire FDCA. It did not do so, but instead wrote a pre-emption clause that applies only to medical devices"). Its silence on the issue, coupled with its certain awareness of the prevalence of state tort litigation, is powerful evidence that Congress did not intend FDA oversight to be the exclusive means of ensuring drug safety and effectiveness.

As shown above from the administrative comments on the standards of identity for milk and the arguments in *Wyeth v. Levine*, intent-based arguments can range from broad references to extremely technical points. These examples also show the general truth that choosing a legal argument means understanding what type of argument is likely to be relevant and persuasive to your audience.

C. Precedent

Precedent-based arguments also range from broad references to extremely technical points. In legal arguments to boards and agencies and decision-makers not formally

---

26. Petitioner's Brief in *Wyett v. Levine*, No. 06-1249, https://www.americanbar.org/content/dam/aba/publishing/preview/publiced_preview_briefs_pdfs_07_08_06_1249_Petitioner.pdf
27. *Wyeth v. Levine*, 555 U.S. 555, 573–574 (2009) (footnotes omitted).

constrained by precedent—in other words, in legal arguments to decision-makers other than courts—precedent-based arguments invoke the audience's general sense of internal consistency and fairness. Legal arguments to courts invoke the courts' adherence to precedent through the doctrine of *stare decisis*. Precedent-based arguments may operate in a direct way based on authority (suggesting the decider should follow what it said or did before) or an indirect way based on analogy (suggesting a prior decision is similar and should be followed for that reason).

In the following excerpted comment, the writer cites the Federal Trade Commission's action in alcohol labeling as a relevant precedent for milk-related beverage labeling:

> Another problem… is the difference in added sugar between dairy and non-dairy milk. Many non-dairy milks are sweetened with rice syrup or barley malt, which can add up to 20g of sugar compared to the 12.5 g of natural lactose seen in 2% milk (Parrish 2018). Many consumers are quite aware of the health implications and dangers that sugar intake can bring. Disguising plant-based milk as dairy milk is very disingenuous and potentially dangerous.
>
> Implementing strict labeling such as the FTC forced Phusion Projects, LLC, the creators of Four Loko to do so. A lawsuit had arisen when the FTC deemed that the Four Loko bottles were misleading by stating a 23.5 ounce can contains the alcohol equivalent of one or two 12-ounce beers and that a person can safely drink a whole can on a single occasion. Their findings were that drinking the beverage in one sitting is similar to drinking five beers at once. In response, an Alcohol Facts panel was to be put on every can that contained over two servings of alcohol, showing the alcohol by volume, servings in the container, and serving size in fluid ounces (Fair 2018). Differentiating the nutritional values such as the sugars or the amount of protein g/oz similarly to the alcohol content is imperative. Implementing not exactly, but similar labels on the milk containers is a potential long term solution.[28]

The idea of "precedent" is extremely broad in an administrative law setting like the regulatory comments on standards of identity shown in this chapter. Thus, as with the example above about legislative intent, we will digress from the comments on standards of identity to show a lawyer's use of precedent-based argument before the Supreme Court. The *Wyeth v. Levine* case provides good examples here as well, with a relevant precedent about federal seat belt standards. If a carmaker that complies with federal law on seat belts cannot be sued under state law for product liability, then why should a pharmaceutical company that complies with federal law on drug labeling be subject to suit under state law for failure to warn? That is the precedent-based argument the pharmaceutical company arguing in favor of preemption asserted:

---

28. Thomas Thorgersen, Comment on The Food and Drug Administration's Comprehensive, Multi-Year Nutrition Innovation Strategy; Public Meeting; Request for Comments, ID No. FDA-2018-N-2381-1032 (Sep. 17, 2018) (available at regulations.gov).

[I]n *Geier v. American Honda Motor Co.*, 529 U.S. 861 (2000), this Court held that state tort law was preempted to the extent that it reached a different balance among several competing objectives than the balance the federal policy had struck. *Id.* at 874–881.

This case presents a conflict between state and federal law analogous to the one the Court addressed in *Geier*. The federal safety regulation at issue in *Geier* "deliberately provided the manufacturer with a range of choices among different passive restraint devices," which "would bring about a mix of different devices introduced gradually over time." 529 U.S. at 864-865, 875. The goal of the federal scheme was not to set minimum airbag standards — seeking "the more airbags, and the sooner, the better," *id.* at 874 — but to accommodate multiple competing concerns, *id.* at 875. This Court held that the federal objective preempted the alleged tort duty because the duty "would have presented an obstacle to the variety and mix of devices that the federal regulation sought" and "stood as an obstacle to the general passive restraint phase-in that the federal regulation deliberately imposed." *Id.* at 881.

Here, as in *Geier*, FDA balanced competing concerns of safety and therapeutic benefit by considering the risks of IV administration of Phenergan and preserving the option for physicians to administer Phenergan by IV push in appropriate cases, subject to carefully crafted warnings and instructions in the labeling.[29]

But arguments from precedent are extremely flexible. A precedent that seems similar and persuasive in one way may be very different in other ways. In its opinion rejecting the pharmaceutical company's argument, the Supreme Court was not persuaded by the narrow analogy to compliance with seat belt laws. It focused instead on a broader point about how Congress, courts, and agencies interact:

In prior cases, we have given "some weight" to an agency's views about the impact of tort law on federal objectives when "the subject matter is technica[l] and the relevant history and background are complex and extensive." *Geier*, 529 U.S., at 883, 120 S.Ct. 1913. Even in such cases, however, we have not deferred to an agency's *conclusion* that state law is pre-empted. Rather, we have attended to an agency's explanation of how state law affects the regulatory scheme. While agencies have no special authority to pronounce on pre-emption absent delegation by Congress, they do have a unique understanding of the statutes they administer and an attendant ability to make informed determinations about how state requirements may pose an «obstacle to the accomplishment and execution of the full purposes and objectives of Congress.» *Hines*, 312 U.S, at 67, 61 S.Ct. 399; see *Geier*, 529 U.S., at 883, 120 S.Ct. 1913; *Lohr*, 518 U.S., at 495-496, 116 S.Ct. 2240. The weight we accord the agency's explanation of state law's impact on the federal scheme depends on its thoroughness, consistency, and persua-

---

29. Petitioner's Brief in *Wyeth v. Levine*, No. 06-1249, at 47-48, https://www.americanbar.org/content/dam/aba/publishing/preview/publiced_preview_briefs_pdfs_07_08_06_1249_Petitioner.pdf

siveness. Cf. *United States v. Mead Corp.*, 533 U.S. 218, 234-235, 121 S.Ct. 2164, 150 L.Ed.2d 292 (2001); *Skidmore v. Swift & Co.*, 323 U.S. 134, 140, 65 S.Ct. 161, 89 L.Ed. 124 (1944).[30]

This precedent-based argument shows how flexible such arguments can be, both in how the writer creates them and in how the decision-maker responds to them.

D. Tradition

Arguments based on tradition may focus on substantive traditions in a community. The following excerpted comment highlights the special role of standards of identity in the food industry:

> *Until and unless Congress changes the statute, FDA should enforce it.* FDA should recognize that standards of identity have a long standing special position within the food safety and food marketing regulatory environment. A commercial enterprise that is gyrating to twist out of the limitations of standards of identity may increase profits; but these games of spin do not protect the consumer. FDA should take enforcement action against the labeled product identity of "almond milk" and comparable food products in the current marketplace.[31]

Arguments based on tradition may also focus on traditional structures and roles for various legal institutions and branches of government. The following excerpted comment combines comments about consumer confusion with arguments for the traditional value that agencies should be neutral among industries:

> I think most consumers, like myself, are delighted that we now have a much greater variety of milks and milk products, including many that are plant-based, readily available than we did a few decades ago. This is a boon to consumers, and government agencies should treat this development as a positive one. It is appropriate for the government to provide nutritional information and other relevant information, such as the impact of animal-based agriculture (including dairy milk) on global climate change.
>
> While I don't know that the FDA has ever done this, certainly other governmental agencies have had discriminatory programs in which they have openly promoted dairy milks. The government should not be in the business of siding with those in certain industries over those in competing industries. While this may not have applied to the FDA, any regulations should follow the general principle that the government should not regulate or subsidize with favoritism. All government agencies, including the FDA, should regulate for the benefit of the whole population without favoritism. Unfortu-

---

30. *Wyeth*, 555 U.S. at 576.

31. James O'Reilly, Comment, Sept. 29, 2018, Regulations.gov, https://www.regulations.gov/document?D=FDA-2018-N-3522-0201

nately, this docket in itself seems to reflect an attempt by the animal-based dairy industry to get favorable treatment by the government. This must be firmly rejected.[32]

And arguments about tradition may merge with textual arguments, as in showing historical understandings of a word:

Almond milk, soy milk etc should be allowed to retain the word milk in the label because they are being used by consumers as dairy milk substitutes. Consumers have accepted the description for years and to change it now would be very confusing. The word milk does not relate to just mammalian lactate. It has been used for over a century to describe fluids with [milk] like consistency such as milk of magnesia a medication for stomach upsets. Please keep the word milk for describing almond or soy milk etc. [C]onsideration of the consumer should supersede the marketing concerns of the dairy board.[33]

The argument above also relies on a type of argument lawyers would refer to as "estoppel." The argument implicitly suggests that the FDA itself allowed labeling such as "soy milk" and "almond milk," so it should not be able to now change its practice that has gone on for years.

E. Policy

In the administrative context, comments can and often should touch on a wide range of policy arguments. The FDA is asking whether it should change its rule. Thus, the real question is what the most effective rule would be, and one way to address that question is with policy arguments about the effect of different rules. Here is an example of a policy argument that also weaves in a legal argument about the United States Constitution:

I am a proud supporter of the Plant Based Foods Association and the plant-based food industry.

I appreciate the opportunity to submit these comments.

Current labeling approach
The entire debate over the use of the term milk and other dairy terms on plant-based foods and beverages is a solution in search of a problem. Companies selling dairy alternatives are using easy to understand, clear, descriptive and truthful language on labels. Many brands use terms such as milk, yogurt, cheese, and cream, all with appropriate qualifiers such as non-dairy, dairy-free, and/or alternative. Plant-based compa-

---

32. William Samuel, Comment on Use of the Names of Dairy Foods in the Labeling of Plant-Based Products, ID No. FDA-2018-N-3522-0269 (Oct. 5, 2018) (available at regulations.gov).

33. Comment from Louise Fung, ID No. FDA-2018-N-3522-1598 (November 7, 2018) (available at regulations.gov).

nies are clear in their intent to convey to the consumer who is making the purchase that these options do not contain cows' milk as that is the primary reason that shoppers are choosing these foods and beverages.

Consumer Understanding of Labels

American consumers are sophisticated and increasingly aware of the origin and ingredients of the foods they are consuming. Consumers who purchase plant-based foods are keenly aware of what they are purchasing and why they are making these choices. Studies show that these shoppers purchase plant-based milks for myriad reasons, including sustainability, health, concerns about allergies, ethics, variety, and taste. If FDA were to require the use of new terminology on principal display panels of plant-based foods, I believe that [it's] highly likely that this will result in more, not less, consumer confusion.

Consumer Understanding of Nutrition

I do not share the concern implied by [FDA's] questions regarding potential risk of poor nutrition due differences between dairy products and plant-based alternatives. To the contrary, many consumers are seeking out plant-based milks and cheeses to avoid certain attributes in dairy such as saturated fat and cholesterol. In addition, many consumers cannot consume dairy due to allergies or intolerance. Consumers can easily obtain nutrients such as protein and calcium from plant-based foods.

Cost of Label Changes

If FDA were to require changes to the way that plant-based foods are labeled, the ensuing changes to manufacturers['] labels would prove to be a significant unexpected and unnecessary financial burden to most companies.

First Amendment and Labeling

The free speech clause of the First Amendment to the U.S. Constitution protects companies that label their foods with truthful, non-misleading names. PBFA's legal analysis indicates [it is] unlikely that these efforts would survive a court challenge under the First Amendment['s] free speech clause.

Conclusion

Enacting new labeling rules would create unnecessary, confusing, and costly label changes that likely violate the First Amendment and would be struck down in court. Ultimately, the question is whether current regulatory definitions can keep up with innovation. We are living in a time of rapid innovation in food and America is leading the way. Consumers are entitled to the benefits of this innovative American spirit and the delicious new plant-based offerings in the marketplace. The FDA has the unique opportunity to support this growing industry and the millions of American consumers who are voting with their dollars.

> I respectfully request that FDA refrain from making any change in its enforcement policy, whether in a guidance document or other form, that would limit the First Amendment rights of companies to label their foods with truthful, non-misleading labels to communicate to consumers who are seeking out plant-based dairy alternative foods and beverages.[34]

The administrative context is particularly appropriate for policy comments because the agencies are generally requesting feedback on the effect of potential rules.

In legal arguments to courts, policy arguments are typically tied to legal sources. A possible conflict between federal and state law and policy outcomes was at the heart of the *Wyeth v. Levine* preemption case. Lawyers for the pharmaceutical company referred to the policy behind the law in shaping their (ultimately unsuccessful) argument for preemption:

> In determining whether a state law interferes with the full purposes and objectives of Congress, courts consider "the entire scheme of the statute"—its text, its context, and the policies underlying it. *Hines*, 312 U.S. at 67 n.20. Here, the regulatory scheme Congress established provides that FDA's drug-approval and labeling decisions must strike a balance between protecting the public from dangerous misuses of drugs and advancing public health by ensuring that beneficial treatments are available to those who need them.[35]

This is just one example of how lawyers arguing to courts may bring up policy in connection with legal arguments and sources. Legal policy arguments may be tightly connected to statutory text or precedent, or they may be more loosely connected, but they should bear *some* connection to legal authority when asserted in a court of law.

This chapter focuses on the practical side of each argument, but Huhn's book goes into more detail on the theoretical background of each. For students interested in legal theory, reading *The Five Types of Legal Argument* would be a good next step.

IV. Enhancements to Persuasive Legal Arguments

In the legal context, written arguments are effective when built on a solid persuasive strategy and crafted with appropriate legal arguments. But is there any way to enhance those basic components? Two options should be considered: narrative persuasion and visual persuasion.

---

34. Comment from Tracy Peters, Plant Based Food Association, ID No. FDA-2018-N-3522-10965 (Feb. 11, 2019) (available at regulations.gov).

35. Petitioner's Brief in *Wyeth v. Levine*, *supra*, at 41, https://www.americanbar.org/content/dam/aba/publishing/preview/publiced_preview_briefs_pdfs_07_08_06_1249_Petitioner.pdf

A. Consider Adding Narrative

Narrative means telling a story. We could stop there, or we could delve into the millions of words that have been written in legal scholarship on how narrative plays out in legal persuasion and decision-making. As law professor Christopher Rideout observed, "Narratives are 'innate' ways of understanding and structuring human experience; this makes them inherently persuasive."[36] Narrative is at the heart of many popular books and movies; one of the most fun and accessible—and useful—examples of legal scholarship on narrative focuses on how to tell a story the way J.K. Rowling portrayed Harry Potter, as an archetypal hero on a journey.[37]

Persuasive narratives should have a beginning, middle, and end. They should not include distracting detail; all the choices should contribute to the structure and the point of the story. Storytelling in movies and books can include anything the author wants to include, but for legal storytelling, it is important to investigate the rules of the forum. Some legal settings require proof of the facts, or they simply disregard stories that are not based in evidence. A school board meeting with an open microphone for comments has much more flexible rules for storytelling than a lawsuit by a parent claiming inadequate accommodation of a child with disabilities.

One decision for the writer is how much "voice" to use in telling the story. Voice is a product of all the writer's decisions such as paragraphing and word choice. A story can be very vivid or very abstract, depending on the situation, the audience, and the writer's persuasive goals. Here is a strong example of personal voice from the comments on the standards of identity for milk:

> I work in dairy, so I get the difference. What I've found when talking to people is that they understand that they are different products and that plant based milk has no dairy in it. What they don't understand is that they have completely different nutritional value.
>
> I know my wife had to do a double take. We have very young children and this can be very dangerous for them. Talking to our pediatrician, our 1 1/2 year old needs the fat, protein, and calcium found in whole milk to stay healthy. If she's not getting it from milk, we need to be aware of it so we can make sure she gets it from somewhere else. In addition to the missing nutritional value of the milk, non-dairy milk has added sugars that you wouldn't want in a young child's diet, or you'd at least want to know about it. We don't give our children juice except on special occasions because it has so much sugar.
>
> Recently we started our daughter at a new in home daycare, and found that they were only giving their children plant based milk, and that they didn't realize that it wasn't a

---

36. Christopher Rideout, *Narrative Rationality, and Legal Persuasion,* 14 J. Leg. Writing 53, 55 (2008).

37. Ruth Anne Robbins, *Harry Potter, Ruby Slippers, and Merlin: Telling the Client's Story Using the Characters and Paradigm of the Archetypal Hero's Journey,* 29 Seattle U. L. Rev. 767 (2006).

substitute for the nutrition in milk. We talked, and they decided they wanted to continue with the Almond juice, but at least now they know so they can make sure their children are getting that nutrition somewhere else. We decided to send milk with our daughter because we don't want her to have that much sugar, and because we plan for the nutrition provided by milk, and don't provide it elsewhere.

If you made it through this, thanks for reading.[38]

A lawyer writing on behalf of a client may decide to let the client's voice speak for itself in quotations and other decisions. Or the lawyer may decide the client's personal voice is not advantageous, and a more abstract voice would be more effective. One way to see the range of voices lawyers use in storytelling is to explore the website SCOTUSblog (www.scotusblog.com). SCOTUSblog has a page for each Supreme Court case decided since 2008, including all the briefs filed in the case. The Petitioner's Brief and the Respondent's Brief are the main "merits briefs" filed in each case. You will also see many other types of briefs, including briefs seeking certiorari (i.e., asking the Supreme Court to hear the case) and amicus briefs ("friend of the court" briefs filed by people and interest groups who are not parties to the case but are allowed to argue). All these briefs are highly stylized and formal, yet they show the vivid voice and storytelling strategies employed by the nation's most prestigious legal advocates in the arguments with the highest stakes.

B. Consider Adding Visuals

Clichés are not persuasive, so we will absolutely *not* begin this section by saying "a picture is worth a thousand words."[39] Charts, images, and photos can be an excellent way to enhance a persuasive message. They can organize data to clarify and make a point. They can provide a timeline of events. They can help the audience visualize the item or property or other subject of an argument. Visual information is a flexible tool for conveying legal information and making legal arguments, and visuals can be used in most communication settings where they are not expressly forbidden, from informal letters to administrative comments to appellate briefs.

In the comments submitted about the standards of identity for milk, comments can be typed into a text box or submitted with an attached document. Writers using the text box would not be able to include a visual due to the nature of the text box itself, but writers submitting attachments can and do include visuals in those attachments. Here is an example of data presented in chart form:[40]

---

38. Matt Michlin, Comment on Use of the Names of Dairy Foods in the Labeling of Plant-Based Products (Oct. 3, 2018), https://www.regulations.gov/document?D=FDA-2018-N-3522-0064.

39. You saw what we did there, didn't you? Sorry about that.

40. Leprino Foods Company, Comment on The Food and Drug Administration's Comprehensive, Multi-Year Nutrition Innovation Strategy; Public Meeting; Request for Comments (Sept. 6, 2018), ID No. FDA-2018-N-2381-0903 (available at regulations.gov) (footnotes omitted).

The myriad products represented as "milk" are difficult to summarize because of the inconsistency associated with the nutritional profile of each product, but the following simple table is demonstrative:

Nutritional Component	Almond "milk" (G/100g)[1]	Soy "milk" (G/100g)[2]	MILK (Skim) (G/100g)[3]
Protein	.42	2.88	3.33
Carbohydrate	6.67	1.65	5.42
Calcium	42	123	125
Potassium	75	123	158
Vitamin C	0	0	1.0
Vitamin D	42	0	42

Charts, images, and photos are just as flexible for persuasion as storytelling. As with telling a story, one key to effective visual persuasion is to avoid unnecessary details or distracting features. When considering including a visual, make sure its form and content work together to serve the document's persuasive purpose. Legal scholars have become increasingly interested in visual persuasion, and the footnote below provides useful further reading in this area.[41]

V. Enhancing Your Persuasion with Editing and Proofreading

Persuasive writing is a fascinating topic with much to think about. This chapter could go on and on with more theories, more examples, and more advice. But no matter what theory you like, what document you're writing, and whom you're writing for and to, here is one final point to keep in mind: *Readers are much more likely to be persuaded by a written message that is carefully edited, formatted, and proofread for errors.* In other words, careful editing and proofreading make any persuasive message even more persuasive.

Why should that be? If the ideas and the words of an argument are persuasive, why should the reader be influenced by the way headings are numbered, the frequency of typos, or the choice of font?[42] At the beginning of this chapter, we mentioned cognitive

---

41. Steven Johansen and Ruth Anne Robbins, *Articulating the Analysis: Systematizing the Decision to Use Visuals as Legal Reasoning*, 20 J. Leg. Writing 57 (2015); *see also* Elizabeth Porter & Kathryn Watts, *Visual Rulemaking*, 91 N.Y.U. L. Rev. 1183 (2016); Elizabeth Porter, *Taking Images Seriously*, 114 Colum. L. Rev. 1687 (2014).

42. Errol Morris, *Hear, All Ye People; Hearken, O Earth (Part I)*, New York Times (August 8, 2012) (discussing a natural experiment asking the same question in different fonts).

biases as one source of persuasive theory. Cognitive biases are the common and sub-conscious mental shortcuts in people's brains that navigate them through the massive amount of information they face every moment. One cognitive bias is the "substitution effect"—taking a mental shortcut by substituting an easy decision for a difficult one. Readers working their way through difficult documents may have questions such as: "Is this right?" or "Should I rely on this?" Especially for readers who do not know much about the document type or subject matter, they may revert to what they actually *do* know and understand: "Does this document look neat?" "Does this document have typos?" "Does this document use the grammatical and punctuation rules I was taught?"

Thus, our final bit of advice on legal persuasion is this: Use all the tools and tech-niques of editing and proofreading reasonably available to you. Chapters 17 and 18 cover techniques for clear and concise writing, with additional advice on editing and proofreading. Higher-quality writing will tend to have more persuasive power. That power is yours for the taking.

Having studied this chapter, you should be able to:

- Reflect on and use basic theories in persuasion
- Examine and assess examples of persuasive writing in a legal context
- Apply techniques for using law in persuasive writing
- Consider enhancements to your persuasive writing such as storytelling and visuals

....

Case Study: Olivia Ralston's Comment Advocating for Oat Milk

Olivia Ralston hopes to open a small coffee shop serving responsibly sourced coffee, as well as oat milk. Ms. Ralston has struggled with a dairy intolerance throughout her life and feels strongly that non-dairy milks should be widely avail-able. She has been following the trends and shortages with oat milk, "Oatly."[43] She believes that offering oat milk in her new business will draw attention and add to her customer base. She has found an oat milk supplier to buy from. Because of her interest in dairy alternatives, she is very interested in recent news that the FDA may change its rules on labeling oat milk and other beverages such as soy milk and almond milk. Specifically, the FDA is considering changing its rules or keep-ing the same rules but changing its enforcement practices. As of 2018, the stan-dards of identity in the Code of Federal Regulations limit the definition of "milk"

---

43. Lily Rose, *Brooklyn's Oat Milk Shortage is Rocking the Hipster Community*, The Daily Meal: All Things Food & Drink (August 15, 2018), https://www.thedailymeal.com/drink/brooklyn-oat-milk-shortage/081518.

to dairy, but the FDA has not enforced this rule, allowing soy and other plant beverages to be labeled as a type of milk.

Ms. Ralston's ultimate goal in this case study is to submit a comment arguing that what she refers to as oat milk and other plant-based drinks should be permitted to be called milk.

Traditions and Trends in Persuasive Legal Writing

Persuasive legal writing has traditionally been a task performed by lawyers writing motions and briefs in litigation—in other words, client advocacy in courts of law. This is not just a custom and practice but also, as discussed in Chapter 3, a regulated monopoly: traditionally, licensed attorneys represent clients in court. Their audience is judges, jurors, and judicial law clerks whom they are trying to persuade, as well as the clients they represent. Those clients maintain autonomy over the objectives of their legal representation, so they indirectly participate in the content of persuasive legal writing on their behalf. But lawyers have their own discretion over the methods for achieving client objectives, which encompasses many tactical decisions including the structure and tone of persuasive legal writing filed on behalf of clients. Because attorneys' duty is to represent their clients, rather than to challenge norms or push boundaries, persuasive legal writing has traditionally been quite traditional. Word processing capabilities and court rules also limited the form of persuasive legal writing such that prose sentences remain the main way of delivering arguments, as opposed to images, photos, or other graphic elements.

These traditions are evolving in a variety of ways. A few legal forums allow non-lawyers to advocate on behalf of others in writing and in person, such as veterans' benefit appeals. Generally, however, the role of legal advocate on behalf of another remains a well-protected stronghold of licensed attorneys. The rules for legal technicians in Washington and Utah do allow specially licensed non-lawyer professionals to assist clients in matters such as family law, landlord-tenant disputes, and debt collection, but not to advocate for those clients in court.

Although who does the advocacy has not changed much, the nature and format of advocacy have evolved to an extent. The influence of pop culture and digital culture have contributed to more use of images and graphics, even in formal legal briefs. Some lawyers have tried a more informal, pop-culture-infused style of legal writing to persuade courts, to mixed results. Legal briefs and video of attorneys' oral arguments often are more widely available for public dissemination and discussion. As noted in chapter 14 on correspondence, demand letters are sometimes made public as well, with the party publicizing the letter—sometimes the sender, sometimes the recipient—seeking to sway public opinion. *See, e.g.*, Ken White, *How to Write a Takedown Request Without Running Afoul of the Streisand Effect*, Popehat: A Group Complaint About Law, Liberty, and Leisure (July 8, 2012), https://www.popehat.com/2012/07/08/how-to-write-a-takedown-request-without-running-afoul-of-the-streisand-effect/

Chapter 17

Accurate and Consistent
Legal Writing

A communication is in plain language if its wording, structure, and design are so clear that the intended readers can easily find what they need, understand what they find, and use that information.

— Center for Plain Language, http://centerforplainlanguage.org/about-plain-language

[G]ood writing is essentially writing that satisfies the needs and desires of the reading audience, and in the context of legal writing, this means writing that promotes the readers' ability to make the important decisions legal readers need to make in the course of their professional duties.

— Mark Osbeck, *What Is "Good Legal Writing" and Why Does It Matter?*, 4 Drexel L. Rev. 417, 422 (2012).

This chapter and the next focus on effective legal writing style. This chapter focuses on editing for *accuracy* and *consistency*. The next chapter focuses on editing for *clarity* and *conciseness*. These goals all go together, but sometimes they have to be balanced against one another. For example, accurately describing a long, complex regulation can be difficult to do concisely. By studying the techniques in this chapter and the next, you will develop a set of specific editing skills to practice as you build your judgment and discretion over time, using these skills in your own line of work.

I. Plain Language and Writing for the Reader

Influences in both chapters include the Plain Language movement in law and the concept from general composition theory of writing for the reader. One of the most famous proponents of Plain Language beginning in the 1970s was Richard Wydick, who wrote an excellent book now in its sixth edition, *Plain English for Lawyers*. (It has been compared favorably to the famous Strunk and White, *Elements of Style*.) You certainly don't have to be a lawyer to learn and implement the lessons of *Plain English for Lawyers* or the Plain Language movement generally.

Within the field of English composition theory and education, a parallel trend has shifted focus from the writer's intent to the needs of the audience, i.e., the reader. Particularly in professional writing, such as technical writing and legal writing, the purpose is not expressive or personal. As a form of professional writing in the workplace, legal writing is effective when it delivers what the reader needs. The chart below summarizes some differences between writer-focused writing and reader-focused writing:

Writer focused	Reader focused
• what writer wanted to express	• what reader needs to know for information or action
• organized by writer's thought process or steps of research	• organized by how reader can easily understand the information
• vocabulary understood by the writer	• vocabulary familiar to the reader

Writing for the reader is in part a mindset that drives other decisions, but it can be learned from the bottom up by practicing techniques such as those throughout this chapter and the next. In a work environment, one way to know that your writing is reader focused is by what *doesn't* happen: You turn in a draft to a supervisor who reads it and does not make many changes. But when supervisors significantly revise a draft, that response often indicates the draft needs to be reoriented toward the reader.

The examples here focus on a controversial current legal issue: When can an employer offer an unpaid internship? This issue is explored in other chapters of this book and has been answered differently by various courts and the Department of Labor. After the United States Court of Appeals for the Ninth Circuit decided a case in 2017 rejecting the Department of Labor's approach since 2010, the Department of Labor updated its guidance on the question to follow the Ninth Circuit's own approach. This guidance is the core legal information used for most examples in this chapter, with the original full text found in Department of Labor's Fact Sheet #71: Internship Programs Under the Fair Labor Standards Act, https://www.dol.gov/whd/regs/compliance/whdfs71.htm (updated January 2018).

II. Accuracy

First and foremost, legal writing must be accurate. If the substance is wrong, the style doesn't matter. Here we focus on three key areas where new legal writers may struggle with accuracy: using legal terms of art, conveying a legal rule's logic without modifying the logic, and quoting sources accurately in context.

A. Using Legal Terms of Art Accurately and Appropriately

Legal literacy entails recognizing legal terms of art and deciding how to use them. Legal terms of art are important and useful because they have a shared meaning in the legal community. Use of legal terms establishes a common understanding. It also demonstrates the person using legal terms to be legally literate, at least when they are used correctly. Correct usage is not a robotic understanding of definitions in a legal dictionary, but a more flexible understanding that draws on the reasonable range of possible interpretations. Using legal terms with legal literacy also means knowing what is *outside* the range of possible interpretations and procedural approaches.[1]

- Legal terms can be substantive and commonly understood, such as "misdemeanor" for a fairly minor crime that is distinct from the serious crimes categorized as felonies.

- Legal terms can be substantive and not commonly understood at all, such as the doctrines of "barratry, champerty, and maintenance." These ancient terms are derived from the old common law in England, were imported to colonial America, and are still influential in some aspects of the American legal system. These doctrines support civil liability and possibly criminal responsibility for harassing litigation or for encouraging lawsuits by lending money to facilitate them. The entire industry of litigation finance — in which law firms and lawyers borrow money to cover the cost of litigating — is a controversial but increasingly popular way to fund lawsuits, and it depends on the abrogation (that

---

1. James Boyd White, *The Invisible Discourse of the Law: Reflections on Legal Literacy and General Education*, 21 Mich. Q. Rev. 420 (1982), reprinted in 54 U. Colo. L. Rev. 143 (1983).

means basically repealing, ending, or removing) of barratry, champerty, and maintenance. A recent New York City Bar ethics opinion, N.Y. City Formal Op. 2018-5, called some litigation finance loans into question. Although it did not even use the term "champerty," its reasoning is grounded in the same basis as those old legal doctrines.

- Legal terms can carry logical meaning, like the difference between a mandatory "element" and a "factor" that must be considered but is not decisive by itself, as discussed further in chapter 5.

- And legal terms can carry procedural meaning, such as "summary judgment" which is the procedure where a judge decides a case based on written evidence and advocacy before that case goes to trial with live witnesses and cross-examinations and opening arguments and so on. Summary judgment is a useful litigation procedure because it saves judicial resources. Even looking at the facts with reasonable inferences drawn in favor of the party that wants to go to trial, the judge has concluded that no reasonable jury would find for that party. Thus, trying the case could waste judicial resources without a benefit in fairness and justice.

These examples show the range of legal terms and how they may function. With this large range of terms and functions, what writers need is a set of practical techniques for communicating about specialized legal terms. To get started, here is a key excerpt from Fact Sheet #71 (with footnotes omitted):

Courts have used the "primary beneficiary test" to determine whether an intern or student is, in fact, an employee under the FLSA. In short, this test allows courts to examine the "economic reality" of the intern-employer relationship to determine which party is the "primary beneficiary" of the relationship. Courts have identified the following seven factors as part of the test:

1. The extent to which the intern and the employer clearly understand that there is no expectation of compensation. Any promise of compensation, express or implied, suggests that the intern is an employee — and vice versa.

2. The extent to which the internship provides training that would be similar to that which would be given in an educational environment, including the clinical and other hands-on training provided by educational institutions.

3. The extent to which the internship is tied to the intern's formal education program by integrated coursework or the receipt of academic credit.

4. The extent to which the internship accommodates the intern's academic commitments by corresponding to the academic calendar.

5. The extent to which the internship's duration is limited to the period in which the internship provides the intern with beneficial learning.

6. The extent to which the intern's work complements, rather than displaces, the work of paid employees while providing significant educational benefits to the intern.

7. The extent to which the intern and the employer understand that the internship is conducted without entitlement to a paid job at the conclusion of the internship.

Courts have described the "primary beneficiary test" as a flexible test, and no single factor is determinative. Accordingly, whether an intern or student is an employee under the FLSA necessarily depends on the unique circumstances of each case.

The information in Fact Sheet #71 is already fairly easy to read, both for highly legally literate readers and general lay readers. But can some of its terminology be simplified even more, without compromising its accuracy? The examples that follow parse through Fact Sheet #71 to reveal options for communicating legal information that contains legal terms:

1. Keeping the Legal Term and Adding an Explanation

Fact Sheet #71 lays out a seven-factor test for whether a student can be an unpaid intern or must be paid as an employee. The Fact Sheet explicitly states, "[N]o single factor is determinative." The words "factor" and "determinative" are themselves common words in legal vocabulary. A factor, as we saw in Chapter 5, is something to consider, not something that must be present or absent. Thus, one factor alone cannot "determine" the answer. The answer requires consideration and balancing of all the factors together. That is what the sentence means when it says "no single factor is determinative." A determinative factor would be a factor that, by itself, controls the whole decision, and in fact we would call that an "element" rather than a factor precisely because it is determinative. A highly legally literate reader would know simply from the word "factor" that no single item in the list of factors is determinative. But the Fact Sheet goes on to explain how factors work when it says "no single factor is determinative." And then it explains the concept again in a way that makes the point even clearer: "whether an intern or student is an employee under the FLSA necessarily depends on the unique circumstances of each case." Thus, this short paragraph shows how legal writing can use legal terms in conjunction with explanations of what those terms mean.

2. Keeping the Legal Term and Adding an Example

Many people prefer to learn by way of concrete examples. For Fact Sheet #71's seven-factor test, one way to show how no single factor is determinative would be to give a specific example. Because the seven-factor test is indeed so flexible, many different examples could work well to illustrate the point. Here is one possibility: "For example, even an internship with a strong training program that resembles clinical education may nonetheless require the interns to be paid if the interns are replacing paid workers and expect to be offered full-time employment after the internship."

3. Replacing a Term, but Cautiously

Sometimes legal terminology is inappropriate or intimidating no matter how many explanations or examples are included. When legal terms will not work for the audience, the writer may consider substituting other words that are more appropriate. We should say here it is never the answer to use a more complicated word. Every reader, regardless of expertise and legal literacy, appreciates efficient writing that does not demand more of the reader's attention than is necessary. As United States Supreme Court Justice Clarence Thomas has said, "[T]he beauty [and] the genius is not to write a 5 cent idea in a ten dollar sentence. It's to put a ten dollar idea in a 5 cent sentence."[2]

With Fact Sheet #71, the original language states, "[N]o single factor is determinative. Accordingly, whether an intern or student is an employee under the FLSA necessarily depends on the unique circumstances of each case." A writer could rephrase these sentences to simplify them along the following lines: "[N]o single factor on the list decides the result. Whether an intern or student is an employee depends on the facts of each case."

Recognizing legal terms and using them accurately yet appropriately for the audience is one of the most difficult—and important—challenges of legal communication. Consult a legal dictionary such as Wex on the Cornell Legal Information Institute's website or the Merriam-Webster onine legal dictionary for comprehensive information on legal terms.

B. Describing the Logic in Legal Information Accurately

Good legal writers preserve the logic and the overall meaning of the information they are describing. Legal writing often depends on legal or factual research that the writer must read and process into an appropriate new written document. Strong reading skills are therefore necessary to be a strong legal writer. Read for key words and for the relationship of ideas. Read key primary sources very closely. For example, if a statute, regulation, or case sets out a legal test, then paraphrases of that test should maintain the same logic of that test. With this information in mind, which of the following examples most accurately preserves the logic of Fact Sheet #71?

Example 1

The "primary beneficiary" test determines whether an intern is a student or an employee. The focus of this test is on the "economic reality" of the relationship.

---

2. Conor Friedersdorf, *Why Clarence Thomas Uses Simple Words in His Opinions*, The Atlantic (Feb. 20, 2013).

Example 2

Whether an intern is a student or an employee depends on the "economic reality" of the relationship. If economic reality weighs in favor of the employer, then the intern is an employee. If economic reality weighs in favor of the intern, then the intern is a student.

Here, Example 1 is better. It preserves the logic of the test, which starts with the primary beneficiary test, and uses economic reality as the measure of that test. Example 2 is attractive because it uses accessible language and two contrasting sentences to clarify the two options. But the logic of Example 2 is not completely accurate because it omits the primary beneficiary test altogether. It does not clarify that the purpose of the economic reality test is to show who is the primary beneficiary of the relationship, and assessing who is the primary beneficiary is the real test. Thus, it does not pass the test of "good legal writing" stated at the beginning of this chapter because it does not help the reader make decisions.

The example above shows an important point about editing: You might find that one passage is more accurate, but another passage is easier to read. Accuracy must prevail, but can you find a way to get the best of both—an accurate paraphrase that is also readable?

Example 3

The "primary beneficiary" test determines whether an intern is a student or an employee. The focus of this test is on the "economic reality" of the relationship: If economic reality makes the employer the primary beneficiary of the intern's work, then the intern is an employee and must be paid. If economic reality makes the intern the primary beneficiary of the intern's own work, then the intern is a student and can be unpaid.

Example 3 above is an attempt to capture the best of both Example 1 and Example 2: it preserves the logic of the legal test, and it adds reader-friendly if/then statements about what the test really means.

You might ask, "If the logic is so crucial to preserve, then why not quote everything, just to be safe?" Paraphrasing source information without changing its meaning is a crucial skill. Source information may be written in a different style that distracts from your main point. Source information may be written for a law-trained audience, whereas you are maybe writing for the general public or a specialized non-lawyer audience. The source information may contain extraneous information such that quoting it means bringing in the extra, unnecessary information. Good legal writers can customize information for their own audience, using paraphrasing skills for achieving that goal.

C. Quoting Accurately and with Integrity

Even with the importance of good paraphrasing, quotation skills are still necessary in legal writing. Some exact text matters very much in legal writing, and quotations allow a writer to incorporate portions of exact text into their own writing. The quotation marks (or use of a block quote) around the quoted text makes a promise to the reader. The promise is that the quoted text comes from another source, exactly as it is written in that source.

Conversely, *not* using quotation marks is a different kind of promise — a promise that the words are the author's, *not* taken from another source. Quoting with integrity means giving credit and preserving exact words in quotation marks. One common rule of thumb is that when you are taking text from a source, quote it when either of the following is true:

- Are you taking more than seven words in a row from the source?
- Are you taking words that are particularly important or original or memorable, and deserve attribution to their source?

When a quotation is needed, the next question is whether to use quotation marks or a block quotation. According to the traditional rules of legal writing, quotations of less than 50 words should generally be in quotation marks. Quotations of 50 words or more should be generally formatted as a block.

Quotation example

Under the approach described in Department of Labor's Fact Sheet #71, "whether an intern or student is an employee under the FLSA necessarily depends on the unique circumstances of each case."

Block-quotation example (more than 50 words)

A student's status as either an unpaid intern or an employee affects several key employment terms:

> If analysis of these circumstances reveals that an intern or student is actually an employee, then he or she is entitled to both minimum wage and overtime pay under the FLSA. On the other hand, if the analysis confirms that the intern or student is not an employee, then he or she is not entitled to either minimum wage or overtime pay under the FLSA.

Outside of very formal legal writing, block quotations can be used for shorter quotations. Block quoting is often used in online writing to emphasize the quoted text, and can work well in less formal legal writing situations.

Example of a flexible block quote

The seven-factor test for determining who is the primary beneficiary of an internship results in a flexible inquiry:

> [W]hether an intern or student is an employee under the FLSA necessarily depends on the unique circumstances of each case.

Note in the example above that the quotation begins with a bracket. The original quote used the word "whether" because the sentence began "Accordingly, whether…" The writer omitted the first transition word. This decision to leave out part of the original quotation is consistent with the value discussed here of quoting with accuracy and integrity. The meaning of the quotation is not changed, and the writer's own text is clearer without the word "Accordingly." But the writer also shows the alteration to the reader: the original text "Accordingly, whether" is changed to "[W]hether" to begin the quoted sentence.

Quoting with integrity also means using ellipses to show that the quotation omits material from the original text. Three periods show an omission within a sentence, and three periods plus the period concluding the sentence show an omission at the end of a quoted sentence. Here are examples that use ellipses, drawn from the Department of Labor's Fact Sheet #71 on Student Internships:

Example 1

Original sentence in source:
Courts have used the "primary beneficiary test" to determine whether an intern or student is, in fact, an employee under the FLSA.

Quotation with internal quotation marks and ellipses:
"Courts have used the 'primary beneficiary test' to determine whether an intern or student is… an employee under the FLSA."

Example 2

Original sentence in source:
Courts have described the "primary beneficiary test" as a flexible test, and no single factor is determinative.

Quotation with internal quotation marks and ellipses:
"Courts have described the 'primary beneficiary test' as a flexible test…."

The examples above quote with accuracy and integrity in another way: They maintain the quotation within the original. The original sentence itself puts quotation marks around "primary beneficiary." The quoted sentence uses double quotation marks, which means it cannot maintain the same double quotation marks for the internal quotation. In U.S. English, double quotation marks are used for the first set of quotations, and single quotation marks are used for a second quotation within a quotation.

Quotation rules and guidelines can become very detailed very fast. Accuracy and integrity are the principles to keep in mind behind these rules. For more information on quotation rules and mechanics, you may want to consult a general source or a law-specific source, such as these:

General sources on quotations:

- Mignon Fogarty, *Grammar Girl's Quick and Dirty Tips for Better Writing*, Ch. 4 (2008).
- Diana Hacker and Nancy Sommers, *Rules for Writers*, Ch. 37 (8th 2016).

Law-specific sources on quotations:

- Anne Enquist, *To Quote or Not to Quote, Perspectives: Teaching Legal Research and Writing* at 16 (Fall 2005), https://info.legalsolutions.thomsonreuters.com/pdf/perspec/2005-fall/2005-fall-5.pdf
- Chris Sprigman et al., *The Indigo Book: A Manual of Legal Citation* at Rules 37-40, Public Resource (2016), https://law.resource.org/pub/us/code/blue/IndigoBook.html#SI

Accurate words and accurate quotations are core components of legal writing style.

III. Consistency

Throughout your career as a writer, you may have been told to make your writing more interesting. You might have even been told to go get a thesaurus and make sure not to use the same word for the same thing over and over because doing so is boring.

Please know:
That advice is terrible for legal writing.

Legal writing thrives on consistency. That is because legal terms have specific meanings. Legal terms with specific meanings should be preserved and used consistently. A legal test for "reasonable efforts" should not be changed to "justifiable attempts." Changing terms in this way is confusing and signals a lack of legal literacy to a legally educated reader. Compare the following two examples:

Example 1

The "primary beneficiary test" is based on the "economic reality" of the relationship between a student and his or her internship provider. If the economic reality of the relationship benefits the student, then the internship provider may treat the student as an unpaid intern. If the economic reality of the relationship benefits the internship provider, then that provider must treat the student as an employee.

Example 2

The "primary beneficiary test" is based on the "economic reality" of the relationship between a student and his or her internship provider. If the situation benefits the intern, then an unpaid internship is allowed. If the employer receives the advantage of the work performed, then the intern is actually an employee and must be paid.

Example 2 above may be exaggerated but shows the problems with inconsistent legal writing—both as to terms and as to concepts. Once the two parties are defined as "student" and "internship provider," those terms should be used consistently. And once the concepts of the "primary beneficiary" based on "economic reality" is introduced, those concepts should be described consistently. Referring to the concept of a primary beneficiary through the more generic word "benefits" is inconsistent. And referring to the same concept (that of the primary beneficiary) with the words "receives the advantage of the work performed" exacerbates the potential for confusion.

Consistency in legal writing may generate objections: It seems monotonous. It's boring. It's not creative. Keep in mind that legal writing can be very creative, but in different ways. Creativity can be defined as "original ideas that are useful."[3] Legal writing prioritizes being useful, and inconsistent terminology makes legal writing far less useful. Legal writing is original in different ways. Perhaps the writer recognizes a need to translate regulations for a general audience. There, the originality is recognizing the need and filling it. Perhaps the writer is advocating for a new policy within an existing legal framework. There, the originality comes from combining aspirations with pragmatism. As you continue to learn and use techniques for legal writing style, we hope you will see how consistent legal writing actually *reveals* creativity.

IV. Punctuation Review

This section gives a quick summary and examples of some selected punctuation rules to follow. We highlight these rules because we have seen them repeatedly broken, both in student and professional writing. Punctuation can create substantive ambiguity, or it can be inaccurate according to the conventions of punctuation itself. Effective legal writing style should use punctuation that is accurate in both senses—accurate in how it communicates the idea, and accurate in the widely understood rules of punctuation.

---

3. Kathleen Elliott Vinson, Samantha Alexis Moppett, and Shailini Jandial George, *Mindful Lawyering: The Key to Creative Problem-Solving* 41 (2018).

A. Using an Apostrophe to Make a Word Possessive, Not to Make a Word Plural

Incorrect	Correct
After hiring the company's first intern, the HR director went on to hire ten more intern's.	After hiring the company's first intern, the HR director went on to hire ten more interns.

If the word is singular, add an apostrophe and an s:

Incorrect	Correct
We received the interns essay on his work experience.	We received the intern's essay on his work experience.

If the word is plural and ends in an s, add an apostrophe:

Incorrect	Correct
We received eight of the intern's essays on their work experience.	We received eight of the interns' essays on their work experience.

These rules should handle most situations. For more complicated situations, keep a writing reference book handy.

B. Using the Oxford Comma

The Oxford comma is the comma before the conjunction and final item in a list of three or more items:

The rule for unpaid interns is derived from legislation, cases, and agency guidance.

This comma is both common and highly recommended in legal writing. The main reason to use it is to be consistent with the conventions of legal writing. There is a theoretical case where the lack of an Oxford comma causes lack of clarity:

Example 1

The intern discussed her unpaid status with her parents, the principal and the intern coordinator.

The problem: Is this sentence saying the intern's parents are "the principal and the intern coordinator"?

Example 2

The intern discussed her unpaid status with her parents, the principal, and the intern coordinator.

The solution: The Oxford comma removes the possible interpretation that "her parents" is a category describing "the principal and the intern coordinator." The sentence with the Oxford comma can be read in only one way, and that is as a list of three items: (1) her parents, (2) the principal, and (3) the intern coordinator.

To see more examples of humorous and sometimes consequential ambiguity caused by the lack of an Oxford comma, search the Internet for "Oxford comma clarity." The small but ever-so-often real risks of ambiguity are why legal writing style is definitely on "Team Oxford comma." Some lawyers on social media even proclaim in their profiles that they are a fan of the Oxford comma. Of course, this does not mean that anyone writing about law anywhere must use the Oxford comma. Journalists and other writers following the Associated Press Stylebook will not use it. For an audience of laypeople, the Oxford comma may not be necessary or even appropriate. But in a document written by or to lawyers or a piece of legal drafting such as a contract, consistently using the Oxford comma is a best practice.

C. Avoiding the Comma Splice

The comma splice is a very common punctuation problem. Comma splices happen when two independent clauses are joined only by a comma:

Examples (comma splices)

The unpaid-intern test relies on seven factors, none is determinative.

The primary beneficiary test governs the decision, it is based in economic reality.

A comma splice can be repaired by adding a conjunction, replacing the comma with a semicolon, or using a period to start a new sentence:

Examples (with comma splices avoided)

The unpaid-intern test relies on seven factors, and none is determinative.

The unpaid-intern test relies on seven factors. None is determinative.

The unpaid-intern test relies on seven factors; none is determinative.

The word "however," can cause particular difficulties with comma splices. Here are some examples of the problem along with some solutions:

Incorrect comma usage with "however" failing to repair a comma splice

Seven factors guide the evaluation, however none is determinative.

Seven factors guide the evaluation, however, none is determinative.

Correct comma usage with "however" and two independent clauses

Seven factors guide the evaluation; however, none is determinative.

Correct comma usage with "however" as an aside within a single clause

Seven factors guide the evaluation. None, however, is determinative.

D. Using a Complete Sentence Before a Colon

The colon introduces a thought that follows. It can introduce a list or another sentence. And it can be used to introduce a block quote. Some writers may shy away from the colon, thinking it's too formal or too risky. But it's actually a very useful tool for clear legal writing because a sentence with a colon helps to introduce a more complicated idea that follows. Here are examples of proper colon use:

Example 1

The seven-factor test focuses on three basic aspects of the employer-intern relationship: their shared expectations, the educational benefit to the intern, and the economic benefit to the employer.

Example 2

As Fact Sheet #71 suggests, the "primary beneficiary" test is different in every case: "[N]o single factor is determinative."

Example 3

The Department of Labor has laid out seven factors for assessing the primary beneficiary of an internship relationship:

> [Then insert the block quote of the seven factors, indented on each side and using justified margins.]

A common error with colons is to use them interchangeably with semicolons; that just isn't right. (See what we did there?) The next subsection addresses some key points on semicolons.

E. Using a Semicolon for Complex Lists and Balanced Independent Clauses

The most commonplace use of semicolons is in lists. To state a list of items in a textual paragraph, use commas in a list of simple items and semicolons for a list of long or complex items:

Example

The "primary beneficiary" test considers the understanding and expectations of the parties; the similarity of training to educational training; connections between the intern's educational program and the internship; the internship's accommodation of the intern's other academic commitments; the internship's duration and alignment with beneficial learning for the intern; any displacement of paid employees' work; and paid job prospects at the end.

Example

The seven factors cover three basic concepts: the understanding between internship provider and intern, the educational benefit to the intern, and replacement of paid work by the intern.

The lists above use semicolons for a complex list and commas for a relatively short list. Either way, you may notice that a long list like this is harder to read in paragraph form. Lists that are broken out into an actual visual list can be much easier to read:

Example

The seven factors cover three basic concepts:

- the understanding between internship provider and intern
- the educational benefit to the intern
- replacement of paid work by the intern.

In very formal legal writing—such as what lawyers file in court—semicolons (or sometimes commas) are used in these lists too, and the writer places an "and" after the semicolon in the second-to-last item:

Example

The seven factors cover three basic concepts:

1. the understanding between internship provider and intern;
2. the educational benefit to the intern; and
3. replacement of paid work by the intern.[4]

But in writing about law for lay readers and the public, the more common style follows business writing conventions and uses either a period or no punctuation at all after each item. Fact Sheet #71 itself uses a list with a period after each of the seven factors. Here is a version with shortened items and no punctuation:

Example

The "primary beneficiary" test considers seven factors:

1. the understanding and expectations of the parties
2. the similarity of training to educational training
3. connections between the intern's educational program and the internship
4. the internship's accommodation of the intern's other academic commitments

---

4. If you use a search engine and search "legal blog primary beneficiary test unpaid intern," you will find a number of law-firm blog posts that write about Fact Sheet #71 with this more formal semicolon style in the list of seven factors.

5. the internship's duration and alignment with beneficial learning for the intern
6. the overlap with paid employees' work
7. paid job prospects at the end

Broken-out lists like these are useful for visually emphasizing the most important information. Make sure to introduce them accurately and punctuate them consistently.

Beyond their use in lists, semicolons are also useful to separate two balanced independent clauses. The keys to using them successfully include recognizing what's an independent clause and determining that a semicolon is actually better than just breaking up the balanced ideas into two separate sentences.

Example

The intern did not displace paid workers; indeed, she slowed them down and took them off task on a regular basis.

In the example above, the semicolon works well to balance and contrast the two clauses. But in many cases, using a semicolon does not work as well because it just makes a long sentence longer. A period is often the better choice, especially when writing to an audience that appreciates clear and simple word choice, sentence structure, and visual design.

V. Accuracy and Consistency with Singular Pronouns: An Evolving Situation

The English language has a rich and wonderful vocabulary for legal concepts, ranging from ancient vocabulary to newer terms. But the English language has a basic problem with its grammar, and that is the lack of a singular pronoun that is also gender-neutral. The following examples show the problem:

Example 1

The intern must register a detailed educational plan with his supervisor.

This style used to be well accepted because, the reasoning went, "his" can be generic and stands in for both male and female references. But the idea of an invisible "her" came to be unacceptable to many. And in a legal setting, the writing should serve the reader; thus, the writer may be comfortable with a generic "he," but it is not a safe assumption that the reader will feel the same.

Example 2

The intern must register a detailed educational plan with their supervisor.

In spoken language and informal writing, "they" is often used to refer to a single individual. Many people also speak "they" as a singular pronoun after an indefinite pronoun like "Everyone": "Everyone must file an education plan before they can obtain credit." For highly formal writing or high-stakes writing such as writing to a state or federal agency, slipping into a generic "they" may seem inconsistently informal.

For individuals who wish to avoid gendered pronouns altogether, there is also an argument that "they" can be singular. The idea is that "they" is easier to use because it's already commonly used, rather than a new pronoun with little acceptance such as "thon," "che," or "ey." Others object to a singular "they" for a known single individual because it is strongly associated with a plural meaning. Some implications of this choice are addressed more fully below.

Example 3

The intern must register a detailed education plan with his/her supervisor.

Slash constructions for alternatives are disfavored under the Associated Press Stylebook and the Chicago Manual of Style. The same is equally if not more true in legal writing style. Slash constructions are informal/ambiguous/imprecise. So the slash construction cannot solve the pronoun problem.

Example 4

The intern must register a detailed education plan with his or her supervisor.

Including both "his or her" is a more inclusive approach, but it is also wordy. It can be tolerated in one or two places in a piece of writing, but repeatedly using it is distracting and seems stilted and verbose.

In some settings, the writer can alternate between "he" and "she" when a singular pronoun is needed. That is the approach in this book. It is risky, however, because the reader may miss the explanation of that choice, see an isolated example of the singular "he," followed by a later reference to the singular "she." The reader may fail to appreciate or understand the writer's attempt to be inclusive, and believe instead that the writer is confused and confusing.

Collected Additional Examples

Another possible solution is to rephrase the sentence, thereby avoiding the issue:

Interns must register a detailed education plan with their supervisors.

Each intern must register detailed education plans with the assigned supervisor.

A detailed education plan must be registered with the intern's supervisor. The intern is responsible for this step.

In the legal field, writers may approach this question with the old practical advice to "know your audience." Some audiences would not notice or would be positively inclined toward a singular "they," while other audiences could be distracted, confused, or grammatically disappointed. For licensed attorneys advocating on behalf of clients, their ethical duty is to serve the client and make writing decisions that will do the same. Thus, attorneys need to tailor their writing decisions to achieving the client's objectives. It is true that attorneys have the discretion to choose the tactics for achieving the client's stated objective, but the tactics should be chosen in light of the client's interest as well.

On the other hand, when writing about a person who has specifically requested certain pronouns, it is respectful to use the pronouns requested by that particular person. This is especially true when writing *to* a person who has made such a request. In a Supreme Court case involving a transgender teenager, the "merits" briefs (meaning the main briefs by the parties in the case) used one pronoun for the teenager, but three advocacy groups filed amicus briefs[5] with a modified caption using a different pronoun. The clerk of the Supreme Court informed the amicus groups they had violated a Supreme Court rule with this modification.[6]

Language experts have predicted that the singular "they" is on its way to becoming widely accepted even in formal professional writing. Until that happens, it is a case study in how good writing requires careful thought about the writer's choices and their effects on the audience.

VI. Unlearning Old Writing Beliefs and Habits

Effective legal writing style has a learning curve, and you may need to "un-learn" some writing lessons ingrained since primary school. As noted above, if you've ever been taught to use a thesaurus so you don't keep using the same word over and over, you will need to re-examine that learning. But the good news is there are many specific and learnable editing techniques. Did you just see how that sentence started with "But"? Starting a sentence with "but" is no longer considered wrong and bad; in fact, it can work nicely as (we think) it does here.

Of course, if you work for a supervisor with strong traditional beliefs, you may not need or want to fight this battle. One space after a period is well accepted now even in highly traditional legal writing, but many supervisors absolutely insist on the more traditional style of two spaces after a period. Learning legal writing style inherently involves learning new rules and challenging preconceptions. You should evaluate what

---

5. An amicus curiae brief, often just described as an amicus brief, is an extra brief filed not by a party in the litigation but by a "a friend of the court" with an interest in the case and something more to contribute.

6. Debra Cassens Weiss, *SCOTUS Clerk Tells Amici to Caption Case of Transgender Teen with Masculine Pronoun*, ABA Journal (March 17, 2017), http://www.abajournal.com/news/article/scotus_clerk_tells_amici _to_caption_case_of_transgender_teen_with_masculine

practices you hope to adopt for your own professional writing and whether you have a realistic chance to do so at your workplace and in your own team.

We began this chapter with a brief exploration of the important question: What is good legal writing? That big question will, we hope, motivate the attention to detail and editing persistence required to produce good legal writing. This chapter focused on accuracy and consistency. The next chapter focuses on clarity and conciseness.

Having studied this chapter, you should be able to:

- Edit your work and that of others for accuracy and precision
- Accurately use terms of art in legal communications
- Selectively use quoted language from legal sources
- Decide when to paraphrase language from legal content
- Avoid the use of "interesting" vocabulary to the detriment of accuracy and consistency
- Make intentional choices about pronoun usage that are effective for your audience in a legal setting
- Edit your work for common punctuation errors in a legal setting

....

Case Study

Ms. Ralston is preparing a blog post to submit to a compliance website. An intern in her business has written a draft for her, and Ms. Ralston is about to sit down and review the draft. Here is what she sees:

Compliance and Unpaid Student Internships

Internships are a great way to gain education and preparation for the workforce. The Fair Labor Standard Act is a crucial federal law that structures employer obligations toward their employee's.

The Law requires that employers pay their employees a minimum wage. It is enforced by the Labor Department, which allows unpaid internships in some circumstances. The DOL's Fact Sheet #71 is an employer's guide to creating an unpaid internship that is not illegal.

Fact Sheet #71 sets up seven requirements for an unpaid internship. Each of these components is addressed here:

1. Does the intern understand there is no salary?
2. Does the internship offer clinical training?
3. Is the internship connected to the university credit?

4. Does the internship respect the intern's scheduling needs?
5. Does the internship end when the intern won't learn anything new?
6. Does the intern get the benefit of the internship?
7. Does the intern know the internship is only temporary?

This is called the primary beneficiary test and analyzes the economic realities of the employer-intern relationship. It comes from a New York case, *Glatt v. Searchlight Pictures, Inc.*, 811 F.3d 528 (2015). There, the court proclaimed that the Department of Labor's old six-factor test should not be used because it did not reflect the realities of the modern educational internship. Instead, the court articulated seven factors for assessing the "economic reality" of the relationship, and those are the same elements listed above. With the Ninth Circuit adopting the same test in late 2017, the Circuits appear to be tilting strongly toward this seven-part test as the definitive rule for the FSLA. But there is still a different approach in the 10th Circuit.

Discuss and edit this draft. In particular, examine how the intern described the seven factors and whether they are accurate to the content of the DOL's Fact Sheet.

Traditions and Trends

Accurate and consistent writing has a strong premium value in legal language, both in primary legal sources produced by government and other authorities and also in legal communication about those sources. The fact that legal writing is sometimes inaccurate and inconsistent does not contradict these values, but rather demonstrates how difficult they are to implement. For a humorous take on the difficulty of drafting simple and effective laws, we suggest an unorthodox law review article, *The Food Stays in the Kitchen* by Hillel Levin.[7] It seems that every general rule stated in beautiful, accessible language opens the door for an argument about a borderline case or a situation left uncovered by the beautiful, accessible language. Yet covering every conceivable situation and closing every loophole may make the rule so unwieldy as to be ridiculous. Similarly, judges endeavor to write accurate, accessible opinions that can be understood by litigants and the public, while also following precedent cases, not all of which are written in accessible language. This tension is not really a "tradition" of legal writing but rather a persistent reality legal writers confront on a daily basis.

One approach offering hope is a model of the writing process imported from general composition theory to legal writing by Bryan A. Garner, a respected expert in the field. This model, debuted by composition professor Betty S. Flowers

---

7. Hillel Y. Levin, *The Food Stays in the Kitchen: Everything I Needed to Know about Statutory Interpretation I learned by the Time I Was Nine*, 12 Green Bag 337 (2009).

in 1979, frames the writing process in four steps: "Madman, Architect, Carpenter, Judge."[8] Some professors find a different way to phrase the "madman" idea, but regardless of its terms, the concept is that writers should start by exploring and producing ideas *without* judging, then design a framework for delivering those ideas, and then draft the text. Only after those three stages does the writer look at everything with a critical eye to edit and proofread. If the judging stage comes too early, the writer might end up blocking good but incomplete ideas, or become unable to generate ideas at all. In contrast, if the writer dawdles while conceiving and producing a draft and fails to reach the judging stage, the written work may be genius but may look sloppy and unreliable. Garner has woven this model into much of his writing and speaking to both legal[9] and business[10] audiences. Although the four-step model can be criticized as artificial and formalistic, it can still be quite helpful. As statistician George Box said, "All models are wrong, but some are useful."

This and other influences from composition theory are deeply grounded in human strengths and weaknesses, and human cognition generally. But a growing trend in writing and editing capitalizes on exactly the opposite: the tireless logic of computers. Since the 1970s, it has been possible to measure language in a mathematical way through readability scores such as the Flesch-Kincaid Grade Level test and early grammar checkers that became commercially available in the 1980s. Editing software and websites are now available to check grammar, target wordy phrases, and find inconsistencies. Some of these services not only highlight language that may have a grammar or style issue, but they also provide explanations and suggest alternatives. These services go beyond checking grammar; the IBM Watson Tone Analyzer can assess text's social and emotional impact, and some grammar-and-style checkers are programmed specifically for legal writing style. These offerings are multiplying and becoming more powerful each year, and writers can definitely learn something by trying them out. Yet human judgment remains essential to any piece of writing that will ultimately inform or persuade other humans.

---

8. Betty S. Flowers, *Madman, Architect, Carpenter, Judge: Roles and the Writing Process*, 44 Proceedings of the Conference of College Teachers of English 7-10 (1979), quoted in Bryan A. Garner, *The Winning Brief: 100 Tips for Persuasive Writing in Trial and Appellate Courts* 4-5 (2003).

9. Bryan A. Garner, *Legal Writing in Plain English: A Text with Exercises* (2d ed. 2013).

10. Sarah Green, *Improve Your Writing: Q&A Interview with Bryan Garner*, Harvard Business Review Blog, https://hbr.org/2013/02/improve-your-business-writing (podcast and transcript).

Chapter 18

Clear and Concise
Legal Writing

> The minute you read something and you can't understand it you can almost be sure that it was drawn up by a lawyer.... If it's in a few words and is plain and understandable only one way, it was written by a non-lawyer.
>
> — Rachel Stabler, *"What We've Got Here Is Failure to Communicate":*
> *The Plain Writing Act of 2010*, 40 J. Legis. 280 (2013)
> (citing Will Rogers, *Weekly Articles: The Lawyers Talking*
> (Steven K. Gragert 6th ed., 1982) (1933–1935)).

Plain, simple writing has many advantages, in legal and nonlegal contexts. A 2005 Princeton study showed that when the reader is able to "fluently" process a piece of writing, he or she is more likely to believe the writer is truthful and worthy of confidence, and even likeable.[1] Conversely, and perhaps surprisingly to many, readers attribute *lower* intelligence to authors who use needlessly complex words. The study consisted of five separate experiments and found an "extremely robust" effect: "needless complexity leads to negative evaluations."[2] Apart from these negative evaluations, an-

---

1. David Oppenheimer, *Consequences of Erudite Vernacular Utilized Respective of Necessity: Problems with Using Long Words Needlessly*, 20 Applied Cognitive Psychology 139, 140 (2006) (citations omitted) ("Simpler writing is easier to process, and studies have demonstrated that processing fluency is associated with a variety of positive dimensions. Fluency leads to higher judgements of truth, confidence ... and even liking.")

2. *Id.* at 151.

other risk of needlessly complex writing in a professional setting is that people won't understand it and therefore won't be able to work effectively.

Clear writing encompasses a broad range of writing decisions: clarity comes from the choice of words, the arrangement of sentences, the flow of paragraphs, and the document's overall design. Writing is clear when it leads readers to understand what the writer wants them to know. Each aspect of clarity is addressed below.

I. Clear and Concise Words

Experts have been discouraging needlessly complex words in legal writing since 1963: "[T]he principle of simplicity would dictate that the language used by lawyers agree with the common speech, unless there are reasons for a difference," David Mellinkoff wrote in *The Language of the Law*,[3] launching the Plain Language movement in the legal field. This section on word choice first addresses word choice generally; and second, word choice with law-specific vocabulary.

A. General Word Choice

Clarity is closely related to precision, using the exact word that pinpoints the writer's intended meaning. (There are exceptions, but to paraphrase Picasso and many others, you should learn the rules before you learn to break them.)

1. Precise Word Choice

Part of precision means choosing the word that most closely defines the thing it describes. The National Archives has a resource, *Principles of Clear Writing*,[4] with an excellent set of examples such as these:

Don't Say	If You Mean
Vehicles	Automobiles
Firearms	Rifles
Aircraft	Helicopters

2. Concrete Word Choice

Another part of clear word choice is *concrete* word choice. "Needlessly complex words" were the target of the Princeton study mentioned in the introduction to this chapter, and needlessly complex words are often very abstract words. An abstract word refers to a concept or a state of events or a diffuse idea. In contrast, a concrete noun is plain and easy to immediately recognize. Here are a few examples:

---

3. David Mellinkoff, *The Language of the Law* vii (1963).

4. National Archives, *Drafting Legal Documents, Principles of Clear Writing*, https://www.archives.gov/federal-register/write/legal-docs/clear-writing.html (last reviewed August 15, 2016).

Abstract	Concrete
Agreement	Contract
Jurisprudence	Case law or (better) the case or the opinion
Legislation	Section 202 of the FLSA
Administrative law	The agency or the regulation or the guidance
Law	The opinion
Law	The regulation
Law	The statute

Common writing advice states that a concrete noun must be detectable by one of the five senses, whereas an abstract noun cannot be directly sensed. Concrete word choice is often much easier to read, increasing fluency and its benefits. As you can see from the final examples above, "law" itself is an abstract noun. Of course you will use it sometimes, but always ask yourself what is your source of law and whether a more concrete description of "the law" would be more precise and helpful for the reader.

3. Minimizing Nominalizations

Abstract writing is particularly associated with a type of noun called a "nominalization." A nominalization uses another part of speech, especially a verb, as a noun:

Examples of nominalizations

The factors' *applicability* is *dependent* on an *assessment* of the circumstances, ultimately supporting the *determination* of the *decision* as to unpaid-intern or employee status.

The sentence is above is exaggeratedly muddled to demonstrate how abstract nouns interfere with clarity. Nominalizations can often be recognized by their word endings such as -ity or –ment or –tion. Changing them requires finding the concrete word—the verb or adjective or other part of speech—hidden inside the noun:

Example with nominalizations removed

How the factors apply depends on the circumstances. The court uses the factors to assess the circumstances and decide whether the intern can be unpaid or must be treated as an employee.

Editing out nominalizations will help any type of writing sound clearer, simpler, and less bureaucratic. There is still room to cut extra words from the passage above, but the example shows how important concrete nouns and verbs are to the goal of clear writing.

B. Concise Word Choice

Cutting extra words is a win-win. The reader wins because reading fewer words takes less time and effort. The writer wins because the reader understands the writer's point more easily and therefore likes the writer better. If concise writing is so fantastic for all concerned, why does so much legal writing seem to be just the opposite—wordy and verbose?

Admittedly, some legal writing is long and detailed because the situation requires an in-depth treatment. That writing may be challenging and even difficult to read, but still concise for its intended purpose. Writing is concise when it delivers a high content-to-word ratio. In other words, conciseness is not about page count or even word count, but rather packing a lot of meaning into relatively few words. A 10-page memo could be very concise, and an email that takes up one full smartphone screen could be very verbose, depending on how many words are really necessary in each situation.

Being concise by hitting the desirable ratio will be different for different situations and audiences. The memorandum of law discussed in chapter 5 and reprinted in full in Appendix A is an example of a detailed analysis that is appropriately concise for a supervising lawyer but might be too long and detailed for a client who just wants to know "the bottom line." One competency of legal literacy is being able to "translate" an in-depth legal analysis written for an expert audience into a shorter but still accurate version of that same message for a different audience.[5]

Verbosity springs from a variety of sources. Lack of time to edit is one, as shown by the famous sign-off from French mathematician Blaise Pascal: "This letter is long because I did not have time to make it shorter." The good news today is that some computer programs can highlight wordy phrases to help the writer recognize and correct them.

Another cause of verbosity is more ingrained: The writer was figuring out what to say as she went along. To write more concisely, plan your writing to efficiently deliver the results of all your work, omitting any unnecessary steps or dead-ends. The solution here is to write and then revise and edit for the reader.

Finally, some writing is verbose because the writer is actively or perhaps subconsciously trying to impress the audience. As the Princeton study points out, using needlessly complex words risks creating the exact opposite impression.

C. Special Focus: Passive Voice

Now we focus on a specific and well-known editing techniques to make your writing more concise: *Minimize or eliminate passive voice.* Many legal readers believe that passive-voice verbs are the single biggest problem with verbose legal writing. Actually, there are sometimes good reasons to use passive verbs, but in legal writing they should

---

5. Chapter 5 addresses this skill by asking textbook readers to translate a lawyer's legal memorandum of law for a client audience.

used carefully and selectively. (The previous sentence uses a passive verb for a good reason as explained below.) A basic understanding of active and passive verbs helps writers know why to minimize their use and when to make an exception. The core idea of a passive verb is how the subject and verb relate. The subject of the sentence "passively" receives the action rather than doing the action:

The interns were classified as unpaid.

The verb provides the action in the sentence, and that action is classifying the interns. But the subject of the sentence — the interns — receive that action. They don't do it. Thus, the subject (the interns) receives the action (were classified as unpaid).

Passive verbs are somewhat a function of word choice, which is why they appear in this section on word choice, but they affect the entire sentence structure. A way to recognize passive verbs is to look for a form of the helping verb "be" plus the past participle of the verb: "were classified." The active verb would be *classify*: "The internship administrator classified the interns as unpaid."

You don't have to know the term "past participle," but you do need to recognize the basic idea of a "be" verb and what seems like a past tense version of the verb. Here's another example: "In order to be educated about legal communication, you should read this book." To make this sentence active, the verb form "to be educated" would need to become "to educate." The revised active sentence would read: "To educate yourself about legal communication, you should read this book." Here are some more examples:

The interns were not paid.
   Active: The summer program did not pay the interns.

The seven-factor test was applied.
   Active: The court applied the seven-factor test.

Paid workers were not displaced.
   Active: The interns did not displace paid workers.

The interns' work schedule was dictated by their academic schedule.
   Active: The interns' academic schedule dictated their work schedule.

The primary beneficiary test was adopted by the Department of Labor.
   Active: The Department of Labor adopted the primary beneficiary test.

The employer's classification of the interns was reversed.
   Active: The court reversed the employer's classification of the interns.

Passive verbs create some well-known problems, most importantly the fact that whatever causes the verb's action is not necessarily present in the sentence:

Example 1

The seven-factor test was applied.

The question is: Applied by whom — the employer, the Department of Labor, the court, or someone else?

Identifying who did the action can be done, but takes extra words:

Example 2

The seven-factor test was applied by the court. (9 words)

Example 3

The court applied the seven-factor test. (7 words)

Because an extra prepositional phrase — "by the court" — is necessary to identify who actually did the action, passive sentences have become closely associated with unnecessarily wordy writing. In addition, almost every computer grammar-and-style checker can flag passive voice in word processing, so it should be easy to catch and edit, unlike more subtle examples of verbosity.

There are some reasons to use passive voice. A passive verb works well when the actor is completely clear from context, or completely unimportant:

Examples of potentially appropriate passive verbs

The district court's decision was later reversed on appeal.
The defendant was arrested on January 3, 2019.
The regulations were issued without proper notice.

In the examples above, the subject of the sentence receives the action, but the actor doing the action is extremely clear from context — the appellate court, the police, and the agency, respectively.

Another reason to perhaps consider using a passive verb is to emphasize or de-emphasize an action. This can be done well or poorly. In the following examples, which is more obvious as an attempt to manipulate the reader's attention away from whomever is responsible?

Example 1

The interns were classified as unpaid.

Example 2

The decision was made to classify the interns as unpaid.

Example 2 above is more obviously manipulative, and therefore less persuasive.

Passive verbs are not only common, but recommended in much scientific writing, such as in describing experiments. Legal writing requires a significantly different mind-set about passive verbs. Writing about law and fact generally *should* identify who is responsible for actions. Unlike in science writing where the scientist and lab workers who did the action fade into the background, in legal writing the party or official or agency or other actor that did the action is usually an important player. Noticeable deviations from this general norm fail to persuade and may bring the reader's judgment on the writer.

D. Can Writing Be Too Concise?

Readers appreciate concise writing. It gets to the point, it is easy to read, and it doesn't waste time. So is it possible for writing to be too concise? Actually, yes.

A common and easily avoidable example is using shorthand terms that the audience won't understand. If you're communicating with a nonexpert audience in just about any field, using expert shorthand terms will be too concise. The number one example of this is acronyms. Acronyms are a form of expert jargon: They streamline communication with experts, but they impair (if not destroy) communication with nonexperts. And even experts can find too many acronyms difficult to wade through. A Circuit Judge in the District of Columbia publicly shamed the attorneys in an energy case for overusing acronyms:

> We … remind the parties that our Handbook of Practice and Internal Procedures states that "parties are strongly urged to limit the use of acronyms" and "should avoid using acronyms that are not widely known." Brief-writing, no less than "written English, is full of bad habits which spread by imitation and which can be avoided if one is willing to take the necessary trouble." George Orwell, "Politics and the English Language," 13 Horizon 76 (1946). Here, both parties abandoned any attempt to write in plain English, instead abbreviating every conceivable agency and statute involved, familiar or not, and littering their briefs with references to "SNF," "HLW," "NWF," "NWPA," and "BRC" — shorthand for "spent nuclear fuel," "high-level radioactive waste," the "Nuclear Waste Fund," the "Nuclear Waste Policy Act," and the "Blue Ribbon Commission."[6]

When writing to an audience that does not share an expert's understanding of key terms in your field, the writing still needs to be concise. It shouldn't use unnecessary

---

6. *Nat'l Ass'n of Regulatory Util. Comm'rs v. U.S. Dep't of Energy*, 680 F.3d 819, 820 n. 1 (D.C. Cir. 2012) (Silberman, J.).

extra words, but adding some words to explain what the audience needs to know is necessary. Here is an example:

Example 1

A split among the Ninth and Tenth Circuits about the unpaid-intern test could lead to a successful cert petition.

Example 2

The Ninth and Tenth Circuits have applied different tests for determining when interns can be unpaid, creating a split among the circuits. Circuit splits can provide the basis for asking the United States Supreme Court to "grant certiorari," meaning agree to decide the case.

Example 1 relies on appellate lawyers' jargon about the Supreme Court. Example 2 is longer, but it explains the same issue with more background for the benefit of non-law professionals in other fields, who do not want to decipher and try to interpret specialized appellate law jargon. This type of explanation from expert to nonexpert helps any professional expert communicate successfully with others. The confusion caused when experts don't explain their key terms to nonexperts is a fact of all professional settings, not just legal communication. Legally literate professionals who do not fully occupy the role of insiders in the legal profession are ideally suited to occupy this middle space, understanding legal jargon but preserving the ability to communicate to others who do not.

II. Clear and Concise Sentences

We now broaden our focus on effective legal writing style from words to sentences. In a book devoted to sentences as the key to good writing, Professor Stanley Fish wrote that "(1) A sentence is an organization of items in the world; and (2) a sentence is a structure of logical relationships."[7] This numbered list is an example of clear and concise writing because it shows the parallel relationship of these two concepts. Whether in a numbered list or just a regular sentence, the information in a sentence should logically and smoothly connect in an easily understandable way. Because sentences deliver the logic of a statement, sentence structure is critical to communication about law, which of course depends on logic. The craft of sentence structure is enough to fill an entire book—such as the one written by Fish—and many more. This section provides a few practical highlights of effective sentences.

---

7. Stanley Fish, *How to Write a Sentence and How to Read One* (2011).

A. Use One Main Idea per Sentence

One of the most common problems with sentences is trying to do too much. A sentence should carry one main idea. It can certainly have add-ons like dependent clauses and prepositional phrases and other offshoots from the main idea. But the sentence should still have one main idea that is easy for a legal reader to identify and understand. Sometimes the metaphor of human digestion is useful: feed information to the reader in small bites. Avoid feeding the reader big clumps of words and ideas that could cause indigestion. If the writing is optional for the reader, long overloaded sentences could make the reader simply turn away and stop reading.

Example 1

The primary beneficiary test measures the economic reality of the relationship between the student and employer. The primary beneficiary is determined by a seven-factor test for evaluating the unique circumstances of each case. No one factor of the test is dispositive.

Example 2

The primary beneficiary test measures the economic reality of the relationship between the student and employer, using a test of seven factors for evaluating the unique circumstances of each case, and no one factor of the test is dispositive.

As shown in Example 2 above, the seemingly innocent word "and" is a common culprit for overloaded sentences. "And" is a fine word, a coordinating conjunction that is extremely helpful in many grammatical situations. And you can start a sentence with "and" without breaking any grammatical rules, even though many people still think it's wrong to begin a sentence with "but" or "and" or any other coordinating conjunction. (See what we did there?)

The problem is using "and" to connect overly long chains of information and reasoning in a single sentence, and thereby linking together multiple ideas, and that is problematic because when a reader faces a long meandering sentence and does not know what to do, the reader may stop reading and blame the writer for the confusion, and that's not the effect any professional writer is aiming to achieve and certainly not what you want. (See what we did there too?) Especially if you've ever been told you tend to write long sentences, it's a good idea to double-check any sentences using "and." Ask yourself why "and" is the best choice to connect ideas in one long sentence. If you spot a meandering sentence, consider breaking it up into two or more shorter ones. As legal writing professor Joe Fore has espoused,[8] consider the benefits of an unexpected "key" to effective legal writing — the period key.

---

8. Joe Fore, Guest Post, *Three Neglected (Keyboard) Keys to Effective Legal Writing*, Lady Legal Writer (June 14, 2016), https://ladylegalwriter.blogspot.com/2016/06/three-neglected-keyboard-keys-in.html.

B. Use a Concrete Subject

In general, the subject of a sentence should be something concrete—in other words, something specific and easily recognizable. Section I.A.2 above compared and contrasted some concrete and abstract nouns. This section revisits the topic because using a concrete subject anchors the whole sentence. Which of the following examples has a more concrete subject?

Example 1

The seven-factor discretionary test used in the assessment of students as unpaid interns means categorical rules do not apply.

Example 2

Unpaid internships are not subject to categorical rules because the test for assessing unpaid interns uses seven discretionary factors.

In law, many concepts are abstract rather than concrete, and the writer should try to choose concrete words whenever possible. Thus, in the sentences above, Example 1 had the following subject: "The seven-factor discretionary test used in the assessment of students as unpaid interns." Example 2 had the following subject: "Unpaid internships." Both sentences are somewhat abstract, but the subject of Example 2 is more concrete. Note also that Example 1 uses a nominalization, "assessment," whereas Example 2 uses a slightly more active verb form of the same word, "assessing." (Technically it is a gerund and still a noun form, but "assessing" seems more active than "assessment." Sometimes editing for grammar means reading a sentence out loud and using your intuition about what sounds better.)

One type of subject has no content at all: the "grammatical expletive" or "dummy subject" or "placeholder subject." These terms all refer to the same thing, an empty subject that merely holds a grammatical place. You can often recognize it by the subject "there" or "it."

Example 1

There are seven factors to the primary beneficiary test.

It has been decided that the primary beneficiary test governs this question.

The sentences in Example 1 use the grammatical expletive "there" and "it" to hold the place of the subject, but do not actually state a concrete subject. What these sentences need is an edit to give them a concrete subject, as shown below.

Example 2

The primary beneficiary test has seven factors.

The Ninth Circuit decided that the primary beneficiary test governs this question.

The sentences in Example 2 have concrete subjects: "the primary beneficiary test" and "the Ninth Circuit." The first sentence also has the benefit of being more concise, cutting eight words in Example 1 down to six words in Example 2. The second sentence has the same number of words, but it is more effective because it delivers more information with the same number of words.

C. Use a Concrete Verb

Verbs provide the action in a sentence and, just as with nouns, concrete verbs are often more effective than abstract verbs. They convey an action that the reader can imagine vividly, rather than a state of being. On that note, the most well-known abstract verb is simply "is" and all its variations—is, was, were, be, been, being.

Example 1

The primary beneficiary test is discretionary and comprised of seven factors.

The test was discretionary and guided by seven factors.

Being that the test is made up of seven factors, it is different in each situation.

Example 2

The primary beneficiary test consists of seven discretionary factors.

Seven factors make up the primary beneficiary test.

The primary beneficiary test is guided by seven discretionary factors.

Because the test requires courts to consider seven factors, it applies differently in each situation.

Example 1 above uses a series of "is" verbs: "is," "was," and—worst of all—"being that." Example 2 uses more concrete verbs: "consists," "make up," "is guided by," "requires," and "applies." As with all writing advice, this advice can be taken too far. Effective legal writing style uses concrete verbs, but that does not mean it uses outlandishly dramatic verbs. The most memorable word choice may seem to be something like "utterly failed" or "wisely discerned" or "plainly decrees." In fact, however, concrete verbs do not need to stretch for creative vocabulary or be adorned with adverbs. The most effective legal writing does not use adverbs much because the verbs themselves communicate the action. The examples below show how appropriate verbs can make a difference.

Example 1

The court found that the students received the primary benefit and thus affirmed the district court's decision they could be unpaid.

Example 2

The court believed that the students received the primary benefit and thus deemed the district court was justified in declaring them unpaid interns.

The first example is effective because it is clear and concrete: It uses commonly accepted legal vocabulary for what courts do: courts *find* facts, they *hold* law, they *state* their reasoning, and ultimately they *grant* or *deny* or *affirm* or *reverse*, or take some other specific action identified in their orders and opinions. All of these legal vocabulary words are concrete, with no need for clarification and no benefit from adornment.

Example 2 above is ineffective because it uses dramatic, emotional words for what the appellate court and district court did: "felt" and "deemed" and "declar[ed]." It also uses an imprecise phrase to describe how the appellate court affirmed the lower court: "deemed the district court was justified." That is a verbose and ambiguous way of saying the appellate court affirmed the district court.

The writer might have chosen this creative phrasing instead of the plain verb "affirmed" to avoid repetition and add variation. Richard Wydick, the author of *Plain English for Lawyers*, introduced the term "elegant variation" to mean using different words to refer to the same thing, in order to sound more interesting and elegant. As noted in chapter 17 on consistent legal writing, elegant variation is not a good thing! It introduces inconsistency and extra verbiage, thus requiring extra effort on the reader's part to interpret the content. The more effective legal writing style should stick with concrete verbs that efficiently convey legal meaning. In general, keep in mind that the creativity in legal writing comes not from incorporating the most vocabulary words, but from the clear selection and concise arrangement of words to achieve a practical goal.

D. Keep Subjects and Verbs Close Together

The advice above about using a concrete subject relates to another technique: keeping subjects and verbs close together. The subject and verb should be relatively close, not separated by a lot of prepositional phrases or other verbiage, so the reader can follow the basic logic of the sentence. Read this and see if you can follow:

Example 1

The seven-factor discretionary test used in the assessment of students as unpaid interns means categorical rules do not apply.

In the example above, the subject is 13 words long. The basic noun at the heart of the subject is "test," and nine words separate that subject from the verb, "means." The separation of the subject and verb makes the sentence much harder to read than it needs to be. There are several ways to improve the sentence, and most of them end up with the subject and verb much closer to each other:

Example 2

The test for assessing students as interns uses seven discretionary factors, and thus categorical rules do not apply.

Categorical rules do not apply to the test for assessing students as interns because the test depends on seven discretionary factors.

The revised sentences in Example 2 show that sometimes you don't need to know exactly what grammar rules apply or why a sentence is hard to follow. Simply noticing that a sentence is hard to follow and trying some alternatives can lead to much more effective legal style.

E. Use Parallel Language for Lists and Parallel Items

Parallel language is an important tool in any legal writer's toolkit. Parallel language means using the same grammatical structure in a sequence or list or other set of ideas. It allows a writer to use grammar to reinforce a logical relationship. For example, a list of required items could be described in the following way:

Unpaid interns need not receive x or y.

In the list above, the words that fill the spots for "x" and "y" should use the same grammatical structure:

Unpaid interns need not receive minimum wage or overtime pay.

Using parallel language requires more intentional and explicit use of grammar rules. Here, both "minimum wage" and "overtime pay" are noun phrases, so this sentence passes the test for parallel grammar. It would be faulty parallelism to use different grammar in the position of "x" and "y":

Unpaid interns need not receive minimum wage or overtime pay is not required.

The example above is an extreme example to show faulty parallelism. There, "x" was a noun ("minimum wage"); therefore, "y" could not be a clause ("overtime pay is not required"). More common examples of faulty parallelism sound somewhat correct:

The primary beneficiary test measures a number of factors including the intern and employer's understanding there is no expectation of compensation and whether the internship provides quasi-educational training.

This example is faulty because the items in the list do not use the same grammatical structure. One way to see this is to line them up with bullet points and compare their structure:

a number of factors including

- the intern and employer's understanding there is no expectation of compensation
- whether the internship provides quasi-educational training

As shown here, the first item in the list is a noun ("understanding") with an attached clause ("there is no expectation of compensation"). The second item in the list is a dependent clause ("whether the internship provides quasi-educational training"). The second item could be edited into a form more parallel with the first:

> The primary beneficiary test measures a number of factors including the intern and employer's understanding there is no expectation of compensation and any quasi-educational training provided by the employer.

In this example, both items in the list are noun phrases. The anchors are *understanding* and *training*. This example passes the test for parallel grammar. Here are some more examples:

> Federal legislation, judicial opinions, and administrative guidance all contribute to the law of unpaid interns.

> Fact Sheet #71 provides legal background, lists the seven factors of the primary beneficiary test, and includes footnotes to sources.

The first sentence above has three parallel nouns in the subject of the sentence: *legislation*, *opinions*, and *guidance*. The second sentence above has three parallel verb phrases in the predicate of the sentence: *provides*, *lists*, and *includes*.

Department of Labor Fact Sheet #71 itself contains several examples of parallel grammar. The list of seven factors demonstrates parallel grammar:

> Courts have identified the following seven factors as part of the test:
>
> 1. The extent to which the intern and the employer clearly understand that there is no expectation of compensation. Any promise of compensation, express or implied, suggests that the intern is an employee — and vice versa.
>
> 2. The extent to which the internship provides training that would be similar to that which would be given in an educational environment, including the clinical and other hands-on training provided by educational institutions.
>
> 3. The extent to which the internship is tied to the intern's formal education program by integrated coursework or the receipt of academic credit.
>
> 4. The extent to which the internship accommodates the intern's academic commitments by corresponding to the academic calendar.
>
> 5. The extent to which the internship's duration is limited to the period in which the internship provides the intern with beneficial learning.
>
> 6. The extent to which the intern's work complements, rather than displaces, the work of paid employees while providing significant educational benefits to the intern.

7. The extent to which the intern and the employer understand that the intern-ship is conducted without entitlement to a paid job at the conclusion of the internship.

The list in Fact Sheet #71 actually uses the exact same words for the beginning of each factor — "the extent to which...." Using the exact same words is not required for parallel grammar and in fact is more the exception than the rule. It would have been possible to use parallel grammar in a different way by using "extent to which" in the introductory language:

Courts use a seven-factor test, evaluating *the extent to which* each of the following factors suggests that the relationship primarily benefits the intern or the employer:

1. Do the intern and the employer clearly understand that there is no expectation of compensation? Any promise of compensation, express or implied, suggests that the intern is an employee — and vice versa.
2. Does the internship provide training that would be similar to that which would be given in an educational environment, including the clinical and other hands-on training provided by educational institutions?
3. Is the internship tied to the intern's formal education program by integrated coursework or the receipt of academic credit?
4. Does the internship accommodate the intern's academic commitments by cor-responding to the academic calendar?
5. Is the internship's duration limited to the period in which the internship pro-vides the intern with beneficial learning?
6. Does the intern's work complement, rather than displace, the work of paid employees while providing significant educational benefits to the intern?
7. Do the intern and the employer understand that the internship is conducted without entitlement to a paid job at the conclusion of the internship?

Fact Sheet #71 contains another example of parallel language that helps readers under-stand the two potential consequences of the determination:

If analysis of these circumstances reveals that an intern or student is actually an employee, then he or she is entitled to both minimum wage and overtime pay under the FLSA. On the other hand, *if the analysis confirms that* the intern or student is not an employee, then he or she is not entitled to either minimum wage or overtime pay under the FLSA.

The parallel grammar in the passage is italicized for emphasis. The passage uses multiple sentences to set up two parallel possibilities using parallel grammar: if the intern *is* an employee, and if the intern *is not* an employee. These examples show that parallel grammar can exist inside one sentence or in a series of related sentences.

III. Clear and Concise Paragraphs

A paragraph is a collection of sentences with a main point — a single main point supported in some way by each sentence. And that main point should be stated in the first sentence of the paragraph. The first sentence is important because "suspense is the enemy of good legal writing." That is a quote from Mary Beth Beazley, a well-known, well-respected, and very funny legal writing professor. Legal writing style aims to be efficient for its reader. Do not make the reader work her way through several sentences to get to the actual point at the end of a paragraph. Start each paragraph with the main point of that paragraph.

Example 1

None of the seven factors used to assess the primary beneficiary is alone determinative. The factors focus on questions such as the intern's expectation of compensation or getting a permanent job after the internship, the benefits to the intern such as education, and the benefits to the employer such as replacing ordinarily paid work with work done by interns. These factors help courts and the Department of Labor assess the "economic reality" of who the primary beneficiary is.

Example 2

Seven factors help courts and the Department of Labor assess the "economic reality" of who the primary beneficiary is. None of the seven factors used to assess the primary beneficiary is alone determinative. The factors focus on questions such as the intern's expectation of compensation or getting a permanent job after the internship, the benefits to the intern such as education, and the benefits to the employer such as replacing ordinarily paid work with work done by interns.

Example 1 above starts with the background idea that these factors aren't determinative. That is not a unique or surprising idea in legal analysis, for reasons discussed in chapters 5 and 17 of this book; legally literate professionals easily understand the notion that factors aren't determinative. Starting with that background idea delays the main point, which is what the test really focuses on: the economic reality of the relationship. In that way, this paragraph is suspenseful because it makes the reader wait until the last sentence to receive the "payoff." Example 2 reverses the ideas, putting the key idea of "economic reality" in the first sentence. Then the background detail and support follow and explain how that idea works.

A vivid way to remember the importance of topic sentences comes from a 1991 circuit-level case: "Judges are not like pigs, hunting for truffles buried in briefs." *United*

States v. Dunkel, 927 F.2d 955, 956 (7th Cir. 1991). Judges aren't alone in not wanting to hunt for truffles. Other types of legal readers do not want to hunt through sentence after sentence to try to find the main point either. Thus, for effective legal writing, write or edit your paragraphs to lead with the main point.

IV. Clarity in Organization and Design

Document organization and design can affect the reader's understanding and the reader's emotional response. It is strange to talk about design being "concise" since that seems to relate only to unnecessary words. But the same concept applies in design: a "cluttered" or "busy" document is the equivalent of a wordy, overwritten, distracting piece of text. It does too much, and some of what it does, does not help the actual goal of the document.

Documents with a clean, uncluttered design are very helpful and much appreciated. Design can enhance understanding by breaking information into pieces. Visual cues, even as simple as bullet points, are also helpful design features. The paragraph itself is a core unit of design; each indented break (or line space between paragraphs) signals to the reader that the next paragraph unit picks up a new point. Design can enhance the reader's emotional response by making a strong positive first impression when the reader first opens and begins to view the document.

For example, which of the following examples seems easier to understand? Which example creates a sense of order and purpose? (The text is generic to keep the focus on design.)

Example 1

Elique rectet re, que con cumqui dignihi ciaepe cum sincta natur? Qui denis sunt et etur, escipsam fugitib usapien duciuritas pro inullo temoluptam experia dolum voloreperore que ped modit, sandae laccae si ressimu scillest et quiat fuga. Rioreiciis quideli quibusa nditasi nvendun dellore ceaquiae eius. Lestium rest, sinus eaquate ctatem et volorum audiscia cus. Enihillique parum ad et (1) Aquas qui quaessunt, illoremporem lignimolupta simpor a sitaquo tem dolorepro quisquis arit, nost, as et arum qui totature pore re, (2) Architat a pelestis rercidelit ex escidit et fugia quis mod quatur, sapid ea si diandam explignam ipietus int volest, ommost et harchil lacepedia con rem. Itaerna turit, si alita verumquia quatur sitasi dissust, ut qui quaecto ius debition commodipsus.

Example 2

Lore, ut velestium rectiore ex est eatque perspicat occae ventis erae. Entotatat estemque liqui undam recus porum labo. Itaquos sinciume imus eaque cusdandit quam quatatet vitatus verfercim et

1. Lorerupt aessimped minia estiasitius ut doluptat ped quatur adis veniendae volupta quid ullesequam niam, vel enis et fugiat laccusam,

2. Otatiand ucidesto desciducia acil mincid quibusa pererib eaquis eumqui dolupta turibus, nustem arum ipis dolendist aligentium et alit

Pudae. Ut vel este nat. Um quas re volupicta nat. Nam, ommodictorum eaquamus isi ium adi tem rati aliquas andigenia quiandam culles quis autaepel il el illuptaere si dererumque.

Example 2 presents the information in small chunks with an introduction, two numbered items, and a conclusion. Its organization and design seem easier to read and more helpful to legal decision-making. Example 1 is a large chunk of text with some numbers in the middle but no visual breaks to help the reader organize the information by looking at it.

Chapter 15, on working with facts, shows some sample timelines that demonstrate basic, helpful design ideas; but a full treatment of design and organization for legal information is beyond the scope of this book. Legal design is a fascinating field involving all types of professionals interested in law, delivery of legal services, legal reform, and access to justice. An excellent resource is Stanford's Legal Tech Design Lab,[9] including its list of design principles.[10] Another aspect of design is typography; the best resource on typography in the legal setting is Matthew Butterick, *Typography for Lawyers* (2d ed. 2015).

V. Conclusion: Reforming "Legalese"

Learning to read legal information may give you a sort of epiphany, wrapped in a strong negative reaction: "It is really unacceptable when legal language is so complex. It doesn't need to be that way! This language protects insiders like lawyers and bureaucrats who maintain control and advantage over others! My mission is to get rid of all the 'legalese' and help make legal vocabulary accessible to everyone!"

This type of zeal can be inspiring, but we also encourage humility and incremental efforts. We assure you, you're not the first person to notice that legal language can be overly complex, and that legal language should serve the public, not just the insider interests of lawyers. The good news is that multiple generations of lawyers and government officials have been working to make legal language more "plain" and thus better. Thanks to the efforts of legal scholars, judges, and practicing lawyers over the past 50 years, the unnecessary verbiage and archaically specialized vocabulary of legal language have been reformed to a great extent. For example, the rules of civil procedure in most jurisdictions now permit "motions for summary judgment" rather than "demurrers," an older Latinate term for pretrial motions. Federal and state laws re-

---

9. Legal Tech Design Lab, http://www.legaltechdesign.com/communication-design/
10. Legal Tech Design Lab, Design Principles, http://www.legaltechdesign.com/communication-design/design-principles/

quiring plain language have not fixed the problem, but they do show resistance to incomprehensible legal jargon.[11] Gaining legal literacy means aspiring to improve legal language and clarify it for the benefit of everyone, with this aspiration balanced against the pragmatic understanding that legal language changes gradually — just like all language. United States law is heavily influenced by the common law tradition, which by its very nature moves slowly, relying on both the results and the specific language of precedent. And apart from its grounding in tradition and history, legal language's function is especially social and utilitarian. Language that people rely on to structure their relationships in a community will evolve only when that community accepts and begins to consistently use new language practices. Language innovations that are not recognized or followed by the relevant language community have thereby failed in their purpose.

Reforming legal language to make it accurate and consistent, as well as clear and concise, is not something that can be achieved in any one person's act of will or mandated from the top down by industry standards. It is a continuing process and a collaborative effort of everyone who creates and relies on legal language. Professionals who use their legal literacy skills to work with law and lawyers occupy a crucially valuable position in this effort. The ability to participate in the legal community with confidence and influence is exactly what this book hopes to teach and encourage.

Having studied this chapter, you should be able to:

- Recognize and avoid common causes of vague and verbose writing
- Edit your writing to make it clearer and more concise
- Use effective topic sentences in paragraphs about legal information
- Avoid overloaded sentences
- Use parallel language to deliver parallel ideas

Case Study: Clear and Concise Editing

Ms. Ralston is preparing a blog post to submit to a compliance website. An intern in her business has written a draft for her, and Ms. Ralston is about to sit down and review the draft. Here is what she sees. This draft needs to be reviewed for clarity and conciseness. The overall meaning should be preserved, but some sentences may need to be restructured or deleted.

---

11. Rachel Stabler, *What We've Got Here Is Failure to Communicate*, 40 J. Legis. 280 (2014) (compiling federal and state laws requiring plain language, and concluding that they have had limited effect in reforming legal language).

Compliance and Unpaid Student Internships

There are a number of mechanisms by which students may accomplish the task of gaining education and preparation to enter the workforce. That unpaid internships under the Fair Labor Standards Act (FLSA) present a key opportunity for such purposes cannot be denied. Employer obligations toward their employees are governed by various provisions in the FLSA including the requirement that a minimum wage be paid to employees. Unpaid internships should be deemed to meet the requirements of the FLSA.

Under the FLSA, it is required that employees are paid a minimum wage. The Department of Labor is the source of enforcement for minimum wage law. An exception to the minimum wage law may be available for student interns when certain requirements are met. The DOL's Fact Sheet #71 is a guide for employers that contains key factors as well as background on the legality of internships provided to student workers without giving minimum wage or wages whatsoever.

Fact Sheet #71 is a key source, giving seven considerations to employers considering the development of an unpaid internship, which are important because these are what the DOL itself considers in deciding whether to bring an enforcement action against an employer for failure to pay the minimum wage:

1. The intern's understanding and lack of expectation for provision of compensation, with any expectations of compensation weighing against the possibility of an unpaid internship

2. The provision of training similar to that which would be provided in an educational environment with clinical training being included in this description

3. Linkages that are present between the internship and the intern's formal course of study

4. Accommodation of the intern's needs in the academic arena through correspondence with the academic calendar

5. Provision of beneficial learning to the intern as it relates to the overall length of time during which the internship is happening

6. Displacement of any paid workers by the intern as well as the receipt of significant educational benefits by the intern

7. Mutual understanding of the intern and employer that a paid job is not an entitlement at the conclusion of the internship

This test is known as the primary beneficiary test and is grounded in an analysis of the economic realities of the relationship between the employer and the intern. This test finds its origination in a case out of New York, *Glatt v. Searchlight Pictures, Inc.*, 811 F.3d 528 (2d Cir. 2015). There, it was proclaimed by the court that the Department of Labor's old test utilizing six factors should not be used in that case because that test caused the economic realities of the educational internship to be disregarded. Instead, seven factors, which do not correspond exactly to the prior six factors but are overlapping with them to some extent, were articulated for assessing the "economic reality" of the relationship, and those are the same elements as listed above. With the same test being adopted by the Ninth Circuit in late 2017, the Circuits appear to be in the process of creating a preference for this seven-part test as the definitive rule for the FSLA. But there is still a different approach needing consideration in the Tenth Circuit, namely the test with six factors used by the DOL before the decision in *Glatt*.

Tess Williams Case File
(re: MegaMart)

- Office Memorandum from Amanda Way to Joshua Mansfield dated August 30, 20XX
- Memorandum of Law dated September 10, 20XX

Way & Wynne, L.L.P.

ATTORNEYS AT LAW
1515 Midway Circle
Arlington, TX 76016

Office Memorandum

To:	Joshua Mansfield
From:	Amanda Way
Date:	August 30, 20XX
Re:	Tess Williams—Potential Claim Against MegaMart Drug Store
	Firm File No. 1242.003

Earlier today, Tess Williams and her parents came to me to discuss whether Tess might have a viable claim against the MegaMart Drug Store, her former employer. The narrative below is based on that interview.

Tess Williams is nineteen years old. She is unmarried and lives at the home of her parents Garret and Angela Williams. In high school she was a member of the drill team. Since she was only five feet tall, she was always on the front line for the team. During her school years, she also worked part time at the concession stand at the movie theater. After graduation from high school, she began working as a cashier at MegaMart. Her MegaMart job was her first full-time job. After one year of service, she was promoted to the cosmetics counter.

MegaMart is part of a national chain of "super-sized" drug stores with separate photo-developing and cosmetics counters. Several of the MegaMart stores are open twenty-four hours. Rocky Malone is the store supervisor at the MegaMart where Tess worked. He is a local hero as he was a lineman on the high school's state championship team twenty years ago and was voted most valuable player on the team. Rocky is now 38 years old, married with two children, and has been an employee of MegaMart for the last ten years. He has regularly received promotions to positions of increasing responsibility at MegaMart, and hopes one day to work his way into a corporate leadership role.

At approximately 3:00 p.m. on July 15, 20XX, Tess was at the cosmetics counter helping her best friend, Caroline, decide on appropriate cosmetics for Caroline's up-coming wedding. Rocky approached the cosmetics counter. He interrupted Tess and Caroline and in a stern voice said, "Tess — I need you to come with me, right now." Tess followed Rocky and claims that she was too surprised and confused to ask any questions about where they were going or why. Rocky had never been so abrupt with her or, to her knowledge, with anyone else in the past.

Rocky, without any explanation, led Tess to a back room. The room was about fifteen feet wide by fifteen feet deep. It had no windows and only one door. The room had a small table and one chair. After they entered the room, Rocky shut, but did not lock, the door. In the room, there were two men dressed in dark suits. Without introduction, one of the men ordered Tess to sit down. The other man, shaking his finger at Tess, demanded: "What did you do with the goods? How long have you been stealing cosmetics?"

Tess was shocked by the demand. She did not know how to respond or defend herself. The man repeated the questions. Tess stammered, "I don't know what you're talking about." The men continued to grill her with similar questions. After about ten minutes, Tess asked to call her dad. The men ignored her request and told her, "If you confess now, the company will go easy on you and it will not be necessary to call the police." Although neither Rocky nor the two other men ever physically restrained Tess, she did not try to leave the room.

Rocky and the two men questioned Tess unremittingly for two hours. Then one of the men slapped a typed confession statement on the table in front of Tess and demanded that she sign it. Reluctantly, Tess signed the confession. One of the men told Tess to go home. Tess claims she signed the confession so that she could leave the room.

Follow-Up Thoughts

These facts have me wondering about the viability of a false imprisonment claim against MegaMart. I recall from a prior matter that the "willful detainment" element is often where false imprisonment claims fail. Please get me a memorandum on that first element, and let us discuss the results so we can help the Williams family decide whether they wish to proceed further. I also need to determine if this claim is one our firm would be willing to take on a contingent-fee basis as the family requested. Your analysis should be helpful on that point.

Memorandum

To:	File
From:	Joshua Mansfield
Date:	September 10, 20XX
Re:	Tess Williams –Willful Detention Element of False Imprisonment Claim against MegaMart (File No. 1242.003)

....

Discussion

Tess Williams can likely prove she was willfully detained by MegaMart and its employees. In a false imprisonment claim, the element of willful detention "may be accomplished by violence, by threats, or by any other means restraining a person from moving from one place to another." *Cuellar v. Walgreens Co.*, 93 S.W.3d 458, 459 (Tex. 2002). Williams was detained in a small room by three men who prevented her from using a phone and who interrogated her, using harsh tones and threatening gestures, until she signed a prepared confession and was permitted to leave. These facts are sufficient to establish willful detention by threat.

False imprisonment in Texas is the willful detention of a person without his or her consent and without the authority of law. *Id.*; *Black v. Kroger*, 527 S.W.2d 794, 796 (Tex. App.—Houston [1st Dist.] 1975). "A willful detention may be accomplished by violence, by threats, or by any other means restraining a person from moving from one place to another." *Cuellar*, 93 S.W.3d at 459. When claiming willful detention by threat, the plaintiff must prove that the threat put her "in just fear of injury to … her person, reputation, or property." *Black*, 527 S.W.2d at 796. Threats to call the police "are not ordinarily sufficient in themselves to effect an unlawful imprisonment." *Cuellar*, 93 S.W.3d at 459 (emphasis added). The threat also must be strong enough to overcome a person's will to leave. *Black*, 527 S.W.2d at 800. Factors that may be considered in assessing whether a person was detained by a force that overcame her free will include the relative age, size, education, experience, sex, and demeanor of the participants, as well as any relationship between interrogator and accused. Courts also consider the physical environment in which the person was confined and any attempts the person made either to leave or to call for help. *Id.* at 800-01; *Cuellar*, 93 S.W.3d at 460.

Factors of age, experience, and education of the claimant relative to her interviewer contributed to a successful false imprisonment claim by the *Black* plaintiff where her counterpart in *Cuellar* failed. Cuellar, a twenty-two-year-old college student and journalist, had worked as a reporter for a television station and two newspapers before beginning her job at Walgreens. She had worked for Walgreens for four months when the store accused her of theft, and she participated in the interview with Walgreens's loss-prevention specialist on terms of intellectual equality. *Cuellar*, 93 S.W.3d at 460-

61. Black, in contrast, was eighteen at the time of the accusation made against her, with a tenth-grade education. Her job at Kroger was the only job she ever held, and she had worked for Kroger for approximately two years when she was accused of theft. *Black*, 527 S.W.2d at 796. Black's mother and husband also worked for Kroger. *Id.* The court in *Black* noted that her limited business experience and the relationship of her family to the store could have made Black particularly unable to resist the authority of her employer. 527 S.W.2d at 800.

The number, gender, demeanor, and relative size of the participants, as well as the physical surroundings in which each interview took place can also aid in establishing willful detention by threat. Black, for example, was taken by her male boss to a small room with one door and no windows, crowded with furniture, in which another man and woman, both claiming to represent Kroger Security, were already present. In sharp tones, they accused her of theft, and they threatened that unless she confessed and re-paid the money, she would be handcuffed and taken to jail and would not see her family "for a long time." *Id.* at 797. Cuellar, on the other hand, was taken to a room normally used for training employees. Her lone interviewer answered her questions calmly, and the only time Cuellar felt intimidated was when her interviewer threatened to call the police. *Cuellar*, 93 S.W.3d at 460. In fact, her interviewer was not in the room when Cuellar wrote her confession. *Id.* at 461.

Tess Williams's claim of willful detention, like Black's, will likely succeed in part because of her relative youth, inexperience, and education as compared to her supervisor. Williams is twenty years old with a high-school education. Her job at MegaMart, for whom she worked for two years, was her first full-time job, so she had limited experience in business or in the world. Williams, like Black and in contrast to Cuellar, has very little business experience and is much more submissive to company authority. Williams was so intimidated by the interrogator's threats and actions that, like Black, she was "unable to exercise her free will to leave the interview and that she was unreasonably detained." *Black*, 527 S.W.2d at 801. In *Cuellar*, the plaintiff's employment and professional experience in journalism enabled her to ask questions and request clarifications, showing she voluntarily remained in the room, a situation unlike that of Williams who asked only to call her father. *See Cuellar*, 93 S.W.3d at 461.

The number, gender, demeanor, and size of MegaMart's employees in the cramped interview space also created an environment in which Williams would reasonably have felt threatened. Williams, the only female in the room, was ordered to sit in the only chair in the room while three men stood around her. In addition, one of the men shook his finger at Williams, accusing her of being a thief by asking her about what she had done with the store's property. These direct accusations continued for two hours without pause before the men "slapped" a pre-written confession on the table and demanded Williams sign it, strongly implying that she could not leave unless she did so. In *Cuellar*, the court determined that because the interrogators did not yell at the plaintiff, call her a thief, or remain in the room when the plaintiff wrote her confession—a notable contrast to Williams's experience—Cuellar was not willfully detained. *See Cuellar*, 93 S.W.3d at 461. Williams's experience more closely parallels the plaintiff's circumstances in *Black*, where the interrogators spoke in a loud tone of voice, called her a thief, and told her to sign "a statement admitting" she took money from the store. *Black*, 527 S.W.2d at 797-98. In fact, Black faced less of a threat of physical harm because another female was in the room and all parties were seated during questioning. *Id.* at 796. The comparative size of the parties—Williams being five feet tall while her supervisor is a former high school linebacker—increased the perceived threat to Williams.

Nonetheless, MegaMart will likely argue that the threat against Williams to call the police was inadequate to prove willful detention by threat because it was not made alongside a threat to Williams's family. Indeed, in *Black*, willful detention was based not only on a threat to call the police, but on such a threat made in the context of a long conversation about Black's family. *Black*, 527 S.W.2d at 801. In Williams's situation, there was no implied threat to her family, and by itself, the threat to call the police would not have been sufficient to establish willful detention. *Cuellar*, 93 S.W.3d at 459. The threat to Williams, however, unlike the threat to Cuellar, did not stand completely alone. The threat to Williams occurred in a context of superior numbers and authority on the employer's side, superior education and experience, cramped surroundings, and the intimidating manner of her interviewers. Furthermore, Williams asked for permission to call for help; not only was the request denied, but followed up by MegaMart's threat to call the police. Such a response would have had a chilling effect on any further attempts by Williams to defend herself. Thus Williams can argue that in context, MegaMart's threat to call police is more like the threat in *Black* than in *Cuellar* and supports her claim for false imprisonment.

The circumstances of Tess Williams's detention are supported by most of the factors Texas courts consider to establish willful detention by threat: the age, experience, and education of the participants; the size and number of participants; the room in which she was detained; and her accusers' demeanor, coupled with their refusal to allow her to call for help. *Id.* at 460; *Black*, 527 S.W.2d at 800-01. Williams accordingly can likely prove the willful detention element of her claim of false imprisonment against MegaMart.

Olivia's Beans Case File
(re: Earth Foods, Inc.)

- Contract for Sale of Goods dated August 12, 20XX
- Website of Federación de Cafeteros Pequeños de Colombia (updated through September 23, 20XX)
- Letter from Raul Proteus to Olivia Ralston (dated September 27, 20XX)
- Memorandum of Law dated October 1, 20XX

Contract for Sale of Goods

This Contract for Sale of Goods ("Contract") is made this **12th day of August, 20XX by and between Olivia's Beans, Inc.,** with its principal place of business at 2200 Central Parkway, Denver, CO 80201 ("Seller") and **Earth Foods, Inc.,** with its principal place of business at 1968 Buckminster Lane, Schenectady, NY 14850 ("Buyer") for the purchase of the goods described below at the price described below:

One hundred thousand (100,000) pounds of Pure Colombian coffee at a total sales price of $705,000.00 (based upon an agreed price of $7.05 per pound) ("Goods").

1. **Term.** This Contract will begin upon its execution and end upon the last delivery unless the parties agree otherwise. Nonetheless, if as of such date, Buyer is in arrears on the account, Seller may then cancel this Contract and sue for its damages, including lost profits, and further recover its cost of suit including attorney fees.

2. **Delivery.** Seller shall arrange for delivery through a carrier chosen by Seller, the costs of which will be borne by Buyer. Delivery will be in ten equal installments of 10,000 pounds each, with each installment to be delivered by no later than the following dates: (1) September 1, 20XX; (2) November 1, 20XX; (3) January 1, 20XY; (4) March 1, 20XY; (5) May 1, 20XY; (6) July 1, 20XY; (7) September 1, 20XY; (8) November 1, 20XY; (9) January 1, 20XZ; and (10) March 1, 20XZ.

3. **Risk of Loss.** The risk of loss from any casualty to the Goods, regardless of the cause, is the responsibility of the Seller until the Goods have been received by the Buyer.

431

4. Acceptance. Buyer may inspect the goods upon receipt. Within three business days after delivery, Buyer must <u>give notice in writing</u> to Seller of any claim for <u>damages</u> on account of condition, quality, or grade of the goods, and Buyer must specify the basis of the claim in detail. Failure of Buyer to comply with these conditions will constitute irrevocable acceptance of the goods by Buyer.

5. **Charges.** The sale price is payable in four equal installments, each of which is due on the first day of the month following the delivery of each shipment until payment in full. <u>Buyer shall pay all charges by no later than thirty days past each due date.</u> Any late payment will bear a <u>late charge of 10%.</u> Late payments will also bear <u>interest at the rate of 12% per year.</u> If Seller undertakes <u>collection or enforcement efforts, Buyer will be liable for all costs</u> thereof, <u>including attorney's fees.</u>

6. **Warranty.** Seller warrants that the goods sold hereunder are new and free from substantive defects in workmanship and materials. Seller's liability under the foregoing warranty is limited to replacement of goods or repair of defects or refund of the purchase price at Seller's sole option.

7. **No other warranty.** No other warranty, express or implied, including the warranty of merchantability, is made by Seller, and none may be imputed or presumed.

8. **Taxes.** All sales taxes, tariffs, and other governmental charges will be <u>paid by Buyer</u> and are Buyer's responsibility except as limited by law.

9. **Governing Law.** This Contract is governed by the <u>laws of the State of New York.</u>

To evidence the Parties' agreement to this Contract, they have executed and delivered it as of the date set forth in the preamble.

Olivia's Beans, Inc. (Seller)
by its President:

Olivia Ralston   *August 12, 20XX*

Olivia Ralston   Date

Earth Foods, Inc. (Buyer)
by its Chief Logistics Officer:

Raul Proteus   *August 12, 20XX*

Raul Proteus   Date

Federación de Cafeteros Pequeños de Colombia

Welcome to our English page.
Haga clic aquí para nuestra página en español.

About Us

The Federación de Cafeteros Pequeños de Colombia (FCPC) is a nonprofit cooperative representing over one hundred small and medium-sized coffee growers in Colombia's Paisa region, commonly known as the "Coffee Triangle." Since 2008, FCPC has been dedicated to sustainable coffee production through small-scale agriculture, employee ownership, and involvement in conservation efforts. FCPC is known internationally for its unique portfolio of coffee strains, as well as its efficient and consistent service.

FCPC routinely deals with international clients directly, or through a network of preferred brokers. If you represent an organization that is interested in partnering with FCPC, please contact FCPC's President, Andrés Barco. An extensive database of client testimonials can be found here.

If you are a coffee grower interested in becoming a FCPC member, please submit a brief statement of interest and a member will reach out to you.

See press releases for recent news and announcements.

Update — September 23, 20XX

Unfortunately, FCPC has suspended its operations indefinitely. We are no longer accepting new orders or membership applications. If you have questions related to FCPC, or if you would like to contact members directly, please email the site administrator: admin@fcpcolombia.org. Be sure to include your name and inquiry type in the subject line.

Earth Foods, Inc.

....

1968 Buckminster Lane, Schenectady, NY 14850
September 27, 20XX

Via Email and Facsimile
Olivia Ralston, President
Olivia's Beans, Inc.
2200 Central Parkway
Denver, CO 80201

Dear Ms. Ralston:

I am deeply troubled by our recent conversation in which you suggested that Olivia's Beans might breach its contract with Earth Foods. Pure Colombian has been Earth Foods' most-popular roast since it debuted earlier this month. The market for sustainably sourced coffee is both lucrative and rapidly expanding, and Earth Foods' place at the forefront of this wave will cement its reputation as America's socially-conscious supermarket. That is why I must insist that you continue to make deliveries pursuant to our agreement.

While I am sympathetic to your difficulties maintaining supplier contracts, that was never a part of our deal. Colombia is one of the world's largest coffee-producing regions, and I have no doubt you can find alternative suppliers. If the prospect of paying them a little more disturbs you, consider the monetary and reputational costs of defaulting on a contract with a nationwide supermarket chain, especially for a newcomer like Olivia's Beans.

Earth Foods' attorneys are prepared to take appropriate legal action to protect its interests if you choose to default. I hope it does not come to that, however. I believe that the mutual benefits we can receive from continued dealings will far outweigh your current difficulty.

Sincerely,

Raul Proteus
Raul Proteus

Memorandum

To: Senior Partner
From: Junior Associate
Date: October 1, 20XX
Re: Olivia's Beans, Inc.—Commercial Impracticability Defense

Question Presented

New York Uniform Commercial Code § 2-615 excuses non-performance or delayed performance of a contract where "performance as agreed has been made impracticable by the occurrence of a contingency the non-occurrence of which was a basic assumption on which the contract was made." Olivia's Beans' ability to perform a long-term contract for the sale of coffee beans to Earth Foods is in jeopardy after its supplier, a Colombian farmers' co-op, went out of business. Can Olivia's Beans be excused for non-performance of the contract?

Brief Answer

Probably not. The impracticability defense in the Uniform Commercial Code excuses performance of a contract due to unforeseeable contingencies that undermine a basic assumption of the contract. The contingencies that qualify are extreme events such as destruction of a factory, not increases in costs, which are generally foreseeable in fixed-cost business arrangements. Moreover, the co-op's dissolution probably did not overturn a basic assumption underlying the Earth Foods contract, because Olivia's Beans contracted with Earth Foods while negotiating but before finalizing its contract with the co-op at the price it now cannot match elsewhere.

Statement of Facts

Olivia's Beans, Inc. is a Colorado corporation, founded and operated by Olivia Ralston, that roasts and sells responsibly-sourced coffee beans to area businesses. On August 12, 20XX, the company entered into a long-term supply contract with Earth Foods, a supermarket chain. The contract is governed by New York law pursuant to its choice-of-law clause. Olivia's Beans is seeking a legal means to excuse itself from that contract because Olivia's Beans has unexpectedly lost its source of supply, and the contract is now unprofitable to perform.

Earth Foods and Olivia's Beans began negotiating an agreement on July 29 under which Olivia's Beans would provide its "Pure Columbia Blend" to Earth Foods. The parties ultimately signed their deal on August 12, giving Earth Foods a volume discount for such a much larger contract than Olivia's Beans had ever handled. Olivia's Beans committed to provide 100,000 total pounds of the Pure Colombian blend at $7.05 per pound. The contract calls for bimonthly shipments of 10,000 pounds of beans starting September 1.

During the July 29 through August 12 negotiating period, Ralston had contacted Colombian farmers' co-ops directly in an effort to reduce costs by "cutting out the middleman." Olivia's Beans received its most attractive bid—$6.50 per pound—from Federación de Cafeteros Pequeños de Colombia (FCPC), a small Colombian co-op. Upon receiving this bid, Ralston executed the August 12 contract with Earth Foods. Then, on August 14, Ralston finalized the contract with FCPC, at the bid of $6.50 per pound.

At these costs, Ralston stood to gain $55,000 on the contract with Earth Foods. Olivia's Beans delivered its first shipment, but now has concerns about the November 1 shipment because FCPC is no longer in business. FCPC dissolved in late September, apparently due to a dispute among the farmers on how to handle profit-splitting. FCPC is now in breach of its contract with Olivia's Beans, but Ralston cannot locate anyone who acts on behalf of the co-op. Thus, Olivia's Beans has no effective remedy available for FCPC's breach. Meanwhile, no other co-op or other supplier has come close to matching the $6.50 per pound of the FCPC contract. The best price available for equivalent roasted Columbian beans, including shipping, is $8.25 per pound. At that price on the remaining 90,000 pounds of the Earth Foods contract, Olivia's Beans will suffer a loss of $108,000 instead of getting its expected profit of $49,500.

Ralston wants to know if any legal strategy would allow Olivia's Beans to be excused from its now-losing contract with Earth Foods. This memo analyzes the commercial impracticability excuse of section 2-615 of the New York Uniform Commercial Code.

Discussion

The impracticability excuse under New York's UCC § 2-615 is probably not available. A party to a sale-of-goods contract may be excused in whole or in part for nonperformance when a contingency occurs "the nonoccurrence of which was a basic assumption" of the contract. N.Y. U.C.C. Law § 2-615(a) (McKinney, Westlaw through L.2019, chs. 1 to 8). But increased cost alone does not make performance impracticable. Id. Here, the increase in cost due to FCPC's dissolution is not excessive enough to create a strong argument. And because Olivia's Beans contracted with Earth Foods before it had actually secured its contract with FCPC, the co-op's continued existence was likely not a basic assumption of the contract.

Under the New York Uniform Commercial Code, a seller is not in breach if it can show performance of the contract is impracticable due to the occurrence of a contingency, "the nonoccurrence of which was a basic assumption" of the contract. Id. Contingencies include "a severe shortage of raw materials ... due to a contingency such as war, embargo, local crop failure, unforeseen shutdown of major sources of supply or the like" which causes a "marked increase" in costs or completely prevents the seller from purchasing the necessary materials. *Dell's Maraschino Cherries Co. v. Shoreline Fruit Growers, Inc.*, 887 F. Supp. 2d 459, 478 (E.D.N.Y. 2012) (applying New York law) (quoting § 2-615 cmt. 4). An increased cost alone is not enough unless that cost is a result of a contingency which "alters the essential nature of performance." *Maple Farms, Inc. v. City Sch. Dist.*, 352 N.Y.S.2d 784, 788 (Sup. Ct. 1974) (quoting § 2-615 cmt. 4). As official comment 4 to § 2-615 makes clear, "a rise or a collapse in the market in itself [is not] a justification, for that is exactly the type of business risk which business contracts made at fixed prices are intended to cover.." N.Y. U.C.C. Law § 2-615 cmt 4. Performance may, however, be excused "where disaster wipes out the means of production." *Id.* at 787. The situation must also be "totally outside contemplation of the parties" and one an experienced draftsman "would not reasonably anticipate." *Moyer v. City of Little Falls*, 510 N.Y.S.2d 813, 815 (Sup. Ct. 1986).

To be excused from performance a seller must show that a contingency made performance impracticable "as a consequence of the occurrence of that contingency." *Dell's Maraschino Cherries*, 887 F. Supp. 2d at 478 (quoting *Canusa Corp. v. A & R Lobosco, Inc.*, 986 F. Supp. 723, 731 n.6 (E.D.N.Y. 1997)) (holding extra time needed to clean raw materials was not a contingency making contract performance impracticable). For example, where a fire completely destroyed a boat manufacturer's factory and thus prevented the building of boats required to fulfill the contract in the time specified, the court excused performance of the contract due to the lost manufacturing capability. *Goddard v. Ishikawajima-Harima Heavy Indus. Co.*, 287 N.Y.S.2d 901, 902 (App. Div. 1968) *aff'd*, 248 N.E.2d 600 (N.Y. 1969). Similarly, where a shipwreck resulted in the total loss of a chartered ship, the court used impracticability to excuse performance. *Asphalt Int'l, Inc. v. Enterprise Shipping Corp., S.A.*, 667 F.2d 261, 266 (2d Cir. 1981) (applying U.C.C. § 2-615). There, a repair cost of $1,500,000 "far exceeded the $750,000 pre-collision fair market value" of the ship. *Id.* The court applied impracticability because the cost to repair the ship, and so continue performance of the contract, was "excessive and unreasonable." *Id.* In contrast, in *Maple Farms*, the sale of "huge amounts" of grain to Russia and unanticipated crop failures, resulting in a 10.4% cost increase, was deemed to not be a contingency for the purposes of impracticability. *Maple Farms*, 352 N.Y.S.2d at 787; *see also La. Power & Light Co. v. Allegheny Ludlum Indus., Inc.*, 517 F. Supp. 1319, 1324-26 (E.D. La. 1981) (applying N.Y. U.C.C. § 2-615) (holding that increased costs of 38% on the contract, diminished plant profits, and the company remaining overall profitable did not support impracticability).

For the impracticability excuse to be available, the contingency must also have been unforeseeable. *See Moyer*, 510 N.Y.S.2d at 814-15. In *Eastern Air Lines, Inc. v. Gulf Oil Corp.*, an embargo that raised the price of foreign oil substantially was sufficiently foreseeable based on the known "volatility of the Middle East situation[.]" *Eastern Air Lines, Inc. v. Gulf Oil Corp.*, 415 F. Supp. 429, 441-42 (S.D. Fla. 1975) (applying U.C.C. § 2-615). Since Eastern Air Lines could not show that the increase was unforeseeable, performance of the contract with Gulf Oil was not impracticable. *Id.* Likewise, in *Maple Farms*, given the inflation of the price of milk in previous years, which was in accordance with the increased price for the year in contest, the increase was held to be foreseeable and not a basis for impracticability. *Maple Farms*, 352 N.Y.S.2d at 789-90; *see also Bende & Sons*, 548 F. Supp. at 1022 (holding a contract clause detailing a different specific contingency indicated that since the parties had considered specific contingencies at the time of contracting, they could "easily have foreseen such an occurrence" in regards to a train derailment).

A cost increase by itself will not support the impracticability defense unless it is excessive. In *Asphalt International*, the repair cost would have been 200% of the lost ship's fair market value. 667 F.2d at 265-66. The court reasoned that although standard maintenance costs were foreseeable pursuant to a contract clause assigning the costs of maintenance to the ship owner, costs from the complete destruction of the ship were not. *Id.* In *Moyer*, the impracticability excuse was successful where the unforeseen closure of one of two landfills created a monopoly, causing a "dramatic increase" of 666% in price (from $1.50 to $10 per cubic yard for use). 510 N.Y.S.2d at 814.

Olivia's Beans likely cannot be excused from its contract with Earth Foods because the price increase for its supplies does not reach a level of "contingency" that New York courts have excused. The dissolution of FCPC does not prevent Olivia's Beans from being able to perform its contract by obtaining coffee beans, unlike the situation in *Goddard* where the boat factory's destruction eliminated the manufacturer's capacity to sell boats. *Goddard*, 287 N.Y.S.2d at 902. Increased cost can be a contingency if it is excessive, such as the 200% of fair-market-value expenditure required to replace the chartered ship in *Asphalt International*. 667 F.2d at 266. The $8.25/lb. replacement coffee beans for Olivia's Beans do cost significantly more than the $6.50/lb. FCPC beans, but the roughly 27% additional cost falls well short of the excess in *Asphalt International*. The increased cost here is much closer to *Maple Farms*, where the 10.4% cost increase was not a contingency, *Maple Farms*, 352 N.Y.S.2d at 787, and it is also closer to the 38% increased costs held insufficient to support impracticability in *Louisiana Power & Light*. 517 F. Supp. at 1324-26. The cost increase suffered by Olivia's Beans is not sufficiently excessive to establish a "contingency" under UCC section 2-615.

Furthermore, even if the Olivia's Beans cost increase were excessive enough to qualify as a contingency, it would not support the impracticability excuse because the increase was not unforeseeable at the time of contracting with Earth Foods. FCPC's specific failure may have been unforeseeable, but price volatility in the coffee bean market was not. Just like the spike in oil prices in *Eastern Air Lines* and the inflation of milk process in *Maple Farms*, changes in the cost of coffee—a common commodity like both oil and milk—is foreseeable. *Eastern Air Lines*, 415 F. Supp. at 441-42; *Maple Farms*, 352 N.Y.S.2d at 789-90. Therefore, similar to the results in *Eastern Air Lines* and in *Maple Farms*, a court is unlikely to recognize impracticability as an excuse for Olivia's Beans to avoid performing the Earth Foods contract. The supply challenge for Ol-

FCPC contract not in place yet

ivia's Beans does not reach the level of unforeseeability that succeeded in *Moyer*. There the city not only faced a price increase of 666% for landfill disposal services, but the increase came about due to an unforeseeable event, the closure of a landfill giving monopoly pricing power to its remaining counterpart. *Moyer*, 510 N.Y.S.2d at 814. In sum, the event now affecting Olivia's Beans' position in performing the contract was generally foreseeable, and thus does not give rise to the excuse of impracticability.

Nonetheless, Olivia's Beans could argue that the price increase on coffee beans for its Earth Foods contract is actually unforeseeable because the dissolution of supplier FCPC is an external event, like the landfill closure in *Moyer*, and not a normal market fluctuation like the milk price increase in *Maple Farms*. Indeed, the unanticipated closure of FCPC is the occurrence surrounding the Earth Foods contract that was arguably unforeseeable by both parties. This argument would likely fail, however, because any unforeseeability here was not part of the "basic assumption on which the contract was made." N.Y. U.C.C. Law § 2-615(a) (emphasis added). At the time Olivia's Beans entered into its contract with Earth Foods, it had not actually secured a contract with FCPC. One of the reasons parties make long-term supply contracts is to insulate themselves from market fluctuations. By agreeing to a particular price, a seller is often betting that market prices will stay the same or fall, while the buyer expects the opposite to occur. In this case, Olivia's Beans took the position that it could find a buyer willing to offer substantial volume discounts when it made the supply contract with Earth Foods. The timing of Olivia's Beans' contracts with Earth Foods (first) and with FCPC (second) strongly cuts against the argument for impracticability because by entering a fixed-price contract with Earth Foods, Olivia's Beans took on the business risk of covering not just increased cost, but even a collapse in the market. N.Y. U.C.C. Law § 2-615 cmt. 4.

Conclusion

Performance by Olivia's Beans of its contract with Earth Foods most likely would not be excused under New York's UCC § 2-615. The increased cost alone does not make performance impracticable, and Ralston negotiated the deal before securing a supply agreement with the Colombian co-op. Neither the coffee beans' price of $6.50/lb., nor the continued existence of FCPC, qualify as a "basic assumption on which the contract was made." Olivia's Beans probably cannot avoid liability for breaching its Earth Foods contract based upon impracticability.

Appendix C

Bibliography of Online Legal Glossaries

Government Websites

United States Courts, *Glossary of Legal Terms*, www.uscourts.gov/glossary

State of Connecticut Judicial Branch, *Common Legal Words*, www.jud.ct.gov/legalterms.htm

Offices of the United States Attorneys, *Legal Terms Glossary*, www.justice.gov/usao/justice-101/glossary

First Judicial Circuit of Florida, *Glossary of Legal Terms*, www.firstjudicialcircuit.org/about-court/glossary

Nevada Judiciary, *English Legal Glossary,* nvcourts.gov/AOC/Programs_and_Services/Court_Interpreter/Documents/For_Public/English_Legal_Glossary/ (PDF, last updated October 22, 2010)

New York State Unified Court System, *Glossary: Common Legal Terms,* accessed February 3, 2019, www.nycourts.gov/courts/6jd/forms/SRForms/glossary_common_legal.pdf

State of Connecticut Judicial Branch Superior Court Operations Division, *Glossary of Legal Terminology - Most Frequently Used Terms,* accessed February 3, 2019, www.jud.ct.gov/external/news/jobs/interpreter/Glossary_of_Legal_Terminology _English.pdf

North Carolina Judicial Branch, *Legal Glossary,* www.nccourts.gov/legal-glossary

Court News Ohio, *CNO Legal Glossary*, www.courtnewsohio.gov/glossary/a.asp#.XFcAyc9KiRs

Tennessee State Courts, *Glossary of Legal Terms*, www.tncourts.gov/media/glossary-legal-terms

West Virginia Judiciary, *Glossary of Legal Terms,* http://www.courtswv.gov/public-resources/press/glossary-of-terms.html

The Second Judicial Circuit of Florida, *Glossary of Legal Terms,* http://2ndcircuit.leoncountyfl.gov/glossary.php

Maryland Courts, *Glossary of Court Terms,* http://mdcourts.gov/reference/glossary

New York State: Office of Mental Health, *The Layperson's Glossary of Legal and Technical Terms,* www.omh.ny.gov/omhweb/forensic/manual/html/appendixe.htm

Indiana Judicial Branch, *Glossary of Legal Terms,* www.in.gov/judiciary/2658.htm

441

Academic Websites

Cornell Law School Legal Information Institute, *Wex*, accessed February 3, 2019, www.law.cornell.edu/wex

University of New Mexico, Judicial Education Center, *Glossary of Legal Terms*, http://jec.unm.edu/manuals-resources/glossary-of-legal-terms

Northern Illinois University College of Law, *Legal Terminology: General Terms*, http://libguides.niu.edu/c.php?g=425200&p=4856514#s-lg-box-15250075 (last updated January 3, 2019)

Other Websites

Gerald and Kathleen Hill, *The People's Law Dictionary: Search Legal Terms and Definitions*, accessed February 2, 2019, http://dictionary.law.com

Edgar Snyder & Associates, *Legal Dictionary*, www.edgarsnyder.com/legal-dictionary/

NOLO, *Nolo's Free Dictionary of Law Terms and Legal Definitions*, accessed February 3, 2019, www.nolo.com/dictionary

SCOTUSblog.com, *Glossary of Supreme Court Terms*, https://www.scotusblog.com/reference/educational-resources/glossary-of-legal-terms/

Translations

State of Connecticut Judicial Branch Superior Court Operations Division, *Glossary of Legal Terminology - English to Spanish*, www.jud.ct.gov/external/news/jobs/interpreter/Glossary_of_Legal_Terminology_English-to-Spanish.pdf

U.S. Diplomatic Mission to Germany, *Common Legal Terms*, http://usa.usembassy.de/etexts/gov/legalterms.htm (last updated August 2002)

State of Washington Administrative Office of the Courts, *Glossary of Selected Legal Terms:* English-Korean, 1994, www.courts.wa.gov/programs_orgs/pos_interpret/content/glossary/Glossary%20of%20Legal%20Terms%20-%20English-Korean.PDF

Wisconsin Court System, *Glossary of Legal Terminology: English-German*, www.wicourts.gov/services/interpreter/docs/germanglossary.pdf

Wisconsin Court System, *Basic Legal Terminology: Some English-Spanish Equivalents*, www.wicourts.gov/services/interpreter/docs/spanishglossary2.pdf

Wisconsin Court System, *Glossary of Legal Terminology: English-Arabic*, www.wicourts.gov/services/interpreter/docs/arabicglossary.pdf

State of Maryland, Administrative Office of the Courts, *Legal Vocabulary: English/French*, www.wicourts.gov/services/interpreter/docs/frenchglossary.pdf

New Jersey Judiciary, *Glossary of Legal (and Related) Terms and Courthouse Signs: English/Haitian Creole*, www.njcourts.gov/forms/11783_glossary_haitian.pdf?cacheID=nDrtJn4 (last updated February 2014)

Index